The Logic of Precedent

Unlike statutory law, which relies on the explicit formulation of rules, common law is thought to emerge from a complex doctrine of precedential constraint, according to which decisions in earlier cases constrain later courts while still allowing these courts the freedom to address new situations in creative ways. Although this doctrine is applied by legal practitioners on a daily basis, it has proved to be considerably more difficult to develop an adequate theoretical account of the doctrine itself. Drawing on recent work in legal theory, as well as artificial intelligence (AI) and law, this book develops a new account of precedential constraint and the balance achieved in the common law between constraint and freedom. This account, which involves construction of a group priority ordering among reasons, is then applied to other topics including the semantics of open-textured predicates and the practice of making exceptions to general rules.

JOHN HORTY is Distinguished University Professor of Philosophy at the University of Maryland. He is the author of three previous books as well as papers on a variety of topics in logic, philosophy, and computer science.

The Logic of Precedent

Constraint, Freedom, and Common Law Reasoning

JOHN HORTY
University of Maryland

CAMBRIDGE
UNIVERSITY PRESS

CAMBRIDGE
UNIVERSITY PRESS

Shaftesbury Road, Cambridge CB2 8EA, United Kingdom

One Liberty Plaza, 20th Floor, New York, NY 10006, USA

477 Williamstown Road, Port Melbourne, VIC 3207, Australia

314–321, 3rd Floor, Plot 3, Splendor Forum, Jasola District Centre, New Delhi – 110025, India

103 Penang Road, #05–06/07, Visioncrest Commercial, Singapore 238467

Cambridge University Press is part of Cambridge University Press & Assessment, a department of the University of Cambridge.

We share the University's mission to contribute to society through the pursuit of education, learning and research at the highest international levels of excellence.

www.cambridge.org
Information on this title: www.cambridge.org/9781009356503

DOI: 10.1017/9781009356480

When citing this work, please include a reference to the DOI 10.1017/9781009356480

First published 2025

A catalogue record for this publication is available from the British Library

A Cataloging-in-Publication data record for this book is available from the Library of Congress

ISBN 978-1-009-35650-3 Hardback

For Lori Frank, Jasper Shide, and Jeremy Shide

Logic (we may say) is generalized jurisprudence.

– Stephen Toulmin

A satisfactory theory of legal reasoning requires and is required by a satisfactory theory of law.

– Neil MacCormick

Contents

Figures

Preface

Ever since I first read Aristotle as an undergraduate, I have been intrigued by the particularist idea – which I believe to be correct – that normative generalizations cannot be formulated carefully enough to apply properly in every situation: there will always be circumstances in which the straightforward application of a normative generalization, no matter how finely articulated, will yield the wrong result. How can we live in a world like this? Except by appealing to normative generalizations, or principles, how can we justify our own actions, or evaluate the actions of others? Questions like these have recently received sustained attention in moral philosophy due, especially, to the work of Jonathan Dancy and other extreme particularists, who argue that principles have no role at all to play in moral justification or evaluation.

Several years ago, I wrote a book, *Reasons as Defaults* (2012), that offered, as I thought, a sensible response to extreme particularism, arguing that moral justification and evaluation could be provided by defeasible principles, and sketching a logic for reasoning with these principles. Still, even if my response was successful in deflecting a broad-scale assault on normative generalizations, it did not address the more detailed problem of explaining how moral justification and evaluation could actually be guided, or constrained, by general principles that might, at any moment, allow for exceptions.

It struck me, as it surely has many others, that we might be able to make progress on this problem by looking carefully at the patterns of reasoning at work in systems of common law. Here we find a relatively stable institution in which, on a daily basis, courts confront new situations against a background of constraints derived from precedent decisions. These constraints are sufficiently firm that decisions in most situations are a matter of routine, but still flexible enough to be adapted to unexpected circumstances. How does the law manage to work with constraints like these?

With this question in mind, I embarked on a haphazard study of the literature on common law reasoning – which is, of course, vast and contentious, touching on central problems in legal theory. As a logician, I tended to focus on theories according to which precedential constraint is carried by rules, rather than on interpretative or coherence theories. My idea was that common law rules should be treated as defeasible, or as default rules, rather than the kind of strict rules familiar from ordinary logic. Logics governing defeasible rules had already been applied, very successfully, in the field of artificial intelligence and law, though primarily for the study of legal argumentation. I was convinced that a useful treatment of common law constraint could be formulated within a similar framework, and set about developing this proposal.

It was at this point that I came across Grant Lamond's extraordinary paper "Do precedents create rules?" (2005), which seemed to contain a genuinely new idea. The idea, as I understood it, was that the concept of common law constraint could best be explicated, not in terms of rules at all, but simply on the basis of relations among reasons. I had argued in my earlier book that reasons themselves could be understood as the premises of default rules. And as soon as I read this paper, I realized that a simplified version of the proposal I was working to develop within default logic could be stated without any appeal to default rules at all but directly in terms of a relation among reasons, just as Lamond had suggested. The result was my first paper on the topic, "Rules and reasons in the theory of precedent" (2011), setting out my own version of the reason model of precedential constraint.

Even after developing this simple version of the reason model, I continued with my original plan of analyzing the concept of precedential constraint within default logic, leading to an account that agrees with the simple reason model where they overlap, but that, while considerably more complex, is also more flexible and more extensible. This book centers around these two accounts – and also a third, based on the more orthodox idea of accommodating unexpected situations through explicit rule modification. I explore the relations among these different accounts, discuss their advantages and disadvantages, extend one or another into new territory, and reflect on the picture they provide of precedential constraint and normative reasoning more generally.

In working out the details of these ideas, I sometimes felt as if I was traveling through a kind of no-man's-land. On one hand, I was trying to understand the concept of precedential constraint using formal tools, and a formal methodology, that would be familiar to anyone working in philosophical logic, but applying these tools and this methodology to a problem that, as far as I know, no contemporary philosophical logician has ever written about. On the other hand, while precedential constraint has, as noted, received extensive attention from legal theorists in the common law tradition, scholars working in this tradition tend not to employ formal methods, and can be skeptical of their value.

Nevertheless, as I made my way through this territory, I was fortunate to find help and support from a number of individuals.

Within artificial intelligence and law – perhaps the unique field in which the application of formal techniques in the study of legal reasoning is expected – I am especially grateful to Trevor Bench-Capon, Henry Prakken, Giovanni Sartor, and Marek Sergot. Trevor, in particular, coauthored the initial paper introducing the ideas presented here to that field, and both he and Henry have continued to find new applications for these ideas, both in artificial intelligence and law and, especially in the case of Henry and his students, in other areas of artificial intelligence.

Within philosophy, I am particularly grateful to Pamela Hieronymi and Mark Schroeder, each of whom provided encouragement, insight, and perspective especially at the beginning of the project, but also at crucial points throughout. This book would not exist without them. Christian List helped me understand crucial aspects of this project that I would not have seen otherwise. I had originally formulated the reason model only in terms of decisions directly favoring a plaintiff or a defendant, but Sam Cumming showed me that the same techniques could be applied in the analysis of vague and open-textured predicates.

Among scholars working in the intersection of law and philosophy, I must thank, first of all, Bruce Chapman and Robin Kar, reviewers of my initial paper on the reason model. Bruce was enthusiastic about the work from the beginning, and exceptionally helpful throughout. Robin, although less immediately tolerant of the formal approach, had the patience to work with me until the paper was more intelligible. Joseph Raz, a reviewer for a later paper, sent me a set of remarks, eventually leading to a correspondence, so extensive and thoughtful that I learn something new every time I read it. Sarah Lawsky is the rare legal scholar who views this project from a standpoint even more rigorous than my own, but who has also, over the years, tempered this rigor with an amazing degree of support and encouragement. And Gabe Broughton, Rob Mullins, and Adam Rigoni have all helped along the way with questions and corrections, and in their own work, adapted versions of the reason model to align more closely with legal practice or with themes in legal theory.

Finally, Ilaria Canavotto arrived in Maryland as a postdoc at a point when I imagined that this manuscript was finished, but proceeded to supply a series of detailed, insightful, and constructive comments that led me to reshape significant portions of the book to reflect her suggestions. More important, Ilaria took a set of ideas that I had thought of as essentially fixed and showed me how they could be extended in new ways, especially in the fields of machine ethics and explanatory artificial intelligence.

Of course, there were many others who helped in many-sided ways, with observations, corrections, or advice. These include: Larry Alexander, Kevin Ashley, Ruth Chang, Luís Duarte d'Almeida, Aleks Knoks, Grant Lamond, Brian Leiter, Sebastian Lewis, Errol Lord, Barry Maguire, David Makinson, Mark McBride, Lynne McFall, Chris Morris, Shyam Nair, Eric Pacuit, Bijan Parsia, Edwina Rissland, Leisa Schwab, Rachel Singpurwalla, Alan Thomas, Rich Thomason, Leon van der Torre, Frank Veltman, and Kai Wehmeier. Mette Gieskes suggested the image used here as a cover illustration, Winslow Homer's *Art-Students and Copyists in the Louvre Gallery, Paris*, which presents a different view of precedential constraint.

In addition to the help I have received from individuals, this project has benefited from valuable institutional support, first from a 2011/12 fellowship at the Center for Advanced Study in the Behavioral Sciences at Stanford University, where the project began, and then from a 2015/16 Fellowship for University Teachers from the National Endowment for Humanities, which allowed me to assemble a first draft. I am grateful to both organizations.

Although this book was written to stand alone, from beginning to end, parts of it draw on previous work. In particular: Chapters 1 and 2 draw on my (2011) and (2012), from *Legal Theory* and *Artificial Intelligence and Law* respectively, the latter coauthored with Trevor Bench-Capon. Chapters 3 and 4 draw on my (2004) and (2015), from *Legal Theory* and *Philosophers' Imprint* respectively. Chapters 5 and 6 develop ideas briefly sketched in my (2016), from *Weighing Reasons*, edited by Errol Lord and Barry Maguire. Chapter 7 draws on my (2019) and (2021), both from *Artificial Intelligence and Law*. The central argument of Section 1.3 appears previously in my (2024), from *Oxford Studies in Philosophy of Law, Volume 5*, edited by Leslie Green and Brian Leiter; likewise, the central argument of Section 4.3 appears previously in my (2023), from *Philosophical Foundations of Precedent*, edited by Timothy Endicott, Hafsteinn Dan Kristjánsson, and Sebastian Lewis.

Introduction

This book presents an account of reasoning, or decision making, against a background of constraints derived from a body of previous authoritative decisions, or precedent cases. The nature and operation of the constraints derived from precedent cases is a central concern of legal theory in the common law tradition and has received its most careful analysis there. In developing my account, I will draw extensively on the literature from legal theory, and the account I present is intended to capture important aspects of precedential constraint in the common law.

At the same time, I want to suggest that the process of reasoning against a background of constraints derived from precedent cases, as in the common law, is not a special style of reasoning learned in law school and practiced only by lawyers. It is, instead, a familiar form of reasoning that we all engage in all the time – in our development of small-scale normative systems, for example, or in our use of open-textured predicates. An important goal of the project is to isolate this form of reasoning as an interesting topic of investigation in its own right, both for philosophy and also for logic, even apart from its varied applications within particular legal institutions. Finally, I will argue that the entire framework – the constraints derived from precedent cases, the associated process of reasoning – is rational, in the sense that it provides, if not a unique optimal solution, then at least one sensible solution to the problem of combining individual preferences and values into a shared priority ordering on reasons that can be used to support decisions affecting members of larger communities. In this sense, the account presented here can be seen as offering a justification for practices in the common law that many writers have taken to be objectionable.

Traditionally, the common law is distinguished from statutory or regulatory law, which is based on a collection of rules crafted by legislators or administrative agencies. Although the proper understanding of statutes and regulations can present complex issues of interpretation, often centered around questions of legislative meaning or intent, the underlying mechanism of constraint, in this case, is at least straightforward. Setting matters of interpretation aside, statutory and regulatory rules work just like any other rules. To take a mundane example, if you are sorting marbles according to a set of directives that includes the rule "Blue marbles must be placed in the blue bin," what this means is that, if you come across a blue marble, you must place it in the blue bin. If, instead, you place a blue marble in the red bin, you fail to satisfy the constraints imposed by the rule – you have violated the rule. In exactly the same way, if a state's motor vehicle code includes the regulation "Vehicles operated on public roads must be registered with the Department of Motor Vehicles," what this means is that, if you operate a vehicle on public roads, that vehicle must be registered with the Department of Motor Vehicles, and you have violated the regulation if you operate a vehicle that is not registered.

The common law, by contrast, is organized around a collection of previous decisions, or precedent cases, rather than a collection of rules. Situations requiring decisions come before authoritative bodies – typically courts – and decisions are rendered. The common law itself is then thought to emerge from these decisions through *stare decisis*, a complex doctrine according to which, on the most common interpretation, decisions reached in earlier, or precedent, cases constrain the decisions available to courts in later cases, while still allowing these later courts a degree of freedom to respond in creative ways to fresh circumstances. In understanding the nature of common law constraint, the central challenge is to determine the precise character of this doctrine of *stare decisis* – or more simply, the doctrine of *precedent*.[1] Although techniques for arguing on the basis of precedent are studied early on in law schools, mastered with relative ease, and applied on a daily basis by legal practitioners, it has proved to be considerably more difficult to arrive at an adequate theoretical account of the doctrine itself. Such an account would have to answer two questions, at least: First, how is it, exactly, that precedent cases constrain future decisions – what is the mechanism of constraint? And second, how is a balance then achieved between the constraints imposed by precedent and the freedoms allowed to later courts for developing the law.

[1] The literature on precedent is immense, but useful introductions are provided in Schauer (1987) and Alexander (1989). An illuminating survey of the issues posed by precedent from a philosophical perspective can be found in Lamond (2006); a detailed discussion of precedent in one particular legal system can be found in Cross and Harris (1991).

Let us begin with the familiar, and very natural, position that constraint in the common law, like statutory or regulatory constraint, also depends on rules. A precedent case normally contains, not only a factual description of some situation together with a decision on the basis of those facts, but some particular rule through which that decision is justified, the *ratio decidendi* of the case. And according to the position under consideration, it is this rule that carries precedential constraint. On this view – which can be described as the *rule model* of precedent – the common law is not so different from statutory or regulatory law.[2] The mechanism of constraint, in each case, depends on previously formulated rules. Just as statutory and regulatory law is based on statutes and regulations, the common law is likewise based on rules, with the sole difference that common law rules are formulated by courts, rather than legislators or administrative agencies.

The general idea that common law constraint is based on rules can be developed in a number of different ways, depending, in the first instance, on the nature of the rules involved. Some writers argue that common law rules are best seen as defeasible – prima facie, or pro tanto – leading to what I will call the *defeasible rule model* of constraint. I have a good deal of sympathy with this position, which has been, I believe, underexplored in legal theory for the simple reason that, until recently, there was no adequate account available of reasoning on the basis of defeasible rules: how could we hope to explicate common law constraint using defeasible rules without understanding the logical behavior of defeasible rules themselves? Now, however, as a result of the sustained study of defeasible, or default, logics carried out during the past several decades within the fields of logic, philosophy, and computer science, we have a much better understanding of defeasible reasoning in general. In my own previous work, I have argued that a particular default logic can be interpreted as providing a precise, mathematical theory of the way in which reasons support conclusions in ethics and epistemology; and later in the book, I will extend this interpretation to show how the central account of precedential constraint developed here can be reformulated

[2] I follow Alexander (1989) and Alexander and Sherwin (2008) in classifying the positions available for understanding precedential constraint into a taxonomy of *models*; my taxonomy, however, differs from theirs both in allowing for more possibilities and in separating certain positions that they group together. In particular, while Alexander and Sherwin use the phrase "rule model" to refer only to the position described below as the "serious rule model," I use this phrase as a more general classification to encompass a variety of positions organized around the manipulation of rules.

within that default logic, a result that I take as a vindication of the defeasible rule model of constraint.[3]

For the present, however, I want to start with the opposite position, that the generalizations expressed by common law rules are not defeasible at all, but strict, or exceptionless. On this view, common law rules are thought to mirror the kind of exceptionless generalizations studied in ordinary symbolic logic. The idea is that rules such as "Vehicles are not allowed in the park," for example, or "Contracts with minors are voidable" are like the statements "All equilateral triangles are equiangular" or "All men are mortal" – there can be no exceptions.

As it turns out, the position that common law rules state exceptionless generalizations can itself be developed in two ways, this time depending, not on the nature, or meaning, of the rules themselves, but on the system of conventions governing their use. Some writers argue that, once a common law rule has been introduced in an earlier case, it must then control any later case in which it is applicable, unless the court in the later case wishes to overrule the earlier decision and has the authority to do so. This hardheaded position can be described as the *serious rule model* of constraint.[4] Other writers favor a more flexible approach, according to which, although only certain courts, depending on their place in the judicial hierarchy, have the authority to overrule earlier decisions, all courts have the power to *distinguish* the fact situation of a case currently under consideration from that of some earlier case in which a precedent rule was formulated – the power, that is, to identify important, or material, differences between the two situations, which the court can then take as justification for modifying the earlier rule in order to avoid an inappropriate application of this rule to the current situation.

The idea that general rules must, on occasion, be modified to avoid inappropriate application in particular situations goes back to antiquity, and receives its most notable treatment in Book V of Aristotle's *Nichomachean Ethics*. There, in the course of his discussion of equity, Aristotle emphasizes that – due to the open-ended variability of human circumstances – it is inevitable that legal generalizations will, at times, yield incorrect results:

[3] See Horty (2012) for my previous work interpreting reasons within default logic.

[4] The position has been developed and defended with great force by Alexander and Sherwin; see Alexander (1989) and then, especially, Alexander and Sherwin (2001, 2008).

> The reason is that all law is universal but about some things it is not possible to make a universal statement which shall be correct. In those cases, then, in which it is necessary to speak universally, but not possible to do so correctly, the law takes the usual case, though it is not ignorant of the possibility of error.[5]

In situations like this, as Aristotle explains, when the straightforward application of legal generalizations leads to a flawed outcome, it is necessary to offer a correction:

> When the law speaks universally, then, and a case arises on it which is not covered by the universal statement, then it is right, when the legislator fails us and has erred by over-simplicity, to correct the omission – to say what the legislator himself would have said had he been present, and would have put into his law if he had known.[6]

And he illustrates his conclusion that legal generalizations must be modified to fit particular cases with a striking analogy to the "Lesbian rule" – a ruler made of soft lead from the island of Lesbos, which could be adjusted to measure irregular shapes:

> In fact this is the reason why all things are not determined by law, viz. that about some things it is impossible to lay down a law, so that a decree is needed. For when the thing is indefinite the rule also is indefinite, like the leaden rule used in making the Lesbian moulding; the rule adapts itself to the shape of the stone and is not rigid, and so too the decree is adapted to the facts.[7]

Turning to the common law proper, a canonical statement of the position that rules are malleable in this way can be found in the work of Edward Levi, who begins his monograph on legal reasoning by considering the hypothesis that the common law could be approached as if it depended on

[5] *NE* 1137b12-17 (Ross translation, here and below).

[6] *NE* 1137b19-24.

[7] *NE* 1137b28-31. Although this concern with the rigidity of general rules is most closely associated with Aristotle, it goes back at least to Plato, who writes in the *Statesman* that law "cannot prescribe with perfect accuracy what is good and right for each member of the community," since "[t]he differences of human personality, the variety of men's activities, and the inevitable unsettlement attending all human experience make it impossible for any art whatsoever to issue unqualified rules holding good on all questions at all times" (294b1-6; Skemp translation, here and below). Unfortunately, as he goes on to say, "the law tends to issue just this invariable kind of rule," and so "it is like a self-willed, ignorant man who lets no one do anything but what he has ordered and forbids all subsequent questioning" (294b8-c2).

> a method of applying general rules of law to diverse facts – in short, as though the doctrine of precedent meant that general rules, once properly determined, remained unchanged, and then were applied, albeit imperfectly, in later cases.[8]

Levi immediately rejects this view, however, writing that, to the contrary, common law rules "change from case to case and are remade with each case," and that "the rules change as the rules are applied."[9] The view that common law rules can be adapted to fit new situations is, arguably, the most prevalent position among legal theorists and provides what I will refer to as the *standard model* of precedential constraint.[10] This standard model is often thought to offer the most accurate picture of ordinary, incremental legal development, through the gradual modification of common law rules in light of later cases. It could be illustrated by tracing the development of an actual common law doctrine, but it will be simpler – and also help to illustrate the point that common law reasoning is already at work in everyday situations – to begin with a more mundane example.[11]

Suppose, then, that Jack and Jo are the parents of two children – Emma, who has just turned nine, and Max, age twelve – and that they have agreed to respect each other's decisions concerning the children, treating these decisions, in effect, as precedents. And imagine that, one night, Emma, who has completed both her chores and her homework, but did not finish dinner, asks Jo if she can stay up and watch TV. This is like a legal case: a situation is presented to an authority, Jo, who must make a decision and, ideally, provide a rationale for her decision. Suppose that Jo resolves the case by granting the request, stating that Emma can stay up to watch TV since she is now nine years old. This decision can be seen as introducing a household version of a common law rule – perhaps, "Children age nine or greater can stay up and watch TV" – fashioned in response to a particular set of circumstances, but applicable to future situations as well.

Now imagine that, the next day, Max, who has likewise completed chores and failed to finish dinner, but who has, in addition, failed to complete

[8] Levi (1949, p. 2).

[9] Ibid., pp. 3–4.

[10] Versions of this position have been developed, not just by Levi but by Simpson (1961), Raz (1979), Eisenberg (1988), and Schauer (1989,1991), along with many others.

[11] For a legal example, see Levi's (1949, pp. 8–27) discussion of the development, within the standard model, of the changing common law rules characterizing the notion of an "inherently dangerous" object. Other artificial examples of the sort considered here can be found in Burton (1985), and especially in Twining and Miers (2010).

homework, asks Jack whether he can stay up and watch TV. And suppose that, in this case, Jack refuses, on the grounds that Max has not completed his homework. Max might reasonably appeal Jack's decision with the complaint, "Ah, but given the precedent established last night, in the case of Emma, our household is now governed by a rule according to which children age nine or greater can stay up and watch TV." And of course, according to the serious rule model of constraint, Max would be right, since the rule established in the case of Emma is applicable in his situation as well. The standard model, however, allows Jack to defend his decision by distinguishing the two cases, arguing that the previous rule should not apply to the new case of Max, since this new case, unlike the previous case of Emma, presents the additional feature that the child in question has not completed his homework. The overall effect of Jack's decision, according to the standard model, is that the household legal system is changed in two ways. It now contains, first of all, a new rule to justify Jack's decision in the case of Max – perhaps the rule, "Children who have not completed their homework cannot stay up and watch TV." And second, the rule previously set out by Jo in the case of Emma has now been modified in order to avoid an unwanted application in the latter case – perhaps reading, "Children age nine or greater can stay up and watch TV, unless they have failed to complete their homework."

Various proposals have been offered about how, exactly, Jack's modification of Jo's previous rule might be justified. Maybe Jack thinks his modified rule provides a better representation than Jo's original formulation of what she had in mind to begin with, or that – whether or not this is what she had in mind – the new rule is the one Jo would have set out had she found herself in, or at least envisioned, the new situation presented by Max.[12] Or maybe Jack simply feels that the overall household regulatory system is sufficiently improved by his modification of Jo's rule. Regardless of justification, however, the fact that the standard model of constraint allows Jack to modify Jo's rule at all leads to a conceptual problem concerning the very notion of rule-based constraint: if Jack is indeed able to reformulate Jo's earlier rule in order to avoid unwanted application in a later case, how can he be thought of as constrained by that rule? Or more generally: if the constraints imposed

[12] The idea that later modifications of a common law rule are meant to capture what the "original court had in mind" is explored by Raz (1979, p. 188); Aristotle's picture is, evidently, based on the counterfactual condition – that a "decree," or rule modification, is meant to represent "what the legislator himself would have said had he been present, and would have put into his law if he had known."

by decisions of earlier courts are supposed to be carried by rules, but later courts are free to modify these rules in order to avoid unwelcome outcomes, how can these rules impose any real constraints at all – how can courts be constrained by rules that they are free to modify at will?

In fact, the literature on the standard model contains a response to this problem – first set out explicitly by Joseph Raz, although, as Raz notes, it owes much to the previous work of A. W. B. Simpson.[13] The central idea is that, although later courts are indeed free to modify the rules set out by earlier courts, they are not free to modify these rules entirely at will. Any later modification of an earlier rule must satisfy two conditions: First, the modification can consist only in the addition of further restrictions, narrowing the original rule. And second, the modified rule must continue to support the original outcome in the case in which it was introduced, as well as in any further cases in which this rule was appealed to as a justification.

The force of these *Raz/Simpson conditions* on rule modification can be illustrated by returning to our domestic example, where Jo's initial rule, "Children age nine or greater can stay up and watch TV," introduced in the case of Emma, was later modified by Jack to read "Children age nine or greater can stay up and watch TV, unless they have failed to complete their homework," in order to block applicability to Max. Here, Jack's modification of the rule satisfies both of the two Raz/Simpson conditions: first, it simply narrows Jo's original rule with a further requirement for applicability, and second, it yields the same result as the original rule in the case in which it was introduced, that Emma can watch TV. Suppose, by contrast, Jack had modified Jo's original rule to read, "Children who are female can stay up and watch TV." Although this replacement would succeed in blocking applicability to Max, it violates the first of the two Raz/Simpson conditions: the new rule is not simply a narrowing of Jo's original rule but instead applies in some situations where the original rule would not – to a seven-year-old female child, for instance. Or suppose Jack had modified the original rule to

[13] See Raz (1979, pp. 180–209) and Simpson (1961). Simpson himself was sharply aware of the problem described in the previous paragraph, describing it as a "paradox," which he presents as follows: "[t]he legal process is conceived of as conditioned by rules, yet in a sense, the rules change from case to case; the very point in having a system of rules to ensure consistency in decision seems to be frustrated if the rules themselves lack fixity" (p. 172). His own approach to this problem was developed in the course of a dialogue with Goodhart and Montrose, going back to Goodhart's (1930) but vigorously pursued in the 1950s. See, in order: Montrose (1956), Montrose (1957a), Simpson (1957), Montrose (1957b), Simpson (1958), Goodhart (1959), and Simpson (1959).

read, “Children age nine or greater who have finished their dinner can stay up and watch TV.” The modification would again block applicability to Max, since he did not finish his dinner, but in this case it violates the second of the two conditions: it fails to justify the original outcome in the original case of Emma, since she did not finish her dinner either.

If we understand the standard model as including the Raz/Simpson conditions on rule modification, then a response to our initial problem concerning constraint is now available: even though later courts are free to modify the rules set out by earlier courts, they are nevertheless constrained by these rules, since they can modify them only in certain ways, those satisfying the Raz/Simpson conditions. This response to our initial problem, however, leads at once to another. Presumably, even if some modification of an earlier rule satisfies the Raz/Simpson conditions, a later court would, all the same, choose not to modify the rule in that way unless the court believed that it could actually improve the rule by doing so. But if a later court believes that it can improve an earlier rule through modification, why should it limit itself to modifications that satisfy the Raz/Simpson conditions? Why should the court not be free to modify the rule in any way at all that leads to an improvement, or if its modifications must be subject to conditions, then why these conditions and not others – in short: what is the justification for this particular set of conditions, the Raz/Simpson conditions, on rule modification?

This book offers an answer to that question, but the answer is arrived at in a roundabout way. My principal aim is to present an entirely different model of constraint – the *reason model* – according to which the mechanism of constraint does not depend on rules at all, whether defeasible or strict, but is instead defined in terms of reasons. The approach derives from an earlier proposal by Grant Lamond and is developed here using ideas from the field of artificial intelligence and law.[14] On this view, what is important about an

[14] See Lamond (2005) for his initial proposal and Lamond (2022) for more recent reflections. The first version of the account presented here occurs in Horty (2011), later developed in Horty (2015, 2016, 2017, 2019, 2021). This account has been related to research in artificial intelligence and law in Horty and Bench-Capon (2012), compared to arguments from analogy and enriched in various ways in Rigoni (2014, 2015), limited in scope in Broughton (2019), explored from a formal perspective in Prakken (2021), and compared to Lamond’s original proposal in Horty (2022). More recently, a different interpretation of Lamond’s proposal, and one that connects it more closely with traditional ideas from legal theory, has been presented in Mullins (2020); interestingly, Mullins shows that his alternative interpretation is, in a precise sense, equivalent to that presented here.

earlier decision is the earlier court's assessment of the importance among the various reasons presented by that case, an assessment that is expressed here as a priority ordering among reasons. Later courts are then constrained, not to follow the rules set out in precedent cases, or even to modify those rules only in certain ways, but simply to reach decisions that are consistent with the priority ordering among reasons that has already been established in earlier decisions. The development of the common law is pictured, not as the elaboration over time of an increasingly complex system of rules, but instead as the gradual construction of an ordering relation among reasons, reflecting their importance, or priority.

A principal advantage of the reason model is that it shows how several of the existing models of precedential constraint can be unified, helping us to see what is correct in each, and how they are related. Because of the link between reasons and default rules, it is possible, first of all, as mentioned earlier, to reinterpret the reason model as a defeasible rule model of constraint – and then to generalize this interpretation, showing how the reason model fits into the framework of defeasible reasoning more broadly. Second, once the reason model of constraint has been defined, it can be shown – somewhat surprisingly – to supply the necessary support for the standard model, by providing a kind of semantic justification for the Raz/Simpson conditions on rule modification; indeed, as we will see, the standard model and the reason model are, in a straightforward sense, equivalent.

A different conception of precedential constraint is provided by the *a fortiori model*, according to which – regardless of any rules or opinions contained in earlier decisions – a later court is constrained at all only if it is facing a situation at least as strong for the winning side of some precedent case as the fact situation of that precedent case itself.[15] Because it disregards case rules entirely, the a fortiori model can be seen as advancing a radical notion of precedential constraint. Nevertheless, we will see that, at least on a charitable interpretation, this conception of constraint can be understood as a special case of the more general reason model.

[15] Alexander (1989) characterizes the model of constraint based on a fortiori reasoning as the "result model," and groups it together with the standard model. Although I adopted this "result model" terminology in Horty (2004), I now think it is better to label this particular conception as the "a fortiori model," in order to make it clear that the standard model and the a fortiori model are distinct.

Finally, there is the *natural model* of constraint, according to which a court confronting a new situation is imagined to reach a decision by engaging in a process of ordinary, or natural, reasoning – based on the various reasons bearing on that situation, possibly including previous cases, and assigning to these reasons the priorities they seem to deserve.[16] On this view, the decisions reached in previous cases are treated as nothing but ordinary events in the natural world, to be taken into account, just like any other ordinary events, in the course of natural reasoning, but not as special sources of law. Here too, it turns out that the natural model can be related to the reason model in a helpful way if, as I have advocated, we understand default logic as providing a precise account of natural reasoning. For we can then see exactly how the process of natural reasoning can itself be constrained – shaped, or modified – by precedent cases to yield results that accord with the reason model.

The book contains seven chapters and an appendix.

Chapter 1 introduces the reason model of constraint, setting out basic definitions and illustrating these definitions with a number of examples, including an application to statements formed from open-textured predicates. Chapter 2 then explores some of the concepts underlying the reason model in more detail.

Chapter 3 presents – for the first time, I believe – a precise formulation of the standard model of constraint. Based on this formulation, it is then established that the standard model and the reason model are equivalent. This chapter also presents a precise formulation of the a fortiori model of constraint, which allows us to see it as a special case of the reason model.

The equivalence between the standard model and the reason model of constraint, though perhaps surprising, is also reassuring, in the way that it is always reassuring when two different analyses of a concept, starting from different initial points and relying on different ideas, agree in outcome. Nevertheless, and in spite of this equivalence, Chapter 4 argues that the reason model is preferable to the standard model, for three reasons: First, the reason model supports a satisfying account of the process of reasoning under the constraints of precedent – described informally in this chapter, and characterized as the process of constrained natural reasoning. Second, the reason model allows us to draw a sharp and principled distinction between the two common law operations of distinguishing and overruling a previous

[16] See Alexander (1989, Section 2) and Alexander and Sherwin (2008, Chapter 2), as well as the references cited there, for a more complete discussion of the natural model.

decision. And third, the reason model allows a deeper understanding of the real mechanism through which common law decisions constrain later courts.

These first four chapters, which presuppose nothing but an acquaintance with set-theoretic notation, provide a thorough introduction to the reason model of constraint. Taken together, they define the reason model, illustrate the model with applications, including an application to open-textured predicates, define the standard and a fortiori models, show that the first of these is equivalent to the reason model while the second is a special case, and finally, defend the reason model. For many readers, this may be all they wish to know about the reason model – and certainly, for some readers, it will be much more than they wish to know. The remaining three chapters suggest some directions in which the reason model can be developed. These chapters are more exploratory, more tentative, and involve formal material that is, although not actually more advanced, at least more intricate than that employed earlier.

Chapters 5 and 6 show how the notion of constrained natural reasoning, described informally in Chapter 4, can be characterized more precisely. Chapter 5 first reviews default logic as a formal theory of natural reasoning and extends this theory to an account of natural reasoning about the problems presented to courts.

Chapter 6 then shows how natural reasoning of this kind can be adapted to respect the constraints derived from precedent cases, resulting, at last, in a precise analysis of constrained natural reasoning. The primary goal of the chapter is to establish that natural reasoning adapted to respect hard, or absolute, constraints from a background case base leads to decisions that satisfy the reason model – this result, as mentioned earlier, can be interpreted as a demonstration that the reason model can be reformulated as a defeasible rule model of constraint. But the chapter has other goals as well: It explores the more complex topic of reasoning against the background of, not only hard constraints but also constraints that are softer – persuasive, but not absolute – and offers, within this setting, an account of overruling a precedent decision. It illustrates the way in which the practice of precedent merges the values of individual courts into a shared priority ordering on reasons. And it shows how the tools of constrained natural reasoning can be employed, once again, to help us understand the phenomenon of open texture.

Finally, Chapter 7 broadens the scope of the reason model to a richer representational setting, where situations are described, not in terms of statements that either do or do not hold but in terms of characteristics that may be present, or not, to a particular degree. The original definition of the reason model seems, at first, to generalize very naturally to this setting but then leads to a new wrinkle, which shows that, in this richer setting, the priority ordering among reasons must itself be refined. Chapter 7 is independent of the earlier Chapters 5 and 6 and can reasonably be read without them.

The Appendix provides, first, a list of fact situations and cases used as examples throughout the book, and then a verification of the various observations noted in the text.

1 The Reason Model

This chapter introduces the reason model of precedential constraint, in the simplest and most straightforward setting. We begin with the underlying representational framework, including factors and reasons, and then move through a series of definitions leading to the central concept of constraint. The theory is illustrated, first, with a brief return to the domestic example set out in the Introduction, and then with a more extended discussion showing how the reason model of constraint can be adapted to provide a semantic account of open-textured predicates.

1.1 Basic Concepts

1.1.1 Factors and Fact Situations

For simplicity, we will refer to any individual or entity with the capacity to render authoritative decisions in some domain as a *court* – thus, for instance, in the domestic example from the Introduction, Jack and Jo function as courts in their household legal system. We will suppose that a situation presented to a court for decision can usefully be represented as a set of *factors*, where a factor is a legally significant property or pattern of properties bearing on that decision, and instantiated in the circumstances under consideration. In our domestic example, the legal, or quasi-legal, issue at hand is whether a child can stay up and watch TV, and the factors involved might reasonably include those already considered – whether the child has reached the age of nine, completed chores, finished dinner, finished homework – as well as countless others, such as whether good behavior was exhibited throughout the day, or whether the child has recently been subjected to any indignities that might merit special compensation, such as a nasty trip to the dentist.

But the factor-based representation of legal situations is not restricted to everyday examples of this kind. In fact, this style of representation has been used to analyze case-based reasoning in a number of complex legal domains within the field of artificial intelligence and law, where it originated in the work of Edwina Rissland and Kevin Ashley.[1] Cases in different areas of the law are characterized by different sets of factors, of course. In the domain of trade-secrets law, for example, where the factor-based analysis has been explored most extensively, a case typically concerns the issue of whether the defendant has gained an unfair competitive advantage over the plaintiff through the misappropriation of a trade secret; and here the factors involved might turn on, say, questions concerning whether the plaintiff took measures to protect the trade secret, whether a confidential relationship existed between the plaintiff and the defendant, whether the information acquired was reverse-engineerable or in some other way publicly available, and the extent to which this information did, in fact, lead to a real competitive advantage for the defendant.[2]

Many factors can naturally be taken to have polarities, favoring one side or another. In our domestic example, being older than nine or completing chores strengthens the child's claim, as plaintiff, that he or she should be allowed to stay up and watch TV; failing to finish dinner or complete homework strengthens the parents' claim, as defendants, that the child should go to bed immediately. In the domain of trade-secrets law, the presence of security measures likewise favors the plaintiff, since it strengthens the claim that the information secured was a valuable trade secret; reverse-engineerability favors the defendant, since it suggests that the information in question might have been acquired through legitimate means. As a simplification, we will assume here, not just that many, or even most, factors have polarities but that all factors are like this, favoring one particular side. In addition, we rely on the further simplifying assumption that the reasoning under consideration involves only a single step, proceeding at once from the

[1] The analysis of legal cases in terms of factors was first introduced by Rissland and Ashley (1987); see Ashley (1990) for a canonical treatment, Rissland (1990) for an overview of research in artificial intelligence and law that places this work in a broader perspective, and Rissland and Ashley (2002) for later reflections on factor-based representation of legal information. An important criticism of this approach can be found in McCarty (1997).

[2] The most detailed study of this domain is presented by Aleven (1997), who analyzed 147 cases from trade-secrets law in terms of a factor hierarchy that includes five high-level issues, eleven intermediate-level concerns, and twenty-six base-level factors. The resulting knowledge base is used in an intelligent tutoring system for teaching elementary skills in legal argumentation, which has achieved results comparable to traditional methods of instruction in controlled studies; see Aleven and Ashley (1997). The formal treatment set out in this book abstracts considerably from this detailed representational work.

factors present in a situation to a decision – to begin with, a decision directly in favor of the plaintiff or the defendant – rather than moving through a series of intermediate legal concepts.

Formally, then, we start by postulating a set F of legal factors bearing on some particular dispute between a plaintiff and a defendant. We will let $F^{\pi} = \{f_1^{\pi}, \ldots, f_n^{\pi}\}$ represent the set of factors favoring the plaintiff and $F^{\delta} = \{f_1^{\delta}, \ldots, f_m^{\delta}\}$ the set of factors favoring the defendant. Given our assumption that each factor favors one side or the other, the entire set of factors will be exhausted by those favoring the plaintiff together with those favoring the defendant: $F = F^{\pi} \cup F^{\delta}$. As this notation suggests, we take π and δ to represent the two sides of a dispute, plaintiff and defendant, and where s is one of these sides, we let $\overline{s}$ represent the other: $\overline{\pi} = \delta$ and $\overline{\delta} = \pi$.

Based on this collection F of factors, a *fact situation* X, of the sort presented to the court for judgment, can then be defined simply as some particular subset of these factors: $X \subseteq F$. And where X is a fact situation, we let X^s represent the factors from X that support the side s, so that $X^{\pi} = X \cap F^{\pi}$ and $X^{\delta} = X \cap F^{\delta}$. Of course, any interesting fact situation will contain factors favoring both sides of a given dispute. For example, the situation $X_1 = \{f_1^{\pi}, f_2^{\pi}, f_1^{\delta}, f_2^{\delta}\}$ contains two factors each favoring the plaintiff and the defendant, with those factors favoring the plaintiff belonging to $X_1^{\pi} = \{f_1^{\pi}, f_2^{\pi}\}$ and those favoring the defendant belonging to $X_1^{\delta} = \{f_1^{\delta}, f_2^{\delta}\}$.

This treatment of factors and fact situations calls for two cautionary notes.

First, the literature in artificial intelligence and law displays a harmless – perhaps even helpful – ambiguity concerning the logical type of factors, which will be continued here: although a factor is supposed to represent a legally significant property, it will occasionally be used to stand, instead, for the proposition that some individual or circumstance under consideration instantiates that property. Returning to our domestic example for illustration, if we let the factor f_1^{π} represent the property of being at least nine years old, this factor might also be used to stand for the proposition that some individual under consideration – Emma or Max, say – exhibits that property. The same ambiguity, which begins with factors, can be found in the discussion of fact situations: although a fact situation, or set of factors, is supposed to represent a set of legally significant properties, it can also be taken to stand for some circumstance in which those various properties are instantiated.

The reason this ambiguity is harmless is that it can be eliminated, though at the cost of some additional complexity. The reason it is helpful is that, in a sense, the ambiguity simply reflects the typical pattern of reasoning in the common law. Decisions are reached in particular circumstances based on propositions, according to which particular individuals in those circumstances instantiate certain properties. These properties, abstracted from the circumstances in which they were first encountered, then provide reasons for similar decisions when they are again encountered in different circumstances, instantiated by different individuals and so resulting in different propositions. The shared properties function as links between these different propositions, and so between the different circumstances in which these properties are encountered.

As a second cautionary note, it is important to emphasize that the mere ability to understand a concrete situation, in all its detail, in terms of the set of factors it presents itself requires a significant degree of legal expertise, which is presupposed here. The account developed in this book begins with situations to which we must imagine that this expertise has already been applied, so that they can be represented directly in terms of the factors involved; we concentrate here only on the subsequent reasoning.

1.1.2 Reasons and Rules

When presented with a fact situation, the court's primary task is to reach a decision, or determine an outcome. Given our assumption that reasoning proceeds in a single step, we can suppose that the *outcome* of a case is a decision directly either in favor of the plaintiff or in favor of the defendant, with these two outcomes likewise represented as π or δ.

In addition to deciding for one side or the other, we generally expect the court to supply a rule, or principle, to serve as justification for its decision.[3] Rules of this kind will be characterized here in terms of reasons, where a *reason for a side* is a nonempty set of factors uniformly favoring that side; a *reason* can then be defined as a set of factors uniformly favoring one side or another. To illustrate: $\{f_1^\pi, f_2^\pi\}$ is a reason favoring the plaintiff, and so a reason, while $\{f_1^\delta, f_2^\delta\}$ is a reason favoring the defendant, and so likewise a reason, but the set $\{f_1^\pi, f_1^\delta\}$ is not a reason, since it contains factors favoring opposite sides. Reasons are to be interpreted conjunctively, so that, for

[3] Although I will refer to case rules as "rules," I take no stand on the question whether they should actually be classified as rules or as principles; I think of these case rules as relatively specific, a property associated with rules, as opposed to principles, by Raz (1972), but also as defeasible, a property associated with principles, as opposed to rules, by Dworkin (1967).

example, the reason $\{f_1^\pi, f_2^\pi\}$ represents the conjunction of the propositions represented by the factors f_1^π and f_2^π, and the reason $\{f_1^\pi\}$ carries the same meaning as the factor f_1^π.

Since reasons, like fact situations, are sets of factors, we can stipulate that a reason U *holds* in a situation X – or using more technical language, that X *satisfies* U – just in case each factor from U belongs to X, so that U is a subset of X – that is, $U \subseteq X$. Even though this idea is entirely straightforward, it will aid later generalization for the idea to be enshrined here in a formal definition. To this end, we introduce the symbol $\models$ to represent the standard relation of logical satisfaction, so that $X \models U$ means that the situation X satisfies the reason U, with the notion defined formally as follows:

Definition 1 (Reason satisfaction) Where X is a fact situation and U is a reason, X satisfies U – written, $X \models U$ – if and only if $U \subseteq X$.

And we can define a relation of strength among reasons for a side according to which, where U and V are reasons for the same side, then *V is at least as strong a reason as U for that side* just in case U is a subset of V – that is, $U \subseteq V$. We introduce the symbol $\leq^s$ to represent this relation of strength for the side s among reasons for that side – again to allow for later generalization – with the concept defined formally as follows:

Definition 2 (Strength for a side among reasons) Where U and V are reasons for the side s, then V is at least as strong a reason as U for s – written, $U \leq^s V$ – if and only if $U \subseteq V$.

To illustrate these two concepts: We can see, first, that the reason $\{f_1^\pi\}$ holds in the previous fact situation $X_1 = \{f_1^\pi, f_2^\pi, f_1^\delta, f_2^\delta\}$, or that X_1 satisfies $\{f_1^\pi\}$ – that is, $X_1 \models \{f_1^\pi\}$ – since $\{f_1^\pi, f_2^\pi\} \subseteq X_1$. And we can see that, of the two reasons $\{f_1^\pi\}$ and $\{f_1^\pi, f_2^\pi\}$, the second favors the plaintiff at least as strongly as the first – that is, $\{f_1^\pi\} \leq^\pi \{f_1^\pi, f_2^\pi\}$ – since $\{f_1^\pi\} \subseteq \{f_1^\pi, f_2^\pi\}$.

It follows from our definition that the relation $\leq^s$ of strength for a side among reasons is a partial ordering: reflexive, transitive, and antisymmetric. That is, for any reasons U, V, and W, all favoring the side s, we have:

$U \leq^s U$,
$U \leq^s V$ and $V \leq^s W$ implies $U \leq^s W$,
$U \leq^s V$ and $V \leq^s U$ implies $U = V$.

The relation of strength for a side is not, however, linear. Given two reasons U and V both favoring the side s, we cannot necessarily conclude that either is at least as strong as the other; we cannot conclude, that is, that either $U \leq^s V$ or $V \leq^s U$. This point can be illustrated by noting that, although both $\{f_1^\pi, f_2^\pi\}$ and $\{f_1^\pi, f_3^\pi\}$ are reasons favoring the plaintiff, we have neither $\{f_1^\pi, f_2^\pi\} \leq^\pi \{f_1^\pi, f_3^\pi\}$ nor $\{f_1^\pi, f_3^\pi\} \leq^\pi \{f_1^\pi, f_2^\pi\}$ – the two reasons, both favoring the plaintiff, are incomparable in strength, since neither is a subset of the other. Is this the right result, from an intuitive standpoint? I think so. Although these two reasons both contain the factor f_1^π, the first contains f_2^π, which is missing from the second, while the second contains f_3^π, missing from the first. Now it may be that the factors f_2^π and f_3^π can be evaluated on the same scale, with f_3^π favoring the plaintiff at least as strongly as f_2^π, in which case it would seem natural to conclude that $\{f_1^\pi, f_2^\pi\} \leq^\pi \{f_1^\pi, f_3^\pi\}$, or with f_2^π favoring the plaintiff at least as strongly as f_3^π, in which case we could conclude that $\{f_1^\pi, f_3^\pi\} \leq^\pi \{f_1^\pi, f_2^\pi\}$. But it is also possible that the two factors f_2^π and f_3^π reflect entirely different values that cannot meaningfully be compared on a single scale at all. It would then be natural to conclude that the reasons $\{f_1^\pi, f_2^\pi\}$ and $\{f_1^\pi, f_3^\pi\}$ are themselves incomparable in strength.

Given this notion of a reason, a *case rule* – or more simply, a *rule* – can be defined as a statement of the form $U \rightarrow s$, where U is a reason supporting the side s.[4] For convenience, we introduce two auxiliary functions – $Premise$ and $Conclusion$ – picking out the premise and conclusion of a rule, so that, if r stands for the rule just mentioned, we would have $Premise(r) = U$ and $Conclusion(r) = s$. And we can say that a rule is *applicable* in a situation whenever the reason that forms its premise holds in that situation, another simple concept that it will be useful to highlight with a formal definition:

[4] A technical aside: What this definition of a rule provides is a one-one function mapping each reason U supporting the side s into a rule $U \rightarrow s$, according to which U supports s. This one-one mapping – convenient, since it supports a close correspondence between reasons and rules – would fail without the requirement that the factor sets representing reasons must be nonempty. Why? Suppose the empty set $\emptyset$ were to count as a reason. In that case, since all the factors from $\emptyset$ favor π, and also favor δ, this set, considered as a reasons, would then favor both π and δ. As a result, the single reason $\emptyset$ would correspond to the two distinct rules $\emptyset \rightarrow \pi$ and $\emptyset \rightarrow \delta$. Of course, there are various ways of allowing empty sets to count as reasons while preserving the one-one mapping from reasons to rules: for example, we might assign types to reasons in accord with the side they favor, requiring that reasons of a certain type contain only factors favoring that side – we could then allow the two typed empty sets $\emptyset^\pi$ and $\emptyset^\delta$ as reasons, corresponding to the two rules $\emptyset^\pi \rightarrow \pi$ and $\emptyset^\delta \rightarrow \delta$. Simply as a means of guaranteeing a one-one mapping from reasons to rules, however, the requirement that the factor sets corresponding to reasons must be nonempty appears to cause the fewest complications elsewhere.

Definition 3 (Rule applicability) Where X is a fact situation and r is a rule, r is applicable in the situation X if and only if $X \models Premise(r)$.

To illustrate: The statement $\{f_1^{\pi}\} \rightarrow \pi$ is a rule, since $\{f_1^{\pi}\}$ is a reason supporting the plaintiff. If we take r_1 to stand for this rule, we would have $Premise(r_1) = \{f_1^{\pi}\}$ and $Conclusion(r_1) = \pi$. And we can see that r_1 is applicable in the situation X_1 above, since $Premise(r_1)$ holds in this situation – that is, $X_1 \models Premise(r_1)$.

The rules defined here are to be interpreted as defeasible, telling us that their premises entail their conclusions, not as a matter of necessity but only by default. Continuing with our illustration, what the rule $r_1 = \{f_1^{\pi}\} \rightarrow \pi$ means, very roughly, is that, whenever the premise $\{f_1^{\pi}\}$ of the rule holds in some situation, then, as a default, the court ought to decide that situation for the conclusion π of the rule – or perhaps more simply, that the premise of the rule provides the court with a pro tanto reason for deciding in favor of its conclusion. This connection between rules, reasons, and oughts can be illustrated with a different sort of normative rule, an ethical generalization, such as "If you make a promise, you ought to keep it." Consider an instance of this generalization, such as "If I promise to have lunch with Alex, I ought to do so," and suppose I have, in fact, promised to have lunch with Alex, so that the rule is applicable in the situation in which I find myself. What is the force of this rule? It cannot mean that I ought to have lunch with Alex, no matter what. Surely other, more important considerations might legitimately interfere – to take a timeworn example, I might be called upon to save the life of a drowning child. Instead, the rule is best interpreted as a default, according to which my promise, the premise of the rule, provides a reason for having lunch with Alex – presumably a very strong reason, since it is based on a promise, but still a reason that might be defeated by stronger reasons supporting an incompatible action.[5]

1.1.3 Cases

Given the concepts introduced so far – fact situations, rules, outcomes – a *case* can be defined as a situation together with an outcome and a rule through which that outcome is justified: such a case can be specified as a triple of the form $c = \langle X, r, s \rangle$, where X is a situation containing the factors presented to

[5] The connections among default rules, reasons, and oughts sketched in this paragraph is explored in detail in Horty (2012).

the court, r is a rule, and s is an outcome. We refer to r as the *rule of the case*, and to $Premise(r)$, the reason that forms the premise of this rule, as the *reason for the decision* in that case – and since reasons and rules are so closely related, we will say, indifferently, that the case is decided *on the basis of* either the rule or the reason that forms its premise. Our representation of cases embodies the simplifying assumption that the rule underlying a court's decision is plain, ignoring the extensive literature on methods for determining the rule, or *ratio decidendi*, of a case, and we suppose, as a further simplification, that a case always contains a single rule, ignoring situations in which a court might offer several rules for a decision, or in which a court reaches a decision by majority, with different members of the court offering different rules, or in which a court might simply render a decision in a case without setting out any general rule at all.[6]

To aid our discussion of cases, we introduce three more auxiliary functions – *Facts*, *Rule*, and *Outcome* – mapping cases into their component parts, so that, in the case c, we would have $Facts(c) = X$, $Rule(c) = r$, and $Outcome(c) = s$. And in order for the concept of a case to make sense, we impose two coherence conditions: first, that the rule of the case is applicable to the fact situation of that case, or equivalently, that the reason for the decision must hold in that fact situation, and second, that the conclusion of the case rule must match the outcome of the case itself. These two coherence conditions can be captured through the general requirements that

$$Facts(c) \models Premise(Rule(c))$$
$$Conclusion(Rule(c)) = Outcome(c)$$

for any case c, or in terms of the particular case displayed above, that $X \models Premise(r)$ and $Conclusion(r) = s$.

These various concepts and conditions can be illustrated with the case $c_1 = \langle X_1, r_1, s_1 \rangle$, where the fact situation of this case is the familiar $X_1 = \{f_1^\pi, f_2^\pi, f_1^\delta, f_2^\delta\}$, where the case rule is the familiar $r_1 = \{f_1^\pi\} \rightarrow \pi$, and where the outcome of the case is $s_1 = \pi$, a decision for the plaintiff. Evidently, the case satisfies our two coherence conditions. The case rule is applicable to the facts since, as we have seen, $X_1 \models Premise(r_1)$, and the conclusion of the case rule matches the case outcome, since $Conclusion(r_1) = \pi$. This particular

[6] An authoritative discussion of the problem of determining the *ratio decidendi* of a case can be found in Cross and Harris (1991, Chapter 2); an interpretation of situations in which a court renders a decision in a particular case without setting out a rule is provided in Section 3.3.3.

case, then, represents a situation in which the court, when confronted with the fact situation X_1, decided for the plaintiff by applying or introducing the rule r_1, according to which the reason $\{f_1^\pi\}$ leads, by default, to a decision for the plaintiff.

Finally, with this notion of a case in hand, we can define a *case base* as a set Γ of precedent cases. It is a case base of this sort – a set of precedent cases – that will be taken to represent the common law in some area.

1.2 Constraint by Reasons

1.2.1 A Priority Ordering on Reasons

How do the cases from a case base constrain future decisions? According to the reason model, what matters about a precedent case is the precedent court's assessment of the relative importance of the reasons presented by that case for each of the opposing sides; this assessment can be represented as a priority ordering on reasons. Later courts are then required to reach decisions that are consistent with the priority ordering derived from the decisions of earlier courts, thereby respecting the assessment of relative importance among reasons determined by these earlier, or precedent, courts.

In order to develop this idea, we need to explain how a priority ordering on reasons can be derived from the decisions of earlier courts, and then what it means for the decision of a later court to be consistent with that ordering.

To begin with, let us return to the case $c_1 = \langle X_1, r_1, s_1 \rangle$ – where $X_1 = \{f_1^\pi, f_2^\pi, f_1^\delta, f_2^\delta\}$, where $r_1 = \{f_1^\pi\} \rightarrow \pi$, and where $s_1 = \pi$ – and ask what information is carried by this case; what is the court telling us with its decision? Well, two things. First of all, with its decision for the plaintiff on the basis of the rule r_1, the court is registering its judgment that $Premise(r_1)$, the reason for its decision, is more important – or has higher *priority* – than any reason for the defendant that holds in X_1, the fact situation of the case.[7] How do we know this? Because if the court had viewed some reason for the defendant that held in the situation X_1 as more important, or higher in

[7] When comparing the relative importance of reasons, it is more common to say, not that one has higher priority than the other, but that one carries greater *weight* than the other. I prefer to speak in terms of priority, rather than weight, for two reasons: first, the priority ordering on reasons to be defined here is nonlinear, while the metaphor of weight tends to suggest linearity; second, the ordering to be defined here allows only ordinal comparisons among reasons, while the metaphor of weight suggests that cardinal comparisons must be available as well. Further discussion of reasons and weight can be found in Section 6.2.1.

priority, than $Premise(r_1)$, the court would have found for the defendant on the basis of that reason, rather than for the plaintiff on the basis of $Premise(r_1)$. Second, if the court is telling us explicitly that $Premise(r_1)$ itself has higher priority than any reason for the defendant that holds in X_1, then the court must also be telling us, at least implicitly, that any other reason for the plaintiff that is at least as strong as $Premise(r_1)$ must likewise have a higher priority than any reason for the defendant that holds in this situation.

Recall that a reason U for the defendant holds in the situation X_1 just in case $X_1 \models U$ – just in case, that is, $U \subseteq X_1$. And a reason V for the plaintiff is at least as strong for the plaintiff as the reason $Premise(r_1)$ just in case $Premise(r_1) \leq^{\pi} V$ – just in case, that is, $Premise(r_1) \subseteq V$. If we let the relation $<_{c_1}$ represent the priority ordering on reasons derived from the particular case c_1, then, the force of the court's decision in this case is simply that: where U is a reason favoring the defendant and V is a reason favoring the plaintiff, we have $U <_{c_1} V$ just in case $X_1 \models U$ and $Premise(r_1) \leq^{\pi} V$. To illustrate, consider the reason $\{f_1^{\delta}\}$ for the defendant and the reason $\{f_1^{\pi}, f_2^{\pi}, f_3^{\pi}\}$ for the plaintiff. Here, we have $X_1 \models \{f_1^{\delta}\}$, since $\{f_1^{\delta}\} \subseteq X_1$. And we have $Premise(r_1) \leq^{\pi} \{f_1^{\pi}, f_2^{\pi}, f_3^{\pi}\}$, since $Premise(r_1) \subseteq \{f_1^{\pi}, f_2^{\pi}, f_3^{\pi}\}$. It therefore follows that $\{f_1^{\delta}\} <_{c_1} \{f_1^{\pi}, f_2^{\pi}, f_3^{\pi}\}$ – the court's decision in the case c_1 entails that the reason $\{f_1^{\pi}, f_2^{\pi}, f_3^{\pi}\}$ favoring the plaintiff is to be assigned a higher priority than the reason $\{f_1^{\delta}\}$ favoring the defendant.

Generalizing from this example, we reach the following definition of the priority ordering among reasons derived from a single case:

Definition 4 (Priority ordering derived from a case) Let $c = \langle X, r, s\rangle$ be a case, and let U and V be reasons favoring the sides $\overline{s}$ and s respectively. Then the relation $<_c$ representing the priority ordering on reasons derived from the case c is defined by stipulating that $U <_c V$ if and only if $X \models U$ and $Premise(r) \leq^{s} V$.

And the pattern of priorities derived from the case $c = \langle X, r, s\rangle$, according to this definition, can then be depicted in Figure 1.1. Here, the outer rectangle represents the entire space F of factors bearing on the issue at hand, divided by the diagonal line into the set F^s of those factors favoring the side s on the right and the set $F^{\overline{s}}$ of those factors favoring the side $\overline{s}$ on the left. We suppose that the fact situation X of the current case straddles this divide, as indicated, containing factors X^s favoring the side s as well as factors $X^{\overline{s}}$ favoring the side $\overline{s}$. By our coherence conditions on cases, we know that the case rule r must be applicable in the fact situation of the case – that is,

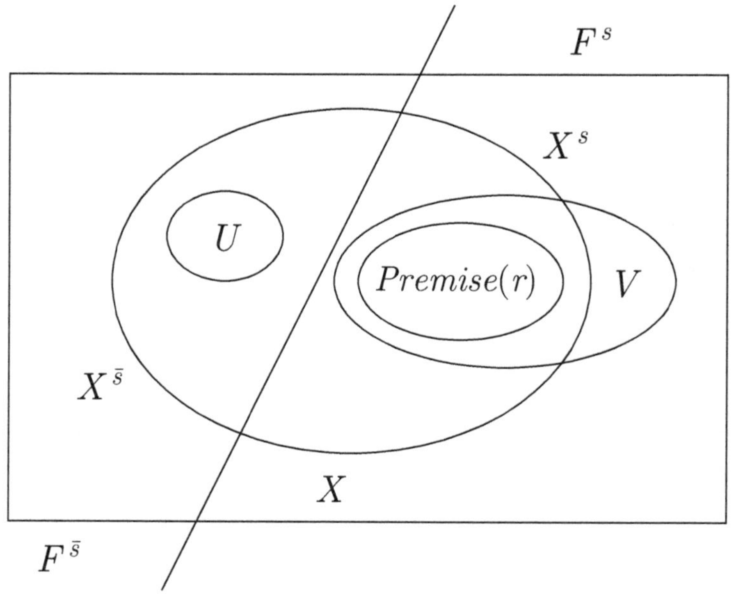

Figure 1.1 The priority $U <_c V$

$X \models Premise(r)$, or $Premise(r) \subseteq X$. And since $Premise(r)$ must itself be a reason favoring the side s – that is, $Premise(r) \subseteq F^s$ – we have $Premise(r) \subseteq X^s$, as indicated. Now suppose, first, that a reason U favoring the side $\bar{s}$ holds in the situation X – that is, $X \models U$, or $U \subseteq X$. Then since U favors $\bar{s}$ – that is, $U \subseteq F^{\bar{s}}$ – we have $U \subseteq X^{\bar{s}}$. And suppose, second, that a reason V for s favors the side s at least as strongly as $Premise(r)$ – that is, $Premise(r) \leq^s V$, or $Premise(r) \subseteq V$. Then again, since V favors s, we also have $V \subseteq F^s$, so that $Premise(r) \subseteq V \subseteq F^s$. What Definition 4 tells us, therefore, is that the priority $U <_c V$ holds whenever the reasons U and V satisfy these two conditions, exactly as depicted in the diagram: first, that $U \subseteq X^{\bar{s}}$, and second, that $Premise(r) \subseteq V \subseteq F^s$.

It follows from Definition 4 that the priority ordering derived from a single case is transitive: $U <_c V$ and $V <_c W$ together imply $U <_c W$ – but only in the trivial sense that $U <_c V$ and $V <_c W$ can never hold together, since, for a particular case c, all reasons standing on left of the $<_c$ relation must favor one side while all reasons standing on the right must favor the other, yet here, the reason V stands on both left and right. By the same argument, the priority ordering derived from a case is irreflexive: $U <_c U$ always fails, since the reason U can favor only one side. And of course, the ordering is not linear either: we need not have either $U <_c V$ or $V <_c U$. Although a particular decision establishes certain priorities among reasons, it leaves others unsettled: from the earlier case c_1, for example, we can conclude that $\{f_1^\delta, f_2^\delta\} <_{c_1} \{f_1^\pi\}$, but we cannot conclude either that $\{f_1^\delta, f_2^\delta, f_3^\delta\} <_{c_1} \{f_1^\pi\}$ or that $\{f_1^\pi\} <_{c_1} \{f_1^\delta, f_2^\delta, f_3^\delta\}$.

It is important to bear in mind the distinction between the relation $\leq^s$ of strength for a side s among reasons, introduced in Definition 2, and the relation $<_c$ of priority among reasons derived from the case c, introduced in Definition 4: $U \leq^s V$ holds when U and V are reasons for the same side s and V favors that side at least as strongly as U, while $U <_c V$ holds when U and V are reasons for opposite sides and it follows from the decision reached in the case c that V carries a higher priority than U. Even though these two relations are separate, however, they interact in important ways – perhaps obvious, but also reassuring. First, if it can be derived from a case c that the reason V favoring s has higher priority than the reason U favoring $\bar{s}$, and some reason W favors s at least as strongly as V, then it follows from c that W likewise has a higher priority than U: together, $U <_c V$ and $V \leq^s W$ imply $U <_c W$. And second, if it can be derived from a case c that the reason V favoring s has higher priority than the reason U favoring $\bar{s}$, and U favors $\bar{s}$ more strongly than some reason W, then it follows from c that V likewise has a higher priority than W: together, $W \leq^{\bar{s}} U$ and $U <_c V$ and imply $W <_c V$.

Once we have defined the priority ordering on reasons derived from a single case, we can introduce a priority ordering $<_\Gamma$ derived from an entire case base Γ, in the simplest possible way, by stipulating that one reason has a higher priority than another according to the case base whenever that priority is supported by some particular case from the case base:

Definition 5 (Priority ordering derived from a case base) Let Γ be a case base, and let U and V be reasons. Then the relation $<_\Gamma$ representing the priority ordering on reasons derived from the case base Γ is defined by stipulating that $U <_\Gamma V$ if and only if $U <_c V$ for some case c from Γ.

This priority ordering, derived from a case base, inherits several properties of the previous priority ordering derived from a single case. For example, the new ordering interacts with the concept of strength for a side in exactly the same way: if U favors $\bar{s}$ and V favors s, then if W likewise favors s, it follows that $U <_\Gamma V$ and $V \leq^s W$ together imply $U <_\Gamma W$, and if W instead favors $\bar{s}$, it follows that $W \leq^{\bar{s}} U$ and $U <_\Gamma V$ together and imply $W <_\Gamma V$. And, like the priority ordering derived from a single case, the ordering derived from an entire case base also fails to satisfy linearity: again, we might have neither $U <_\Gamma V$ nor $V <_\Gamma U$. More surprisingly, this new ordering now fails to satisfy transitivity as well: it is possible for $U <_\Gamma V$ and $V <_\Gamma W$ to hold without entailing that $U <_\Gamma W$. The issues surrounding transitivity are vexed; we will consider some of these issues in more detail later, in Section 2.2.3.

Using this concept of a priority ordering derived from a case base, we can now define a case base itself as inconsistent if its derived ordering yields conflicting information about the priority among reasons – telling us, for some pair of reasons, that each has a higher priority than the other – and consistent otherwise:

Definition 6 (Consistent and inconsistent case bases) Let Γ be a case base with $<_\Gamma$ its derived priority ordering. Then Γ is inconsistent if and only if there are reasons U and V such that $U <_\Gamma V$ and $V <_\Gamma U$, and consistent otherwise.

Is this a good definition of case base inconsistency, and so consistency, from an intuitive point of view? Well, the condition isolated by the definition is almost certainly sufficient with respect to our intuitive notion of inconsistency – surely any case base from which it can be derived that, of two conflicting reasons, each has a higher priority than the other would have to be classified as inconsistent from an intuitive standpoint. But is the suggested condition also necessary? Perhaps a case base might exhibit some other anomaly that would lead us to classify it, from an intuitive standpoint, as inconsistent. Suppose, for example, that the case base contains two precedent cases of the form $\langle X, r, s\rangle$ and $\langle X, r', \overline{s}\rangle$ in which the very same fact situation leads to decisions for opposing sides; surely there is some kind of intuitive inconsistency in a case base like this. True enough, but as it turns out, this particular anomaly entails that the formal condition set out in our definition of inconsistency has been met, so that it cannot be used to challenge the claim that the formal condition is necessary: if a case base Γ contains two cases of the form $\langle X, r, s\rangle$ and $\langle X, r', \overline{s}\rangle$, then Γ is inconsistent in the formal sense of Definition 6. This result follows from Observation 9, established below in Section 3.3.1, which shows that a slightly more general anomaly also entails case base inconsistency, providing further support for the claim that our formal definition of consistency provides necessary as well as sufficient conditions.

1.2.2 Constraint

Building on this concept of case base consistency, we now present the reason model of constraint itself. The guiding idea, once again is that a constrained court is required simply to preserve consistency of a background case base.

Suppose, more exactly, that the court, working against the background of a consistent case base Γ, is confronted with a new fact situation X. Then what the reason model requires is that the court should reach a decision in the situation X that is itself consistent with Γ – the court, in other words, is permitted to reach a decision only if that decision preserves case base consistency.

The reason model applies, in the first instance, to the rules on the basis of which a court is permitted to justify its decisions, specified in the following definition:

Definition 7 (Reason model of constraint on rule selection) Let Γ be a consistent case base and X a fact situation confronting the court. Then against the background of Γ, the reason model of constraint on rule selection permits the court to base its decision in X on a rule r, applicable in X and supporting the side s, if and only if the augmented case base $\Gamma \cup \{\langle X, r, s\rangle\}$ is consistent.

And given this definition, we can now state the central result that a court working against the background of a consistent case base, and presented with a new fact situation, will always be able to reach a decision that satisfies the reason model of constraint on rule selection. The court will never be forced to introduce an inconsistency – there will always be some rule available on the basis of which the court is permitted to justify its decision:

Observation 1 Let Γ be a consistent case base and X a fact situation confronting the court. Then there exists some rule r applicable in X and supporting the side s such that the augmented case base $\Gamma \cup \{\langle X, r, s\rangle\}$ is consistent.

The definitions leading up to the reason model, and the model itself, can be illustrated by imagining, first, a background case base $\Gamma_1 = \{c_1\}$, containing as its single member the familiar case $c_1 = \langle X_1, r_1, s_1\rangle$ – where, again, $X_1 = \{f_1^\pi, f_2^\pi, f_1^\delta, f_2^\delta\}$, where $r_1 = \{f_1^\pi\} \rightarrow \pi$, and where $s_1 = \pi$. Now suppose that, against this background, the court confronts the fresh situation $X_2 = \{f_1^\pi, f_2^\pi, f_1^\delta, f_2^\delta, f_3^\delta\}$ and considers finding for the defendant in this situation on the basis of the reason $\{f_1^\delta, f_2^\delta\}$, leading to the decision $c_2 = \langle X_2, r_2, s_2\rangle$, where X_2 is as above, where $r_2 = \{f_1^\delta, f_2^\delta\} \rightarrow \delta$, and where $s_2 = \delta$. Can the court do this, according to the reason model – against the background of the case base Γ_1, is the court permitted to decide the situation X_2 for the defendant on the basis of the rule r_2?

Well, as we can see, $Premise(r_1) = \{f_1^{\pi}\}$, the reason for the decision in the initial case, holds in the new situation X_2 as well – that is, $X_2 \models \{f_1^{\pi}\}$. And of course, the new reason $Premise(r_2) = \{f_1^{\delta}, f_2^{\delta}\}$ favors the defendant at least as strongly as itself – that is, $Premise(r_2) \leq^{\delta} Premise(r_2)$, or $Premise(r_2) \leq^{\delta} \{f_1^{\delta}, f_2^{\delta}\}$. It therefore follows from Definition 4 that c_2, the court's envisaged decision, would assign the reason $\{f_1^{\delta}, f_2^{\delta}\}$ for the defendant a higher priority than the reason $\{f_1^{\pi}\}$ for the plaintiff – that is, $\{f_1^{\pi}\} <_{c_2} \{f_1^{\delta}, f_2^{\delta}\}$. But Γ_1 already contains the case c_1, from which, in a similar fashion, we can derive the priority relation $\{f_1^{\delta}, f_2^{\delta}\} <_{c_1} \{f_1^{\pi}\}$, telling us exactly the opposite. Since the augmented case base

$$\begin{aligned} \Gamma_2 &= \Gamma_1 \cup \{c_2\} \\ &= \{c_1, c_2\} \end{aligned}$$

resulting from the court's envisaged decision contains both these cases, we would then have both $\{f_1^{\delta}, f_2^{\delta}\} <_{\Gamma_2} \{f_1^{\pi}\}$ and $\{f_1^{\pi}\} <_{\Gamma_2} \{f_1^{\delta}, f_2^{\delta}\}$ by Definition 5, so that, by Definition 6, this augmented case base would be inconsistent. From Definition 7, we can therefore conclude that the court is not permitted to decide for the defendant in the situation X_2 on the basis of the rule r_2, since c_2, the resulting decision, would introduce an inconsistency into the background case base.

Of course, it does not follow from the fact that the court is not permitted to decide the situation X_2 for the defendant on the basis of the particular rule r_2 that it is not permitted to decide this situation for the defendant at all – in this situation, there are other rules on the basis of which the court is permitted to reach a decision for the defendant. Suppose, for example, that the court considers finding for the defendant on the basis of the reason $\{f_1^{\delta}, f_3^{\delta}\}$, leading to the decision $c_3 = \langle X_3, r_3, s_3 \rangle$, where $X_3 = X_2$, where $r_3 = \{f_1^{\delta}, f_3^{\delta}\} \rightarrow \delta$, and where $s_3 = \delta$. The augmented case base

$$\begin{aligned} \Gamma_3 &= \Gamma_1 \cup \{c_3\} \\ &= \{c_1, c_3\} \end{aligned}$$

resulting from this decision would then be consistent. As before, the previous case c_1 supports the priority $\{f_1^{\delta}, f_2^{\delta}\} <_{c_1} \{f_1^{\pi}\}$, and the new decision c_3 would now support the priority $\{f_1^{\pi}\} <_{c_3} \{f_1^{\delta}, f_3^{\delta}\}$, so that we would then have both the case base priorities $\{f_1^{\delta}, f_2^{\delta}\} <_{\Gamma_3} \{f_1^{\pi}\}$ and $\{f_1^{\pi}\} <_{\Gamma_3} \{f_1^{\delta}, f_3^{\delta}\}$. But there is nothing inconsistent about this pair of priorities, as we can see, informally at least, with another homely scenario: one can easily imagine a teenager thinking, and thinking consistently, that going to the movies is more fun than going to the beach with her parents, but that going to the beach with her friends is more fun than going to the movies.[8] And since the decision c_3 is consistent with the background case base, it follows from Definition 7 that a decision for the defendant on the basis of the new rule r_3 would be permitted.

Now imagine that the court does, in fact, decide the situation X_2 in this way, augmenting the background case Γ_1 with the new decision c_3, leading to the case base $\Gamma_3 = \Gamma_1 \cup \{c_3\}$. According to the reason model, this decision would then represent a step in the normal development of a legal system, which proceeds more generally as follows: A court confronts a new situation X against the background of a consistent case base Γ, with an associated ordering $<_\Gamma$ on reasons. The court is permitted to base its decision only on a rule r supporting an outcome s such that the case base $\Gamma' = \Gamma \cup \{\langle X, r, s\rangle\}$ is consistent, with the result that the background case base is augmented with this new decision. The next court confronting the next new situation Y must then work against the background of the augmented case base Γ', which gives rise to the strengthened ordering $<_{\Gamma'}$ on reasons. This new court is likewise permitted to base its decision only on a rule r' supporting an outcome s' such that the case base $\Gamma'' = \Gamma' \cup \{\langle Y, r', s'\rangle\}$ is consistent, thus further augmenting the case base, further strengthening the underlying priority ordering on reasons, and the process continues.

The hypothesis of the reason model is that this is how the common law develops in the normal, incremental case – by building up a stronger and stronger priority ordering on reasons through a series of decisions that are, at each stage, consistent with the existing case base.

1.2.3 The Domestic Example

All of this has been very abstract. For a more concrete illustration of legal development according to the reason model, we return to the domestic example set out in the Introduction. The example centered around a situation in which Jack and Jo have two children: Emma, age nine, who completed chores and homework but failed to finish dinner, and Max, age twelve, who likewise completed chores, but neither finished dinner nor completed homework. Both children wanted to stay up and watch TV. We imagined that Emma first asked Jo, who granted the request to watch TV, justifying her decision with the rule "Children age nine or greater can stay up and watch TV."

[8] A discussion of the process of establishing that a case base is consistent, as well as a verification that this particular case base is consistent, can be found in Section 2.2.1.

Next, we imagined, Max asked Jack, who denied the request to watch TV, distinguishing this case from that of Emma by appeal to the fact that Max failed to complete his homework, and introducing the new rule "Children who have not completed their homework cannot stay up and watch TV."

With Max and Emma as plaintiffs, and with Jack and Jo functioning – as parents do – both as defendants and as adjudicators, or courts, this example can be cast in our framework by letting the factor f_1^π represent the fact that the child in question is at least nine years old, by letting f_2^π represent the fact that the child in question completed chores, and then letting f_1^δ and f_2^δ represent, respectively, the facts that the child failed to finish dinner and failed to complete homework. The initial situation presented by Emma to Jo can then be represented as $X_4 = \{f_1^\pi, f_2^\pi, f_1^\delta\}$, which Jo then decided for Emma on the basis of the rule $r_4 = \{f_1^\pi\} \to \pi$, leading to the decision $c_4 = \langle X_4, r_4, s_4 \rangle$, where X_4 and r_4 are as above, and where $s_4 = \pi$. As a result of this initial decision, the case base representing the common law of the household, at least as it pertains to staying up and watching TV, is $\Gamma_4 = \{c_4\}$, with $<_{\Gamma_4}$ as its associated ordering on reasons.

Next, the situation presented by Max to Jack can be represented as $X_5 = \{f_1^\pi, f_2^\pi, f_1^\delta, f_2^\delta\}$. In keeping with our story, we can suppose that Jack would like to decide against Max on the basis of the rule $r_5 = \{f_2^\delta\} \to \delta$, leading to the decision $c_5 = \langle X_5, r_5, s_5 \rangle$, where X_5 and r_5 are as above, and where $s_5 = \delta$. Is he permitted to do so, according to the reason model, against the background of the case base Γ_4? The answer is Yes. From Jo's earlier decision, we can conclude that the reason $\{f_1^\pi\}$ is to be assigned a higher priority than the reason $\{f_1^\delta\}$ – that $\{f_1^\delta\} <_{c_4} \{f_1^\pi\}$, so that $\{f_1^\delta\} <_{\Gamma_4} \{f_1^\pi\}$ as well. And Jack's decision would force us to conclude also that the reason $\{f_2^\delta\}$ must be assigned a higher priority than the reason $\{f_1^\pi\}$ – that $\{f_1^\pi\} <_{c_5} \{f_2^\delta\}$. But there is no conflict between this priority and the previous priority, derived from Jo's decision – a reasonable individual might, for example, prefer chocolate ice cream to vanilla and vanilla to strawberry. And because the background case base Γ_4 currently contains only Jo's decision, it follows that Jack's decision in the case of Max is consistent with this case base as well. The reason model thus permits Jack to carry through with his decision, resulting in

$$\begin{aligned}\Gamma_5 &= \Gamma_4 \cup \{c_5\} \\ &= \{c_4, c_5\}\end{aligned}$$

as the updated case base now representing the household common law, with $<_{\Gamma_5}$ as its strengthened ordering on reasons.

1.2.4 Decisions for a Side

The reason model as set out in Definition 7 characterizes the rules on the basis of which a court is permitted to justify its decisions. But of course, once this idea is in place, it can be used to define the conditions under which a court is permitted, or required, to reach a decision for one side or another – through the natural stipulation that a court is permitted to reach a decision for a side if some rule on the basis of which it is permitted to justify its decision supports that side, and required to reach a decision for a side if every rule on the basis of which it is permitted to justify its decision supports that side:

Definition 8 (Reason model of constraint on decision for a side) Let Γ be a consistent case base and X a fact situation confronting the court. Then against the background of Γ, the reason model of constraint on decision for a side permits the court to decide X for the side s if and only if some rule permitted by the reason model of constraint on rule selection supports that side; the reason model requires the court to decide X for the side s if and only if every rule permitted by the reason model of constraint on rule selection supports that side.

For illustration, we can return to the domestic example just considered. Here, as we have seen, Jack is permitted, against the background of the case base Γ_4 containing only Jo's decision in the case of Emma, to decide the new situation X_5 presented by Max for the defendant. Of course, Jack is also permitted to decide X_5 for the plaintiff, perhaps on the basis of the rule r_4 originally formulated by Jo in the case of Emma. The example developed thus far presents no interesting requirements, but suppose that Jack and Jo have another child, Chris, who would also like to stay up and watch TV, and of whom it is known only that she is older than nine but failed to finish dinner, so that the situation she presents is $X_6 = \{f_1^\pi, f_1^\delta\}$. Jack is then required to decide the new situation X_6 for the plaintiff, since every rule on the basis of which he is permitted to justify his decision supports the plaintiff.

As our definitions show, the reason model is centered around deontic ideas – it tells us what a court is permitted or required to do. The deontic character of the model is especially evident in the reason model of constraint on decision for a side, which defines notions of permission and requirement that satisfy familiar principles of standard deontic logic. Suppose that, against the background of a consistent case base, a court is considering some situation X. Then it follows immediately from Definition 8 that the court is permitted to decide X for the side s just in case it is not required to decide X for $\bar{s}$, the opposite side, and likewise required to decide X for s just in case it is not permitted to decide X for $\bar{s}$. By Observation 1, we know, further, that there must be some rule on the basis of which the court is permitted to justify its decision in X – the set of permissible rule is not empty. From this it follows that the court will never face conflicting requirements: if the court is required to decide X for the side s, it will also be permitted to decide X for s, so that the court will never be required to decide X for s and also required to decide X for $\bar{s}$. And we can likewise be assured that the court will find itself in exactly one of three circumstances: either it will be required to decide X for s and not permitted to decide X for $\bar{s}$, or it will be required to decide X for $\bar{s}$ and not permitted to decide X for s, or it will be permitted to decide X for s and also permitted to decide X for $\bar{s}$.

1.3 Open Texture: Hart

1.3.1 A Semantic Theory

We have concentrated so far on disputes concerning an issue that is to be resolved directly either for a plaintiff or for a defendant. But it is also possible that the issue under dispute might concern, instead, the proper application of a predicate to a particular individual or situation – and then, of course, the applicability of that predicate might itself figure into a larger dispute to be resolved for a plaintiff or defendant, or it might not. At times, the application conditions for predicates are determined by definitions. To decide whether a plane figure is a "triangle," for example, we determine whether it is a polygon with three sides. To decide whether a natural number is "even," we determine whether it is divisible by two. But it is more difficult to develop a definitional account of this kind outside of mathematics and a very few other formal disciplines.

Suppose, for example, that Jack and Jo have established a household rule according to which Max can go out and play with his friends Saturday mornings once his room is clean. What does it mean, in this setting, for Max's room to be "clean" – how can it be determined whether this predicate applies to Max's room? Jack and Jo might attempt a definitional account, perhaps stipulating that Max's room is clean just in case the floor is vacuumed and the bed is made up with fresh sheets. But what if the shelves have not been dusted and are covered with clutter? On the other hand, what if the bed is not made up with fresh sheets, but the reason is that no fresh sheets are available and Emma is using the washing machine? Jack and Jo might try to refine their initial definition, perhaps leading to: Max's room is clean just in case the floor is vacuumed, shelves are dusted, and the bed is made up with fresh sheets unless no fresh sheets are available and the laundry room is busy. But what if the trash has not been emptied? What if clothes are not folded and put away? Given the unbounded collection of possible complicating considerations, and especially the open-ended nature of this collection, it is hard to imagine how any definitional account of what it means for Max's room to be clean could be successful.[9]

The phenomenon at work in this example is what H. L. A. Hart describes as *open texture*, a feature of ordinary predicates that he illustrates with his famous example of vehicles in the park:

> A legal rule forbids you to take a vehicle into the public park. Plainly this forbids an automobile, but what about bicycles, roller skates, toy automobiles? What about airplanes? Are these, as we say, to be called "vehicles" for the purpose of the rule or not?

And just as famous as Hart's example is his semantic proposal – involving a "core" and a "penumbra" – for understanding the meaning of open-textured predicates:

> If we are to communicate with each other at all, and if, as in the most elementary form of law, we are to express our intentions that a certain type of behavior be regulated by rules, then the general words we use – like "vehicle" in the case I consider – must have some standard instance in which no doubts are felt about its application. There must be a core of settled meaning, but there will be, as well, a penumbra of debatable cases in which words are neither obviously applicable nor obviously ruled out. These cases will each have some features in common with the standard case; they will lack others or be accompanied by features not present in the standard case.[10]

[9] Recent discussions of the problems confronting definitional accounts of predicate meaning can be found in Elbourne (2011, Chapter 1) and throughout Ludlow (2014); a classic account, focusing on theories of sentence comprehension and concept learning, is provided by Fodor et al. (1980).

[10] The passages quoted in this paragraph are from Hart (1958, Section 2), where he first discusses the concept of an open-textured predicate, although in this paper he describes these predicates using the phrase "open character" instead. This discussion is then elaborated upon and extended in Hart (1961, Chapter 7), where the concept of open character is now described as "open texture," a phrase that Hart adopted from Waismann (1945) as detailed in Section 6.3.

According to Hart's proposal, then, an open-textured predicate – such as "clean," applied to Max's room – is associated with a core of settled meaning, which determines a set of cases to which the predicate clearly apples, as well as a set of cases to which it clearly fails to apply. The predicate would clearly apply, for example, to a glittering room: bed crisply made, fresh sheets, floor perfectly vacuumed, clothes neatly folded and put away, shelves dusted, trash properly disposed of. The predicate would clearly fail to apply to a filthy and chaotic room: bed unmade, dirty sheets, clothes and trash scattered around an unvacuumed floor, cluttered, dust-covered shelves. In addition to these clear cases, however, Hart's view allows for a range of penumbral cases to which the predicate neither clearly applies nor clearly fails to apply. It is not hard to imagine that the room of a typical twelve-year-old, such as Max, would fall within this penumbra: bed sloppily made though perhaps with fresh sheets, floor vacuumed toward the center but debris visible around the edges, trash disposed of, shelves still cluttered but haphazardly dusted.

Although Hart illustrates his concept of open texture with the hypothetical example of vehicles in a park, the problems of determining applicability of particular open-textured predicates in various penumbral situations are common in the law. Sometimes these problems seem to be comical, even ludicrous, until the stakes are appreciated. For example, the British court system once considered the question whether Pringles could properly be classified as "potato chips." The reason this question found its way into the courts is that, in the United Kingdom, food is generally exempt from the value-added tax, with only a few exceptions – including potato chips. In an effort to avoid this tax, amounting to roughly $160 million, the manufacturer of Pringles was therefore intent on establishing that Pringles should be classified, not as potato chips but rather as "savory snacks," on the grounds that they contain corn, rice, and wheat, in addition to potato flour.[11] At other times, the importance of the problems involved in determining the applicability of open-textured predicates is almost self-evident. These include the various cases in employment law testing the distinction between "employees" and "contractors," as well as the range of cases exploring applicability of such socially fraught predicates as "marriage" or "rape" or "person."[12]

[11] After multiple levels of appeal, this effort failed, with the result that Pringles were officially classified as "potato chips" and the manufacturers were forced to pay a value-added tax; see Cohen (2009).

[12] A useful discussion of the changing conditions for applicability of the predicates "rape" and "person" can be found in Schiappa (2003).

Because of the intrinsic interest and practical importance of the issues surrounding open-textured predicates, a substantial literature on the topic has evolved within legal theory.[13] For the most part, however, this literature focuses on what might be thought of as broader issues related to open texture – the role of defeasible legal rules, policy arguments concerning the application of these rules, the impact of open-textured predicates on theories of legal interpretation. The legal literature on the topic does not provide anything like a semantic account of open-textured predicates, or at least, not in the sense that a contemporary semanticist would recognize.

The goal of this section is to offer such an account, particularly of open-textured predicates in the law, but an account that may be applicable to uses of these predicates in language more broadly.[14] The intuition underlying this account is that judgments involving open-textured predicates – whether Max's room is clean, whether Pringles are potato chips – are evaluated against a background set of previous authoritative decisions involving these predicates, and that these previous decisions then constrain later applications of the same predicates in accord with a natural generalization of the reason model.[15]

This intuition is developed in several steps. The first is to interpret π and δ – previously regarded simply as grammatically indeterminate symbols indicating a decision for the plaintiff or the defendant – explicitly as predicates, so that, where X is a fact situation, the application of π to X means that the situation is decided for the plaintiff, while the application of δ to X means that the situation is decided for the defendant. If π and δ are predicates, it

[13] Some highlights include Baker (1977), Bix (1991), MacCormick (1991), Lyons (1999), Tur (2001), and Schauer (2008, 2013).

[14] The idea that an account along these lines can be applied in language more broadly, not just legal language, arose in discussion with Cumming, and is currently under development in joint work; see Cumming (2023) for an initial proposal.

[15] Because the account presented here draws on the mechanism of precedential constraint to help explain the use of open-textured predicates, it falls within a strong tradition of research connecting work in the philosophy of language with issues in legal theory; see Endicott (2022) for an overview. Much of the work in this tradition concentrates on the illumination, or lack thereof, to be derived from an application within legal theory of ideas originally developed in logic or the philosophy of language, such as formal treatments of vagueness; see, for example, Endicott (2000) and the papers in Keil and Poscher (2016). What distinguishes the present proposal is that it moves in the opposite direction – rather than exploring the application of ideas from logic and the philosophy of language within legal theory, it applies ideas first developed in the study of legal reasoning to illuminate an issue within the philosophy of language itself, the phenomenon of open texture.

seems clear that they must be open-textured predicates, since a judgment about their applicability in some situation is determined, not by appeal to definition but by assessing the various competing considerations that might favor a decision for the plaintiff or the defendant. And it is clear also that the predicates π and δ are contraries, in the traditional sense that they cannot both apply in a particular situation, but that, at any given point, it may not yet be determined which applies.

Once we have agreed to regard π and δ as open-textured predicates, the next step is simply to generalize the analysis already set out for the particular predicates π and δ to open-textured predicates more broadly. We begin by stipulating that, just as π and δ can be thought of as contraries, each open-textured predicate p is associated with some contrary p'. To illustrate: If p represents the predicate "clean," applied to Max's room, then p' represents the predicate "not clean." If p represents the predicate "potato chips," applied to a manufactured comestible, such as Pringles, then p' represents the predicate "not potato chips." If p represents the predicate "employee," applied to an individual performing a service for pay, such as an Uber driver, then p' represents the predicate "contractor." A pair consisting of an open-textured predicate p and its contrary p' represents the two sides of a *dispute*. As before, we will let s range over these two sides, and where s is one of the sides, $\overline{s}$ is the other: $\overline{p} = p'$ and $\overline{p'} = p$.

For each dispute between a pair of open-textured predicates p and p', we postulate a set $F^p = \{f_1^p, f_2^p, \ldots, f_n^p\}$ of factors favoring the decision that the predicate p should be applied to some object or situation under consideration, and a set $F^{p'} = \{f_1^{p'}, f_2^{p'}, \ldots, f_n^{p'}\}$ of factors favoring the judgment that, instead, the predicate p' should be applied. If we take p and p' to represent "clean" and "not-clean," for example, then F^p might include the factors that, in Max's room, the bed is crisply made, or the floor carefully vacuumed, while $F^{p'}$ might include the factors that unfolded clothes are strewn about, or that trash has not been emptied. If we take p and p' to represent the predicates "potato chips" and "not potato chips," then F^p might include the factor that a particular manufactured comestible contains at least 40 percent potato flour, while $F^{p'}$ might include the factor that it contains other ingredients as well, such as corn, rice, or wheat flour. If we take p and p' to represent the predicates "employee" and "contractor," then F^p might include the factors that, for a particular individual, the company directs "when, where, and how" that individual's work is done or that the individual is required to "undergo company-provided training," while $F^{p'}$

might include the factors that there is no need for the individual in question to perform "on-site services" or that the individual performs the required services using "independently-obtained supplies or tools."[16]

Following our earlier pattern, we let $F^{p/p'} = F^p \cup F^{p'}$ represent the entire set of factors bearing on the dispute between p and p'. And we define a fact situation X that *gives rise* to this dispute as some subset of $F^{p/p'}$ – that is, $X \subseteq F^{p/p'}$ – divided into those factors $X^p = X \cap F^p$ favoring application of the predicate p and those factors $X^{p'} = X \cap F^{p'}$ favoring application of the predicate p'. Again, the most interesting situations are those containing factors favoring opposite sides of some dispute, such as the situation presented by Max's room, as described earlier, the situation presented by Pringles, which contain 42 percent potato flour but substantial amounts of corn, wheat, and rice flour, and the situation presented by Uber drivers, who undergo company-provided training but perform services off-site using their independently provided vehicles.

From this point forward, the account set out already, centered around the dispute between application of the particular open-textured predicates π and δ, generalizes in a straightforward way to any dispute between application of the open-textured predicates p or p' more broadly. A reason U for a side s of the dispute between p and p' is defined as a set of factors uniformly favoring that side – that is, $U \subseteq F^s$ – and a reason bearing on this dispute is defined as a reason for one side of the dispute or the other. As before, the reason U is said to hold in a fact situation X just in case each factor from U belongs to X, or $U \subseteq X$. A rule for the side s of the dispute between p and p' has the form $U \rightarrow s$, where U is a reason for s, and such a rule is applicable in some situation X just in case the reason U that forms its premise holds in that situation. A case *bearing on* the dispute between p and p' then has the form $c = \langle X, r, s \rangle$, where X is a fact situation giving rise to this dispute and r is a rule applicable in that fact situation and supporting the side s. And a case base Γ bearing on this dispute is a set of cases bearing on the dispute.

Exactly as before, a priority ordering among reasons supporting opposite sides of the dispute between p and p', and derived from a particular case bearing on this dispute, can be set out as in Definition 4, and then extended to a priority ordering derived from a case base as in Definition 5. The notion of a consistent case base can be set out as in Definition 6. Finally, against the background of a case base Γ bearing on the dispute between p and p',

[16] These particular factors are extracted from the United States Internal Revenue Service 20-factor test for differentiating employees from contractors.

the rules on the basis of which the court is permitted to arrive at a decision in a particular situation X giving rise to this dispute can be specified as in Definition 7, and the decisions that the court is required or permitted to reach specified as in Definition 8.

1.3.2 The Super Scoop

We now shift from Max's room, Pringles, and Uber drivers to another example, based on a series of United States federal court cases involving the question whether the Super Scoop – a dredge, at the time the largest in the world – could properly be classified as a "vessel." The issue was originally brought before the courts by Willard Stewart, a marine engineer working on the Super Scoop, who was injured on the job through, as he claimed, the company's negligence, and sought compensation for damages. Stewart had two routes to recovery. He could file a claim through the Longshoreman and Harbor Workers' Compensation Act, a federal statute that would provide the equivalent of workers' compensation but would exclude negligence. Or he could file under the Jones Act, another federal statute specifically enacted to protect seamen, due to the extraordinary perils of work at sea, containing the language

> Any seaman who shall suffer personal injury in the course of his employment may, at his election, maintain an action for damages at law, with the right of trial by jury …

and so allowing recovery for negligence.[17]

Because Stewart hoped to claim negligence under the Jones Act, it was necessary for him to establish that he had been employed by Dutra as a "seaman" at the time of his injury. Although this term is not defined in the Jones Act itself, a gloss on the statute specifies that whether or not an individual is a seaman depends on that individual's connection with a vessel. The nature of Stewart's connection with the Super Scoop was never an issue, since all parties acknowledged that he had been employed as a member of its crew. The question remained, however, whether the Super Scoop could legitimately be classified as a "vessel" – or more exactly, a "vessel in navigation" – as this predicate was understood in the Jones Act, and on that issue, there were considerations naturally favoring different

[17] 46 U.S.C. App. §688(a). The Act has since been further amended and recodified at 46 USC 30104.

sides. On one hand, the Super Scoop shared a number of characteristics with more typical vessels. It had a captain and crew, as well as various marine appurtenances, such as ballast tanks and navigation lights, and, importantly, it was registered with and subject to regulations of the United States Coast Guard. On the other hand, the Super Scoop was incapable of self-propulsion but had to be towed from one location to another, and its primary purpose was construction, rather than navigation.

Stewart's suit against Dutra began in the District Court of Massachusetts, which found that the Super Scoop was not a vessel, so that Stuart could not proceed under the Jones Act, a decision that was upheld by the First Circuit Court of Appeals in *Stewart v. Dutra Construction Co., Inc.*[18] The decision was then appealed again to the United States Supreme Court, which reversed the Appeals Court judgment, ruling instead that the Super Scoop was a vessel, and allowing Stewart to proceed with his Jones Act suit.[19]

We will not consider here the reasoning either of the District Court or of the Supreme Court but focus only on the decision of the First Circuit Court of Appeals, which was explicitly based on the precedent established in *Di Giovanni v. Traylor Bros., Inc.*, an earlier case before the same court, and dealing with the same issue.[20] This case concerned, not a dredge, but a barge, the Betty F, bearing a crane used for bridge construction. The Betty F was similar, in many ways, to the Super Scoop, with a captain and crew, requiring Coast Guard registration, but without the capacity for self-propulsion, and with construction rather than navigation as its primary business; in addition, at the time of the incident in question, the Betty F had been largely stationary for over a month. This incident occurred when Rocco Di Giovanni, a workman on the Betty F, slipped and fell, due to the negligence of Traylor in failing to address a hydraulic fluid leak. Like Stewart, Di Giovanni hoped to bring suit as a seaman under the Jones Act. Again, the sole point of contention was whether or not the Betty F could be classified as a vessel, a question that had been presented to the First Circuit Court of Appeals, which decided that the Betty F could not be so classified, on the grounds that "if a barge, or other float's 'purpose or primary business is *not* navigation or commerce,' then workers assigned thereto ... are to be considered seamen only when it is in actual navigation or transit."[21] Confronted with an analogous issue

[18] 230 F.3d 461 (1st Cir. 2000).
[19] 543 U.S. 481 (2005).
[20] 959 F.2d 1119 (1st Cir. 1992).
[21] 959 F.2d at 1123 (1st Cir. 1992).

in *Stewart*, the court felt that it was bound by its own precedent, and so concluded that the Super Scoop could not be classified as a vessel either.

To model, or at least approximate, the situation confronting the First Circuit Court in *Stewart* within the current framework, we let the open-textured predicates v and v' represent the judgments that some marine platform is or is not a vessel. Among the factors favoring v, that the object is a vessel, we let f_1^v indicate that it has a captain and crew and f_2^v that it is subject to Coast Guard regulations. Among the factors favoring v', that the object is not a vessel, we let $f_1^{v'}$ indicate that it is not capable of self-propulsion, $f_2^{v'}$ that its primary business is not navigation, and $f_3^{v'}$ that it has been largely stationary for at least a month.

Using this notation, the situation presented by the Betty F to the *Di Giovanni* court can be represented as $X_7 = \{f_1^v, f_2^v, f_1^{v'}, f_2^{v'}, f_3^{v'}\}$ – and we simplify by imagining that the court was considering this situation against the background of an empty case base $\Gamma_6 = \emptyset$ containing no decisions at all concerning applicability of the predicate "vessel."[22] Given this information, and reasoning, as we imagine, against this background case base, the court then concluded that the Betty F should not be classified as a vessel on the grounds that its primary business was not navigation – that is, on the basis of the rule $r_7 = \{f_2^{v'}\} \rightarrow v'$ – leading to the decision $c_7 = \{X_7, r_7, s_7\}$, where X_7 and r_7 are as above and where $s_7 = v'$. The augmented case base resulting from this earlier decision, and constraining the reasoning of the later *Stewart* court, is therefore

$$\begin{aligned}\Gamma_7 &= \Gamma_6 \cup \{c_7\} \\ &= \{c_7\},\end{aligned}$$

with the situation presented by the Super Scoop to the *Stewart* court itself represented as $X_8 = \{f_1^v, f_2^v, f_1^{v'}, f_2^{v'}\}$, differing from that presented by the Betty F situation only in omitting $f_3^{v'}$, and so forming a slightly stronger case for the conclusion v.[23] Nevertheless, as the reader can verify, the reason model of constraint requires a judgment for v' in the situation X_8 considered against the background of Γ_7 – that is, a decision that the Super Scoop is not a vessel, just as the *Stewart* court itself concluded. In fact, the court justified its decision through a further application of the *Di Giovanni* rule, leading to

[22] This is a significant simplification, since, by the time of *Di Giovanni*, there was already a substantial body of case law concerning applicability of the predicate "vessel."

[23] The precise sense in which X_8 presents a stronger case than X_7 for v will be defined in Section 3.3.1.

$c_8 = \{X_8, r_8, s_8\}$ as the decision in *Stewart*, where X_8 is as above, where $r_8 = r_7$, and where $s_8 = v'$.

1.3.3 Comparisons

Having set out our semantic account of open-textured predicates, it will be useful to draw two comparisons: first, between the present account and the more standard truth-conditional treatment, and second, relating the present account to Hart's own approach.

The comparison of the present account with truth-conditional semantics is short and stark. The goal of truth-conditional semantics is to specify, in a systematic way, the conditions under which sentences are true – so, for example, the conditions under which a sentence like "The Super Scoop is a vessel" is true. The goal of the present account, by contrast, is not to specify the conditions under which sentences are true, but instead, the conditions under which the court is required or permitted to affirm certain kinds of statements – whether, for example, against the background of a set of previous decision, the court is required to affirm that the Super Scoop is a vessel, required to affirm that it is not a vessel, or permitted either to affirm that it is a vessel or to affirm that it is not a vessel. The present account is thus developed at an entirely different level from the standard truth-conditional treatment: it is normative, working at the level of requirements and permissions, rather than factual. And this level of analysis seems to be appropriate for the subject. It is hard to see how it could ever be established, as a purely factual matter, whether or not the Super Scoop is a vessel, for example. But it is easy to imagine situations in which we might have reasons for classifying the Super Scoop as a vessel, or for denying that it should be so classified – especially when the concept of a vessel plays a role in a regulatory system, so that the classification has consequences.

Turning to Hart, his own view, presented in the canonical passage quoted at the beginning of this section, can be compared to the current account as follows: Hart argues that an open-textured predicate has a "core of settled meaning," which determines a range of cases in which "no doubts are felt about its application," but that such a predicate may also allow for a range of penumbral cases in which the predicate is neither "obviously applicable nor obviously ruled out." The current account, however, does not postulate a separate core of settled meaning to determine situations in which no doubts are felt about the applicability of an open-textured predicate. Instead, it relies only on a background set of precedent cases that requires the application of that predicate in certain situations and requires the application of its contrary in others. In the same way, the current account does not postulate a set of penumbral situations in which an open-textured predicate is neither obviously applicable nor obviously ruled out but supposes only that there may be a range of situations in which the background set of precedent cases requires application neither of the predicate nor of its contrary but permits the decision to go either way.

I think of the current account of open texture as providing a sympathetic reconstruction of Hart, capturing in a formal semantic theory much of what is most important in his proposal. At the same time, I also want to argue that an explicit reliance on a background set of precedent decisions, as in the current account, has advantages over any appeal to a separate core of settled meaning. I will try to establish this point by, first, deflecting Hart's own argument, if it is interpreted as favoring a separate core of settled meaning, and then highlighting one benefit of relying, instead, on a background set of precedents.

We begin, then, with Hart's argument for a core of settled meaning. The argument is brief and contained in the canonical passage already quoted. Here, Hart takes as his premise the claim: "If we are to communicate with each other at all ... then the general words we use – like 'vehicle' in the case I consider – must have some standard instances in which no doubts are felt about its application." And from this he moves directly to his conclusion: "There must be a core of settled meaning." But this argument fails if it is interpreted as favoring a separate core of settled meaning, apart from the background set of precedent cases. After all, in the example we have just considered, once the court had decided that the Betty F cannot be classified as a vessel, it follows at once that it is no longer permissible to apply the predicate "vessel" to the Super Scoop either – there is, in Hart's language, no longer any doubt about application of this predicate to the Super Scoop. Yet this judgment does not depend on any separate core meaning of the predicate "vessel" but only on the relation between the situation at hand and the background set of precedents.

Moving on to our positive argument: the current account, with its explicit reliance on a background set of precedent decision, seems to allow a better explanation than an account based on a core of settled meaning for the linkage, or coordination, between judgments concerning the applicability of open-textured predicates to different items that were originally in the penumbra. Imagine, for example, the state of affairs as it existed before applicability of the predicate "vessel" had been investigated for either of the two marine platforms under consideration, the Betty F and the Super Scoop – imagine, once again, that the background set of decisions on the issue was simply $\Gamma_6 = \emptyset$. At that point, it is natural to suppose that either decision concerning applicability of the open-textured predicate to each of these items would have been permissible, or in Hart's terminology, that both would have fallen within the predicate's penumbra. Once it was decided in *Di Giovanni* that the Betty F should not be classified as a vessel, however – that is, once the background case base had shifted from Γ_6 to $\Gamma_7 = \{c_7\}$ – the later *Stewart* court was required to reach the same decision concerning the Super Scoop, since the *Di Giovanni* rule applied to the Super Scoop as well, and the Super Scoop displayed no features on the basis of which it could be distinguished.

What can explain the Super Scoop's change of status – from an item lying within the penumbra of the open-textured predicate "vessel," for which either decision concerning applicability would have been permitted, to an item whose exclusion from the category of vessels is now required? The current account offers an explanation, since the required classifications depend on the background set of precedent cases, and this set has changed, from Γ_6 to Γ_7 – it now contains *Di Giovanni*, which, in accord with the reason model, requires the judgment that the Super Scoop is not a vessel. It is more difficult to find an explanation for this change of classification on any view according to which the classification of an item – as a vessel, not a vessel, or lying in the penumbra – is supposed to depend on a separate core of settled meaning for the open-textured predicate.

One way to understand the difficulty is to ask: if there is a separate core of settled meaning for the predicate "vessel," did this core of settled meaning change with the *Di Giovanni* decision? And here we face a dilemma. If the core of settled meaning did not change, and the core of settled meaning is what determines the classification of an item, then, since the Super Scoop lay within the penumbra prior to the *Di Giovanni* decision, it should remain in the penumbra afterward. On the other hand, if the core of settled meaning for the predicate "vessel" did change with the *Di Giovanni* decision, then that could explain the change of classification, of course. But in that case, if the core of settled meaning of an open-textured predicate can vary with the set of precedent decisions concerning applicability of that predicate, and variation in this set of precedent decisions can account for changes of classification all on its own, as in the reason model, then it is natural to wonder what additional work the separate core of settled meaning is supposed to be doing.

2 Exploring the Reason Model

Having introduced the reason model of constraint in Chapter 1, we now explore certain aspects of this model in more detail. We focus, first, on case rules and the dynamics of case base development, considering some important concepts from the traditional theory of precedent as well as the relation between the reason model of constraint and constraints derived from rules. We then turn to a number of issues bearing on the definitions set out in Chapter 1 but not considered there: methods for determining case base consistency, applications of the reason model to inconsistent case bases, transitivity of the priority ordering on reasons, and some foundational problems concerning the factor-based representation of legal information.

2.1 Case Rules and Case Base Dynamics

Cases contain rules, in addition to fact situations and outcomes. But so far, at least, the only function of these rules has been to isolate the reasons for decisions. According to the reason model, constraint is then defined entirely in terms of relations among these reasons, while the rules themselves remain idle.

Since the underlying case rules have no real role to play in the definition of constraint, it is natural to wonder why these rules should be included in our representation of cases at all. Later, in Chapter 6, we will explore one answer to this question in detail: the reason model of constraint can be reformulated as a defeasible rule model, in which these defeasible case rules play an important part. In this section, we consider some other motives for including rules in the representation of cases. The availability of case rules allows us to see, first, how certain concepts from the traditional theory of precedent, such as the concepts of following a rule or distinguishing a case, can be explicated within the current setting. In addition, and somewhat paradoxically, the explicit inclusion of rules helps us to understand why the constraints derived from a set of common law cases cannot simply be identified with the constraints derived from the rules contained in those cases.

2.1.1 Binding Case Base Rules

In order to explore the role of rules in the current framework, we begin by defining the set of rules contained in a case base as those contained in the cases from that case base. This idea can be captured simply by extending the function *Rule*, which extracts the rule from a single case, to apply to a set of cases as well, so that the set of rules contained in a case base Γ can be characterized as

$$Rule(\Gamma) = \{Rule(c) : c \in \Gamma\}.$$

To illustrate, we return to the case base $\Gamma_3 = \{c_1, c_3\}$ considered in Chapter 1, with $c_1 = \langle X_1, r_1, s_1 \rangle$, where $X_1 = \{f_1^\pi, f_2^\pi, f_1^\delta, f_2^\delta\}$, where $r_1 = \{f_1^\pi\} \rightarrow \pi$, and where $s_1 = \pi$, and with $c_3 = \langle X_3, r_3, s_3 \rangle$, where $X_3 = \{f_1^\pi, f_2^\pi, f_1^\delta, f_2^\delta, f_3^\delta\}$, where $r_3 = \{f_1^\delta, f_3^\delta\} \rightarrow \delta$, and where $s_3 = \delta$. The rules contained in this case base, then, are those belonging to $Rule(\Gamma_3) = \{r_1, r_3\}$, since $Rule(c_1) = r_1$ and $Rule(c_3) = r_3$.

Next, having defined the entire set of rules from a case base, we turn to the concept of a *binding case rule* – where, from an intuitive standpoint, the case rules that are binding in some fact situation are those that have the greatest bearing on that situation. The concept of a binding rule depends on two background ideas. The first is the notion of a rule that is applicable in a particular situation, already introduced in Definition 3 from Section 1.1.2 as a rule whose premise holds in that situation. Since case rules are defeasible, however, not every rule from a case base that is applicable in some situation can be classified as binding in that situation. Some will be, as we say, defeated by more important, or higher priority, case rules supporting conflicting outcomes.[1]

When can we say that one rule from a background case base carries higher priority than another? The force of a case rule, we recall, is that the premise of that rule provides the court with a reason for deciding in favor of the side specified in its conclusion. It is natural, then, to suppose that case rules can be prioritized in accord with the reasons that form their premises, or, more

[1] The concepts of applicable, defeated, and binding rules at work here, and in Chapter 1, are simplifications for the present setting of concepts that will be defined more generally later, in Chapter 5, in the setting of a full default logic.

exactly, that the relation $<_\Gamma$ introduced in Definition 5 from Section 1.2.1 as a priority ordering on reasons derived from a case base Γ can be lifted from the premises of case rules to the rules themselves:

Definition 9 (Priority ordering on rules derived from a case base) Let Γ be a case base, and let r and r' be rules from $Rule(\Gamma)$. Then r' is assigned a higher priority than r by the case base Γ – written, $r <_\Gamma r'$ – if and only if $Premise(r) <_\Gamma Premise(r')$.

Given this priority ordering on rules, we can now define an applicable rule as defeated in the context of a case base whenever that case base contains another applicable rule carrying higher priority than the first and supporting the opposite side:

Definition 10 (Defeat in the context of a case base) Let Γ be a case base and X a fact situation. Then a rule r that is applicable in X is defeated in the context of Γ if and only if there is another rule r' belonging to $Rule(\Gamma)$ which is also applicable in X, but which is such that (1) $r <_\Gamma r'$ and (2) $Conclusion(r') = \overline{Conclusion(r)}$.

Finally, we can define the rules from a case base that are binding in some fact situation as those that are applicable in that situation but not defeated:

Definition 11 (Binding case base rules) Let Γ be a case base and X a fact situation. Then a rule r from $Rule(\Gamma)$ is binding in the situation X in the context of the case base Γ if and only if r is applicable in the situation X and not defeated in the context of Γ.

The concept of a binding case base rule can be illustrated by returning to $\Gamma_3 = \{c_1, c_3\}$ as a background case base and considering the new fact situation $X_9 = \{f_1^\pi, f_2^\pi, f_3^\pi, f_1^\delta, f_3^\delta, f_4^\delta\}$. It is easy to see that both the rules r_1 and r_3 belonging to $Rule(\Gamma_3)$ are applicable in X_9, since both $Premise(r_1)$ and $Premise(r_3)$ hold in this situation. The first of these rules, however, is defeated by the second in the context of the case base Γ_3. The two rules favor different sides, of course, with r_1 favoring the plaintiff and r_3 favoring the defendant. And the second of these rules is assigned a higher priority than the first in the context of Γ_3, since, as we saw in our earlier discussion, from Section 1.2.2, we have $Premise(r_1) <_{c_3} Premise(r_3)$, from which it follows that $Premise(r_1) <_{\Gamma_3} Premise(r_3)$, so that $r_1 <_{\Gamma_3} r_3$. Because both the rules r_1 and r_3 are applicable in the fact situation X_9, but r_1 is defeated in the context of Γ_3, only r_3 is binding in this fact situation.

2.1.2 Following and Distinguishing

The reason model of precedential constraint is extraordinarily simple, requiring courts only to preserve consistency of the background case base; the account makes no appeal at all to concepts from the traditional theory of precedent, such as following a rule or distinguishing a case. Simplicity is a virtue, but at the same time, we cannot just ignore the ideas that have been fashioned by legal theorists in an effort to characterize their practice. We now show, therefore, how some important concepts from the traditional theory can be explicated within the present framework.

Imagine, then, that a court working against the background of a consistent case base Γ is confronted with a new fact situation X, and suppose, to begin with, that none of the rules belonging to $Rule(\Gamma)$ is even applicable in X. A situation like this is our theoretical analogue to the legal notion of *a case of first impression*, presenting issues that have not previously been addressed within the law, so that established precedents have no bearing.[2] What the reason model tells us is that, in such a situation, the court is free to assess the issues presented by the fact situation X in whatever way it thinks best, and then to formulate a rule r as a justification for its preferred outcome s, leading to a decision of the form $\langle X, r, s\rangle$. Any such decision will be permitted, since the updated case base is guaranteed to preserve consistency:

Observation 2 Let Γ be a consistent case base with $Rule(\Gamma)$ the set of rules contained in this case base, and let X be a fact situation in which none of the rules from $Rule(\Gamma)$ is applicable. Then where r is some newly formulated rule applicable in X and supporting the side s, the augmented case base $\Gamma \cup \{\langle X, r, s\rangle\}$ is also consistent.

In a case of first impression, then, there is no precedential constraint at all.

Next, still imagining that a court working against the background of the case base Γ is confronted with the new situation X, let us suppose that some rule r from $Rule(\Gamma)$ is, in fact, binding in this new situation. According to the traditional theory of precedent, the court then has a disjunctive obligation: it must either follow this binding rule, or distinguish the new situation from the previous situation in which the binding rule was formulated or

[2] See, for example, the discussion in Cross and Harris (1991, pp. 200–206); at times, other, more complicated situations are also referred to as cases of first impression, such as situations in which multiple precedent rules apply yet none clearly defeats the other, or situations in which entirely novel factors are present.

applied.[3] How can these traditional concepts of following and distinguishing be understood in the current setting?

Let us assume that the rule r from *Rule*(Γ) that is binding in the new situation X is found in some previous case $\langle Y, r, s\rangle$ from Γ, so that r supports the side s. We will then say that the court *follows* the rule r whenever it reaches a decision of the form $\langle X, r, s\rangle$, leading to $\Gamma \cup \{\langle X, r, s\rangle\}$ as an augmented case base. Following a binding rule presents, in a way, the most straightforward scheme for case base update: the court decides a new situation simply by applying a binding rule that was already established in a previous case. As we have seen, the reason model of constraint is not defined in terms of binding rules, but there is a connection between bindingness and constraint. Although satisfying the reason model of constraint does not require following a binding rule, it turns out that following a binding rule is sufficient to guarantee that the reason model of constraint is satisfied, in the sense that the resulting decision is permitted:

Observation 3 Let Γ be a consistent case base with *Rule*(Γ) the set of rules contained in this case base, X a fact situation confronting the court, and r a rule from *Rule*(Γ), supporting the side s, that is binding in the context of Γ. Then the augmented case base $\Gamma \cup \{\langle X, r, s\rangle\}$ is consistent.

According to the traditional theory of precedent, however, even though the rule r found in some previous case $\langle Y, r, s\rangle$ from Γ is binding in the new situation X, the court is nevertheless free to distinguish this new situation – that is, not to follow the rule r but instead to decide X for $\overline{s}$, the opposite side, on the basis of some reason favoring $\overline{s}$ that holds in this new situation but not in the previous situation Y. To characterize this idea formally, we will say that, when a rule r from the case $\langle Y, r, s\rangle$ is binding in the new situation X, the court *distinguishes* this new situation in the face of the binding rule r just in case it decides X on the basis of a rule r' supporting $\overline{s}$, the opposite side, in

[3] See Lamond (2006), who writes that a later court is not required simply to follow binding precedents, but instead that "the more accurate statements of the doctrine of precedent are to the effect that a later court must *either* follow *or* distinguish a binding precedent – a disjunctive obligation" (Section 2.1.2); see also Simpson (1961), who writes that being "bound clearly implies the existence of some sort of obligation, and the content of the obligation may be quite simply stated ... [it is] an obligation to *follow* or *distinguish*" (p. 150), and Schauer (1987), who writes that "a binding precedent is one that must either be followed or distinguished" (p. 593). Of course, depending on its standing in the judicial hierarchy, a court might have the further option of overruling a binding precedent; we will consider the topic of overruling in Sections 4.2 and 6.2.

a way that leads to an augmented case base $\Gamma \cup \{\langle X, r', \overline{s} \rangle\}$ that is consistent, so that the decision is permitted by the reason model of constraint.

Both the ideas of following a binding rule and of distinguishing a new situation in the face of a binding rule can be illustrated with our current example, in which a court constrained by the case base $\Gamma_3 = \{c_1, c_3\}$ confronts the new fact situation $X_9 = \{f_1^\pi, f_2^\pi, f_3^\pi, f_1^\delta, f_3^\delta, f_4^\delta\}$. Here, as we noted earlier, the rule $r_3 = \{f_1^\delta, f_3^\delta\} \rightarrow \delta$, formulated in the context of the earlier case $c_3 = \langle X_3, r_3, s_3 \rangle$, where $X_3 = \{f_1^\pi, f_2^\pi, f_1^\delta, f_2^\delta, f_3^\delta\}$ and where $s_3 = \delta$, is the unique rule from the background case base that is binding in X_9. The court therefore follows this binding rule if it reaches the decision $c_9 = \langle X_9, r_9, s_9 \rangle$, where $r_9 = r_3$ and where $s_9 = \delta$, leading to $\Gamma_3 \cup \{\langle X_9, r_9, s_9 \rangle\}$ as an updated case base, which we know from Observation 3 to be consistent. Even though the rule r_3 is binding in the new situation X_9, however, the court is also free to distinguish this situation on the basis of some reason favoring the plaintiff that holds in X_9, but that did not hold in X_3. For example, the court might distinguish c_9 on the basis of $\{f_3^\pi\}$, a reason for the plaintiff that holds in X_9 but not in X_3, resulting in the decision $c_{10} = \langle X_{10}, r_{10}, s_{10} \rangle$ – where $X_{10} = X_9$, where $r_{10} = \{f_3^\pi\} \rightarrow \pi$, and where $s_{10} = \pi$ – and leading to the consistent $\Gamma_3 \cup \{\langle X_{10}, r_{10}, s_{10} \rangle\}$ as an updated case base.

With these notions of following and distinguishing a rule before us, we close with two further points.

The first is a point of clarification. We said informally that, in distinguishing a new situation X in the face of a binding rule r from a previous case $\langle Y, r, s \rangle$, the court must decide the new situation for $\overline{s}$, the opposite side, on the basis of some reason favoring $\overline{s}$ that holds in X but did not hold in Y. Yet our formal characterization of distinguishing requires only that the court should decide the new situation for $\overline{s}$ on the basis of some rule r' such that the resulting decision $\langle X, r', \overline{s} \rangle$ is consistent with the background case base, and so permitted by the reason model. Do we know, then, that a decision for $\overline{s}$ in the new situation that satisfies our formal characterization of distinguishing, with $\langle X, r', \overline{s} \rangle$ consistent, also satisfies our informal characterization – that it must be based on some reason that did not hold in the previous situation Y in which the binding rule r was formulated or applied? Yes, we do:

Observation 4 Let Γ be a consistent case base, X a fact situation confronting the court, and $\langle Y, r, s \rangle$ a case from Γ such that the rule r of that case is binding in X in the context of Γ. Then, if we suppose, where r' is a rule applicable in X and supporting the side $\overline{s}$, that the case base $\Gamma \cup \{\langle X, r', \overline{s} \rangle\}$ is consistent, it follows that we do not have $Y \models \mathit{Premise}(r')$.

What this observation tells us, in other words, is that, where the court offers the reason $Premise(r')$ as a justification for its decision for $\bar{s}$ in the situation X, this reason must contain at least some factor favoring $\bar{s}$ that was not present in the previous situation Y.

Our second closing point is that, although the traditional theory of precedent requires a court confronting a situation to which a binding rule applies either to follow that binding rule or to distinguish the new situation, the reason model is apparently more general, presenting the court with options that do not fall within this traditional classification. To illustrate, we return to the example just considered of a court confronting the situation $X_9 = \{f_1^{\pi}, f_2^{\pi}, f_3^{\pi}, f_1^{\delta}, f_3^{\delta}, f_4^{\delta}\}$ against the background of the case base $\Gamma_3 = \{c_1, c_3\}$, with $r_3 = \{f_1^{\delta}, f_3^{\delta}\} \rightarrow \delta$ as the unique rule from the background case base that is binding in X_9. As we have seen, rather than following this binding rule, the court might feel that the new reason $\{f_3^{\pi}\}$ for the plaintiff, which holds in X_9 but not in the previous situation in which the rule r_3 was formulated or applied, has higher priority than the previous reason $\{f_1^{\delta}, f_3^{\delta}\}$ for the defendant, and so decide the new situation X_9 for the plaintiff on this basis, leading to the decision $c_{10} = \langle X_{10}, r_{10}, s_{10}\rangle$, as specified above. But we could also suppose that the court, while still thinking that the new reason $\{f_3^{\pi}\}$ for the plaintiff has higher priority than the previous reason $\{f_1^{\delta}, f_3^{\delta}\}$ for the defendant, believes in addition that the new reason $\{f_4^{\delta}\}$ for the defendant, likewise present in X_9 for the first time, itself has higher priority than $\{f_3^{\pi}\}$. On this basis, the court might then reach the decision $c_{11} = \langle X_{11}, r_{11}, s_{11}\rangle$ – where $X_{11} = X_9$, where $r_{11} = \{f_4^{\delta}\} \rightarrow \delta$, and where $s_{11} = \delta$ – which is, again, permitted by the reason model, since $\Gamma_3 \cup \{\langle X_{11}, r_{11}, s_{11}\rangle\}$ is consistent.

In this scenario, although both the decision and the train of thought leading to it seem to make perfect sense, it would be hard to describe the court's decision in terms of the traditional vocabulary of either following a binding rule or distinguishing the current fact situation from that in which the rule was previously formulated. The court is not following the binding rule r_3 since its decision is not based on this rule, and indeed, the court feels that the current situation X_9 presents a reason $\{f_3^{\pi}\}$ for the plaintiff with higher priority than the reason $\{f_1^{\delta}, f_3^{\delta}\}$ for the defendant, which forms the premise of r_3. But the court is not distinguishing the new fact situation X_9 from that in which the binding rule r_3 was formulated either, since it reaches a decision for the plaintiff, the side favored by that rule. The present framework, then, seems to provide a vocabulary for characterizing patterns of reasoning and justification that cannot be characterized in terms of the traditional vocabulary of following and distinguishing.

2.1.3 Is the Common Law a System of Rules?

Finally, the present framework, with its explicit inclusion of rules, allows us to understand a feature of the common law that can seem very puzzling from a more traditional perspective – the idea that simply following a binding rule can lead to a change in the law. This idea is often alluded to in the legal literature. Levi writes, for example, that "the rules change from case to case and are remade with each case," and later, that "the rules change as the rules are applied."[4] And, Simpson, after discussing the operations of following or distinguishing a precedent rule, writes that "the development of the law is normally brought about by just these two activities," suggesting that following as well as distinguishing leads to legal development.[5]

These remarks can be hard to understand. It is easy enough to see how distinguishing a new situation in the face of a binding rule might change the law. As we have seen, distinguishing typically involves introducing a new rule into the case base. But if a court simply follows a binding rule – if it does no more than draw a binding rule from some precedent case and apply that same rule to a new fact situation – how can we say that "the rules change," or that the law is affected at all?

The reason model gives us the resources to answer this question, as long as we take phrases such as "the rules change as the rules are applied" to refer not necessarily to the set of case rules themselves but, in a more metaphorical way, to the constraints derived from the underlying case base. We can then see that, although simply following a binding rule, applying a familiar rule in a new situation, does not lead to any modification in the set of rules contained in a case base, it may well affect the constraints derived from that case base. According to the reason model, these constraints depend not on rules but on consistency with a background case base. Consistency itself is defined in terms of a priority ordering on reasons derived from a case base. And it turns out that this priority ordering is determined not only by the rules contained in a case base but by the situations in which those rules are applied: two case bases Γ and Γ' containing exactly the same rules might lead to different priority orderings if those rules are applied in different

[4] See Levi (1949, pp. 2–4).

[5] See Simpson (1961, p. 172), who himself cites Levi.

situations – even if the sets $Rule(\Gamma)$ and $Rule(\Gamma')$ of rules contained in the two case bases are identical, the derived priority orderings $<_\Gamma$ and $<_{\Gamma'}$ might still differ.

How can this happen, exactly? How can following a binding rule – simply applying a familiar rule in a new situation, so that the overall set of rules is unchanged – affect the priority ordering on reasons derived from a case base, and so change the law? Put abstractly, the answer is this: By following a familiar rule, favoring a particular side, in a new situation, the court registers its judgment that whatever new reasons favoring the other side might hold in the new situation, and might, conceivably, have been viewed as important enough to justify distinguishing that situation, are in fact not important enough. This judgment concerning the relative unimportance of any new reasons found in the situation is then encoded in the court's decision, and becomes part of the priority ordering derived from the updated case base containing that decision. As a result, the options open to the court when it encounters those same reasons in the future are limited, so that, in that sense, the law is changed.[6]

The point can be illustrated by returning to our initial example, in which a court constrained by the background case base $\Gamma_1 = \{c_1\}$ – with $c_1 = \langle X_1, r_1, s_1 \rangle$, where $X_1 = \{f_1^\pi, f_2^\pi, f_1^\delta, f_2^\delta\}$, where $r_1 = \{f_1^\pi\} \to \pi$, and where $s_1 = \pi$ – is confronted with the fresh situation $X_2 = \{f_1^\pi, f_2^\pi, f_1^\delta, f_2^\delta, f_3^\delta\}$. As we saw in our earlier discussion of this example, from Section 1.2.2, the reason model permits the court, working against the background of Γ_1, to base its decision in this new situation on the reason $\{f_1^\delta, f_3^\delta\}$, leading to the decision $c_3 = \langle X_3, r_3, s_3 \rangle$, where $X_3 = X_2$, where $r_3 = \{f_1^\delta, f_3^\delta\} \to \delta$, and where $s_3 = \delta$. Although the initial case c_1 supports the priority $\{f_1^\delta, f_2^\delta\} <_{c_1} \{f_1^\pi\}$, from which it follows that $\{f_1^\delta, f_2^\delta\} <_{\Gamma_1} \{f_1^\pi\}$, and the new decision c_3 supports the priority $\{f_1^\pi\} <_{c_3} \{f_1^\delta, f_3^\delta\}$, this new priority was consistent with that derived from Γ_1, so that the updated case base $\Gamma_1 \cup \{c_3\}$ was itself consistent.

Suppose, however, that, prior to confronting the fact situation X_2 above – and so, still working against the background of the case base

[6] Lamond (2005) makes exactly this point, that following, as well as distinguishing, a previous precedent rule can change the law; following a rule, he writes, leads to a change in legal doctrine because "every time a precedent is followed, further facts are added to the list of those regarded as insufficient to defeat the reason provided by the *ratio*" (p. 17; see also p. 20). Although there was a slight technical difficulty in Lamond's formulation of this point, mentioned in Horty (2011, p. 21, fn. 22), the basic idea is clear enough and the difficulty corrected in Lamond (2022).

$\Gamma_1 = \{c_1\}$ – the court is faced with the fact situation $X_{12} = \{f_1^\pi, f_1^\delta, f_3^\delta\}$. The rule r_1 from the case c_1 is binding in this new situation, so imagine that the court simply applies this binding rule to the new situation, leading to the decision $c_{12} = \langle X_{12}, r_{12}, s_{12}\rangle$, where X_{12} is as above, where $r_{12} = r_1$, and where $s_{12} = \pi$, resulting in

$$\begin{aligned}\Gamma_8 &= \Gamma_1 \cup \{c_{12}\} \\ &= \{c_1, c_{12}\}\end{aligned}$$

as an augmented case base. Since the rule r_{12} – that is, r_1 – is binding in the context of Γ_1, it follows that this augmented case base is itself consistent. And of course, since the new case c_{12} contained in Γ_8 is decided on the basis of a rule already contained in the previous Γ_1, these two case bases contain the same rules – $Rule(\Gamma_8)$ and $Rule(\Gamma_1)$ are identical. Nevertheless, although it does not affect the set of case base rules, the new decision c_{12} does change the priority orderings derived from these two case bases – $<_{\Gamma_8}$ differs from $<_{\Gamma_1}$. By following the binding rule $r_1 = \{f_1^\pi\} \rightarrow \pi$ in the new situation X_{12}, the court registers its judgment that the familiar reason $\{f_1^\pi\}$ for the plaintiff carries higher priority than any new reason for the defendant that might hold in this situation, a judgment that is then encoded in c_{12}, the court's new decision. In particular, c_{12} tells us that $\{f_1^\pi\}$ carries higher priority than the new reason $\{f_1^\delta, f_3^\delta\}$ for the defendant – that is, we have $\{f_1^\delta, f_3^\delta\} <_{c_{12}} \{f_1^\pi\}$, from which it now follows that $\{f_1^\delta, f_3^\delta\} <_{\Gamma_8} \{f_1^\pi\}$.

And this changed priority ordering also changes the notion of constraint: as we noted, a court working against the background of the case base Γ_1 is permitted to reach the decision $c_3 = \langle X_3, r_3, s_3\rangle$, but this decision is no longer permitted against the background of Γ_8. Why not? Well, as just verified, we now have $\{f_1^\delta, f_3^\delta\} <_{\Gamma_8} \{f_1^\pi\}$. But it is easy to see that the decision c_3 would tell us exactly the opposite – that is, $\{f_1^\pi\} <_{c_3} \{f_1^\delta, f_3^\delta\}$. The decision c_3 is therefore inconsistent with Γ_8, so that the augmented case base $\Gamma_8 \cup \{c_3\}$ would be inconsistent as well.

To sum up: In moving from the case base Γ_1 to the case base Γ_8, the underlying set of case rules does not change – once again, $Rule(\Gamma_8)$ and $Rule(\Gamma_1)$ are identical. Nevertheless, the priority orderings derived from these two case bases do change – $<_{\Gamma_8}$ differs from $<_{\Gamma_1}$ – and change in a way that affects the permitted options available to future courts: the decision c_3 is permitted against the background of Γ_1 but not against the background of Γ_8. Since the options permitted to future courts change, the law must change as well. And since the law changes while the set of case rules does not, it follows that the law cannot be identified with the set of case rules.

2.2 Variations and Elaborations

We now consider some issues bearing on the series of definitions from Chapter 1, leading to our formulation of the reason model.

2.2.1 Determining Consistency

We begin by returning to our discussion from Section 1.2.2 and focus in more detail on the claim that the case base $\Gamma_3 = \{c_1, c_3\}$ is consistent, with $c_1 = \langle X_1, r_1, s_1 \rangle$, where $X_1 = \{f_1^\pi, f_2^\pi, f_1^\delta, f_2^\delta\}$, where $r_1 = \{f_1^\pi\} \rightarrow \pi$, and where $s_1 = \pi$, and with $c_3 = \langle X_3, r_3, s_3 \rangle$, where $X_3 = \{f_1^\pi, f_2^\pi, f_1^\delta, f_2^\delta, f_3^\delta\}$, where $r_3 = \{f_1^\delta, f_3^\delta\} \rightarrow \delta$, and where $s_3 = \delta$. In our earlier discussion, after noting that this case base supported both the priorities $\{f_1^\delta, f_2^\delta\} <_{\Gamma_3} \{f_1^\pi\}$ and $\{f_1^\pi\} <_{\Gamma_3} \{f_1^\delta, f_3^\delta\}$, we argued that these priorities were consistent through a kind of analogy – pointing out that a teenager might prefer going to the movies to going to the beach with her parents but also, consistently, prefer going to the beach with her friends to going to the movies. This kind of argument is suggestive, of course, but does not count as a real verification of case base consistency, and verification, as it turns out, is not entirely trivial.

Let us define an *inconsistency contained in a case base* Γ as a pair of opposing reasons U and V such that $U <_\Gamma V$ and $V <_\Gamma U$ – that is, such that each of these reasons is assigned a higher priority than the other. According to Definition 6, then, a case base is inconsistent if it contains an inconsistency, and consistent otherwise. It is therefore relatively straightforward to demonstrate that a case base Γ is inconsistent, since that involves only exhibiting an inconsistency contained in the case base: some pair of opposing reasons U and V such that $U <_\Gamma V$ and $V <_\Gamma U$. By contrast, it is more difficult to demonstrate that Γ is consistent, since that involves showing that there is no inconsistency contained in the case base: no pair of opposing reasons U and V such that $U <_\Gamma V$ and $V <_\Gamma U$. Establishing a negative claim of this kind can be challenging. In the worst case, it might require searching through a large space of pairs of opposing reasons and verifying individually, for each such pair, that it does not count as an inconsistency.

How large would the search space be? Well, suppose we restrict attention to the plaintiff/defendant factors mentioned so far in this book – the three factors f_1^π, f_2^π, and f_3^π favoring the plaintiff and the four factors $f_1^\delta, f_2^\delta, f_3^\delta$, and f_4^δ favoring the defendant. Since reasons are defined as sets of factors uniformly favoring one side or the other, it follows that even these limited materials would allow for construction of $2^3 = 8$ reasons favoring the plaintiff and $2^4 = 16$ reasons favoring the defendant, so that we would have to consider $8 \times 16 = 128$ pairs of opposing reasons in order to verify case base consistency through an exhaustive search. More generally, a domain with m factors favoring one side and n factors favoring the other would present a search space containing $2^m \times 2^n = 2^{m+n}$ pairs of opposing reasons, a number that could be huge in any realistic setting, with a multitude of factors present.[7] Of course, analytic techniques might allow us to trim the overall search space in various ways, avoiding a fully exhaustive search.[8] But since the search space grows exponentially with the number of factors present, the task of establishing consistency of a case base by considering pairs of conflicting reasons individually is likely to remain overwhelming, in spite of any efficiencies that might be introduced.

Fortunately, a simplification is available. By our formal definition again, a case base is inconsistent if it contains an inconsistency – a pair of opposing reasons each of which it ranks as having a higher priority than the other. It turns out, however, that a case base that is inconsistent in this sense will exhibit an inconsistency of a very special sort, involving only reasons that function as premises of rules from that case base:

Observation 5 Let Γ be a case base. Then Γ is inconsistent if and only if there are cases $c = \langle X, r, s \rangle$ and $c' = \langle Y, r', \overline{s} \rangle$ belonging to Γ such that $Premise(r') <_c Premise(r)$ and $Premise(r) <_{c'} Premise(r')$.

And from this it follows that, in trying to establish the consistency of a case base, rather than searching through the entire space of pairs of opposing reasons for an inconsistency, it is necessary to consider only those pairs of opposing reasons that function as premises of case rules. If no inconsistency can be found among these, then the entire case base is consistent.

The resulting search space is, in general, smaller, and so verification of consistency more tractable: if the case base contains p cases decided for one side and q cases decided for the other, then there can be at most $p \times q$ pairs of case rule premises favoring opposite sides, a search space that is polynomial in the number of cases, rather than exponential in the number of factors.

7 As mentioned earlier, the analysis of trade-secrets cases presented in Aleven (1997) involves twenty-six base level factors, thirteen favoring the plaintiff and thirteen favoring the defendant. In this domain, we would therefore have to consider $2^{26} = 67,108,864$ pairs of opposing reasons in order to establish lack of conflict through an exhaustive search.

8 For example, Bench-Capon (2017) presents a graph-based representation, suggesting various more efficient search procedures, of the priority relations among the reasons based on a given set of factors.

The point can be illustrated by returning to our original task of verifying that the case base $\Gamma_3 = \{c_1, c_3\}$ is consistent. Here, we note that the case base contains only the single case c_1 for the plaintiff and the single case c_3 for the defendant. Rather than examining all 128 pairs of opposing reasons constructible from the underlying set of factors, determining whether any such pair counts as an inconsistency, it is necessary to consider only whether the $1 \times 1 = 1$ pair of opposing reasons that function as premises of the two case rules constitutes an inconsistency – whether, that is, we have both $Premise(r_3) <_{c_1} Premise(r_1)$ and $Premise(r_1) <_{c_3} Premise(r_3)$. As the reader can verify, we do have $Premise(r_1) <_{c_3} Premise(r_3)$, since $X_3 \models Premise(r_1)$ and $Premise(r_3) \leq^{\delta} Premise(r_3)$. But we do not have $Premise(r_3) <_{c_1} Premise(r_1)$, since, although $Premise(r_1) \leq^{\pi} Premise(r_1)$, we do not have $X_1 \models Premise(r_3)$. We can therefore conclude that the single pair of opposing reasons that function in Γ_3 as premises of case rule does not constitute an inconsistency, and so by Observation 5 that the case base itself is consistent.

2.2.2 The Reason Model with Inconsistency

Continuing with the theme of consistency, we now note that, since the reason model constraint on rule selection, set out in Definition 7 from Section 1.2.2, permits a court to reach a decision only if the result of augmenting the background case base with that decision is consistent, the model depends on the assumption that the background case base is consistent to begin with. This is, of course, an unrealistic assumption. Given the vagaries of judicial decision, with a body of case law developed by a number of different courts, at different places and different times, it would be surprising if any nontrivial case base were actually consistent. But in fact, this assumption is not essential. The notion of inconsistency at work in the reason model is not like logical inconsistency – it is local, not pervasive. A case base might be inconsistent in certain areas, providing conflicting information about the relative priority of particular reasons, while remaining consistent elsewhere. It is possible, therefore, to generalize the reason model in order to apply also to inconsistent case bases, by requiring of a court, not necessarily that its decision should preserve the consistency of a consistent case base, but only that its decision should introduce no new inconsistencies, which were not present before, into a case base that may already be inconsistent.

To state this idea precisely, we recall from the previous section that an inconsistency in a case base Γ is defined as a pair of opposing reasons U and

V such that $U <_\Gamma V$ and $V <_\Gamma U$. The idea that a court should introduce no new inconsistencies into a case base can then be captured through the requirement that every inconsistency present after the court's decision must already have been present prior to that decision, leading to the following generalization of our earlier statement of the reason model:

Definition 12 (Reason model constraint on rule selection: generalization) Let Γ be a case base and X a fact situation confronting the court. Then against the background of Γ, the general version of the reason model constraint on rule selection permits the court to base its decision in X on a rule r, applicable in X and supporting the side s, if and only if, where $\Gamma' = \Gamma \cup \{\langle X, r, s\rangle\}$ is the augmented case base resulting from this decision, then: for any reasons U and V, whenever $U <_{\Gamma'} V$ and $V <_{\Gamma'} U$, it also holds that $U <_\Gamma V$ and $V <_\Gamma U$.

In situations in which a background case base may already be inconsistent, this generalization of the reason model of constraint on rule selection can be used in place of the previous version, set out in Definitions 7, which permits a decision only if the result of updating the background case base with that decision is consistent; as the reader can verify, however, this generalization of the reason model agrees with the previous version when applied to a consistent case base.[9]

The more general definition of the reason model can be illustrated by considering the case base $\Gamma_9 = \{c_{13}, c_{14}\}$ with $c_{13} = \langle X_{13}, r_{13}, s_{13}\rangle$, where $X_{13} = \{f_1^\pi, f_1^\delta, f_2^\delta\}$, where $r_{13} = \{f_1^\pi\} \to \pi$, and where $s_{13} = \pi$, and with $c_{14} = \langle X_{14}, r_{14}, s_{14}\rangle$, where $X_{14} = \{f_1^\pi, f_1^\delta\}$, where $r_{14} = \{f_1^\delta\} \to \delta$, and where $s_{14} = \delta$. This case base is inconsistent, of course, since it yields both $\{f_1^\delta\} <_{\Gamma_9} \{f_1^\pi\}$ and $\{f_1^\pi\} <_{\Gamma_9} \{f_1^\delta\}$. But now, suppose that, against the background of this case base, the court confronts the new fact situation $X_{15} = \{f_1^\pi, f_2^\delta\}$. According to our original Definition 7, the court simply cannot satisfy the reason model – no decision is permitted, since no decision results in a consistent case base. According to the new Definition 12, however, one of the two decisions available to the court satisfies our more general definition of the reason model while the other does not.

[9] It is also worth asking whether, when considering a new situation against the background of an inconsistent case base, there is always some rule on the basis of which the court is permitted to justify its decision in the sense of Definition 12 – does this new definition, that is, support an analogue to the previous Observation 1? The answer is Yes, as established in Canavotto (2022).

The decision that satisfies our more general definition in the situation X_{15} is a decision for the plaintiff on the basis of $\{f_1^\pi\}$, leading to $c_{15} = \langle X_{15}, r_{15}, s_{15}\rangle$, where X_{15} is as above, where $r_{15} = \{f_1^\pi\} \rightarrow \pi$, and where $s_{15} = \pi$; the reader can verify that the augmented case base $\Gamma_9{}' = \Gamma_9 \cup \{\langle X_{15}, r_{15}, s_{15}\rangle\}$ contains no inconsistencies that are not already present in Γ_9: whenever $U <_{\Gamma_9{}'} V$ and $V <_{\Gamma_9{}'} U$, it also holds that $U <_{\Gamma_9} V$ and $V <_{\Gamma_9} U$. The decision that fails to satisfy even our more general definition of the reason model is a decision for the defendant on the basis of $\{f_2^\delta\}$, leading to $c_{16} = \langle X_{16}, r_{16}, s_{16}\rangle$, where $X_{16} = X_{15}$, where $r_{16} = \{f_2^\delta\} \rightarrow \delta$, and where $s_{16} = \delta$, and resulting in $\Gamma_9{}'' = \Gamma_9 \cup \{\langle X_{16}, r_{16}, s_{16}\rangle\}$ as an augmented case base. This decision would introduce a new inconsistency into the background case base, since, as the reader can again verify, we would then have both $\{f_2^\delta\} <_{\Gamma_9{}''} \{f_1^\pi\}$ and $\{f_1^\pi\} <_{\Gamma_9{}''} \{f_2^\delta\}$, even though it did not previously hold that both $\{f_2^\delta\} <_{\Gamma_9} \{f_1^\pi\}$ and $\{f_1^\pi\} <_{\Gamma_9} \{f_2^\delta\}$.

2.2.3 Transitivity

Next, we return to the vexed issues surrounding transitivity of the priority ordering derived from an entire case base. As noted earlier, in Section 1.2.1, the relation $<_\Gamma$ introduced in Definition 5 to represent the priority ordering among reasons derived from the case base Γ is not transitive: $U <_\Gamma V$ and $V <_\Gamma W$ do not entail $U <_\Gamma W$. Indeed, quite the opposite. As we can see from the definitions advanced in our earlier discussion, whenever $U <_\Gamma V$, the two reasons U and V must favor opposite sides of some dispute. Hence, given $U <_\Gamma V$ and $V <_\Gamma W$, we can conclude that U and W, both lying opposed to V, must themselves favor the same side, from which it follows that $U <_\Gamma W$ fails.

What blocks transitivity, then, is the assumption – built into our definition – that two reasons can be related by the $<_\Gamma$ relation only if they favor opposite sides. This assumption is not unnatural. The $<_\Gamma$ relation is built on top of the $<_c$ relation, representing the priority ordering among reasons derived from the single case c, and what the court decides in any single case is whether the reasons presented for one side do or do not have higher priority than the reasons presented for another; any observation that a reason for one side happens to have higher priority than another reason for that same side would likely be taken as mere dicta, and not authoritative in future decisions.

But even if a priority comparison between reasons favoring the same side cannot be derived from a single case, perhaps such a comparison can be derived by combining information from several cases within a case base. Suppose, for example, that our background case base is $\Gamma_{10} = \{c_{17}, c_{18}, c_{19}\}$, with $c_{17} = \langle X_{17}, r_{17}, s_{17} \rangle$, where $X_{17} = \{f_1^\pi, f_1^\delta\}$, where $r_{17} = \{f_1^\pi\} \to \pi$, and where $s_{17} = \pi$, with $c_{18} = \langle X_{18}, r_{18}, s_{18} \rangle$, where $X_{18} = \{f_1^\pi, f_2^\delta\}$, where $r_{18} = \{f_2^\delta\} \to \delta$, and where $s_{18} = \delta$, and with $c_{19} = \langle X_{19}, r_{19}, s_{19} \rangle$, where $X_{19} = \{f_2^\pi, f_2^\delta\}$, where $r_{19} = \{f_2^\pi\} \to \pi$, and where $s_{19} = \pi$. From these three cases, taken individually, we know that $\{f_1^\delta\} <_{c_{17}} \{f_1^\pi\}$, that $\{f_1^\pi\} <_{c_{18}} \{f_2^\delta\}$, and that $\{f_2^\delta\} <_{c_{19}} \{f_2^\pi\}$; and then, since each of these cases is contained in the case base Γ_{21}, we have:

$$\{f_1^\delta\} <_{\Gamma_{21}} \{f_1^\pi\},$$
$$\{f_1^\pi\} <_{\Gamma_{21}} \{f_2^\delta\},$$
$$\{f_2^\delta\} <_{\Gamma_{21}} \{f_2^\pi\}.$$

However, at least according to the Definition 5 treatment of priority derived from a case base, we do not have, as transitivity might suggest, the further conclusion $\{f_1^\delta\} <_{\Gamma_{21}} \{f_2^\pi\}$. There is no case c belonging to Γ_{21} such that $\{f_1^\delta\} <_c \{f_2^\pi\}$ – indeed, there is no case belonging to Γ_{21} whose fact situation satisfies both the reasons $\{f_2^\pi\}$ and $\{f_1^\delta\}$, and so the comparative priority of these two reasons is never even considered. Nevertheless, we can imagine the following form of argument in favor of the idea that the case base Γ_{21} should support the conclusion that $\{f_2^\pi\}$ has higher priority as a reason for the plaintiff than $\{f_1^\delta\}$ as a reason for the defendant:

> From c_{18} and c_{19}, we have $\{f_1^\pi\} <_{c_{18}} \{f_2^\delta\}$ and $\{f_2^\delta\} <_{c_{19}} \{f_2^\pi\}$ – that $\{f_2^\delta\}$ has higher priority as a reason for the defendant than $\{f_1^\pi\}$ as a reason for the plaintiff, and that $\{f_2^\pi\}$ has higher priority as a reason for the plaintiff than $\{f_2^\delta\}$ as a reason for the defendant. Since both c_{18} and c_{19} are contained in Γ_{21}, these results can be combined to yield the Γ_{21} conclusion that $\{f_2^\pi\}$ itself has higher priority as a reason for the plaintiff than $\{f_1^\pi\}$ does – otherwise, why would $\{f_2^\pi\}$ but not $\{f_1^\pi\}$ have higher priority than $\{f_2^\delta\}$? From c_{17}, we have $\{f_1^\delta\} <_{c_{17}} \{f_1^\pi\}$ – that $\{f_1^\pi\}$ has higher priority as a reason for the plaintiff than $\{f_1^\delta\}$ as a reason for the defendant. Since c_{17} is also contained in Γ_{21}, this result can be combined with the previous conclusion, that $\{f_2^\pi\}$ has higher priority as a reason for the plaintiff than $\{f_1^\pi\}$ does, to yield the further Γ_{21} conclusion that $\{f_2^\pi\}$ likewise has higher priority as a reason for the plaintiff than $\{f_1^\delta\}$ as a reason for the defendant.

This argument is appealing, in many ways, and there is no technical difficulty involved in capturing the underlying idea – transitivity of the priority ordering – in the current framework. To do so, we need only replace our canonical treatment of case base priority from Definition 5 with an alternative definition that incorporates transitivity, leaving all other definitions unchanged:

Definition 13 (Transitive priority ordering derived from a case base) Let Γ be a case base, and let U and V be reasons. Then the relation $<_\Gamma$ representing the priority ordering on reasons derived from the case base Γ is defined by stipulating that $U <_\Gamma V$ if and only if there is some sequence $c_1, \ldots c_n$ of cases from Γ and some sequence $W_1, \ldots W_{n+1}$ of reasons such that (1) $W_1 = U$ and $W_{n+1} = V$ and (2) $W_i <_{c_i} W_{i+1}$ for i from 1 through n.

On the basis of this transitive definition, we can now reach the conclusion that $\{f_1^\delta\} <_{\Gamma_{21}} \{f_2^\pi\}$ from the previous observations that $\{f_1^\delta\} <_{c_{17}} \{f_1^\pi\}$, that $\{f_1^\pi\} <_{c_{18}} \{f_2^\delta\}$, and that $\{f_2^\delta\} <_{c_{19}} \{f_2^\pi\}$, since each of c_{17}, c_{18}, and c_{19} belong to Γ_{21}. And of course, with other definitions unchanged, this new, stronger notion of transitive priority affects the overall concept of constraint as well. Suppose, for example, that, working against the background of Γ_{21}, the court is confronted with the new fact situation $X_{20} = \{f_2^\pi, f_1^\delta\}$, and wishes to find for the defendant on the basis of $\{f_1^\delta\}$, leading to the decision $c_{20} = \langle X_{20}, r_{20}, s_{20}\rangle$, where X_{20} is as above, where $r_{20} = \{f_1^\delta\} \rightarrow \delta$, and where $s_{20} = \delta$. Is the court permitted to decide as it wishes? According to our earlier formulation of the reason model, based on the canonical treatment of priority from Definition 5, this decision is indeed permitted, since the updated case base $\Gamma_{21} \cup \{\langle X_{20}, r_{20}, s_{20}\rangle\}$ is consistent. But according to the version of the reason model now under consideration, based on the transitive notion of priority set out in Definition 13, this decision would not be permitted: the updated case base would be inconsistent, since the proposed decision supports the priority $\{f_2^\pi\} <_{c_{20}} \{f_1^\delta\}$, which would then conflict with the priority $\{f_1^\delta\} <_{\Gamma_{21}} \{f_2^\pi\}$ derivable from the transitive definition.

Which version of the reason model is right, the canonical formulation, based on the original Definition 5, or the new version, based on the transitive Definition 13? I am not sure. Even though the argument displayed above is appealing, and the extension to a transitive treatment of priority is straightforward, I am not entirely convinced that we should adopt this extension. My concerns have to do with transitivity itself, and in particular, with the way in which transitivity allows the priority orderings among different reasons established by different courts to be amalgamated together into a group ordering, even though the various reasons involved may never have been compared with each other by any single court – as in our example, where the separate judgments of the c_{17}, c_{18}, and c_{19} courts are combined to support the overall judgment that the reason $\{f_2^\pi\}$ has higher priority than the reason $\{f_1^\delta\}$, even though no single court has ever compared these two reasons. The prospect of shifting to a transitive priority ordering on reasons would introduce a number of complex issues concerning the amalgamation of judgments and preferences from different sources.[10] In order to avoid these additional complexities, we concentrate in the remainder of this book only on the canonical formulation of the reason model, relying on the case base priority ordering set out in Definition 5, leaving the promises and problems associated with any possible transitive extension of this canonical formulation for another time.

2.2.4 Factors, Again

The present account depends on a particular factor-based representation of legal information that itself raises a number of issues. We close this chapter simply by mentioning two of these issues, each of which suggests the need for substantial generalization of the current representational format.

The first is that the fact situations at work here are specified only in terms of the factors they contain, not the factors they fail to contain; but often, the explicit absence of a factor is as important to the meaning of a case as its presence. The current representation of a fact situation simply as a set of positive factors leaves us with no middle ground: if a factor is not listed as present in a fact situation, it must be regarded as absent. Indeed, this perspective is sometimes adopted by legal theorists: Raz, for example, suggests that it is reasonable to suppose that a case can be characterized as one in which *not-F* whenever "there is no record whether it was a case of *F* or of *not-F*."[11] This style of reasoning – from the absence of positive information to the presence of negative information – is known in the computer science literature as "closed world reasoning."[12] It is certainly appropriate in some situations: if the Air France flight schedule does not explicitly list a flight from New York to Paris at 5:00pm on Saturday, we can conclude from this that there is no such flight; if I do not know that I have a brother, it is

[10] Any reader who is unfamiliar with these issues is invited to consult Kornhauser and Sager (1986) and the extensive literature on judgment aggregation spawned by this paper; an authoritative review of this work by one of its central figures is found in List (2012).

[11] Raz (1979, p. 187).

[12] The classic reference is Reiter (1978); see also Minker (1988).

reasonable to conclude from this that I have no brother. But there are other situations in which closed world reasoning is much less appropriate: to take an extreme example, if I do not happen to know that President Biden is wearing a blue suit today, it would be unreasonable for me to conclude from this that he is, in fact, not wearing a blue suit.

Rather than assuming that closed world reasoning applies uniformly for legal factors, or that it uniformly fails, some writers, such as Vincent Aleven, suppose, more sensibly, that this form of reasoning applies for some factors but fails for others.[13] In the domain of trade-secrets law, for example, Aleven argues that closed world reasoning can be applied to the factor representing the existence of an explicit confidentiality agreement between plaintiff and defendant: lacking positive information indicating such an agreement, that is, the court can legitimately conclude that there is none. But he denies that this form of reasoning can be applied to the factor representing the existence simply of a confidential relationship between plaintiff and defendant: even lacking explicit information indicating such a relationship, the court cannot conclude that no such relationship exists – the presumption of confidentiality is too strong.

If this analysis is correct, then the presence of a negative factor cannot be defined as nothing but the absence of the corresponding positive factor. A fact situation cannot therefore be represented simply as a list of positive factors, with all negative factors calculated, implicitly, through closed world reasoning. Instead, both positive and negative factors must, at times, be listed as basic components of the fact situation; fact situations must be allowed to contain both factors and their negations explicitly. And in that case, many of our fundamental ideas, which currently apply to fact situations containing only positive factors, will have to be generalized to apply to these richer fact situations as well.

The second issue mentioned here is that, as noted earlier, the present account relies on the idea that every factor favors one side or the other of some dispute – in our standard case, either the plaintiff or the defendant. This is, in many ways, a plausible assumption, especially for relatively mature areas of the law, or other straightforward fields of normative dispute. It is hard, for example, to think of a factor that, while legally relevant, does not favor one side or another; and certainly, the analysis mentioned earlier of actual legal cases by Ashley and his colleagues involves only factors favoring

[13] See Aleven (1997, pp. 239–247) for a list of various legal factors to which closed world reasoning does or does not apply.

some particular side. Still, there are arguments within moral philosophy suggesting that the polarity of certain factors, the side they favor, might vary depending on the context in which they appear – that a particular factor might favor one side when taken together with one group of factors, and a different side when taken together with a different group.[14] The basic idea can be illustrated with an example entirely outside the moral or legal domain, by considering a situation in which an individual is trying to decide whether conditions are favorable for an afternoon run. It is easy to imagine that both heat and rain might count as unfavorable factors, tending to rule out a run, but that a combination of heat and rain together is acceptable, perhaps even refreshing. On one natural interpretation, what this example suggests is that neither heat nor rain itself has any independent polarity with respect to the classification of a situation as favorable for running, since each of these features tends to make the situation less favorable in one context, when present alone, but more favorable in another, when both features are present together.

The issues surrounding examples like this are complicated, and of course, other interpretations are possible as well; perhaps what this particular example shows is that the basic factors involved in the domain are actually heat-without-rain and rain-without-heat, both of which would have negative polarity, and heat-and-rain-together, which would have positive polarity. Nevertheless, such examples, as well as other considerations from the literature, give life to the possibility that certain factors might have variable polarity, favoring different sides of an issue depending on the context in which they occur. If this turns out to be true, the ideas presented here will again have to be altered in important ways to allow for this possibility.[15]

[14] See Dancy (1993, 2004) for arguments in favor of this position; my own views on Dancy's argument are developed in Horty (2012).

[15] Prakken and Sartor (1998) develop a model of precedential reasoning with polarity-free factors; the idea is explored in Horty (1999) as well. More recently, Lamond (2022) has argued for the advantages of a case representation built from components that do not favor one side or the other – "features," he calls them, rather than "factors."

3 Some Alternative Models

We have now presented the reason model of precedential constraint – the central topic of this book – setting out basic definitions in Chapter 1 and then investigating the model in more detail in Chapter 2. In this chapter, we consider two alternative models and explore their relations to the reason model.

The first of these alternatives is the standard model, discussed informally in the Introduction, according to which precedential constraint is carried through ordinary logical rules, but which allows these rules to be modified in accord with the Raz/Simpson conditions. This chapter provides – for the first time, I believe – a precise formulation of the standard model of constraint and then establishes the surprising result that the standard model and the reason model are, in a straightforward sense, equivalent.

The second alternative is the a fortiori model of constraint, also mentioned in the Introduction, according to which a court is constrained only when it is presented with a situation that is at least as strong for the winning side of some precedent case as the fact situation of that precedent case itself. After providing a precise formulation of the a fortiori model, we show that it can be understood as a special case of the reason model.

3.1 The Standard Model

The reason model, as we have seen, is based on a picture of cases as containing defeasible rules, where conflicts between these defeasible rules are resolved by a priority ordering on the reasons that form their premises. The standard model, by contrast, is based on the idea that the rules contained in cases are strict – universal, or exceptionless. Conflicts between these rules are not resolved but rather avoided entirely, through a process of rule modification designed to guarantee that two rules supporting conflicting outcomes are never both applicable in the same fact situation. Of course, as we discussed in the Introduction, a body of precedent cases could not constrain later courts at all if these courts were free to modify the rules contained in earlier cases at will. Instead, constraint in the standard model results from the fact that modification of earlier rules by later courts is subject to the two Raz/Simpson conditions: first, that rule modification can consist only in the addition of further restrictions, narrowing the original rule; and second, that the modified rule must continue to support the same outcome as the original rule in all previous cases in which the original rule was applied.

But how, exactly, does this work: how do the Raz/Simpson conditions on rule modification lead to a notion of constraint? Let us say – informally for now, but soon to be rendered more precisely – that a new decision can be accommodated within an existing case base whenever: if the case base is augmented with that new decision, then existing rules from the case base can be modified in accord with the Raz/Simpson conditions in such a way that, after modification, two rules supporting different outcomes are never both applicable in any fact situation from the case base.[1] Using this notion of accommodation, the basic idea underlying the standard model notion of constraint can be put very simply: given a background case base and a new fact situation, a court is permitted to reach a particular decision in that situation only if the decision can be accommodated within the background case base – the court, in other words, is not permitted to reach a decision that requires existing rules to be modified in ways that violate the Raz/Simpson conditions in order to prevent conflicting rules from applying to the same fact situation.

So that is the basic idea. To state things more precisely, we first describe the framework in which the standard model is developed, with strict rules and cases. We refer to this framework as the *strict framework* – and for purposes of clarity, to heighten contrast, we will also refer in the chapter to the framework set out previously as the *defeasible framework*. After describing the strict framework in which the standard model is developed, we then set out the model itself.

3.1.1 Strict Rules and Cases

We begin with strict case rules. There are two differences between these rules and the defeasible case rules that we have focused on thus far. The first involves strength of implication. Where U is a reason favoring the side s, a

[1] The precise version of this definition can be found in Section 3.1.3.

defeasible rule has the form $U \rightarrow s$, telling us that, in any situation in which U holds, that fact provides the court with a pro tanto reason for deciding in favor of the side s. The corresponding strict rule has the form $U \Rightarrow s$, where the stronger arrow indicates greater implication strength, and the rule itself is taken to mean that, in any situation in which U holds, the court not only has a reason to decide in favor of the side s but is required to do so. To illustrate, what the strict rule $\{f_1^\pi\} \Rightarrow \pi$ means is that, in any situation in which the reason $\{f_1^\pi\}$ for the plaintiff holds, the court is required to decide for the plaintiff. The second difference between strict and defeasible case rules is that strict rules allow for more complicated premises, containing explicit qualifications, or hedges. For example, where, as usual, the symbols $\wedge$ and $\neg$ indicate conjunction and negation, the strict rule $\{f_1^\pi\} \wedge \neg\{f_1^\delta, f_3^\delta\} \Rightarrow \pi$ is taken to mean that, in any situation in which the reason $\{f_1^\pi\}$ for the plaintiff holds and the reason $\{f_1^\delta, f_3^\delta\}$ for the defendant does not, the court is required to decide for the plaintiff.

This second difference between strict and defeasible case rules may seem puzzling. We have said that strict rules are supposed to be universal, or exceptionless – yet it might seem that the rule $\{f_1^\pi\} \wedge \neg\{f_1^\delta, f_3^\delta\} \Rightarrow \pi$ contains an exception, so that it cannot be universal. Is this a problem? The answer is No, it is not a problem, and the impression that it might be results from confusing universality with generality. The rule $\{f_1^\pi\} \wedge \neg\{f_1^\delta, f_3^\delta\} \Rightarrow \pi$ is indeed less general than the previous rule $\{f_1^\pi\} \Rightarrow \pi$, in the sense that it requires a definite course of action in a narrower range of situations. But the two rules are equally universal, both applying to any situation whatsoever. In particular, the rule $\{f_1^\pi\} \wedge \neg\{f_1^\delta, f_3^\delta\} \Rightarrow \pi$ tells us that, in any situation whatsoever, if the reason $\{f_1^\pi\}$ holds and the reason $\{f_1^\delta, f_3^\delta\}$ does not, then the court is required to decide for the plaintiff.[2]

The notion of a strict case rule can now be specified formally as follows: where U is a reason favoring the side s and $V_1, \ldots, V_n$ are n reasons, for some integer n, favoring the opposite side $\bar{s}$, then a formula of the form

$$U \wedge \neg V_1 \wedge \ldots \wedge \neg V_n \Rightarrow s$$

[2] The distinction between universality and generality described in this paragraph is discussed in application to moral principles by Hare (1963), at various points, but especially throughout Chapter 3, where he provides the following illustration: "The moral principle 'One ought never to make false statements' is highly general; the moral principle 'One ought never to make false statements to one's wife' is much more specific. But both are universal; the second one forbids *anyone* who is married to make false statements to his wife" (p. 40).

is a *strict rule* supporting the side s. As with defeasible rules, we appeal to the auxiliary functions $Premise$ and $Conclusion$ to pick out a rule's premise and conclusion, and now also to a new function $Premise^s$ to pick out the positive part of a rule's premise – that is, where a rule supports the side s, the part of the rule's premise that lends positive support to that side. These functions are defined so that, where r is the rule displayed above, we have

$$Premise(r) = U \wedge \neg V_1 \wedge \ldots \wedge \neg V_n,$$
$$Premise^s(r) = U,$$
$$Conclusion(r) = s.$$

And again, as with defeasible rules, we will say that a strict rule is *applicable* in any fact situation in which its premise holds, where this idea is now defined formally as follows, to accommodate the additional complexity of strict rule premises:

Definition 14 (Strict rule applicability) Where X is a fact situation and r is a strict rule of the form $U \wedge \neg V_1 \wedge \ldots \wedge \neg V_n \Rightarrow s$, then r is applicable in the situation X if and only if $X \models U$ and, for each i from 1 to n, it is not the case that $X \models V_i$.

Working through these definitions, we can now verify that the earlier formula $\{f_1^\pi\} \wedge \neg\{f_1^\delta, f_3^\delta\} \Rightarrow \pi$ is, in fact, a strict rule supporting the plaintiff, since $\{f_1^\pi\}$ is a reason favoring the plaintiff and $\{f_1^\delta, f_3^\delta\}$ is a reason favoring the defendant. If we let r stand for this rule, we have $Premise(r) = \{f_1^\pi\} \wedge \neg\{f_1^\delta, f_3^\delta\}$ and $Premise^\pi(r) = \{f_1^\pi\}$, as well as $Conclusion(r) = \pi$. And it is easy to see that this rule is applicable in the situation $X_1 = \{f_1^\pi, f_2^\pi, f_1^\delta, f_2^\delta\}$, for example, since $X_1 \models \{f_1^\pi\}$ but it is not the case that $X_1 \models \{f_1^\delta, f_3^\delta\}$.

A *strict case*, like a defeasible case, is a structure of the form $c = \langle X, r, s\rangle$ in which, as before, X is a fact situation and s is an outcome, but in which r is now a strict rule. Again, we will refer to r as the *rule of the case*, but here, we do not take the entire premise of this rule but only the positive part – that is, $Premise^s(r)$ – as the *reason for the decision* in the case; and we will say, indifferently, that the case is decided *on the basis of* either the strict rule r or the reason $Premise^s(r)$.[3] If the situation X_1 happens to be decided for

[3] Some writers argue that the entire premise of the case rule should be taken as a reason for the decision – that is, the positive consideration favoring the outcome together with statements indicating that various considerations favoring the other side are not present. This issue is discussed in Dancy (2004, pp. 38–52), and also in Horty (2012, pp. 53–59, 141–146).

the plaintiff on the basis of the rule $r = \{f_1^\pi\} \wedge \neg\{f_1^\delta, f_3^\delta\} \Rightarrow \pi$, for example, then the reason that forms the basis of this decision is not $Premise(r) = \{f_1^\pi\} \wedge \neg\{f_1^\delta, f_3^\delta\}$, the entire premise of this rule, but only $Premise^\pi(r) = \{f_1^\pi\}$, the component of the premise that actually favors the plaintiff.

Just as with defeasible cases, we suppose that the functions *Facts*, *Rule*, and *Outcome* pick out the fact situation, rule, and outcome of a case, and we again require, as coherence conditions on the concept of a case, both that the case rule must actually be applicable in the fact situation of the case and that the conclusion of the case rule must match the case outcome. This first coherence condition – that the case rule must be applicable in the fact situation – will turn out to be particularly important when it comes to formulating the standard model of constraint.

Finally, we define a *strict case base* as a set Γ containing only strict cases.

3.1.2 Case Base Refinement

In order to motivate the standard model of constraint, we begin by tracing two simple examples of legal development in accordance with this model; for ease of comparison, both of these examples mirror those used to illustrate the reason model.

Suppose, then, that a court confronts the familiar fact situation $X_1 = \{f_1^\pi, f_2^\pi, f_1^\delta, f_2^\delta\}$ and decides this situation for the plaintiff on the basis of the strict rule $\{f_1^\pi\} \Rightarrow \pi$, leading to the decision $c_{21} = \langle X_{21}, r_{21}, s_{21}\rangle$, where $X_{21} = X_1$, where $r_{21} = \{f_1^\pi\} \Rightarrow \pi$, and where $s_{21} = \pi$. This case is similar to the earlier $c_1 = \langle X_1, r_1, s_1\rangle$, decided on the basis of the defeasible rule $r_1 = \{f_1^\pi\} \rightarrow \pi$, where the same fact situation was confronted, and where the same decision was reached for the same reason. The difference is that, since the case c_1 is defeasible, the force of the decision in that case is simply that, in the future, the reason $\{f_1^\pi\}$ for the plaintiff is to be assigned higher priority than any reason for the defendant that was itself supported by X_1, the fact situation of that case. The force of the decision in the strict case c_{21}, by contrast, is that, in any future situation in which the reason $\{f_1^\pi\}$ holds, the court is required to decide for the plaintiff.

Now imagine that, as a result of the initial court's decision, the background case base is now $\Gamma_{11} = \{c_{21}\}$, and that, against this background, a court is confronted with the fact situation $X_2 = \{f_1^\pi, f_2^\pi, f_1^\delta, f_2^\delta, f_3^\delta\}$, also considered earlier. And let us suppose that, as in our earlier scenario, the court takes the presence of the new factor f_3^δ in conjunction with the previous f_1^δ – that is, the reason $\{f_1^\delta, f_3^\delta\}$ – as sufficient, in this situation, to justify a decision for the defendant. Of course, the earlier strict rule $r_{21} = \{f_1^\pi\} \Rightarrow \pi$ is also applicable in this new situation, apparently requiring a decision for the plaintiff. But according to the standard model, the court can decide for the defendant on the basis of the reason $\{f_1^\delta, f_3^\delta\}$ all the same by distinguishing the new fact situation from that of the case in which the earlier rule was introduced – pointing out that the new situation, unlike that of the earlier case, is one in which the new reason $\{f_1^\delta, f_3^\delta\}$ for the defendant holds, and so declining to apply the earlier rule on that basis.

The result of this decision, according to the standard model, is that the case base $\Gamma_{11} = \{c_{21}\}$ is modified in two ways. First, by deciding the new situation for the defendant on the basis of the reason $\{f_1^\delta, f_3^\delta\}$, the court augments the existing case base with the new case $c_{22} = \langle X_{22}, r_{22}, s_{22}\rangle$, where $X_{22} = X_2$, where $r_{22} = \{f_1^\delta, f_3^\delta\} \Rightarrow \delta$, and where $s_{22} = \delta$. And second, by declining to apply the earlier $r_{21} = \{f_1^\pi\} \Rightarrow \pi$ to the new situation on the grounds that this situation satisfies the reason $\{f_1^\delta, f_3^\delta\}$ supporting the other side, the court, in effect, modifies this earlier rule to accommodate its new decision, so that the earlier rule now carries the force of $r_{21}{}' = \{f_1^\pi\} \wedge \neg\{f_1^\delta, f_3^\delta\} \Rightarrow \pi$. The new case base is thus $\Gamma_{12} = \{c_{21}{}', c_{22}\}$, with c_{22} as above, and with the new case $c_{21}{}' = \langle X_{21}{}', r_{21}{}', s_{21}{}'\rangle$ as a modification of the previous case c_{21}, where $X_{21}{}' = X_{21}$, where $r_{21}{}'$ is as above, and where $s_{21}{}' = s_{21}$.

Note that the rule modification involved here – from the earlier r_{21} to the modified $r_{21}{}'$ – is a genuine accommodation, as we have defined this term, since it satisfies the two Raz/Simpson conditions. First, the modified rule $r_{21}{}'$ simply narrows the existing r_{21}, by supplementing its premise with an additional clause that must be satisfied to guarantee applicability. And second, the modified rule continues to support the same outcome as the original rule in the situation in which the original rule was introduced; as we have already seen, $r_{21}{}'$ is applicable in the situation X_{21}, and likewise supports a decision for the plaintiff.

So far, we have retraced a familiar path: the transition from the initial case base $\Gamma_{11} = \{c_{21}\}$ to the modified and augmented $\Gamma_{12} = \{c_{21}{}', c_{22}\}$ simply recapitulates in the standard model the transition from the initial case base $\Gamma_1 = \{c_1\}$ to the augmented $\Gamma_3 = \{c_1, c_3\}$, explored in our earlier illustration of the reason model, from Section 1.2.2. But of course, the process could continue. Suppose that, against the background of the new case base $\Gamma_{12} = \{c_{21}{}', c_{22}\}$, a court is now confronted with the further fact situation

$X_{23} = \{f_1^{\pi}, f_2^{\pi}, f_4^{\delta}\}$, and takes the reason $\{f_4^{\delta}\}$ as sufficient to justify a decision for the defendant, in spite of the fact that even the modified rule r_{21}' requires a decision for the plaintiff. What this suggests is that the initial rule must be modified even further, to take the reason $\{f_4^{\delta}\}$ into account as an additional qualification, or hedge. Again, then, the court's new decision would change the existing case base $\Gamma_{12} = \{c_{21}', c_{22}\}$ in two ways: first, augmenting this case base with a new case representing the current decision, and second, further modifying the initial rule to accommodate this new decision as well. The resulting case base would be $\Gamma_{13} = \{c_{21}'', c_{22}, c_{23}\}$, with c_{22} as before, with $c_{23} = \langle X_{23}, r_{23}, s_{23}\rangle$ representing the new decision, where X_{23} is as above, where $r_{23} = \{f_4^{\delta}\} \Rightarrow \delta$, and where $s_{23} = \delta$, and with $c_{21}'' = \langle X_{21}'', r_{21}'', s_{21}''\rangle$ as a modification of the previous c_{21}', where $X_{21}'' = X_{21}'$, where $r_{21}'' = \{f_1^{\pi}\} \wedge \neg\{f_1^{\delta}, f_3^{\delta}\} \wedge \neg\{f_4^{\delta}\} \Rightarrow \pi$, and where $s_{21}'' = s_{21}'$.

For a second, more concrete example, we return to the domestic situation first set out in the Introduction and then examined from the standpoint of the reason model in Section 1.2.3. Again, as we recall, the children, Max and Emma, who would like to stay up and watch TV, function as plaintiffs presenting cases to their parents, Jack and Jo, who function as both defendants and adjudicators. The situations involved are characterized by taking the factor f_1^{π} to represent the fact that the child in question is at least nine years old, by taking f_2^{π} to represent the fact that the child in question completed chores, and then taking f_1^{δ} and f_2^{δ}, respectively, to represent the facts that the child failed to finish dinner and failed to complete homework.

The initial situation presented by Emma to Jo was represented as $X_4 = \{f_1^{\pi}, f_2^{\pi}, f_1^{\delta}\}$, which Jo then decided for Emma on the grounds that Emma was at least nine years of age – that is, in the current strict framework, on the basis of the rule $r_{24} = \{f_1^{\pi}\} \Rightarrow \pi$. In the current framework, this decision would be represented as $c_{24} = \langle X_{24}, r_{24}, s_{24}\rangle$, where $X_{24} = X_4$, where r_{24} is as above, and where $s_{24} = \pi$, leading to $\Gamma_{14} = \{c_{24}\}$ as the initial case base representing the household common law. Against the background of this case base, we then imagined that the situation presented by Max to Jack was represented as $X_5 = \{f_1^{\pi}, f_2^{\pi}, f_1^{\delta}, f_2^{\delta}\}$, and that, in spite of the applicability of the rule formulated in the earlier case, Jack wished to decide against Max on the grounds that he had failed to complete homework – that is, on the basis of the rule $r_{25} = \{f_2^{\delta}\} \Rightarrow \delta$.

Once again, the result of Jack's decision is that the initial case base $\Gamma_{14} = \{c_{24}\}$ is modified in two ways. First, by deciding against Max, Jack augments this case base with the new case $c_{25} = \{X_{25}, r_{25}, s_{25}\}$, where $X_{25} = X_5$, where

r_{25} is as above, and where $s_{25} = \delta$. And second, the effect of Jack's refusal to apply the previous rule $r_{24} = \{f_1^\pi\} \Rightarrow \pi$ to the new situation, on the grounds that this situation satisfies the reason $\{f_2^\delta\}$, is that this rule is now modified to carry the force $r_{24}' = \{f_1^\pi\} \wedge \neg\{f_2^\delta\} \Rightarrow \pi$. The new case base is thus $\Gamma_{15} = \{c_{24}', c_{25}\}$ with c_{25} as above, and with $c_{24}' = \langle X_{24}', r_{24}', s_{24}' \rangle$ as a modification of the previous c_{24}, where $X_{24}' = X_{24}$, where r_{24}' is as above, and where $s_{24}' = s_{24}$.

Each of these examples presents a scenario in which fact situations are confronted, decisions are reached, new rules are formulated to justify these decisions, and existing rules are modified in accord with the Raz/Simpson conditions to accommodate the new decisions. In the examples as presented here, fact situations are confronted and decisions reached in some particular sequence. This way of presenting things offers, of course, the most realistic picture of a legal system evolving over time. However, it turns out that, as long as all decisions from a case base can be accommodated within that case base, with rules modified appropriately, then the exact sequence in which these decisions are reached is irrelevant. Indeed, the decisions need not be reached in any particular sequence at all: if a set of decisions from a case base is capable of being accommodated through rule modifications satisfying the Raz/Simpson conditions, then all the rules that need to be modified can be modified at once, through a process to be characterized here as *case base refinement*:

Definition 15 (Refinement of a case base) Where Γ is a strict case base, its refinement – written, Γ^* – is the set that results from carrying out the following procedure. For each case $c = \langle X, r, s \rangle$ belonging to Γ:

1. Let

$$\Gamma_c = \{c' \in \Gamma : c' = \langle Y, r', \bar{s} \rangle \;\&\; Y \models Premise^s(r)\}$$

2. For each case $c' = \langle Y, r', \bar{s} \rangle$ from Γ_c, let

$$d_{c,c'} = \neg Premise^{\bar{s}}(r')$$

3. Define

$$D_c = \bigwedge_{c' \in \Gamma_c} d_{c,c'}$$

4. Replace the case $c = \langle X, r, s \rangle$ from Γ with $c^* = \langle X, r^*, s \rangle$, where r^* is the new rule

$$Premise^s(r) \wedge D_c \Rightarrow s$$

The instructions contained in this procedure for transforming a case base Γ into its refinement Γ^* can be described more informally as follows. First, for each case c belonging to Γ, decided for some side s and for some particular reason, collect together into Γ_c all of the cases from Γ in which that reason holds but which were decided for the other side $\overline{s}$. Second, for each such case c' from Γ_c, let $d_{c,c'}$ – the consideration that distinguishes c from c' – be the negation of the reason for which c' was decided. Third, conjoin these various distinguishing considerations together into a single statement D_c, which then distinguishes c from all cases in Γ_c at once. And fourth, replace the original case $c = \langle X, r, s\rangle$ from Γ with a new case $c^* = \langle X, r^*, s\rangle$ just like the original except that the rule r from c is replaced with a new rule r^* whose premise is formed by conjoining $Premise^s(r)$, the reason for the original decision, with the distinguishing statement D_c – resulting in a rule that will no longer apply to any other case in which the reason for the original decision holds but which was decided for the opposite side.

Using this notion of case base refinement, we can now verify that, in the examples considered thus far, the case base resulting from our suggested modifications is identical with the case base that would have resulted simply from deciding the same fact situation for the same reasons, augmenting the existing case base with this new decision, and then refining the result.

To illustrate, suppose a court decides the situations X_{21}, X_{22}, and X_{23} for exactly the reasons set out above but without concerning itself with any form of rule modification to avoid the applicability of conflicting rules. The result would be the case base $\Gamma_{16} = \{c_{21}, c_{22}, c_{23}\}$, with $c_{21} = \langle X_{21}, r_{21}, s_{21}\rangle$, where $X_{21} = \{f_1^\pi, f_2^\pi, f_1^\delta, f_2^\delta\}$, where $r_{21} = \{f_1^\pi\} \Rightarrow \pi$, and where $s_{21} = \pi$, with $c_{22} = \langle X_{22}, r_{22}, s_{22}\rangle$, where $X_{22} = \{f_1^\pi, f_2^\pi, f_1^\delta, f_2^\delta, f_3^\delta\}$, where $r_{22} = \{f_1^\delta, f_3^\delta\} \Rightarrow \delta$, and where $s_{22} = \delta$, and with $c_{23} = \langle X_{23}, r_{23}, s_{23}\rangle$, where $X_{23} = \{f_1^\pi, f_2^\pi, f_4^\delta\}$, where $r_{23} = \{f_4^\delta\} \Rightarrow \delta$, and where $s_{23} = \delta$. This case base is, in a sense, flawed, since it contains multiple rules supporting different outcomes that are applicable in the same fact situation: both the rules r_{21} and r_{22} are applicable in the fact situation X_{22} but support different outcomes, and both r_{21} and r_{23} are likewise applicable in X_{23}, again supporting different outcomes.

But let us now refine the case base Γ_{16} in accord with our refinement procedure. The procedure asks us to apply its four-step procedure to each case from Γ, and so we begin with c_{21}. First, we collect together as $(\Gamma_{16})_{c_{21}} = \{c_{22}, c_{23}\}$ the set of cases from Γ_{16} in which the reason for the decision in c_{21} holds but which were decided for the opposite side. Second, for each case c' belonging to $(\Gamma_{16})_{c_{21}}$, we let $d_{c_{21},c'}$ – the consideration that distinguishes c' from c_{21} – be the negation of the reason for which c' was decided. Since $Premise^{\delta}(r_{22}) = \{f_1^{\delta}, f_3^{\delta}\}$ and $Premise^{\delta}(r_{23}) = \{f_4^{\delta}\}$, this gives us $d_{c_{21},c_{22}} = \neg\{f_1^{\delta}, f_3^{\delta}\}$ and $d_{c_{21},c_{23}} = \neg\{f_4^{\delta}\}$. Third, we conjoin these various distinguishing considerations together into the statement $D_{c_{21}} = \neg\{f_1^{\delta}, f_3^{\delta}\} \wedge \neg\{f_4^{\delta}\}$, which distinguishes c_{21} from each of the cases belonging to $(\Gamma_{16})_{c_{21}}$ at once. Finally, we replace the case $c_{21} = \langle X_{21}, r_{21}, s_{21}\rangle$ from Γ_{16} with the new case $c_{21}{}^* = \langle X_{21}, r_{21}{}^*, s_{21}\rangle$, where $r_{21}{}^* = \{f_1^{\pi}\} \wedge \neg\{f_1^{\delta}, f_3^{\delta}\} \wedge \neg\{f_4^{\delta}\} \Rightarrow \pi$ results when the premise of the original rule r_{21} is replaced by a statement that conjoins the reason $Premise^{\pi}(r_{21}) = \{f_1^{\pi}\}$ for the original decision with the new distinguishing statement $D_{c_{21}}$. Having applied the four-step refinement procedure to c_{21}, we must now move on to c_{22} and c_{23}, the remaining cases from Γ_{16}. Fortunately, however, both $(\Gamma_{16})_{c_{22}}$ and $(\Gamma_{16})_{c_{23}}$ are empty, since the reasons for the decisions in these cases do not hold in any cases that were decided for the opposite side. As a result, no further changes are made to the original case base, and the output of the refinement procedure, applied to $\Gamma_{16} = \{c_{21}, c_{22}, c_{23}\}$, is simply $\Gamma_{16}{}^* = \{c_{21}{}^*, c_{22}, c_{23}\}$.

Inspection now reveals that the case $c_{21}{}^*$ is identical to the earlier $c_{21}{}''$, so that the refined case base $\Gamma_{16}{}^* = \{c_{21}{}^*, c_{22}, c_{23}\}$ is identical to the earlier $\Gamma_{13} = \{c_{21}{}'', c_{22}, c_{23}\}$ – supporting our claim that, at least in this example, the rule modifications suggested earlier to accommodate the new decisions coincide with those that would be arrived at simply from deciding the same fact situations for the same reasons, augmenting the background case base with these new decisions, and then refining the result. The diligent, or skeptical, reader is invited to confirm that this claim holds also for our second example – that is, where $\Gamma_{17} = \{c_{24}, c_{25}\}$, the refinement $\Gamma_{17}{}^* = \{c_{24}{}^*, c_{25}\}$ of this case base is identical to the earlier $\Gamma_{15} = \{c_{24}{}', c_{25}\}$.

3.1.3 Accommodation, Consistency, and Constraint

The intuition underlying the standard model, once again, is that a court is permitted to reach a particular decision just in case that decision can be accommodated within the background case base, with conflicts avoided through modifications of existing case rules in accord with the Raz/Simpson conditions. In the examples we have considered thus far, where a new decision can indeed be accommodated within a background case base, the appropriate rule modifications can be arrived at by, first, augmenting the case base with that new decision, and then applying the refinement procedure from Definition 15 to the result. But what if a particular decision cannot be accommodated within a background case base? What does the refinement procedure lead to then? Our hypothesis is that, when a case base is augmented with a decision that cannot be accommodated through rule modifications satisfying the Raz/Simpson conditions, the formal refinement procedure will then alter certain case base rules in such a way that they fail to apply in their corresponding fact situations – so that, strictly speaking, the resulting items would no longer be cases, and the resulting set no longer a case base.[4]

To illustrate, we return to the scenario in which the court is considering the fact situation $X_2 = \{f_1^\pi, f_2^\pi, f_1^\delta, f_2^\delta, f_3^\delta\}$ against the background of the strict case base $\Gamma_{11} = \{c_{21}\}$, with $c_{21} = \langle X_{21}, r_{21}, s_{21}\rangle$, where $X_{21} = \{f_1^\pi, f_2^\pi, f_1^\delta, f_2^\delta\}$, where $r_{21} = \{f_1^\pi\} \Rightarrow \pi$, and where $s_{21} = \pi$. This time, however, imagine that the court would like to find for the defendant on the basis of the reason $\{f_1^\delta, f_2^\delta\}$, leading to the decision $c_{26} = \langle X_{26}, r_{26}, s_{26}\rangle$, where $X_{26} = X_2$, where $r_{26} = \{f_1^\delta, f_2^\delta\} \Rightarrow \delta$, and where $s_{26} = \delta$. Such a decision would be an analogue, in the present, strict framework, of the earlier decision $c_2 = \langle X_2, r_2, s_2\rangle$ against the background of the defeasible case base $\Gamma_1 = \{c_1\}$. As we saw in our previous discussion, from Section 1.2.2, this earlier decision was not permitted by the reason model of constraint, and it turns out that the analogous $c_{26} = \langle X_{26}, r_{26}, s_{26}\rangle$ cannot be accommodated within the strict case base $\Gamma_{11} = \{c_{21}\}$ either. Suppose, then, that we augment the existing case base with this new decision, leading to

$$\begin{aligned}\Gamma_{18} &= \Gamma_{11} \cup \{c_{26}\}\\ &= \{c_{21}, c_{26}\},\end{aligned}$$

and then refine the result. As the reader can verify, the refinement of this augmented case base is the set $\Gamma_{18}{}^* = \{c_{21}{}^*, c_{26}{}^*\}$, with $c_{21}{}^* = \langle X_{21}, r_{21}{}^*, s_{21}\rangle$ where $r_{21}{}^* = \{f_1^\pi\} \wedge \neg\{f_1^\delta, f_2^\delta\} \Rightarrow \pi$, and with $c_{26}{}^* = \langle X_{26}, r_{26}{}^*, s_{26}\rangle$ where $r_{26}{}^* = \{f_1^\delta, f_2^\delta\} \wedge \neg\{f_1^\pi\} \Rightarrow \delta$. And this set is not a case base, in our technical sense, since $c_{21}{}^*$ and $c_{26}{}^*$ are not, in this same technical sense, cases, both failing to satisfy our criterion that the rule of a case must be applicable in its fact situation: the rule $r_{21}{}^*$ is no longer applicable in the fact situation X_{21}, and the rule $r_{26}{}^*$ is no longer applicable in the fact situation X_{26}.

Our hypothesis, then, is that what holds in the particular examples we have considered also holds in general: When a decision can be accommodated

[4] Recall from Section 3.1.1 that a strict case base is defined as a set of strict cases, where a strict case is subject to the coherence condition that the rule of a case must apply in its fact situation.

within a background case base, the appropriate accommodations can be arrived at by augmenting the case base with that decision and refining the result. When a decision cannot be accommodated, refinement of the augmented case base winds up modifying certain case rules in such a way that they are no longer applicable to their corresponding fact situations – leading to items that can no longer be classified as cases, so that the output of the refinement procedure is, technically, no longer a case base.

Based on this hypothesis, and since the link between accommodation and refinement goes in both directions, we can now provide a precise explication of accommodation in terms of refinement as follows: a decision can be *accommodated* within a case base just in case the result of augmenting the case base with that decision can be refined into a case base. And we can introduce a new notion of *accommodation consistency*, according to which a strict case base is accommodation consistent just in case it can accommodate each case it contains – just in case, that is, the refinement of that case base is itself a case base:

Definition 16 (Accommodation consistent and inconsistent case bases) Let Γ be a strict case base. Then Γ is accommodation consistent if and only if its refinement Γ^* is itself a case base, and inconsistent otherwise.

We have just seen, for example, that Γ_{18} is not accommodation consistent, since its refinement $\Gamma_{18}{}^*$ is not a case base. By contrast, our argument at the end of Section 3.1.2 shows that Γ_{16} is accommodation consistent, since $\Gamma_{16}{}^*$ is a case base. Both Γ_{16} and Γ_{18} contain rules leading to conflicting results when applied to fact situations from the case base. Since Γ_{16} is accommodation consistent, however, the conflicts in this case base can be resolved through the process of refinement, while the conflicts in Γ_{18} cannot be resolved, except by modifying rules in a way that violates the Raz/Simpson conditions.

Drawing on this notion of accommodation consistency, we can now, at last, formulate the standard model of constraint, and in a way that parallels our earlier formulation of the reason model. Imagining a court confronting a new situation X against the background of an accommodation consistent case base Γ, we first specify that a decision on the basis of a particular rule is permitted just in case it preserves accommodation consistency:

Definition 17 (Standard model constraint on rule selection) Let Γ be an accommodation consistent strict case base and X a fact situation confronting the court. Then against the background of Γ, the standard model of constraint on rule selection permits the court to base its decision in X on a rule r, applicable in X and supporting the side s, if and only if the augmented case base $\Gamma \cup \{\langle X, r, s\rangle\}$ is accommodation consistent.

To illustrate this definition, we return once again to our previous example in which the court is considering the fact situation $X_2 = \{f_1^\pi, f_2^\pi, f_1^\delta, f_2^\delta, f_3^\delta\}$ against the background of the strict case base $\Gamma_{11} = \{c_{21}\}$, with $c_{21} = \langle X_{21}, r_{21}, s_{21}\rangle$ as above. It follows from our previous discussion that, according to the standard model, the court is permitted to base its decision on the rule $r_{22} = \{f_1^\delta, f_3^\delta\} \Rightarrow \delta$, since the augmented case base $\Gamma_{11} \cup \{\langle X_{22}, r_{22}, s_{22}\rangle\}$ is accommodation consistent, where $X_{22} = X_2$ and where $s_{22} = \delta$. But as we have seen, the court is not permitted to base its decision on the rule $r_{26} = \{f_1^\delta, f_2^\delta\} \Rightarrow \delta$, since, where $X_{26} = X_2$ and $s_{26} = \delta$, the augmented case base $\Gamma_{11} \cup \{\langle X_{26}, r_{26}, s_{26}\rangle\}$ is not accommodation consistent.

Once this constraint on rule selection is in place, then – just as in our exposition of the reason model – the standard model can be extended to permit a decision for a particular side whenever some permitted rule supports that side, and to require a decision for a side whenever every permitted rule supports that side:

Definition 18 (Standard model of constraint on decision for a side) Let Γ be an accommodation consistent strict case base and X a fact situation confronting the court. Then against the background of Γ, the standard model of constraint on decision for a side permits the court to decide X for the side s if and only if some rule permitted by the standard model of constraint on rule selection supports that side; the standard model requires a decision for the side s if and only if every rule permitted by the standard model of constraint on rule selection supports that side.

The reader is invited to illustrate this definition by transposing into the strict framework the illustrations of Definition 8 already offered in Section 1.2.4.

3.2 Equivalence to the Reason Model

3.2.1 The Result

We now have before us two models – the standard model described here and the reason model from Chapters 1 and 2 – which offer strikingly different pictures both of precedential constraint and of legal development. According to the standard model, what is important about a background case base is the set of rules it contains. These rules are to be thought of as strict, or exceptionless. However, in reaching a decision concerning a new fact situation, a court is permitted to modify existing rules in ways that satisfy certain conditions – the Raz/Simpson conditions – in order to accommodate its decision. Constraint results from the fact that accommodation in accord with the Raz/Simpson conditions is not always possible; legal development involves the modification of existing rules, together with the introduction of new rules from new decisions. According to the reason model, case rules are to be thought of as defeasible and play a secondary role. What is most important about a case base is the priority ordering on reasons derived from the decisions it contains. In confronting a new fact situation, a court is required only to reach a decision that is consistent with this existing priority ordering. Constraint results from the fact that not all possible decisions are consistent; legal development involves strengthening the existing priority ordering with new priorities derived from new decisions.[5]

[5] A different kind of contrast between the standard model and the reason model of constraint emerges when we reflect that, according to the standard model, the rules offered by courts to justify their decisions are universal generalizations, yet, as these courts well know, their universal generalizations are likely to be judged as incorrect in the future, and so distinguished, or modified – or, to put it even more bluntly: the standard model paints a picture according to which courts justify their decisions by offering universal generalizations that they might as well assume will later be judged as incorrect. This feature of the model is highlighted by MacCormick (1987, pp. 162–165), who argues that justification of a decision requires it to be put "on the footing that *because* the facts are F1, F2, ... Fn, the judgment j ought to be pronounced," and – in keeping with his general treatment of legal explanation from MacCormick (1978) – that "such a '*because*...' requires a commitment to the universal, 'whenever $f1, f2, \ldots fn$, then j', coupled with: 'and in this case, F1, F2, ... Fn, which are instances of $f1, f2, \ldots fn$' " (p. 162). But then he asks, paraphrasing a criticism raised by Burton (1988), how the court could "ever be satisfied that [it] has exhaustively considered every possible relevant set of facts ... so as to decide exactly how to state some ruling ... of the kind which we have formulated in the terms: 'Whenever $f1, f2, \ldots fn$, then j'?" (p. 163). MacCormick's response is to grant the point of Burton's criticism, that a court is unlikely to be able to formulate a correct universal generalization, while insisting that Burton has not shown that "the logical properties of a good justifying principle ... are other than those of universality" (p. 164), but to reconcile the apparent conflict between these two ideas by allowing that courts have a low "quality of commitment" to the universal generalizations they formulate to justify their decisions – in other words, as he writes, the court's "rulings should be universalized or at the very least universalizable; but [its] commitment to them can and should be relativistic, open-ended, and therefore revisable" (p. 165). On the view advocated by MacCormick, then, courts working with the standard model are to be thought of as justifying their decisions with very strong rules, universal generalizations, but committing themselves only weakly to these rules, realizing that they are subject to

In spite of the very different pictures associated with these two models, we show in this section that the two models are equivalent, in a sense that can be approximated as follows: against the background of a given case base, a decision in some new situation on the basis of a particular rule satisfies the standard model of constraint just in case the same decision satisfies the reason model. This approximation will have to be refined, of course, since the two models are developed within different frameworks – the standard model is developed in the framework of strict rules and case bases, while the reason model is developed in the framework of defeasible rules and case bases – so that, taken literally, the very same decision can never satisfy both models. In order to provide a more accurate formulation of equivalence between the standard model and the reason model, therefore, we must establish a correspondence between items from the strict and defeasible frameworks.

A primary task of this section is to introduce such a correspondence – call it, k – between the two frameworks, such that: (1) if r is a strict case rule, then r^k is the corresponding defeasible case rule; (2) if r is a defeasible case rule, then r^k is the corresponding strict case rule; and (3) if Γ is a case base, strict or defeasible, then

$$\Gamma^k = \{\langle X, r^k, s\rangle : \langle X, r, s\rangle \in \Gamma\}$$

is the corresponding case base, defeasible or strict, that results when each case $\langle X, r, s\rangle$ from Γ is replaced by a case $\langle X, r^k, s\rangle$ exactly like the initial case $\langle X, r, s\rangle$ except that the rule r from the initial case is replaced by the corresponding rule r^k.

On the basis of this correspondence, we will be able to establish a kind of equivalence between the two concepts of case base consistency at work in this book, the Definition 6 concept of consistency for defeasible case bases and the Definition 16 concept of accommodation consistency for strict case bases:

Observation 6 Let Γ be a defeasible case base. Then Γ is consistent if and only if the corresponding strict case base Γ^k is accommodation consistent. Likewise, let Γ be a strict case base. Then Γ is accommodation consistent if and only if the corresponding defeasible case base Γ^k is consistent.

later modification. By contrast, courts working with the reason model can be thought of as justifying their decisions with weaker rules, defeasible generalizations, while committing themselves to these rules more strongly – even when later situations are distinguished, according to the reason model, the defeasible rules formulated in previous cases remain intact.

Using this equivalence between the central consistency concepts of our two models of constraint, the reason model and the standard model, we can show these models are equivalent as well, beginning with their respective notions of constraint on rule selection, set out in Definitions 7 and 17:

Observation 7 Let Γ be a consistent defeasible case base and X a fact situation confronting the court. Then against the background of Γ, the reason model permits the court to base its decision in X on the defeasible rule r, applicable in X and supporting the side s, if and only if, against the background of the corresponding strict case base Γ^k, the standard model permits the court to base its decision in X on the corresponding strict rule r^k, also applicable in X and supporting s. Likewise, let Γ be an accommodation consistent strict case base and X a fact situation confronting the court. Then against the background of Γ, the standard model permits the court to base its decision in X on the strict rule r, applicable in X and supporting the side s, if and only if, against the background of the corresponding defeasible case base Γ^k, the standard model permits the court to base its decision in X on the corresponding defeasible rule r^k, also applicable in X and supporting s.

And then, of course, given this equivalence between the reason model and standard model notions of constraint on rule selection, it is easy to establish the equivalence between their corresponding notions of constraint on decision for a side, set out in Definitions 8 and 18:

Observation 8 Let Γ be a consistent defeasible case base and X a fact situation confronting the court. Then against the background of Γ, the reason model permits the court to decide X for the side s if and only if, against the background of the corresponding strict case base Γ^k, the standard model permits the court to decide X for the same side. Likewise, let Γ be an accommodation consistent strict case base and X a fact situation confronting the court. Then against the background of Γ, the standard model permits the court to decide X for the side s if and only if, against the background of the corresponding defeasible case base Γ^k, the reason model permits the court to decide X for the same side.

With this equivalence result before us, we can now return to a question set out in the Introduction. There, after explaining that the standard model required case rules to be modified only in accord with the Raz/Simpson conditions, we asked why rule modifications should be limited in just this way: why not limit rule modifications in accord with some other set of conditions – what, exactly, is so special about the Raz/Simpson conditions? Our equivalence result shows how the reason model of precedential constraint can be used to answer this question, by supplying a kind of semantic justification for the Raz/Simpson conditions on rule modification. Suppose that, taking the reason model as fundamental, we imagine a notion of constraint based instead on the accommodation of new decisions through rule modification and search for conditions on rule modification that will guarantee its equivalence with the reason model. Then what our equivalence result shows is that it is exactly the Raz/Simpson conditions that do the job. The Raz/Simpson conditions supply a syntactic encoding, at the level of explicit rule modification, of the semantic ideas underlying the reason model of constraint.

This result – that there exists an equivalence between the standard model and the reason model, based on a correspondence between the strict and defeasible frameworks – is the primary point of the current section. The precise details of the correspondence used to establish this equivalence are less important, and any reader who is not concerned with these details is invited to skip ahead to Section 3.3. Some readers, however, enjoy details, and for those readers, details are now provided.

3.2.2 The Correspondence

Our correspondence k depends on two auxiliary functions: $+$, which maps items from the defeasible framework into items from the strict framework, and $-$, which maps items from the strict framework into items from the defeasible framework. Both $+$ and $-$ are defined first for rules.

Where r is a defeasible case rule of the form $U \rightarrow s$, we define r^+ as the corresponding strict rule $U \Rightarrow s$. Evidently, the strict rule r^+ simply strengthens the defeasible rule r, replacing a defeasible implication with a strict, or exceptionless, implication. Next, where U is a reason favoring the side s and $V_1, \ldots, V_n$ are reasons favoring the opposite side, and taking r as the strict rule $U \wedge \neg V_1 \wedge \ldots \wedge \neg V_n \Rightarrow s$, we define r^- as the corresponding defeasible rule, of the form $U \rightarrow s$. In this case, the relation between the strict rule r and the defeasible rule r^- is more complicated, since r^- does not just weaken r by replacing a strict with a defeasible implication but might also remove various qualifications from r.

These mappings between strict and defeasible case rules can be illustrated by recalling, first, that $r_1 = \{f_1^\pi\} \rightarrow \pi$, so that $r_1{}^+ = r_{21} = \{f_1^\pi\} \Rightarrow \pi$.

And evidently, we also have ${r_{21}}^- = r_1 = \{f_1^\pi\} \rightarrow \pi$. This example illustrates the general fact that, for a defeasible case rule r, we invariably have $(r^+)^- = r$. The converse does not always hold: there are strict case rules r for which we do not have $(r^-)^+ = r$. To illustrate, we need only recall the strict rule ${r_{21}}' = \{f_1^\pi\} \wedge \neg\{f_1^\delta, f_2^\delta\} \Rightarrow \pi$, which has $({r_{21}}')^- = r_1 = \{f_1^\pi\} \rightarrow \pi$ as its corresponding defeasible rule. As we have seen, however, the strict rule corresponding to the defeasible r_1 is r_{21} rather than ${r_{21}}'$; thus we have $(({r_{21}}')^-)^+ = {r_1}^+ = r_{21}$. This fact reflects the feature of our definitions according to which, in moving from a strict rule to its defeasible counterpart, not only is the strict implication replaced by a defeasible implication, but various qualifications can be stripped away – and then, moving back, from that defeasible rule to the corresponding strict rule, implication is strengthened once again to a strict relation, but the qualifications are not replaced.

We now turn from rules to case bases, and here, our definitions move in parallel. Where Γ is a defeasible case base, we define its corresponding strict case base as

$$\Gamma^+ = \{\langle X, r^+, s\rangle : \langle X, r, s\rangle \in \Gamma\},$$

resulting from the original through the replacement of each defeasible rule from each case by the corresponding strict rule; and in the same way , where Γ is a strict case base, we define its corresponding defeasible case base as

$$\Gamma^- = \{\langle X, r^-, s\rangle : \langle X, r, s\rangle \in \Gamma\},$$

resulting from the original through the replacement of strict case rules by their defeasible counterparts.

To illustrate, we recall the defeasible case base $\Gamma_3 = \{c_1, c_3\}$, with $c_1 = \langle X_1, r_1, s_1\rangle$, where $r_1 = \{f_1^\pi\} \rightarrow \pi$, and with $c_3 = \langle X_3, r_3, s_3\rangle$, where $r_3 = \{f_1^\delta, f_3^\delta\} \rightarrow \delta$. The corresponding strict case base is ${\Gamma_3}^+ = \{c_{21}, c_{22}\}$, with $c_{21} = \langle X_{21}, r_{21}, s_{21}\rangle$, where $X_{21} = X_1$, where $r_{21} = \{f_1^\pi\} \Rightarrow \pi$, and where $s_{21} = s_1$, and with $c_{22} = \langle X_{22}, r_{22}, s_{22}\rangle$, where $X_{22} = X_3$, where $r_{22} = \{f_1^\delta, f_3^\delta\} \Rightarrow \delta$, and where $s_{22} = s_3$. Again, we can see here that $({\Gamma_3}^+)^-$ is simply the original Γ_3, illustrating the general fact that $(\Gamma^+)^- = \Gamma$ for any defeasible case base Γ. Once more, however, the converse does not hold: there are strict case bases Γ for which we do not have $(\Gamma^-)^+ = \Gamma$. This can be illustrated by considering the more recent $\Gamma_{12} = \{{c_{21}}', c_{22}\}$ with ${c_{21}}' = \langle {X_{21}}', {r_{21}}', {s_{21}}'\rangle$, where ${X_{21}}' = X_{21}$, where ${r_{21}}' = \{f_1^\pi\} \wedge \neg\{f_1^\delta, f_3^\delta\} \Rightarrow \pi$, and where ${s_{21}}' = s_{21}$, and with c_{22} as above. As we have seen, $({r_{21}}')^- = r_1 = \{f_1^\pi\} \rightarrow \pi$, on the basis of which, and together with identities noted elsewhere in this paragraph, the reader can calculate that $\Gamma_{12}^{-} = \Gamma_3$. And then, of course, $(\Gamma_{12}^{-})^{+} = \Gamma_3^{+}$. But the case base $\Gamma_3^{+} = \{c_{21}, c_{22}\}$ differs from the original case base $\Gamma_{12} = \{c_{21}', c_{22}\}$, since the case c_{21} differs from the case c_{21}'. Again, the failure of the identity $(\Gamma^{-})^{+} = \Gamma$ to hold for strict case bases in general reflects the fact that the transformation of a strict case base Γ into its defeasible counterpart Γ^{-} might remove rule qualifications that are not then replaced by the transformation of the defeasible case Γ^{-} base into $(\Gamma^{-})^{+}$, its own strict counterpart.[6]

Given the auxiliary functions $+$ and $-$, we can now define our correspondence k between the strict and defeasible frameworks very simply as follows:

Definition 19 (Strict/defeasible framework correspondence) For case base rules, if a rule r is defeasible, then r^k is r^{+}, and if r is strict, then r^k is r^{-}. And likewise for case bases, if a case base Γ is defeasible, then Γ^k is Γ^{+}, and if Γ is strict, then Γ^k is Γ^{-}.

And on the basis of this correspondence, it is then a straightforward matter to verify our previous Observations 6 and 7.

3.3 The A Fortiori Model

The second alternative model of constraint to be considered in this chapter is the a fortiori model, according to which constraint depends, not on any on rules or opinions expressed in previous cases, but only on the relation of some current fact situation to the fact situations of those previous cases. More exactly, according to the a fortiori model, a later court is constrained by a precedent case only when it confronts a fact situation that is at least as strong for the winning side of that precedent case as the fact situation of the precedent case itself. In ignoring explicitly formulated case rules in favor of relations among facts, the a fortiori model echoes the long history of legal skepticism behind the idea that a court's own efforts at justifying

[6] It is interesting to note that there is one special circumstance in which something like this identity holds: if Γ is a case base that happens to be identical with its own refinement – that is, if $\Gamma^* = \Gamma$ – then it follows that the refinement of $(\Gamma^{-})^{+}$ is itself identical to Γ – that is, $((\Gamma^{-})^{+})^* = \Gamma$. Here, as long as Γ is identical with its refinement, then, although the transformation of the strict Γ into the defeasible Γ^{-} may again remove rule qualifications that are not replaced in the transformation of this defeasible case base back into the strict $(\Gamma^{-})^{+}$, the refinement of this case base into $((\Gamma^{-})^{+})^*$ reinstates exactly those rule qualifications found in the original Γ. The diligent reader can verify this fact in general, or confirm a particular instance by noting that, since $\Gamma_{12}^* = \Gamma_{12}$, for example, we also have $((\Gamma_{12}^{-})^{+})^* = \Gamma_{12}$.

its decisions should carry less weight than the decisions themselves. This history goes back at least to Arthur Goodhart's view that legal decisions are often influenced by principles of which the court is unaware, or which the court misunderstands; accordingly, Goodhart locates the meaning of a case, its *ratio decidendi*, not in some rule explicitly formulated by the court, but simply in the material facts of that case together with the decision reached on the basis of those facts.[7] Nevertheless, we will see that, in spite of the radical nature and pedigree of the a fortiori model, this conception of constraint can be understood as a special case of the more general reason model.

3.3.1 Ordering the Fact Situations

Evidently, the a fortiori model must be based on some ordering through which different fact situations can be compared in strength for one side or another. To motivate our definition, we consider the familiar situation $X_1 = \{f_1^\pi, f_2^\pi, f_1^\delta, f_2^\delta\}$ along with the new situation $X_{27} = \{f_1^\pi, f_2^\pi, f_2^\delta\}$. Because X_{27} contains all the factors from X_1 that favor the plaintiff and no factors favoring the defendant that are not already found in X_1, it seems that the new situation X_{27} is at least as strong for the plaintiff as the earlier situation X_1. We record this fact by writing $X_1 \leq^\pi X_{27}$. By dual reasoning, we can conclude that the earlier situation X_1 is at least as strong for the defendant as the new situation X_{27}, a fact recorded as $X_{27} \leq^\delta X_1$.

Generalizing from this example, we will say that the situation Y is at least as strong for the side s as the fact situation X whenever Y contains all the factors from X that support s, and X contains all the factors from Y that support $\bar{s}$, the opposite side. If we let $\leq^s$ represent the ordering of strength for the side s among fact situations, this idea can then be defined formally as follows:

Definition 20 (Strength for a side among fact situations) Let X and Y be fact situations. Then Y is at least as strong as X for the side s – written, $X \leq^s Y$ – if and only if $Y^{\bar{s}} \subseteq X^{\bar{s}}$ and $X^s \subseteq Y^s$.

The symbol $\leq^s$ used here to represent the ordering of strength for a side among fact situations is the same symbol used earlier, in Definition 2 from Section 1.1.2, to represent strength for a side among reasons. This is not an accident. Formally, the concept of a fact situation is a generalization of the

[7] See Goodhart (1930); an interesting discussion of the influence of the American legal realists on Goodhart's thinking is found in Duxbury (2005, pp. 80–90).

concept of a reason: while reasons are collections of factors favoring a single side, fact situations are collections that may contain factors favoring both sides of a dispute. And just as the concept of a fact situation generalizes the concept of a reason, the strength ordering defined here on fact situations generalizes the strength ordering previously defined on reasons: the present Definition 20 applies to reasons as well as to fact situations in general, and collapses, in that case, to the previous Definition 2.

It is easy to verify that the ordering defined here on fact situations, like the earlier ordering on reasons, is a partial ordering: reflexive, transitive, and antisymmetric. That is, for any fact situations X, Y, and Z, we have:

$X \leq^s X$,
$X \leq^s Y$ and $Y \leq^s Z$ implies $X \leq^s Z$,
$X \leq^s Y$ and $Y \leq^s X$ implies $X = Y$.

The ordering also satisfies a duality property, according to which the fact situation Y is at least as strong for the side s as the fact situation X whenever X is at least as strong for $\overline{s}$ as Y:

$X \leq^s Y$ if and only if $Y \leq^{\overline{s}} X$.

As with reasons, the ordering of strength for a side is not linear. Given two situations X and Y, we cannot necessarily conclude that one is at least as strong for some particular side as the other – we cannot conclude, that is, that either $X \leq^s Y$ or $Y \leq^s X$. Of course, this result already follows from the failure of linearity for the strength ordering among reasons, since strength for a side among reasons is a special case of strength for a side among fact situations. But the generalization to fact situations allows for a different kind of illustration, which we can see by comparing $X_1 = \{f_1^\pi, f_2^\pi, f_1^\delta, f_2^\delta\}$ to the situation $X_{14} = \{f_1^\pi, f_1^\delta\}$, also considered earlier. Here, the relation $X_{14} \leq^\pi X_1$ fails because, even though the situation X_1 contains each factor favoring the plaintiff found in X_{14}, the situation X_{14} does not contain each factor favoring the defendant found in X_1; and $X_1 \leq^\pi X_{14}$ fails as well because, even though the situation X_1 contains each factor favoring the defendant found in X_{14}, the situation X_{14} does not contain each factor favoring the plaintiff found in X_1.

We can now note, also, that this ordering of strength for a side among fact situations allows us to buttress our earlier argument that the notion of consistency for case bases introduced in Definition 6 is intuitively correct, in the sense that it classifies case bases exhibiting various anomalies as inconsistent. We claimed toward the end of Section 1.2.1, without verification, that a case base containing two cases of the form $\langle X, r, s\rangle$ and $\langle X, r', \overline{s}\rangle$ – that is, two cases in which the same fact situation X is decided for opposite sides – would be classified as inconsistent. We can now verify that a case base is likewise inconsistent if it contains cases in which one situation X is decided for the side s while another situation Y that is at least as strong for the side s as X is decided for $\overline{s}$, the opposite side:

Observation 9 Let Γ be a case base containing two precedent cases of the form $c = \langle X, r, s\rangle$ and $c' = \langle Y, r', \overline{s}\rangle$ where $X \leq^s Y$. Then Γ is inconsistent.

Since any fact situation is at least as strong as itself for either side, this result generalizes our earlier claim, and so provides further support for our notions of consistency and inconsistency.

3.3.2 Constraint

With this strength ordering on fact situations in place, we can now define the a fortiori model of constraint. The idea, once again, is that a court faced with a fact situation X is required to reach a decision for the side s whenever X is at least as strong for s as the fact situation of some precedent case whose outcome was a decision for that side:

Definition 21 (A fortiori model of constraint on decision for a side) Let Γ be a case base and X a fact situation confronting the court. Then against the background of Γ, the a fortiori model of constraint requires the court to decide X for the side s if and only if there is some case c from Γ such that $Outcome(c) = s$ and $Facts(c) \leq^s X$; the a fortiori model permits a decision for the side s if and only if it does not require a decision for the side $\overline{s}$.

To illustrate, suppose the background case base is the familiar $\Gamma_1 = \{c_1\}$, containing as its single member the familiar case $c_1 = \langle X_1, r_1, s_1\rangle$ – where, again, $X_1 = \{f_1^\pi, f_2^\pi, f_1^\delta, f_2^\delta\}$, where $r_1 = \{f_1^\pi\} \rightarrow \pi$, and where $s_1 = \pi$ – and imagine that the court is now confronted with the fact situation $X_{27} = \{f_1^\pi, f_2^\pi, f_2^\delta\}$. Then the a fortiori model of constraint requires a decision in this situation for the plaintiff, since $Outcome(c_1) = \pi$ and, as we have seen, $Facts(c_1) \leq^\pi X_{27}$.

The a fortiori model differs in two ways, one stylistic and one substantive, from the previous models of constraint considered thus far. The stylistic difference – just worth mentioning – is this: in both of these previous models, the reason model and the standard model, it seemed most natural to focus first on what a court is permitted to do, and then to define requirement in terms of permission, but in the case of the a fortiori model, it seems better to go the other way around, first defining what a court is required to do, and then characterizing permission as lack of requirement. The second, more substantive difference is that both the reason model and the standard model are developed on two levels, initially as constraints on rule selection, and then as constraints on decision for a side, but the a fortiori model is developed only on the single level of decision for a side. Neither rules nor reasons play any role at all in the a fortiori model. Instead, the model presents a picture of precedential constraint that depends entirely on the comparative strength for a side of current fact situation relative to the fact situation of some precedent case, regardless of the rule explicitly formulated by the court.

3.3.3 Relation to the Reason Model

We have seen that the standard model of constraint is equivalent to the reason model. What, then, is the relation between the a fortiori model of constraint and the reason model? Well, we can verify, first of all, that constraint according to the a fortiori model entails constraint according to the reason model, in the sense that, in any situation in which the a fortiori model requires a decision for some particular side, the reason model requires that same decision:

Observation 10 Let Γ be a consistent case base and X a fact situation confronting the court. Then against the background of Γ, if the a fortiori model of constraint requires the court to decide X for the side s, then the reason model of constraint also requires the court to decide X for the side s.

Next, it is easy to see that the converse entailment does not hold: there are situations in which the reason model of constraint requires the court to reach a decision that is not required by the a fortiori model. Suppose, for example, that the background case base is the familiar set $\Gamma_1 = \{c_1\}$, with c_1 as above, and that, against this background, the court is now confronted with $X_{14} = \{f_1^{\pi}, f_1^{\delta}\}$ as a new fact situation. Here, because $\{f_1^{\delta}\} <_{\Gamma_1} \{f_1^{\pi}\}$, the reason model requires the court to decide X_{14} for the plaintiff, since a decision for the defendant on the basis of $\{f_1^{\delta}\}$, the strongest reason for the defendant that holds in this situation, would be inconsistent with the background case base. But the a fortiori model does not require the court to decide X_{14} for the plaintiff, since X_{14} is not as strong for the plaintiff as some case from the case base already decided for the plaintiff; there is only one such case – c_1, with fact situation X_1 – and as we have seen, $X_1 \leq^{\pi} X_{14}$ fails. Instead, the a fortiori model permits the court to decide X_{14} for the defendant.

Putting these two observations together, we can conclude that constraint according to the a fortiori model entails, but is not entailed by, constraint according to the reason model: in any situation in which the a fortiori model of constraint requires a particular decision, the reason model requires that same decision, but there are some situations in which the reason model requires decisions that the a fortiori model does not. Furthermore, we can begin to see how it is, exactly, that the formulation of explicit rules, or reasons, allows the reason model to strengthen the a fortiori model of constraint.

Imagine that a court, working against the background of a case base containing the single case $c = \langle X, r, s \rangle$, is considering the new fact situation Y. Since *Outcome*$(c) = s$ and *Facts*$(c) = X$, it follows from Definition 21 that the a fortiori model requires the court to reach a decision in this situation for the side s just in case $X \leq^{s} Y$ – or, by Definition 20, just in case

(∗) $Y^{\overline{s}} \subseteq X^{\overline{s}}$ and $X^{s} \subseteq Y^{s}$.

Unwinding definitions – an exercise left for the reader – we can also see that the reason model requires the court to reach a decision for the side s just in case

(∗∗) $Y^{\overline{s}} \subseteq X^{\overline{s}}$ and $Premise(r) \subseteq Y^{s}$,

where $Premise(r)$ is the premise of rule from the case c above. Since the premise of a case rule is required to hold in the fact situation of the case, but may not exhaust even the positive part of that fact situation, we are guaranteed to have $Premise(r) \subseteq X^{s}$, although $X^{s} \subseteq Premise(r)$ may fail. From this it follows that any situation Y satisfying (∗) also satisfies (∗∗), so that a decision required by the a fortiori model must be required by the reason model as well, but that it is possible for Y to satisfy (∗∗) without satisfying (∗), so that a decision can be required by the reason model though not by the a fortiori model.

This relation between the reason model and the a fortiori model of constraint is illustrated in Figure 3.1, constructed in accord with the conventions governing the earlier Figure 1.1: The outer rectangle represents the entire space F of factors, divided by the diagonal line into the set F^{s} favoring s on the right and the set $F^{\overline{s}}$ favoring $\overline{s}$ on the left. The fact situation X of the case

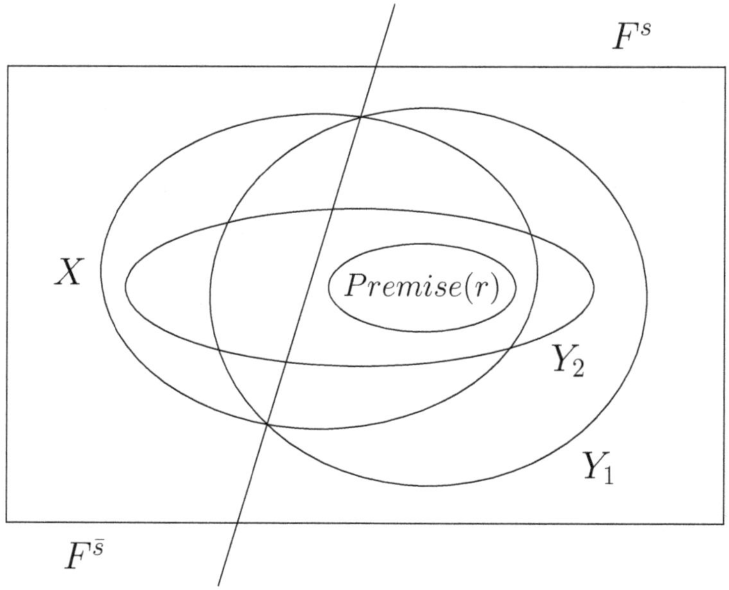

Figure 3.1 Comparing models of constraint

$c = \langle X, r, s\rangle$ straddles this diagonal, containing factors favoring both sides, and our coherence conditions on a case tell us that $Premise(r) \subseteq X^s$. We consider two additional fact situations, Y_1 and Y_2, as indicated. Since $Y_1^{\bar{s}} \subseteq X^{\bar{s}}$ and $X^s \subseteq Y_1^s$, it follows from (∗) that, if we suppose that c belongs to the background case base, the a fortiori model requires the court to decide Y_1 for the side s. Turning to Y_2, although we have $Y_2^{\bar{s}} \subseteq X^{\bar{s}}$, we do not have and $X^s \subseteq Y_2^s$, so that the a fortiori model does not require a decision for s in this situation. We do, however, have $Premise(r) \subseteq Y_2^s$, and so by (∗∗) the reason model requires the situation to be decided for s. The formulation of an explicit rule r, then, allows the court to justify its decision for a side s in the situation X by appeal to a reason $Premise(r)$ that may be weaker than the strongest reason X^s supporting s that holds in X, thus enabling the court to weaken the conditions necessary for constraint, and so to formulate precedents with broader reach.

The same point can be seen from the other direction as well. Rather than considering the way in which the appeal to rules in the reason model adds expressive power to the a fortiori model, we can instead view the a fortiori model itself as a special case of the reason model in which rules are restricted to a particular form. Consider again a fact situation X that is decided for s. As we have seen, the reason model allows the court, by formulating a rule r, to justify its decision, not necessarily on the basis of X^s, the strongest reason favoring s that holds in the situation X, but only on the basis of $Premise(r)$, a subset of X^s that may be considerably weaker. But suppose the court does, in fact, base its decision for s on the very strong reason X^s, by formulating a rule of the form $r = X^s \rightarrow s$, so that $Premise(r)$ and X^s coincide. In that case, as we can see by comparing ($*$) and ($**$) above, the court's decision will have the same force, requiring a judgment for s in exactly the same set of future situations, according to both the reason model and the a fortiori model. More generally, if we suppose that courts are limited to rules of this special form, the reason model of constraint collapses into the a fortiori model:

Observation 11 Let Γ be a consistent set of cases of the form $\langle X, r, s\rangle$ in each of which the case rule r has the form $X^s \rightarrow s$, and let Y be a fact situation confronting the court. Then against the background of Γ, the reason model of constraint requires the court to decide Y for some particular side if and only if the a fortiori model of constraint requires the court to decide Y for that same side.

This result suggests two lines of interpretation, which are simply mentioned here. It provides us, first of all, with a way of interpreting within the reason model the occasional case in which a court reaches some decision on the basis of a fact situation but fails to supply an explicit rule justifying that decision: if the fact situation is X and the court reaches a decision for the side s, we can imagine that the court is working with an implicit rule of the form $X^s \rightarrow s$, according to which the entire set of factors from X favoring the side s is taken as the premise of a rule leading to s as its conclusion. And second, the result also suggests a charitable interpretation of Goodhart's material facts version of the rule of a case, mentioned earlier. On Goodhart's view, once again, less emphasis should be placed on whatever rule is explicitly formulated by the court to justify its decision, and more emphasis on, we might as well say, an implicit rule that has as its premise the material facts of the case and as its conclusion the outcome arrived at by the court. But surely not all the material facts of a given case can be taken to support this outcome. If the fact situation is X and the outcome arrived at by the court is s, only those facts belonging to X^s actually support s as an outcome; the others – those facts belonging to $X^{\overline{s}}$ – instead support $\overline{s}$, the opposite side. Goodhart can thus be interpreted as holding that, regardless of the rule explicitly formulated by the court, the principle actually guiding the court's decision for s in the situation X is simply the rule $X^s \rightarrow s$.

4 Supporting the Reason Model

We have focused thus far on two central models of precedential constraint and legal development. The first is the reason model, set out in Chapters 1 and 2, according to which precedential constraint is based on a priority ordering among reasons, and legal development involves strengthening that ordering; as we have seen, the reason model has the a fortiori model as a special case. The second is the standard model, discussed informally in the Introduction and then set out precisely in Chapter 3, according to which constraint is based on rules, and legal development involves modification of these rules in a way that respects the Raz/Simpson conditions. Although these two models present very different pictures of precedential constraint and legal development, it was established in Chapter 3 that they are, in fact, equivalent. This equivalence was interpreted as showing that the reason model, itself taken as fundamental, could be viewed as providing a semantic justification for the Raz/Simpson conditions on rule modification.

In light of the equivalence between the standard model and the reason model, however, it is natural to ask why we should view the reason model as the more fundamental of the two – why not take the standard model as fundamental, so that it is the reason model that needs to be justified, or, more plausibly, why not simply take the two models of precedential constraint as providing two different theoretical treatments of the same phenomenon, which just happen to agree, without supposing that either is more fundamental than the other? Given their equivalence, what are the advantages of understanding precedential constraint from the standpoint of the reason model, rather than the standard model – why should we think of the common law as organized around reasons and priorities among reasons, rather than around complex, exception-laden rules?

This question is the topic of the current chapter, which presents three advantages of the reason model.[1] The first is that the reason model supports an attractive account not only of precedential constraint itself but also of the process of reasoning, or decision making, against a background set of precedent cases. The second is that the reason model allows for a principled distinction between the concepts of distinguishing and overruling a previous decision. The third is that the reason model provides a deeper understanding of the way in which previous common law decisions constrain later courts.

4.1 Reasoning with Precedents

A model of precedential constraint is different from an account of reasoning, or decision making, on the basis of that model. The first provides an answer to the question: against the background of a set of precedent cases, what decisions are permitted in some new situation? The second provides an answer to the question: how could a court reason its way to a permitted decision? These two questions are sometimes run together, sometimes almost inevitably so, when the relation between a model of constraint and the associated account of reasoning are particularly close. For example, the natural model of constraint, mentioned in the Introduction and discussed in more detail later in the current section, characterizes permitted decisions as those that might be arrived at through a process of natural, or ordinary, reasoning – so

[1] The question whether norms and normative development are best understood in terms of reasons whose priorities can be adjusted or in terms of rules that can be modified arises for moral as well as legal norms. For example, Hare (1952, pp. 49–55, 60–65) argues that moral development involves a process of modification of the moral principles guiding our actions very much like the process of rule modification in the standard model; he later summarizes the view by writing that "our moral development, as we grow older, consists in the main in making our moral principles more and more specific, by writing into them exceptions and qualifications to cover kinds of case of which we have had experience" (1963, p. 40). Likewise, Richardson (1990) argues that, in order to avoid conflicts, moral norms can be "specified" as they are applied, drawing explicit analogy to the way in which common law allows "scope for the judge to modify the rules to fit the case at hand" (p. 287). I suspect, but have not verified, that Richardson's specification proposal would be equivalent to a proposal that relies, instead, on prioritization of reasons, or defeasible rules, of the sort described in Horty (2012). Even so, however, there would remain the further question whether there are any advantages to presenting the proposal within one framework or the other, specification of moral rules or prioritization of moral reasons. The arguments set out here do not apply to this broader question concerning norms more generally, including moral norms, but are focused only on legal norms.

that, here, the notion of constraint is simply defined in terms of an associated account of reasoning. Likewise, the serious rule model – also mentioned in the Introduction and discussed later in this section – defines permitted decisions in terms of serious rules, so that it is sensible to imagine that any associated account of reasoning would involve the application of those rules.

Nevertheless, these two questions – concerning the definition of permitted decisions, or the reasoning involved in reaching, or justifying, those decisions – are distinct, as we can see by considering the reason model itself, which sets out a notion of constraint without any appeal to an associated account of reasoning. The goal of this section, then, is to argue that the reason model of constraint can be supported by an attractive account of reasoning in accord with that model, and to provide a preliminary overview of this account.

4.1.1 Serious Rules and Natural Reasoning

The task of developing an account of reasoning, or decision making, against a background of precedent cases is vexed in the literature, because this kind of reasoning often appears to slip between two familiar accounts of legal decision making, each with its own advantages and disadvantages.

The first of these two accounts can be characterized as decision making based on *serious rules*. This form of reasoning corresponds to the position described in the Introduction as the serious rule model of constraint – the idea, advocated by Larry Alexander and Emily Sherwin, that constraint is determined by precedent rules that cannot be modified once they are introduced but must be applied exactly as stated.[2] In accord with this view, decision making in a new situation would consist simply in applying the serious rules from precedent cases to this situation. Of course, the application even of serious rules is not entirely straightforward. The predicates contained in these rules could require interpretation, a process that may itself be guided by precedent.[3] And there could be gaps or gluts within the system of rules: at times, decisions may need to be reached in situations in which no rule is applicable, while at other times, multiple rules supporting conflicting results may be applicable. But at least in situations in which some rule is

[2] See, once again, Alexander (1989, Section 2), and Alexander and Sherwin (2008, Chapter 2).

[3] Recall, for example, our discussion in Section 1.3 of the predicate "vessel," as applied to objects such as the Super Scoop.

applicable – conflict aside, and modulo interpretation – this account is one in which outcomes are determined entirely through the application of rules.

Decision making based on serious rules offers several advantages, which have been discussed at length by a number of writers, and of which I mention only a few here.[4] It is, first of all, simple, involving nothing more than a straightforward application of rules, and so leading to the advantage of efficiency.[5] It possesses, in addition, the advantage described by Melvin Eisenberg as "replicability," according to which individuals who are affected by a court's decisions can replicate the reasoning underlying those decision.[6] Other virtues follow from replicability. For example, as Eisenberg notes, individuals who can replicate a court's reasoning are in a better position to appreciate the competence of that court, and so more likely to comply with its decisions; or, in case of incompetence, those who can replicate the court's reasoning are in a better position to question that reasoning at the appropriate points.

Most important, replicability implies a degree of predictability, since individuals who can replicate a court's reasoning in previous cases will be able, in the same way, to predict its reasoning in future cases. And if individuals are able to predict the decisions a court might reach in future cases, they can plan their actions accordingly, fostering social coordination. Imagine, for example, that Ann would like to construct a shopping center on her property, while, at the same time, Bob is considering an adjacent property as the site for his new vacation home, and suppose that zoning decisions are determined by a set of serious rules. Then, since reasoning with serious rules is predictable, Ann can apply these rules to conclude

[4] For further discussion, and a guide to the literature, see especially Schauer (1991) and Alexander and Sherwin (2008).

[5] Raz (1979, pp. 181–182) questions this advantage, arguing that even the straightforward application of rules can be difficult: he defines a "regulated dispute" as one governed by rules whose application does not require interpretation, claims that "regulated cases can be complex and more difficult to decide than unregulated cases," and illustrates this claim by noting that the "difficulty in solving a complex tax problem according to law may be much greater than that of solving a natural justice problem according to moral principles." I agree with this, of course – regulatory problems can be arbitrarily complex. But the difficulties presented by these complexities are of a special sort, reflecting our own information-processing limitations as much as anything else. In the field of artificial intelligence and law, where the focus is on machines with a very different pattern of cognitive limitations, pure rule-based reasoning is relatively unproblematic even in complex regulatory domains; see, for example, Bench-Capon (1991).

[6] See Eisenberg (1988, pp. 10–12); the idea is also discussed by Lamond (2005, p. 7).

that a shopping center is allowed, or her representatives can do so.[7] She can therefore proceed with construction, without worrying that Bob might convince a court to halt the project. And Bob, applying the same rules, will be able to reach the same result – that he cannot convince a court to halt Ann's construction – and conclude, therefore, that he should not buy the adjacent property, unless he is willing to accept the possibility of a shopping center next door. Coordination is thus achieved, with minimal judicial involvement.

Reasoning with serious rules, then, has these advantages – efficiency, replicability, predictability, social coordination – as well as many others. Indeed, its sole disadvantage seems to be that, by screening off from consideration all features of particular situations except those that trigger the application of existing rules, this form of reasoning can lead, at times, to suboptimal decisions, or to decisions that do not seem to be best, all things considered.[8] Everyone is familiar with situations in which an important benefit is denied because of a minor violation of rules – perhaps a form was filed containing a trivial error, or a correct form filed just slightly past deadline.[9] Here, the direct application of rules designed to promote the bureaucratic goals of order and efficiency interferes with achievement of the different, but arguably more important, goals of benevolence and equity. The suboptimality of decision making based on serious rules is even more notable when the direct application of these rules interferes with the achievement, not of different goals, even of more important goals, but of the very goals that the rules were introduced to advance – as when, for example, speed limits are put in place to assure that traffic flows smoothly and with minimal risk, but a driver finds that she can both enhance traffic flow and reduce risk by adjusting her speed to that of the surrounding vehicles, thus joining her fellow drivers in breaking the law.[10]

7 Eisenberg emphasizes (1988, p. 11) that replicability, and so predictability, is what allows for so many legal issues to be resolved by a professional class of lawyers, taking pressure off the judicial system.

8 This feature of rule-based decision making, and its consequences, are explored at length in Schauer (1991); see also Schauer (2009, Chapter 2) and the papers cited there.

9 Schauer (2009, p. 10) discusses a case in which the United States Supreme Court decided that an individual should be denied a benefit because he filed a form on December 31 while the relevant statute read that the form should be filed "prior to December 31" – even though everyone agreed that the language of the statute reflected a drafting error, and that what Congress had meant to say was that the form should be filed "on or prior to December 31."

10 The difficulties pointed out in this paragraph are, of course, standard objections to one version of rule utilitarianism.

The second of the two familiar accounts of reasoning considered here, already alluded to above as the basis of the natural model of constraint, will be characterized as decision making based on *natural reasoning*.[11] A court reasoning about a new situation in this way proceeds through two stages: first, surveying the reasons that bear on the situation at hand and assigning these reasons the priorities they seem to deserve, and then, second, arriving at whatever results these reasons and their assigned priorities seem to support.

This description of natural reasoning calls for two comments. It is, to begin with, radically incomplete, since there are no clear, generally accepted answers to the questions of how the range of reasons bearing on some situation is to be established, how priorities are to be assigned to those reasons, or how reasons along with their priorities support the results they do. Some of these issues will be addressed below, in Chapter 5, which reviews an account of natural reasoning developed in my own earlier work and shows how it can be adapted to the reasoning underlying judicial decisions. In the current chapter, however, we will continue to work only with the very high-level sketch of natural reasoning provided here, taking the idea of decision making purely on the basis of reasons as sufficiently well-understood for our present purposes – it is, after all, how most of us make most of the decisions we do.

As a second comment, it is important to bear in mind that among the features of a situation that might be relevant to a decision – even a decision entirely based on reasons – is the existence of rules. If there are rules, there may also be expectations that these rules will be followed, and both the rules and the resulting expectations may function as reasons for one decision or another. There is nothing about natural reasoning that prevents rules from being taken into account in this way. All this account of decision making requires is that the rules themselves do not determine the resulting decisions. Instead, the facts that there are rules, and that these rules may lead to expectations, constitute reasons, which can then be prioritized along with other reasons to support one decision or another. Even if the resulting decisions conform to the rules, it is the reasons generated by these rules that determine the decision, not the rules themselves.

[11] Although we use the phrase "natural reasoning" here, this form of reasoning has been described in various ways – as "pure" reason-based decision making, as "all-things-considered" decision making, or as decision making that is "open-ended," "unconstrained," or "particularistic."

The central advantage of decision making on the basis of natural reasoning is that, in contrast to decision making based on serious rules, it is guaranteed to lead to an optimal decision. How do we know this? By stipulation, or nearly so. When we say that the direct application of serious rules leads to a suboptimal result in some situation, what we mean is that it leads to a result different from the result we would have endorsed if we had taken into account all the reasons bearing on that situation, with each assigned its proper priority, and arrived at a decision on that basis. But a decision arrived at through natural reasoning simply is one reached on the basis of all relevant reasons, with each assigned its proper priority. This style of reasoning, therefore, can be taken as defining what it means for a decision to be optimal.

The central disadvantage of decision making based on natural reasoning is that, in allowing for full consideration of all reasons bearing on a particular situation, it sacrifices the various advantages discussed earlier associated with decision making based on serious rules. Natural reasoning need not be particularly efficient: while the direct application of rules is straightforward, reflection on reasons, their priorities, and the decisions they support can be slow and agonizing. Nor is this form of reasoning, by and large, replicable: different courts facing the same situation may well identify different reasons as relevant, or assign the same reasons different priorities, so that different outcomes will be supported when these reasons are considered along with their priorities. Since those affected by the judgments of decision makers will no longer be able to replicate the reasoning behind these judgments, they will have less confidence in the judgments themselves, and will be less likely to comply; and if they wish to question this reasoning, they will find it more difficult to do so in a useful way.

Most important, if the reasoning behind a court's previous decisions cannot be replicated, it is unlikely that the court's future reasoning can be predicted either – with the result that individuals will no longer be able to anticipate judicial decisions, and the advantages of social coordination will be lost. Returning to our earlier example, just imagine a system in which zoning decisions were made, not through the uniform application of serious rules, but on the basis of natural reasoning, with the possibility that different courts might well assign different priorities to the various reasons in play. The result would be chaos, or paralysis. Ann could never begin to build her shopping center without worrying that a court that happens to prioritize environmental concerns, or on the rights of Ann's neighbors to enjoy their property, might force her to halt construction. Bob could never buy property for his vacation home without worrying that a court that prioritizes commercial development would allow construction of a shopping center next door.

The contrast between the two accounts of decision making considered here – decision making based on serious rules, or on natural reasoning – is especially stark when it is considered from the perspective of the balance between constraint and freedom in common law reasoning. The first account, based on serious rules, emphasizes constraint at the expense of freedom: courts are constrained to follow the existing rules exactly as they have been formulated, without any freedom to modify these rules to avoid suboptimal outcomes. The second account, based on natural reasoning, emphasizes freedom at the expense of constraint: courts are free to consider all reasons bearing on a particular situation, along with their priorities, in order to reach the best decision possible in that situation, without any constraint at all from the rules articulated in previous decisions, except to the extent that those rules may themselves provide reasons, to be balanced against others in reaching a judgment.

4.1.2 Constrained Natural Reasoning

As mentioned earlier, it often appears that the correct picture of common law decision making lies somewhere between the two accounts described here, with their attendant advantages and disadvantages – allowing more freedom than reasoning based on serious rules alone but requiring more constraint than natural reasoning.[12] And there are, in the literature, two reactions to this idea. The first is to deny that there is, in fact, any defensible middle ground lying between these two familiar accounts, so that we are forced to assimilate common law decision making to one of these accounts or the other, with no further options. This hard-headed position is advocated most forcefully by Alexander and Sherwin, who go on to argue that it is best for everyone, both theorists and practitioners, to understand common

[12] Alexander (1989) makes this point by alluding to the children's story, writing of readers presented only with these two models that, "Like Goldilocks and the bowls of porridge and beds, they will complain that the natural model of precedent is too weak to capture their sense of how precedents operate and that the rule model of precedent is too strong" (p. 28).

law deliberation as reasoning based on serious rules.[13] The second reaction is to try to define a middle ground, and argue that it is defensible. This project has been pursued by a number of writers, in different ways, but a representative, and very attractive, proposal can be found in Frederick Schauer's "presumptive positivism."[14] According to this proposal, common law reasoning proceeds on the basis of serious rules in the vast run of cases, even in cases in which the direct application of these rules leads to moderately suboptimal outcomes. There is therefore a strong presumption in favor of rule application, and so constraint. The exception, according to Schauer, is that, in cases in which the suboptimality resulting from pure rule-based decision making threatens to become extreme, the rules can then be ignored in favor of natural reasoning, allowing courts the freedom to avoid the most egregious outcomes.

The account of decision making suggested by the reason model of constraint is different. It is not an attempt to combine reasoning based on serious rules with natural reasoning; indeed, there is no appeal to rules at all. Instead, this account is entirely reason-driven, just like decision making based on natural reasoning but with the sole difference that a common law decision maker, constrained by the precedents from a background case base, must adapt their own priority ordering on reasons so that it respects that derived from the case base. Because this form of reasoning is like natural reasoning, but with the priority ordering on reasons constrained to respect the priority ordering derived from a background case base, I refer to it as *constrained natural reasoning*.

A precise description of constrained natural reasoning will be set out in Chapter 6, building on the precise description of natural reasoning to be presented in Chapter 5. Once again, though, we can make do in the current chapter with a high-level and largely informal overview of the process – which may well be enough for most purposes. As we recall, decision making on the basis of natural reasoning depends on two things: first, the reasons the court sees as bearing on the situation at hand, and second, the priorities that the court assigns to those reasons. We will simplify here by imagining that the reasons bearing on some situation X are clear, and let us suppose that $<_i$ represents the priority ordering assigned by some court i to those reasons, so that it is this ordering on reasons that would guide the court's own natural

13 See Alexander (1989) throughout, and then Alexander and Sherwin (2001, pp. 136–156; 2008, pp. 27–127).

14 See Schauer (1989, pp. 469–471; 1991, p. 117n, pp. 196–206).

reasoning concerning the situation. All that differs, then, when the court is engaged in constrained natural reasoning, against the background of a case base Γ, is that the court's own priority ordering $<_i$ on reasons must be revised to respect the ordering $<_\Gamma$ derived, in accord with Definition 5 from Section 1.2.1, from this background case base – leading to, let us say, $<_{i/\Gamma}$ as a new priority ordering on reasons – and that it is this new ordering, rather than the original $<_i$, that now guides the court's reasoning in arriving at a decision.

How is the revised ordering $<_{i/\Gamma}$ to be determined, given the court's original priority ordering $<_i$ together with the ordering $<_\Gamma$ derived from the background case base? We can assume that the revised ordering must be consistent – that we cannot have both $U <_{i/\Gamma} V$ and $V <_{i/\Gamma} U$, for reasons U and V. And since the court's reasoning is supposed to be constrained by the derived priority ordering $<_\Gamma$, we require also that the revised ordering $<_{i/\Gamma}$ should extend $<_\Gamma$ – that we have $U <_{i/\Gamma} V$ whenever $U <_\Gamma V$, so that the revised ordering tells us that V has higher priority than U whenever this relation can be derived from the background case base, no matter how the court might originally have ranked these reasons.

Beyond these two conditions, there is little of a systematic nature to be said. It may be tempting, from a conservative perspective, to imagine that the revised ordering $<_{i/\Gamma}$ should represent some minimal modification of the court's original ordering $<_i$ – or more technically, that $<_{i/\Gamma}$ should result from combining the ordering $<_\Gamma$ derived from the background case base with some maximal subset of the agent's original ordering $<_i$ that is consistent with $<_\Gamma$. But it is hard to think of any justification for such a strong requirement. Of course, some particular court might take such a resolute, unyielding stance toward its own ordering on reasons that the court is unwilling to accept any modifications at all, apart from those strictly necessary for reconciling this ordering with that derived from the background case base. But it is also possible for a court to adopt a more open-minded, or receptive, attitude, perhaps extrapolating from the actual decisions contained in the background case base to a broader theory underlying those decisions, and then, in light of this broader theory, modifying its own priority ordering on reasons in ways that go beyond those strictly necessary for achieving consistency with the background case base. Which attitude the court adopts, and how, exactly, the court's original ordering on reasons is modified to respect that derived from the case base might depend on a number of variables – including structural facts about the relation between the court's original ordering and that derived from the case base, substantive facts about the nature of the reasons under consideration, and psychological facts about the individuals constituting the court.

Once the court has revised its own original ordering of reasons $<_i$ to respect the ordering $<_\Gamma$ derived from the case base, leading to the new ordering $<_{i/\Gamma}$, the suggestion, again, is that, to reach a decision in some new situation X, the court simply reasons in the natural way about this situation, except with the priority ordering on reasons given by the revised $<_{i/\Gamma}$ rather than the original $<_i$. Suppose that, reasoning in this way, the court arrives at a decision in favor of the side s, say, on the basis of the rule r. The case base Γ will then be supplemented with this new decision, resulting in the augmented case base $\Gamma' = \Gamma \cup \{\langle X, r, s\rangle\}$ and the strengthened ordering $<_{\Gamma'}$, which will then constrain the reasoning of the next court deciding the next case. At each succeeding stage, then, the case base will be further augmented, and the derived priority ordering further strengthened, in a way that reflects each particular court's own priority ordering among the reasons bearing on the situation at hand, but only after that court's ordering has been revised to respect the ordering derived from the existing case base.

What of constraint and freedom, and of the respective advantages and disadvantages associated with decision making on the basis of serious rules or natural reasoning? Unlike decision making based on serious rules, which provides constraint without freedom, or decision making based on natural reasoning, which allows freedom without constraint, decision making based on constrained natural reasoning strikes a reasonable balance between the two. In considering some new situation against the background of an existing case base, the court is constrained by the requirement that the reasons bearing on this situation must be evaluated, not in accord with the priorities that the court would naturally assign to them, but instead, in accord with a priority ordering that has been revised to respect that derived from the existing case base. Once this requirement has been satisfied, however, the court is free to engage in an open-ended process of deliberation that brings all reasons bearing on that situation into play, and that proceeds in the natural way.

Constrained natural reasoning, then, offers this balance between constraint and freedom, but it is important to note that the balance will shift as the law matures. Initially, while the law in some area is just beginning to develop, the background case base Γ will contain few decisions, so that the derived priority ordering $<_\Gamma$ will be weak. This derived priority ordering will therefore have relatively little impact on the revised ordering $<_{i/\Gamma}$, so that reasoning in accord with this revised ordering will approximate reasoning in accord with the court's original ordering $<_i$. At this early stage, constrained natural reasoning will share many of the advantages and disadvantages of unconstrained reasoning: courts will have a good deal of freedom to reach decisions they consider to be optimal, but their reasoning will be less predictable, and advantages of social coordination will be sacrificed. As the law is developed, and the case base Γ becomes more populated with decisions, the ordering $<_\Gamma$ derived from this case base will grow stronger. Because the revised priority ordering $<_{i/\Gamma}$ must extend the derived ordering $<_\Gamma$, this derived ordering will have an increasing influence on the nature of the revised ordering, so that reasoning in accord with this revised ordering will diverge more significantly from reasoning based on the court's original ordering. In these later stages of legal development, constrained natural reasoning will come to share the characteristics of reasoning on the basis of serious rules: courts will have less freedom to reach decisions they view as optimal, but their decisions will become more predictable, supporting social coordination.

It is also worth noting that – although we cannot explore this topic in any detail here – our account of constrained natural reasoning yields the entirely new benefit of allowing us to reflect on the process of common law development from the standpoint of preference aggregation. What the common law generates, according to the reason model, is a social ordering on reasons, constructed as a result of decisions by individual courts engaged in constrained natural reasoning, each deciding cases on the basis of their own personal ordering on reasons, once this ordering has been modified to respect the social ordering already established. The common law can thus be seen as the realization of a particular kind of preference aggregation procedure – a particular way of aggregating individual preferences, or priorities, among reasons into a group preference. Unlike the preference aggregation functions usually studied in social choice theory, however, the procedure realized by the common law does not simply take a collection of individual preferences as inputs and output a group preference, all at once. Instead, the common law constructs its group preference ranking on reasons through a procedure that is piecemeal, distributed, and responsive to particular circumstances. Especially given the challenges to the overall coherence of common law reasoning that have been advanced over the years, it will be interesting to explore the extent to which the preference aggregation procedure realized by the common law can be justified using ideas from social choice theory.

4.2 Distinguishing and Overruling

4.2.1 Constructive and Destructive Operations

We now turn to the second advantage of the reason model of constraint over the standard model: unlike the standard model, the reason model allows for a principled distinction between the operations of distinguishing a new situation and overruling a previous decision. The difference between distinguishing and overruling is generally taken as central to the common law. All courts are thought to have the power of distinguishing, through which they carry out a process of gradual, incremental, adaptive legal development. Overruling, by contrast, is viewed as a more radical operation, generally available only to courts either above or, sometimes, at the same level as the court that arrived at the decision to be overruled. Even then, this option is avoided whenever possible, since the resulting legal transformations can be abrupt and extreme: when a precedent case is overruled, it is as if the case were, in the words of Rupert Cross, "wiped off the slate," or as Raz writes, removed "root and branch."[15]

In order to illustrate the difference between distinguishing and overruling, we return to our initial domestic example, first set out in the Introduction, and then considered from the perspective of the reason model in Section 1.2.3 and from the perspective of the standard model in Section 3.1.2. The example involved two children, Max and Emma, both of whom wanted to stay up and watch TV, presenting their cases as plaintiffs to their parents, Jack and Jo, who function as defendants and adjudicators. The situations presented by the children were characterized through combinations of the factors f_1^π and f_2^π, respectively representing the facts that the child in question is at least nine years old and has completed chores, and the factors f_1^δ and f_2^δ, respectively, representing the facts that the child failed to finish dinner and failed to complete homework.

Let us begin by reviewing our treatment of this example within the standard model. As we recall, the initial situation presented by Emma to Jo, represented as $X_4 = \{f_1^\pi, f_2^\pi, f_1^\delta\}$, was decided in favor of Emma on the basis of the strict rule "Children age nine or greater can stay up and watch TV" – that is, in the strict framework, on the basis of the strict rule $r_{24} = \{f_1^\pi\} \Rightarrow \pi$, leading to the decision $c_{24} = \langle X_{24}, r_{24}, s_{24}\rangle$, where $X_{24} = X_4$, where r_{24}

[15] See Cross and Harris (1991, pp. 127–128), who attribute the phrase to Lord Dunedin, and Raz (1979, p. 189).

is as above, and where $s_{24} = \pi$. Next, we supposed that, working against the background of the case base $\Gamma_{14} = \{c_{24}\}$ containing only the decision reached by Jo in the case of Emma, Jack was confronted by Max with the situation $X_5 = \{f_1^{\pi}, f_2^{\pi}, f_1^{\delta}, f_2^{\delta}\}$, which he decided against Max on the grounds that Max had not completed his homework – that is, on the basis of the strict rule $r_{25} = \{f_2^{\delta}\} \Rightarrow \delta$. The effect of this decision, according to the standard model, was both to augment the existing case base with the new case $c_{25} = \{X_{25}, r_{25}, s_{25}\}$, where $X_{25} = X_5$, where r_{25} is as above, and where $s_{25} = \delta$, and also to modify Jo's original rule r_{24} so that it can now be read as "Children age nine or greater can stay up and watch TV, unless they have failed to complete their homework," represented as $r_{24}{}' = \{f_1^{\pi}\} \wedge \neg\{f_2^{\delta}\} \Rightarrow \pi$. Since Jack's modification of Jo's rule satisfied the Raz/Simpson conditions – merely narrowing her original rule, and doing so in a way that continued to support her previous decision – this decision was classified as a legitimate instance of distinguishing, leading to the new case base $\Gamma_{15} = \{c_{24}{}', c_{25}\}$, with c_{25} as above and with $c_{24}{}' = \{X_{24}{}', r_{24}{}', s_{24}{}'\}$ as a modification of the previous c_{24}, where $X_{24}{}' = X_{24}$, where $r_{24}{}'$ is as above, and where $s_{24}{}' = s_{24}$.

Suppose, however, that Jack had disagreed more sharply with Jo's original decision, which downplays the significance of failing to finish dinner as a factor for the defendant, and chose to use the case of Max to reaffirm the importance of this factor. We can then imagine that, rather than proceeding as in the initial scenario, Jack would instead have justified his decision with the new rule "Children who have not finished their dinner cannot stay up and watch TV," represented here as $r_{28} = \{f_1^{\delta}\} \Rightarrow \delta$, and so leading to the new decision $c_{28} = \langle X_{28}, r_{28}, s_{28}\rangle$, where $X_{28} = X_5$, where r_{28} is as above, and where $s_{28} = \delta$. This decision of Jack's can no longer be accommodated within the case base $\Gamma_{14} = \{c_{24}\}$ containing Jo's original decision – any modification of Jo's rule that respects the Raz/Simpson conditions would allow both Jack's rule and Jo's modified rule, which support different outcomes, to apply to some fact situation from the case base. As a result, Jack must now be taken, not simply as distinguishing, but as overruling Jo's previous decision.

How can this operation of overruling be modeled in the present framework? If an overruled case is indeed to be "wiped off the slate," or "removed root and branch," then it is natural to suppose that one logical effect of this operation is that the overruled case should be removed from the case base entirely.[16] On this view, Jack can be seen as adding his new decision to

[16] There may be other logical effects as well. Perhaps, in overruling a case, a court should be taken as removing from the case base not only that particular case, but every other

the background case base and then, not modifying, but simply removing Jo's previous decision, leading to

$$\Gamma_{19} = (\Gamma_{14} - \{c_{24}\}) \cup \{c_{28}\}$$
$$= \{c_{28}\}$$

as the updated case base, where c_{28} is as above.

From an intuitive standpoint, a comparison between these two different paths of legal development – taking us from the original case base Γ_{14} to the new case base Γ_{15}, or from the original Γ_{14} to the new Γ_{19} – seems to support the generally accepted view that distinguishing and overruling previous decisions are very different ways of modifying the law. It does seem, for example, that the rule Jack sets out in the second scenario, when he overrules, presents a much more radical challenge to Jo's decision than the rule he sets out in the first scenario, when he distinguishes. It almost seems that, with his second rule, Jack is contradicting Jo's opinion, rather than just working to refine it; and if this is so, we can understand why, in a stable legal system, only certain courts should be able to challenge earlier decisions in such a radical way. Nevertheless, in spite of the intuitive force of the distinction between these two ways of modifying the law, a number of theorists have questioned whether there is, in fact, any real difference between the operations of distinguishing and overruling. Schauer, for example, writes of a rule that is "subject to modification when the features of the case demand" – that is, of a rule that can be modified through the process of distinguishing – that "the rule itself furnishes no constraint," much like a rule that can simply be eliminated.[17] And Alexander and Sherwin are even more explicit, arguing that the insistence on a difference between distinguishing and overruling is both confused and dangerous. On confusion, they write that we should not

> distinguish between overruling precedent rules and modifying or "distinguishing" them. When a judge makes an exception to a rule to accommodate a particular case, the judge is effectively eliminating the precedent rule and announcing a new rule in its place.[18]

case that shares the same rule; or perhaps there is a temporal dimension, so that the court should be taken as removing every other case sharing the same rule as the original that was decided at a later date. Overruling can be a complex operation, but there is no need to consider its complexities here, since our example contains only a single case to be overruled.

17 Schauer (1991, pp. 175, 177); earlier, he claims that a rule of this kind, which can be modified at the moment of application, is "in an important way not a rule at all" (p. 117).

18 Alexander and Sherwin (2008, pp. 114–115; see also pp. 59, 84).

And on danger:

> The practice of distinguishing precedent rules is dangerous to the stability of rules because it creates an illusion of modesty. Judges may intervene more often when they believe they are merely modifying, rather than overruling, established rules. This belief is mistaken because modifying or distinguishing precedent rules just *is* overruling them.[19]

And indeed, when the matter is considered from the perspective of the standard model, I believe these objections to the distinction between distinguishing and overruling make good sense. From a purely logical point of view, we must agree with Alexander and Sherwin that, even in instances of legal development that are typically classified as distinguishing, where a previous rule is modified in accord with the Raz/Simpson conditions, a later court is not, strictly speaking, modifying the earlier rule at all but instead, removing that rule from consideration and introducing one or more new rules in its place; these new rules may have more or less similarity to the original, but they are nevertheless different rules, exhibiting different syntactic forms and yielding different results in a variety of situations. In the first of our two scenarios, for example, which was classified as an instance of distinguishing, Jack removes Jo's original rule $r_{24} = \{f_1^{\pi}\} \Rightarrow \pi$ and introduces the two new rules $r_{24}' = \{f_1^{\pi}\} \wedge \neg\{f_2^{\delta}\} \Rightarrow \pi$ and $r_{25} = \{f_2^{\delta}\} \Rightarrow \delta$; in the second scenario, which was classified as an instance of overruling, Jack again removes Jo's original rule and introduces the new rule $r_{28} = \{f_1^{\delta}\} \Rightarrow \delta$. In each of these scenarios, then, Jo's original rule is eliminated entirely, and none of the new rules support the same result as the original in the new fact situation presented by Max. Why, then, should we think that Jack's challenge to Jo's decision in the first scenario is any less radical than his challenge in the second – why should we think of distinguishing as any less radical than overruling?

This problem for the standard model, with its emphasis on rule modification, has a happy solution when the matter is viewed from the perspective of the reason model, which allows a clear semantic distinction between distinguishing and overruling to be drawn in terms of the priority ordering on reasons derived from a background case base. Since decisions that distinguish and decisions that overrule both change the case base, both kinds of decisions change the derived priority ordering as well, but they do so in very different ways. A court that distinguishes a previous decision merely

[19] Ibid. p. 124.

expands the existing case base through the addition of a new decision, with the result that the new derived priority ordering on reasons is stronger than the original. But a court that overrules a previous decision both expands the existing case base with a new decision and contracts it through the removal of a previous decision, with the result that the new derived priority ordering is strengthened in some ways but weakened in others, and is therefore incomparable to the original.

To illustrate this point, we consider the same two scenarios – in which Jack first distinguishes, and then overrules Jo – from the standpoint of the reason model, beginning with the original scenario, exactly as it was originally set out in Section 1.2.3. There, as we recall, Jo's initial decision in the case of Emma was represented as $c_4 = \langle X_4, r_4, s_4 \rangle$, where $X_4 = \{f_1^\pi, f_2^\pi, f_1^\delta\}$, where $r_4 = \{f_1^\pi\} \rightarrow \pi$, and where $s_4 = \pi$, leading to $\Gamma_4 = \{c_4\}$ as the case base representing the household legal system. Jack's decision in the case of Max was then represented as $c_5 = \langle X_5, r_5, s_5 \rangle$, where $X_5 = \{f_1^\pi, f_2^\pi, f_1^\delta, f_2^\delta\}$, where $r_5 = \{f_2^\delta\} \rightarrow \delta$, and where $s_5 = \delta$. Since Jack decided for the defendant in spite of Jo's binding rule for the plaintiff – and since Jack's decision is consistent with the background case base – this decision counts as a legitimate instance of distinguishing, according to our Section 2.1.2 analysis of this concept within the reason model, leading, as we saw earlier, to $\Gamma_5 = \{c_4, c_5\}$ as an augmented case base. But what about the second scenario, in which Jack chooses to challenge Jo's decision more directly? Within the reason model, Jack's decision in this second scenario can be represented as $c_{29} = \langle X_{29}, r_{29}, s_{29} \rangle$, where $X_{29} = X_5$, where $r_{29} = \{f_1^\delta\} \rightarrow \delta$, and where $s_{29} = \delta$. Since this decision is no longer consistent with the background case base, it must therefore be taken as overruling Jo's earlier decision, removing it "root and branch," and so leading to

$$\begin{aligned} \Gamma_{20} &= (\Gamma_4 - \{c_4\}) \cup \{c_{29}\} \\ &= \{c_{29}\} \end{aligned}$$

as an updated case base, where c_{29} is as above.

In the first of these scenarios, then, where Jack distinguishes Jo's earlier decision, moving from the original case base Γ_4 to the new case base Γ_5, the derived priority ordering is strengthened: it is easy to see that $U <_{\Gamma_4} V$ implies $U <_{\Gamma_5} V$ for any reasons U and V, and that the new ordering yields $\{f_1^\pi\} <_{\Gamma_5} \{f_2^\delta\}$ while, previously, we did not have $\{f_1^\pi\} <_{\Gamma_4} \{f_2^\delta\}$. But in the second scenario, where Jack overrules Jo's decision, now moving from the original case base Γ_4 to the new Γ_{20}, the resulting derived priority ordering is incomparable to the original: it is stronger in some ways, since we have $\{f_1^\pi\} <_{\Gamma_{20}} \{f_1^\delta\}$ but not $\{f_1^\pi\} <_{\Gamma_4} \{f_1^\delta\}$, but it is also weaker in some ways, since we have $\{f_1^\delta\} <_{\Gamma_4} \{f_1^\pi\}$ but not $\{f_1^\delta\} <_{\Gamma_{20}} \{f_1^\pi\}$.

Let us return, now, to our previous question: why should we think that Jack's challenge to Jo's decision in the first scenario, where he distinguishes, is less radical than his challenge in the second, where he overrules? From the perspective of the reason model, with its focus on the priority ordering among reasons, the answer is clear. The force of Jo's initial decision is simply that being at least nine years of age is a more important reason for the plaintiff than failing to finish dinner is for the defendant, reflected in the initial case base priority $\{f_1^\delta\} <_{\Gamma_4} \{f_1^\pi\}$. In the first scenario, when Jack distinguishes, moving from Γ_4 to Γ_5, he is not challenging Jo's initial judgment at all, but simply augmenting her initial decision with a further, consistent decision. The augmented case base continues to support $\{f_1^\delta\} <_{\Gamma_5} \{f_1^\pi\}$, reflecting Jo's initial decision, but now also supports $\{f_1^\pi\} <_{\Gamma_5} \{f_2^\delta\}$, reflecting Jack's further decision that, although being at least nine years of age is a more important reason for the plaintiff than failing to finish dinner is for the defendant, failing to complete homework is a more important reason for the defendant than being at least nine years of age is for the plaintiff. In the second scenario, by contrast, when Jack overrules Jo's initial decision, moving from Γ_4 to Γ_{20}, the resulting case base no longer supports Jo's initial judgment, but instead, the opposite, that failing to finish dinner is more important than being at least nine years of age, or that $\{f_1^\pi\} <_{\Gamma_{20}} \{f_1^\delta\}$. This decision presents a radical challenge to Jo's decision because it removes information about the priority among reasons that was supported by Jo's decision and replaces it with conflicting information.

Stepping back from this particular example – and drawing on technical terminology from computer science – what our discussion shows is that overruling previous decisions is a radical way of changing the law precisely because it is a *destructive* operation, removing existing information from the overall priority ordering in addition to adding new information. The operation of distinguishing can likewise appear to be destructive when it is viewed from the perspective of the standard model, since it involves the removal of existing rules – this is Alexander and Sherwin's point. But when it is viewed from the perspective of the reason model, we can see that this operation is entirely *constructive*, merely adding new information to the priority ordering, not removing any existing information. The reason model thus provides us with a principled way of explicating the traditional common law distinction between the distinguishing and overruling, as a distinction between operations that lead to constructive versus destructive changes in the priority ordering on reasons derived from the resulting case base.

4.2.2 Negative Distinguishing

Suppose that the rule r from a case $\langle Y, r, s\rangle$ belonging to a background case base Γ is binding in a new situation X confronting the court. Earlier, in Section 2.1.2, we stipulated that the court distinguishes this new situation just in case it decides X on the basis of a rule r' supporting $\overline{s}$, the opposite side, in a way that leads to a consistent case base $\Gamma \cup \{\langle X, r', \overline{s}\rangle\}$; we then showed, with Observation 4, that the premise $Premise(r')$ of the new rule r' favoring the side $\overline{s}$ cannot hold in the fact situation Y of the previous case in which the binding rule r was formulated or applied. Because the court's decision is based on the presence of a new reason $Premise(r')$ favoring the new decision, which holds in the new situation but which did not hold in the previous situation, we can refer to this form of distinguishing as *positive distinguishing*. With this vocabulary, it is apparent that, for example, Jack's decision for the defendant in the case of Max, in spite of the binding rule favoring the plaintiff formulated in the previous case of Emma, involves positive distinguishing, since it is based on a reason favoring the defendant – failure to complete homework, or $\{f_2^\delta\}$ – that holds in the new situation presented by Max but not in the previous situation presented by Emma. The question now arises: in addition to positive distinguishing, is there a corresponding form of *negative distinguishing*, based, not on the presence in the new situation of a new reason favoring a new decision, but on the absence in the new situation of a reason that favored the previous decision in the previous situation, but was simply not included in the rule justifying that decision?[20]

To give this question concrete meaning, we return to our familiar domestic situation, with the factors f_1^π and f_2^π representing the facts that some child in question is at least nine years old and has completed chores, and with the factors f_1^δ and f_2^δ representing the facts that the child has failed to finish dinner and failed to complete homework. And let us consider, once again, Jack and Jo's third child, Chris, introduced in Section 1.2.4, who also hopes to stay up and watch TV, and who is at least nine years old but failed to

[20] I am grateful to Gabriel Broughton for forcing me to consider this question.

finish dinner. The situation presented by Chris, then, is $X_6 = \{f_1^\pi, f_1^\delta\}$; note that this situation differs from the earlier $X_4 = \{f_1^\pi, f_2^\pi, f_1^\delta\}$ presented by Emma in not containing the factor f_2^π – it is not part of the current situation that Chris has completed chores.

We begin by considering the matter from the perspective of the standard model, with $\Gamma_{14} = \{c_{24}\}$ as the background case base, containing only Jo's previous decision for the plaintiff in the case of Emma – that is, in the strict setting, the case $c_{24} = \langle X_{24}, r_{24}, s_{24}\rangle$, where $X_{24} = X_4$, where $r_{24} = \{f_1^\pi\} \Rightarrow \pi$, and where $s_{24} = \pi$. Imagine that, against the background of this case base, the situation $X_6 = \{f_1^\pi, f_1^\delta\}$ presented by Chris now comes before Jack. And suppose that Jack wishes to distinguish this new situation by deciding for the defendant, not on the grounds that some new reason favoring the defendant holds in the case of Chris – in fact, there is no such reason – but instead, on the grounds that some reason for the plaintiff that held in the previous case of Emma fails to hold in the new situation presented by Chris. Suppose, to be specific, that Jack wants to distinguish the new situation on the grounds that Emma had both reached the age of nine and completed chores, while Chris has not – that is, on the grounds that the reason $\{f_1^\pi, f_2^\pi\}$, which held in the situation presented by Emma, fails to hold in the situation presented by Chris.

In that case, working within a framework that allows modification of existing rules, Jack might reinterpret Jo's previous rule to mean that Emma can stay up and watch TV, not because she has simply reached the age of nine, but because she has both reached the age of nine and completed chores – modifying the previous $r_{24} = \{f_1^\pi\} \Rightarrow \pi$, that is, to carry the force of $r_{24}'' = \{f_1^\pi, f_2^\pi\} \Rightarrow \pi$. And he might then justify his decision for the defendant in the case of Chris on the grounds that Chris failed to finish dinner, while noting that the modified justification of a decision for the plaintiff in the case of Emma no longer applies to Chris – that is, Jack might base his decision on the rule $r_{30} = \{f_1^\delta\} \Rightarrow \delta$. The resulting case base would be $\Gamma_{21} = \{c_{24}'', c_{30}\}$ with $c_{24}'' = \langle X_{24}'', r_{24}'', s_{24}''\rangle$ as Jack's modification of Jo's previous decision in the case of Emma, where $X_{24}'' = X_{24}$, where r_{24}'' is as above, and where $s_{24}'' = s_{24}$, and with $c_{30} = \langle X_{30}, r_{30}, s_{30}\rangle$ as Jack's new decision in the case of Chris, where $X_{30} = X_6$, where r_{30} is as above, and where $s_{30} = \delta$.

The question we face is, if Jack proceeds in this way, is he merely distinguishing the new situation presented by Chris from the previous situation presented by Emma, in which Jo's original rule was formulated, or is he actually overruling Jo's previous decision? What makes this question interesting is that Jack's modification of Jo's previous rule appears to satisfy the two Raz/Simpson conditions: first, the modified rule merely narrows the original rule, and second, the modified rule yields the same outcome as the original in all situations to which the original was applied. Furthermore, Raz himself, in his own commentary on these conditions, can be understood as suggesting that rule modifications of the kind introduced by Jack should count as distinguishing:

> The second condition above [that the modified rule yields the same outcome as the original in all previous cases] makes it tempting to say that the modified rule was really the rule the original court had in mind but which it failed to articulate clearly. Often enough this may indeed be the case. It may be that the court in [the case of Emma] was influenced by the fact that the case was one [in which the factor f_2^π was present], but somehow perhaps they took this feature too much for granted, they failed to specify its existence among the operative conditions of their *ratio*.[21]

On the other hand, it is also easy to see that, against the background of the case base $\Gamma_{14} = \{c_{24}\}$ containing Jo's original decision, Jack's decision in the case of Chris does not satisfy our official version of the standard model, set out in Definition 17 from Section 3.1.3, which stipulates that a decision is permitted only if the result of augmenting the existing case base with that decision is accommodation consistent. And here, as the reader can verify, the case base $\Gamma_{14} \cup \{\langle X_{30}, r_{30}, s_{30}\rangle\}$ that would result from augmenting Γ_{14} with Jack's decision is not accommodation consistent.

At this point, we face two options. We could, first of all, agree with what seems to be Raz's suggestion that Jack's decision in the case of Chris should count as distinguishing, rather than overruling, Jo's previous decision in the case of Emma. We would then be forced to admit that our official characterization of the standard model, in Definition 17, is too restrictive, since it allows only for positive distinguishing, such as Jack's decision in the case of Max, but not for negative distinguishing, such as Jack's decision in the case of Chris. The challenge would then be to provide a less restrictive definition of the standard model, allowing for negative distinguishing as well as positive distinguishing. Since our Definition 17 characterization of

[21] Raz (1979, p. 188), with prose slightly adapted to apply to the present example, rather than to the example in Raz's text; I am grateful, once again, to Broughton for calling my attention both to this passage and to its relevance to the current question.

the standard model coincides with the reason model, we could no longer expect such agreement from a new, more liberal version.

Alternatively, we could conclude that, in spite of Raz's apparent endorsement of negative distinguishing as a form of distinguishing, Jack's decision in the case of Chris does not just distinguish but actually overrules Jo's earlier decision in the case of Emma. There are reasons for thinking this. First, in the passage from Raz displayed above, although I adapted his remarks to our present example, and so interpreted Raz as suggesting that what the precedent court took for granted was the presence of a positive factor favoring its decision, Raz's own discussion does not rely on factors with polarity, favoring one side or another.[22] It is therefore hard to tell whether he means to suggest that what the precedent court took for granted, and so failed to mention as part of its ratio, was actually the presence of a positive factor favoring its decision, or instead, the absence of a negative factor favoring the other side – without factor polarities, it is hard to tell whether Raz really is advocating for negative distinguishing, or simply for the more familiar form of positive distinguishing. Second, even if Raz himself may endorse negative distinguishing as a legitimate form of distinguishing, there is strong evidence that Simpson does not.[23]

[22] See our earlier discussion of factors without definite polarity, from Section 2.2.4.

[23] The evidence occurs in a complex passage from Simpson (1961, p. 174), which explicitly considers the idea that a court can "distinguish two cases by emphasizing some circumstances in the earlier case which the judge in the earlier case did not think important or material" – that is, in our language, the idea of negative distinguishing – and argues against this idea by presenting an example that may at first seem to require negative distinguishing, but in fact does not. Simpson's example centers around the old-fashioned parietal rules governing visitation in college dormitories – and I apologize for the sexist nature of the example, but the issue is subtle enough that I do not know how to support my claim, which is about Simpson interpretation after all, without relying on the example he actually presents. He begins by imagining that a "College Dean has a power to make and enforce rules of conduct in his College, and that he does not publish a set of carefully drafted rules, but applies a rough and ready doctrine of precedent," and then considers the Dean's decisions in two cases. First, the Dean "fines Jones £5 and explains to him that he has done so because Jones kept Miss Doe, his girl friend, in the College until 9.30 and that he has always fined undergraduates £5 if they allow ladies to stay in College after 9 p.m." Next, two days later, the Dean "discovers that Smith allowed Miss Styles to remain in until 9.10 p.m. because she had been stung by a bee and was in considerable pain," distinguishes this second case from the first, and chooses not to issue a fine. Simpson argues that the Dean's decision in the second case "would surely be justifiable" and emphasizes that the Dean can justify this decision without "having to show that in Jones' case he had emphasized the rude health of Miss Doe, or treated it as in any way material ... but only that in Smith's case he finds a circumstance which

Which of these options is correct – should we accept negative distinguishing as another form of distinguishing, or should we view it, instead, as overruling? Here we can turn to the reason model for help. When the issue is viewed from that perspective, rather than from the perspective of the standard model, it then becomes apparent that negative distinguishing is best understood, not as a legitimate form of distinguishing but as a form of overruling.

To see this, let us place our current example within the framework of the reason model, with $\Gamma_4 = \{c_4\}$ as the background case base containing $c_4 = \langle X_4, r_4, s_4 \rangle$ as a representation of Jo's initial decision regarding Emma, where $X_4 = \{f_1^{\pi}, f_2^{\pi}, f_1^{\delta}\}$, where $r_4 = \{f_1^{\pi}\} \to \pi$, and where $s_4 = \pi$; and suppose that Jack now considers the situation $X_6 = \{f_1^{\pi}, f_1^{\delta}\}$ presented by Chris against this background. It follows at once from the reason model that Jack is not permitted to base his decision in this situation on the rule $r_{31} = \{f_1^{\delta}\} \to \delta$, the defeasible rule corresponding to the previous strict $r_{30} = \{f_1^{\delta}\} \Rightarrow \delta$, since the resulting augmented case base $\Gamma_4 \cup \{\langle X_{31}, r_{31}, s_{31} \rangle\}$ is inconsistent, where $X_{31} = X_6$, where r_{31} is as above, and where $s_{31} = \delta$. According to the reason model, then, Jack can decide for the defendant in this situation only if he is willing to overrule Jo's previous decision.

Just suppose, however, that, in a kind of hybrid reason/standard model, Jack has the ability to modify even the defeasible rule from the background case base as suggested above, so that it carries the force of $r_4' = \{f_1^{\pi}, f_2^{\pi}\} \to \pi$, and then proceeds to decide the new situation presented by Chris on the basis of the rule $r_{31} = \{f_1^{\delta}\} \to \delta$. We would then have $\Gamma_{22} = \{c_4', c_{31}\}$ as the resulting case base, with $c_4' = \langle X_4', r_4', s_4' \rangle$, where $X_4' = X_4$, where r_4' is as above, and where $s_4' = \pi$, and with $c_{31} = \langle X_{31}, r_{31}, s_{31} \rangle$ as above. As the reader can verify, the resulting case base $\Gamma_{22} = \{c_4', c_{31}\}$ would be consistent, suggesting that, as long as Jack is able to modify Jo's rule as above, from r_4 to r_4', his decision in the case of Chris might be interpretable as distinguishing, rather than overruling. However, it turns out that even the move from the initial case base $\Gamma_4 = \{c_4\}$ to the augmented case base

makes it very different from Jone's case" – that is, the bee sting. Taking the Dean as plaintiff and both Smith and Jones as defendants, then, in our language, what Simpson is emphasizing with his example is that the Dean's decision in Smith need not involve negative distinguishing, relying on factors favoring the plaintiff that were present but not mentioned in the rule supporting the original decision for the plaintiff; instead, the Dean's decision can be justified through positive distinguishing, relying only on a new factor supporting the defendant, the bee sting, that was present in Smith but not in Jones.

$\Gamma_{22} = \{c_4{}', c_{31}\}$ still results in a destructive modification of the derived priority ordering – priority information is still lost, since we have $\{f_1^{\delta}\} <_{\Gamma_4} \{f_1^{\pi}\}$ but not $\{f_1^{\delta}\} <_{\Gamma_{22}} \{f_1^{\pi}\}$. Therefore, given our earlier analysis of the distinction between distinguishing and overruling as a distinction between case base operations that result in constructive versus destructive modifications of the derived priority ordering, a decision for the defendant in this situation – and negative distinguishing more generally – must be understood, not as true distinguishing, but as a kind of overruling.

4.3 The Real Mechanism of Precedential Constraint

4.3.1 The Alligator and the Ocelot

Finally, we turn to the third advantage of the reason model over the standard model: the reason model allows us to formulate a response to what may be the deepest objection, or at least the most common, to the standard model idea that common law rules are malleable. The objection is that, as long as the rules set out by courts can be modified through the process of distinguishing – even if the modifications involved are required to satisfy the Raz/Simpson conditions – common law decisions cannot really constrain future courts at all, since, as the objection goes, no two situations are ever entirely alike: there will always be features available for future courts to use in distinguishing the situations they face from those confronted earlier.

This objection is set out forcefully by Alexander and Sherwin, who illustrate the point with their story, adapted here, of the alligator and the ocelot.[24] Imagine, first, that Albert, as defendant, wishes to keep a pet alligator on his property but that the local neighborhood association, as plaintiff, brings suit against Albert asking him to remove the alligator on the grounds that it is a dangerous wild animal. Albert argues that he should be allowed to keep his alligator, since it resides on his private property, but the

[24] See Alexander and Sherwin (2008, pp. 84–86). For ease of exposition, the original story set out by Alexander and Sherwin is modified here, in two ways. First, rather than focusing, as Alexander and Sherwin do, on the question whether the alligator and the ocelot should be classified as "nuisances" – a question, that is, concerning the application of an open-textured predicate – the issue is cast here as one directly between a plaintiff who wants the animals to be removed and a defendant who wants to keep them. Second, rather than taking the ocelot as precedent and distinguishing the alligator on the grounds that it is not furry, we take the alligator as precedent and distinguish the ocelot on the grounds that it is furry.

court is not convinced and justifies its decision for the plaintiff with the rule "Residents are not allowed to keep dangerous wild animals." Next, suppose that another resident, Olive, acquires a pet ocelot, and the neighborhood association again brings suit for removal. This time, however, imagine that the case comes before a court that is sympathetic to the ocelot, wishes to arrive at a decision for the defendant in the case at hand, but is aware that it must distinguish the situation from the previous case of the alligator in order to do so. The court therefore notes that ocelots, but not alligators, are furry, and proceeds to distinguish on that basis, modifying the previous rule to read, "Residents are not allowed to keep dangerous wild animals, unless they are furry," and, we might as well suppose, justifying its own decision for the plaintiff with the new rule "Residents are allowed to keep furry wild animals."

By modifying the earlier rule in this way, the later court has rendered it inapplicable to the ocelot, providing itself the freedom to decide the new case as it wishes, without constraint from the rule. And as Alexander and Sherwin emphasize, this instance of rule modification satisfies the Raz/Simpson conditions, merely narrowing the previous rule, and narrowing it in such a way that the modified rule continues to support the decision arrived at in the previous case. The example thus highlights the fact that any two cases can be differentiated in any number of ways, even if many of these differences are either entirely incidental or of only marginal importance – that one dangerous wild animal but not the other is furry, or that the defendant in one case but not the other has freckles, or plays the harmonica, or has an aunt living in Idaho. And if all a court needs to do in order to shield the decision it wishes to reach from some previous rule is to narrow that rule by appeal to one of these incidental or marginal differences, it really does begin to seem, at least from the perspective of the standard model, that decisions arrived at in earlier cases cannot constrain later courts at all.

But let us look at the example more closely. Suppose the court considering Olive's ocelot actually does believe that the ocelot's furry nature provides a reason for allowing Olive to keep it on her property, and indeed a stronger reason than that provided for the opposite conclusion by the fact that it is a dangerous wild animal. In that case, it would be right, at least from an internal perspective, for the court to reach exactly the decision described in the example – that the new situation should be distinguished, and the ocelot allowed because it is furry. The court, after all, has an obligation to reach the decision it sincerely thinks is best.

What is so odd about this result, and what gives the example its force, is not some problem with the idea of distinguishing but simply the assumption that the court might actually conclude, in all sincerity, that this particular decision is best – that the court could somehow conclude that the ocelot's furry nature, if it is even a reason at all, is a strong enough reason that it should outweigh an important consideration favoring the other side. How could this conclusion be justified? Surely a court that reasoned its way to a conclusion like this would be subject to criticism, just as those who engage in poor reasoning in any other domain are subject to criticism.[25]

And it is by focusing on this idea – that common law decisions are subject to substantive criticism and require substantive justification – that we can locate a response to the objection that, as long as distinguishing is allowed, any situation can be distinguished from any other, so that constraint is illusory. In fact, this line of response has already been explored by Simpson, who notes that, when we ask whether or not a court can distinguish a case, we are not asking about the "can" of human ability:

> When one is talking in this context of what judges can and cannot do under the rules of the legal system one is not making a simple statement of fact, of what is as a matter of fact humanly possible. If one were, it would be true to say that a case can always be distinguished, for this would only amount to saying that two cases will always involve some factual difference, which it is possible for a judge to point out.[26]

Instead, he writes, we are asking about the "can" of permissibility. What we want to know is not whether it is "humanly possible" to find some difference between two cases – of course it is – but whether, in distinguishing on the basis of this difference, the court's action will be seen as permissible, in the sense that the factual distinction highlighted by the court will be accepted as a justification for failing to follow a binding rule, or whether, instead, the court will be subject to criticism, by the standards at work in the legal system or in society at large:

25 There is also the suggestion in Alexander and Sherwin's own presentation of the example that the court, by introducing the ocelot's furry nature as a consideration at all, is being insincere, or disingenuous. But then, this move would be criticizable as well – not in the way that poor natural reasoning is criticized, but in the way that we might criticize a person who is deceitful or hypocritical.

26 Simpson (1961, p. 175).

> From this [factual difference] it does not follow that it is always permissible for a judge to distinguish a case; that he can do so whilst conforming to the rules of the legal system, or that he can do so without becoming liable to be criticized for having acted improperly. Distinguishing does not simply involve pointing out a factual distinction between two cases; it involves further the use of this factual distinction as a justification for refusal to follow the earlier case ....[27]

It is important to emphasize, and to tease apart, two distinct notions of permissibility at work in this passage, and in Simpson's paper more generally. There is, first of all, the notion according to which a decision is permissible if it satisfies the relevant legal norms – it is this notion that is explicated by the reason model of constraint, set out formally in Definition 7 from Section 1.2.2, which classifies a decision as permissible if it is consistent with the existing case base. But, second, there is also the notion according to which a decision is permissible if it can be justified by more general social standards. In the remainder of this section, I refer to the first of these notions as "formal permissibility" and to the second as "social permissibility," and will try to illustrate how the real mechanism of constraint arises from an interplay between these two notions.[28]

4.3.2 Two Notions of Permissibility

We begin by coding the alligator/ocelot example in our representational framework, taking f_1^π as the factor, favoring the neighborhood association as plaintiff, that some wild animal under consideration is dangerous, and taking f_1^δ as the factor, favoring the resident as defendant, that the wild animal is kept on private property. The initial situation presented by Albert's alligator, a dangerous wild animal kept on private property, is therefore represented as $X_{32} = \{f_1^\pi, f_1^\delta\}$. And let us assume that the background case base concerning animals in the neighborhood is initially empty, so that the alligator presents a case of first impression.

Now suppose that, of the two conflicting reasons that hold in this situation, danger and private property – that is, $\{f_1^\pi\}$ and $\{f_1^\delta\}$ – neither is generally recognized as more important than the other: the priority relation between

[27] Ibid.

[28] This distinction between formal and social permissibility, and the use to which it is put here, runs parallel to the distinction between doctrinal and social propositions, and its use, in Eisenberg (1988).

these reasons is a matter about which reasonable people can disagree. Imagine, however, that the case of Albert's alligator comes before a court that, while recognizing the matter as one of legitimate disagreement, itself happens to assign greater priority to the danger posed by the alligator – imagine, that is, that this court prioritizes $\{f_1^\pi\}$ over $\{f_1^\delta\}$. Given its own priorities, we can suppose, therefore, that the court finds in favor of the plaintiff in the case of the alligator on the basis of its danger, leading to the decision $c_{32} = \langle X_{32}, r_{32}, s_{32} \rangle$ – where X_{32} is as above, where $r_{32} = \{f_1^\pi\} \rightarrow \pi$, and where $s_{32} = \pi$ – and resulting in $\Gamma_{23} = \{c_{32}\}$ as the augmented case base on the issue.

In rendering this decision, the court introduces a legal proposition. This proposition, according to the reason model, is not a rule, like "Residents are not allowed to keep dangerous wild animals," but instead a statement about the relative priority of various reasons – the proposition that, as a matter of law, danger as a reason for the plaintiff now carries a higher priority than private property as a reason for the defendant, or that $\{f_1^\delta\} <_{\Gamma_{23}} \{f_1^\pi\}$. Since, in introducing this proposition into the law, the alligator court simply elevates its own particular opinion concerning the relative priority of reasons to the status of legal doctrine, it is necessary to ask whether this decision is permissible, in each of our two senses: Is it socially permissible? Is it formally permissible?

The answer is that, at least given a certain sensible assumption, the decision is indeed socially permissible. We have already stipulated that the priority relation between danger and private property is a matter about which reasonable people can disagree. So all we need to assume – sensibly, it seems – is that it is socially permissible for a court to take some particular side on a contentious issue about which reasonable people can disagree: surely it is too much to require that a court's decision is socially permissible only if it is something that all reasonable people would agree with. And of course, the alligator court's decision is formally permissible as well, by the standards of the reason model, since the initial case base is empty and any decision at all is consistent with an empty case base.[29]

Next, we turn to Olive's ocelot – like Albert's alligator, a dangerous wild animal kept on private property but one that is, in addition, furry. In representing this example, we will assume that the ocelot's furry nature, here

[29] This fact follows at once by Observation 2 from Section 2.1.2, in case it is not already obvious.

taken as f_2^δ, is a factor that favors the defendant, though very weakly. (Furry wild animals, especially large furry felines, tend to be beautiful in a way that, for most people, alligators are not; and we can assume that preservation of beauty in the neighborhood is at least a very weak reason for allowing the ocelot.) The situation presented by the ocelot is therefore $X_{33} = \{f_1^\pi, f_1^\delta, f_2^\delta\}$.

Since we have assumed that the priority between danger and private property is a matter about which reasonable people can disagree, let us now imagine that the ocelot case comes before a court that happens to prioritize property rights over danger – we imagine, that is, that this court, unlike the previous alligator court, prioritizes $\{f_1^\delta\}$ over $\{f_1^\pi\}$. Given its own priority ordering, the current ocelot court would prefer to find for the defendant on the basis of private property, leading to the decision $c_{33} = \langle X_{33}, r_{33}, s_{33}\rangle$, where X_{33} is as above, where $r_{33} = \{f_1^\delta\} \rightarrow \delta$, and where $s_{33} = \delta$. And of course, by an argument exactly parallel to that just offered for the alligator court, this decision, taken on its own, would have been socially permissible. Unfortunately for the ocelot court, however, it is not considering the new situation against the background of an empty case base, but against the background of the case base $\Gamma_{23} = \{c_{32}\}$ containing the previous alligator decision. And in this context, the ocelot court's preferred decision is not formally permissible, since it would introduce an inconsistency into the background case base – the new priority $\{f_1^\pi\} <_{c_{33}} \{f_1^\delta\}$ resulting from the ocelot court's preferred decision would now conflict with the derived priority $\{f_1^\delta\} <_{\Gamma_{23}} \{f_1^\pi\}$ already established in the case of the alligator.

The effect of the alligator decision, then, is to block, on formal grounds, the ocelot court from reaching a decision for the defendant in what would have been, from the social standpoint, the most straightforward and easily justifiable way, on the basis of private property. But does the court have another option? Yes, at least from a purely formal perspective. As Alexander and Sherwin suggest, the ocelot court might decide for the defendant on the grounds of the ocelot's furry nature, leading to the decision $c_{34} = \langle X_{34}, r_{34}, s_{34}\rangle$ – where $X_{34} = X_{33}$, where $r_{34} = \{f_2^\delta\} \rightarrow \delta$, and where $s_{34} = \delta$ – resulting in $\Gamma_{24} = \{c_{32}, c_{34}\}$ as an augmented case base. Since this new case base is consistent, the court's decision would be permissible by the formal standards of the reason model. But it is hard to imagine how such a decision by the ocelot court could ever be classified as socially permissible: the proposition that the court would then introduce into the law – that a furry nature as a reason for the defendant has higher priority than danger as a reason for the plaintiff, or $\{f_1^{\pi}\} <_{\Gamma_{24}} \{f_2^{\delta}\}$ – is so peculiar that it would surely be subject to intense criticism on substantive grounds.

There is also a more complicated possibility. While respecting the previous court's decision for the plaintiff – and so taking on board the legal proposition that danger carries a higher priority than private property, or that $\{f_1^{\delta}\} <_{\Gamma_{23}} \{f_1^{\pi}\}$ – the ocelot court might argue that, although danger is now, as a matter of law, prioritized over private property, the comparison between these two reasons is close enough that adding even the very weak reason for the defendant provided by the ocelot's furry nature tips the balance to the other side. In that case, the court could decide for the defendant on the basis of the rule $r_{35} = \{f_1^{\delta}, f_2^{\delta}\} \rightarrow \delta$, leading to the decision $c_{35} = \langle X_{35}, r_{35}, s_{35}\rangle$ – where $X_{35} = X_{33}$, where r_{35} is as above, and where $s_{35} = \delta$ – resulting in $\Gamma_{25} = \{c_{32}, c_{35}\}$ as an augmented case base. Since this case base is consistent, the decision would be permissible by the formal standards of the reason model. Moreover, this decision would not require the court to justify the implausible view that the ocelot's furry nature, on its own, carries higher priority than the danger it poses. But it does require the court to provide a justification for the complex position it then advances – that, while danger is prioritized over private property, private property together with a furry nature is prioritized over danger, or that $\{f_1^{\delta}\} <_{\Gamma_{25}} \{f_1^{\pi}\}$ but $\{f_1^{\pi}\} <_{\Gamma_{25}} \{f_1^{\delta}, f_2^{\delta}\}$. Although it may be possible to justify this position – with the result that the decision would then be classified as socially permissible as well – constructing such a justification would be considerably more difficult than justifying a decision for the defendant directly on the basis of private property, if that option had not already been ruled out by the alligator precedent.

This particular example, then, illustrates the mechanism of common law constraint, which relies on our two notions of permissibility to work together: decisions must be both formally permissible and socially permissible – neither is sufficient alone. Without the requirement of formal permissibility, nothing would prevent the ocelot court from reaching the decision c_{33}, allowing Olive to keep her ocelot on the grounds that it resides on private property – even though the ocelot is also dangerous, and it was previously decided by the alligator court in c_{32} that danger is prioritized over private property. Without the requirement of social permissibility, nothing would prevent the ocelot court from reaching one of the decisions c_{34} or c_{35}, allowing Olive to keep her ocelot on the grounds that it is furry, or else both furry and residing on private property – even though the first of these decisions would require the assignment of an inordinately high priority to what seems, intuitively, to be a very weak reason, and the second would require a complex and delicate argument for its justification.

More generally, the real mechanism of constraint associated with the reason model works like this: Earlier courts constrain later courts, not by preventing these later courts from reaching decisions for a particular side entirely through the application of formal standards, but by restricting the formally permissible decisions for that side to those that are more difficult to justify in a satisfactory way. Each decision settles the priority relations among certain reasons, and so, on formal grounds, restricts later courts from making decisions that would introduce conflicting priorities. After a sufficient number of decisions have been reached, the formal priority relations among the important reasons in some domain are settled to the extent that – as in our example – it becomes difficult to distinguish later cases without introducing further claims of priority among reasons that are harder to justify on substantive grounds, and so more likely to be classified as socially impermissible.

A question remains: Since the reason model provides an account of formal permissibility that is meant to work in conjunction with an account of social permissibility, it is natural to ask how the appropriate standards of social permissibility should be formulated. Unfortunately, since this question opens up a new direction of inquiry, it is not something I can address in any detail here, apart from mentioning a few options. The idea that distinguishing, in addition to meeting formal standards, also requires substantive justification, is found in Raz, for instance. In his view, the rule modifications involved in distinguishing should satisfy, not only the formal Raz/Simpson conditions, but also the more substantive condition that, as he puts it, a modified rule "can usually be justified only by reasoning very similar to that justifying the original rule," so that the modification of a particular rule must "preserve its fundamental rationale."[30] And of course, Raz's picture could be adapted to the current setting as well: we might suppose that, in order for a later decision that distinguishes an earlier decision to be classified as socially permissible, the priorities derived from that later decisions must respect the fundamental rationale justifying the priorities derived from the earlier decision. Alternatively, there is a long tradition according to which

[30] Raz (1979, pp. 187, 188); but see, for example, Eisenberg (1988, p. 52) for a challenge to the idea that later rules must preserve some fundamental rationale.

considerations of overall coherence play an important part in justification.[31] This approach could also be adapted to the current setting, so that, after a decision is distinguished, social permissibility requires that the entire set of derived priorities must still exhibit a kind of overall coherence.

My own view is that, rather than assuming that the justification of priorities among reasons should satisfy some global standard – preservation of fundamental rationale, or overall coherence – we should adopt a more piecemeal, or pluralist, approach, imagining that justifications of the priorities resulting from common law decisions might be based on a range of principles, or values, and that a central function of the common law is to reconcile conflicts among these competing values as they apply in concrete situations. In this, I agree with Simpson, who writes that it would be "as hopeless to attempt to catalogue the possible justifications of distinguishing as it would be hopeless to catalogue the factors which influence the making of law and recommend it to a nation."[32] But, perhaps in contrast to Simpson, I do not take this hopelessness of arriving at a fixed catalog of justifications to entail pessimism about systematic work on the nature or structure of these justifications for priority relations among reasons. Indeed, some of the most interesting recent research in artificial intelligence and law is focused on exactly this issue.[33]

[31] See Dickson (2016) for a discussion and references.

[32] Simpson (1961, p. 175).

[33] This work tends to start with the premise that what makes a consideration a legal reason at all is the fact that deciding an issue on the basis of that consideration promotes or defends some value that the legal system should promote or defend, and then moves to the conclusion that the importance of a consideration as a reason depends on the importance of the value that it promotes and the extent to which a decision on the basis of that reason promotes that value. The literature on this topic began with Berman and Hafner (1993), a paper whose importance was later emphasized by Bench-Capon (2002); highlights in the resulting stream of research include Prakken (2002), Bench-Capon and Sartor (2003), Sartor (2010), and Grabmair and Ashley (2011). Within philosophy, an analysis of reasons similar in many ways to that at work in this literature from artificial intelligence and law, but with independent motivation, is provided by Maguire (2016).

5 Natural Reasoning

Chapter 4 provided an informal account of a court's reasoning, or decision making, against a background set of authoritative precedent cases. The general idea underlying this account of reasoning – characterized as constrained natural reasoning – was that a court, considering a new situation against a background case base, engages in a process just like natural reasoning, but with the exception that, constrained by precedents from the case base, the court must adapt its own priority ordering on reasons to respect the ordering derived from the case base. The goal of this chapter and the next is to explore one way in which the informal sketch of constrained natural reasoning provided in Chapter 4 can be developed as a formal theory.

Any precise account of constrained natural reasoning would have to be built on top of a precise account of natural reasoning, so that we can see exactly what is being constrained and how the relevant constraints are supposed to operate. I will rely here on the account of natural reasoning developed in my own earlier work, which is driven by two theses.[1] The first is that natural reasoning involves reasons. This thesis may seem to be uncontroversial – it has a ring of etymological plausibility, at least. But it is not. The intuitive notion of a reason plays little role in the most prominent formal treatments of reasoning, such as ordinary logic, decision theory, or heuristic search in artificial intelligence. One hypothesis for this neglect is the impression that there is no formal framework – no *calculus ratiocinator* – available for studying the role of reasons in natural reasoning. This may have been true until recently, but it is no longer true, which brings me to my second thesis: that the role of reasons and their interaction in supporting

[1] See Horty (2012), the central ideas of which are summarized in Sections 5.1 and 5.2 of the present chapter; any reader who is already familiar with this earlier work is invited to skim these two sections for notation alone and then jump ahead to Section 5.3.

conclusions can, at least to a first approximation, be modeled within certain nonmonotonic logics, such as default logic.[2]

The current chapter begins, therefore, by reviewing a very simple prioritized default logic, where defaults represent reasons, the priorities among defaults correspond to the importance of the reasons they represent, and the logic itself models the way reasons interact to support conclusions; the system is motivated with an analysis of some elementary patterns of natural reasoning. Continuing our review, we then consider two elaborations of this simple default logic, in which the reasoner can be thought of as reasoning, also by default, about the priorities that guide their own default reasoning, and about the possibility of excluding certain defaults from consideration.

On the basis of this more elaborate default logic, developed as a formal account of natural reasoning in general, we can then turn to the central topic of the current chapter: showing how the logic can be used to provide, in particular, an account of natural reasoning about the situations presented to a court for adjudication. Once we understand natural reasoning about these fact situations, we will then be in a position, in Chapter 6, to see how this kind of reasoning can be adapted in the face of constraints derived from a background case base.

5.1 Default Logic

5.1.1 Fixed Priority Default Theories

Our prioritized default logic is developed against the background of an ordinary logical system in which $\wedge$, $\vee$, $\supset$, and $\neg$ are the operations of conjunction, disjunction, implication, and negation, and in which $\top$ is the trivially true proposition. The turnstile $\vdash$ indicates ordinary logical consequence, so that $\mathcal{E} \vdash X$ means that the proposition X follows from the set of propositions $\mathcal{E}$. We define $\mathit{Closure}(\mathcal{E}) = \{X : \mathcal{E} \vdash X\}$ as the logical closure of $\mathcal{E}$, the set of propositions that follow from $\mathcal{E}$ through ordinary logical consequence.

Where X and Y are propositions, we take $X \rightarrow Y$ as the *default rule* – or simply, the *default* – that allows us to conclude Y, by default, once X has

[2] The general subject of default logic was introduced in Reiter (1980); the particular default logic employed in this chapter derives from Horty (2012). Although we rely on default logics here, because of their simplicity, other nonmonotonic logics could have been used as well. Of special interest are the argumentation frameworks growing out of Dung (1995), which have been employed extensively for the analysis of legal argument within artificial intelligence and law; see Prakken and Sartor (2015) for an overview.

been established. To illustrate: if we suppose that B is the proposition that Tweety is a bird and F is the proposition that Tweety flies, then $B \rightarrow F$ is the rule that allows us to conclude that Tweety flies, by default, once it has been established that Tweety is a bird.

In fact, we have already encountered default rules in this book; the defeasible case rule $\{f_1^\pi\} \rightarrow \pi$, for example, can now be understood as a default rule according to which the reason $\{f_1^\pi\}$ supports, by default, a decision for the plaintiff. More generally, let us now describe the reasons considered thus far – that is, sets of factors uniformly favoring one side or the other – as *factor reasons*, to distinguish them from the various other reasons to be considered in this chapter and the next. Then, where U is a factor reason favoring the side s, the rule $U \rightarrow s$ can be interpreted as a special kind of default rule, which we now refer to as a *factor default*. The current chapter can be read as showing how the factor defaults that we have been considering all along can be embedded within a more general theory of default reasoning.

We assume that the two functions $Premise$ and $Conclusion$ defined earlier for factor defaults can be broadened to apply to default rules in general: if r is the default $X \rightarrow Y$, then $Premise(r)$ is the proposition X and $Conclusion(r)$ is the proposition Y. The second of these functions is lifted from individual defaults to sets of defaults in the obvious way: where $\mathcal{S}$ is a set of defaults, $Conclusion(\mathcal{S}) = \{Conclusion(r) : r \in \mathcal{S}\}$ is the set of conclusions of those defaults belonging to $\mathcal{S}$.

Default rules can be thought of as expressing the reason relation. In the case of our example, what the default $B \rightarrow F$ indicates is that the premise that Tweety is a bird functions as a reason for the conclusion that Tweety flies. It is this reason relation that allows default rules to mediate the inferences they do: we are able to conclude, by default, that Tweety flies once we know that Tweety is a bird precisely because the premise that Tweety is a bird functions as a reason for the conclusion that Tweety flies. In general, the reasons expressed by default rules can be either practical or epistemic – reasons for actions, or reasons for conclusions. The information that Tweety is a bird might be said to provide an epistemic reason supporting the conclusion that Tweety flies. By contrast, if Jack promises to meet Jo for lunch, his promise is most naturally interpreted as providing a practical reason. It does not necessarily support the conclusion that Jack will meet Jo for lunch but provides Jack with a reason for doing so.

Some defaults, as well as their corresponding reasons, have greater importance, or higher priority, than others. This information is represented through an ordering relation $<$ on default rules, where the statement $r < r'$ means that the default r' has a higher priority than the default r. Suppose, for example, that P is the proposition that Tweety is a penguin, so that $P \to \neg F$ is the default allowing us to conclude that Tweety cannot fly once it is established that Tweety is a penguin. Then if we take $r_B = B \to F$ as our earlier default and $r_P = P \to \neg F$ as this new default, it is natural to assume that $r_B < r_P$ – that the default concerning penguins has higher priority than the default concerning birds. Although the ordering relation $<$ on defaults is usually thought of as a partial ordering, we suppose here that it satisfies only the weaker asymmetry property according to which, for any defaults r and r', if $r < r'$, then it is not the case that $r' < r$. We do not suppose that the ordering on default rules must, in general, satisfy transitivity as well, since we will eventually want to mirror the priority ordering on reasons derived from a case base in our ordering on default rules, and, as noted in Section 1.2.1 and explored in Section 2.2.3, that ordering is not transitive; of course, transitivity can still be imposed separately on classes of defaults for which a transitive priority ordering is appropriate.

The priority relations among defaults, and their corresponding reasons, can have different sources. In the Tweety example, the priority of the penguin default r_P over the bird default r_B seems to depend on specificity: a penguin is a specific kind of bird, and so information about penguins in particular has higher priority than information about birds in general. Reliability is another source of priority relations, at least for epistemic default rules. We tend, by default, to accept what we are told – but what if one source of information asserts that climate change is a hoax while a different, much more reliable source asserts that it is real? In that case, we would tend to agree that climate change is real, discounting the information supplied by the less reliable source. And once we move from epistemic to practical reasons, then authority provides yet another source for priority relations. Just as there are defaults according to which we tend to accept what we are told, there are defaults according to which we ought to do as we are told, at least by appropriate authorities. But authorities come in different levels. National laws are typically prioritized over state or municipal laws, and more recent court decisions are prioritized over older decisions; in a military setting, orders from higher-ranking officers are prioritized over orders from lower-ranking officers, and direct orders are prioritized over standing orders.

Finally, one of the most important sources of priority among default rules is our very own reasoning, indeed our default reasoning, about which defaults, or reasons, have higher priority than others. Just as we reason about ordinary things in the world – birds, penguins, climate change – so we reason about our own reasons, offering further reasons for taking some of our reasons more seriously than others, for supposing that some sources of information are more reliable than others, or that some authorities are more important than others; we can then offer further reasons for evaluating those higher-level reasons, and still further reasons for evaluating those. The process through which priorities among defaults can themselves be established through default reasoning, or through which the strength of reasons is established by appeal to further reasons, will be described in the following section.

We begin, in this section, with *fixed priority* default theories – default theories, that is, in which all priorities among default rules are fixed in advance, so that there is no need to consider either the source of these priority relations or the way in which they are established, but only their effect on the conclusions reached through default reasoning. A theory of this kind contains three components. The first is a set of ordinary propositions, the second a set of defaults, and the third a priority ordering on these defaults:

Definition 22 (Fixed priority default theories) A fixed priority default theory is a structure of the form $\Delta = \langle \mathcal{W}, \mathcal{D}, < \rangle$, in which $\mathcal{W}$ is a set of ordinary propositions, $\mathcal{D}$ is a set of default rules, and $<$ is an asymmetric ordering on $\mathcal{D}$.

Such a structure – a collection of ordinary propositions, taken as settled, or *hard*, information, together with an ordered collection of default rules – is supposed to represent the initial data provided to an agent as a basis for its reasoning.

Since defaults are special rules of inference that can be used to extend the conclusions derivable from a body of hard information beyond its ordinary logical consequences, the conclusion sets supported by default theories are generally referred to as *extensions*. We will concentrate here, however, not directly on these conclusion sets, or extensions, but on the more fundamental notion of a *scenario*, where a scenario based on a default theory $\Delta = \langle \mathcal{W}, \mathcal{D}, < \rangle$ is defined simply as some subset $\mathcal{S}$ of the set $\mathcal{D}$ of defaults contained in that theory. From an intuitive standpoint, a scenario is supposed to represent the particular subset of available defaults that have actually been selected by a reasoning agent as providing sufficient support for their conclusions – the particular subset of defaults to be used by the agent in extending the initial information from $\mathcal{W}$ to a full set of conclusions. More exactly, where $\mathcal{S}$ is a scenario based on the default theory $\Delta = \langle \mathcal{W}, \mathcal{D}, < \rangle$, we can say that the conclusion set $\mathcal{E}$ is *generated* by that scenario just in case

$$\mathcal{E} = \mathit{Closure}(\mathcal{W} \cup \mathit{Conclusion}(\mathcal{S})).$$

The agent arrives at the conclusion set $\mathcal{E}$ generated by the scenario $\mathcal{S}$, therefore, by first extracting the conclusions from the defaults belonging to that scenario, then combining this set of conclusions with the hard information from $\mathcal{W}$, and finally taking the logical closure of the entire thing.

Not every scenario based on a default theory is intuitively acceptable, of course; some might contain what seem to be the wrong selection of defaults. Our first task, then, is to characterize, as we will say, the *proper scenarios* – those sets of defaults that might be accepted by an ideal reasoning agent on the basis of the information contained in a particular default theory. Once this notion of a proper scenario is in place, the traditional concept of an extension of a default theory can be defined quite simply, as a conclusion set that is generated by a proper scenario.

These ideas can be illustrated by returning to the Tweety example, with P, B, and F as the propositions that Tweety is a penguin, a bird, and that he flies. The information from our example, then, can be captured by the default theory $\Delta_1 = \langle \mathcal{W}, \mathcal{D}, < \rangle$ where $\mathcal{W} = \{P, P \supset B\}$, where $\mathcal{D} = \{r_B, r_P\}$ with $r_B = B \rightarrow F$ and $r_P = P \rightarrow \neg F$, and where $r_B < r_P$. The set $\mathcal{W}$ contains the hard information that Tweety is a penguin and that this entails that he is a bird; the set $\mathcal{D}$ contains the two defaults concerning birds and penguins, and the ordering tells us that the penguin default carries higher priority than the bird default.

It is often possible, and where possible it is often helpful, to depict default theories as *inference graphs*, with nodes representing propositions and links between nodes representing both ordinary and default entailment relations between these propositions. The conventions for interpreting these graphs are as follows: A strict link of the form $X \Rightarrow Y$ indicates that, according to the theory under consideration, the proposition X materially implies the proposition Y; as a special case, the link $\top \Rightarrow Y$ indicates that Y is materially implied by the true proposition, or more simply, that Y is true. In order to make the inference relations among propositions more perspicuous, a strict positive link $X \Rightarrow \neg Y$, with a negated proposition on its tail, is often written as the strict negative link $X \not\Rightarrow Y$, and two strict negative links of

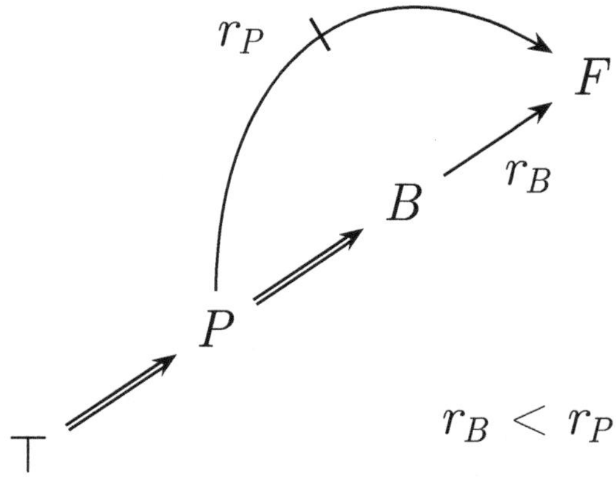

Figure 5.1 The Tweety Triangle

the form $X \not\Rightarrow Y$ and $Y \not\Rightarrow X$ are often merged into a single link $X \not\Leftrightarrow Y$, indicating that the propositions X and Y are inconsistent, that each implies the negation of the other. A default link of the form $X \rightarrow Y$ indicates that the proposition Y follows from X by default, where, again, a positive default link $X \rightarrow \neg Y$, pointing at a negated proposition, is often abbreviated as $X \not\rightarrow Y$. Given these conventions, the theory currently under consideration can be represented as in Figure 5.1 – this theory is often referred to as the Tweety Triangle, because of its roughly triangular shape when depicted as an inference graph.

Evidently, this particular theory allows four possible scenarios – $\mathcal{S}_1 = \emptyset$, $\mathcal{S}_2 = \{r_B\}$, $\mathcal{S}_3 = \{r_P\}$, or $\mathcal{S}_4 = \{r_B, r_P\}$ – corresponding to the situations in which the reasoning agent endorses neither of the two available defaults, only the bird default, only the penguin default, or both. From an intuitive standpoint, it seems that the agent should accept the penguin default r_P, and only that default, leading to the conclusion that Tweety does not fly. Therefore, only the third of these four scenarios, $\mathcal{S}_3 = \{r_P\}$, should be classified as proper. Following our recipe, we can then define the extension of this default theory, the conclusion set generated by the unique proper scenario allowed by the theory, as

$$\begin{aligned}\mathcal{E}_3 &= \mathit{Closure}(\mathcal{W} \cup \mathit{Conclusion}(\mathcal{S}_3)) \\ &= \mathit{Closure}(\{P, P \supset B\} \cup \{\neg F\}) \\ &= \mathit{Closure}(\{P, P \supset B, \neg F\}),\end{aligned}$$

arrived at by combining the conclusion of the single default rule from $\mathcal{S}_3$, the proposition $\neg F$, with the hard information from $\mathcal{W}$, the propositions P and $P \supset B$, and then taking the logical closure of the result.

5.1.2 Binding Defaults

As this example shows, the process of constructing an extension from a proper scenario, once one has been identified, is routine. How, then, can we define the proper scenarios?

The definition provided here depends on the concept of a binding default. If defaults correspond to reasons in general, then binding defaults correspond to those that can be classified as good reasons, in the context of a particular scenario. This reference to a scenario is not accidental: the idea is that the set of defaults that might correspond to good reasons will depend on the set of defaults already endorsed, the reasoning agent's current scenario. Formally, the concept of a binding default is defined in terms of three preliminary ideas, which we consider first – applicability, conflict, and defeat.[3]

The defaults that are applicable in a scenario are defined as those whose premises are entailed by that scenario – those defaults, that is, whose premises follow from the hard information from the default theory together with the conclusions of the defaults already endorsed:

Definition 23 (Applicable defaults) Let $\Delta = \langle \mathcal{W}, \mathcal{D}, < \rangle$ be a fixed priority default theory, and $\mathcal{S}$ a scenario based on this theory. Then the defaults from $\mathcal{D}$ that are applicable in the context of the scenario $\mathcal{S}$ are those belonging to the set

$$\mathit{Applicable}_{\mathcal{W},\mathcal{D}}(\mathcal{S}) = \{r \in \mathcal{D} : \mathcal{W} \cup \mathit{Conclusion}(\mathcal{S}) \vdash \mathit{Premise}(r)\}.$$

This idea can be illustrated by returning to the Tweety Triangle – once again, the theory $\Delta_1 = \langle \mathcal{W}, \mathcal{D}, < \rangle$ where $\mathcal{W} = \{P, P \supset B\}$, where $\mathcal{D} = \{r_B, r_P\}$ with $r_B = B \to F$ and $r_P = P \to \neg F$, and where $r_B < r_P$. Suppose we consider the scenario $\mathcal{S}_1 = \emptyset$. In the context of this scenario, both the defaults r_B and r_P are applicable, since $\mathcal{W} \cup \mathit{Conclusion}(\mathcal{S}_1) \vdash \mathit{Premise}(r_B)$ and $\mathcal{W} \cup \mathit{Conclusion}(\mathcal{S}_1) \vdash \mathit{Premise}(r_P)$.

Applicability is a necessary condition that a default must satisfy in order to be classified as binding in a scenario, but it is not sufficient. Even if some

[3] The concepts of applicability, defeat, and bindingness defined here in the setting of a full default logic are generalizations of the concepts introduced earlier, in Definition 3 from Section 1.1.2 and Definitions 10 and 11 from Section 2.1.1, in a much more limited setting. The defaults characterized here as applicable coincide with those that I have referred to earlier, in Horty (2012), for example, as triggered.

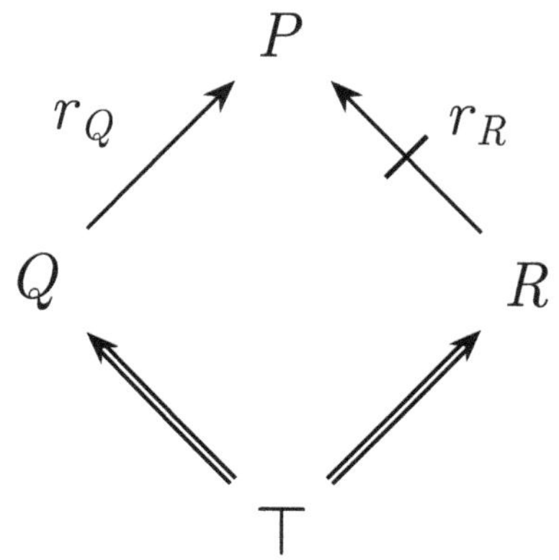

Figure 5.2 The Nixon Diamond

default is applicable, it might not be binding – the reason it provides might not be a good reason. Two further aspects of the situation could interfere.

The first is easy to describe. An applicable default will not be classified as binding in the context of a scenario if it is conflicted – that is, if the agent is already committed to the negation of its conclusion:

Definition 24 (Conflicted defaults) Let $\Delta = \langle \mathcal{W}, \mathcal{D}, < \rangle$ be a fixed priority default theory, and $\mathcal{S}$ a scenario based on this theory. Then the defaults from $\mathcal{D}$ that are conflicted in the context of the scenario $\mathcal{S}$ are those belonging to the set

$$Conflicted_{\mathcal{W},\mathcal{D}}(\mathcal{S}) = \{r \in \mathcal{D} : \mathcal{W} \cup Conclusion(\mathcal{S}) \vdash \neg Conclusion(r)\}.$$

This idea can be illustrated through another example, centered around Richard Nixon, the 37th President of the United States. Suppose that Q, R, and P are the statements that Nixon is a Quaker, that Nixon is a Republican, and that Nixon is a pacifist; and consider the defaults $r_Q = Q \to P$ and $r_R = R \to \neg P$, according to which the fact that Nixon is a Quaker supports the conclusion that he is a pacifist while the fact that he is a Republican supports the conclusion that he is not. Because Nixon was, in fact, both a Quaker and a Republican, the information from this example can be represented through the theory $\Delta_2 = \langle \mathcal{W}, \mathcal{D}, < \rangle$ – depicted in Figure 5.2 and known as the Nixon Diamond – where $\mathcal{W} = \{Q, R\}$, where $\mathcal{D} = \{r_Q, r_R\}$, and where $<$ is empty, since we can suppose that neither default from this theory carries higher priority than the other. Now imagine that, on whatever grounds, an agent presented with this information decides to endorse one of these two defaults – say r_Q, supporting the conclusion P – and is therefore reasoning on the basis of the scenario $\mathcal{S}_5 = \{r_Q\}$. In this context, the other default – r_R, supporting the conclusion $\neg P$ – will be conflicted, since $\mathcal{W} \cup Conclusion(\mathcal{S}_5) \vdash \neg Conclusion(r_R)$.

The second restriction governing the notion of a binding default is that, even if it is applicable, and even if it is not conflicted, a default still cannot be classified as binding if it happens to be defeated. Although the concept of defeat is surprisingly difficult to define in full generality, the idea is simple enough, and can serve as the basis of a definition adequate for the present setting.[4] Very roughly, a default will be classified as defeated in the context of a scenario based on a particular default theory whenever that theory contains another default that is applicable in that scenario, that is stronger than the original, and that supports a conflicting conclusion:

Definition 25 (Defeated defaults) Let $\Delta = \langle \mathcal{W}, \mathcal{D}, < \rangle$ be a fixed priority default theory, and $\mathcal{S}$ a scenario based on this theory. Then the defaults from $\mathcal{D}$ that are defeated in the context of the scenario $\mathcal{S}$ are those belonging to the set

$$\begin{aligned} \mathit{Defeated}_{\mathcal{W},\mathcal{D},<}(\mathcal{S}) = \{r \in \mathcal{D} : \text{ there is a default } r' \in \mathit{Applicable}_{\mathcal{W},\mathcal{D}}(\mathcal{S}) \text{ such that}\\ r < r',\\ \mathcal{W} \cup \{Conclusion(r')\} \vdash \neg Conclusion(r)\}. \end{aligned}$$

This idea can be illustrated by returning once again to the Tweety Triangle – the theory $\Delta_1 = \langle \mathcal{W}, \mathcal{D}, < \rangle$ described above – and imagining that a reasoning agent presented with this information has not yet endorsed either of the two defaults r_B or r_P from this example, so that the agent's initial context is $\mathcal{S}_1 = \emptyset$ and neither default is conflicted. Still, even with the empty scenario as context, the default r_B is defeated, since the applicable default r_P has higher priority and supports a conflicting conclusion – that is, we have both $r_B < r_P$ and $\mathcal{W} \cup \{Conclusion(r_P)\} \vdash \neg Conclusion(r_B)$.

With the concepts of applicability, conflict, and defeat in place, we can now define a default as binding in the context of a particular scenario just in case it is applicable, but neither conflicted nor defeated:

Definition 26 (Binding defaults) Let $\Delta = \langle \mathcal{W}, \mathcal{D}, < \rangle$ be a fixed priority default theory, and $\mathcal{S}$ a scenario based on this theory. Then the defaults from $\mathcal{D}$ that are binding in the context of the scenario $\mathcal{S}$ are those belonging to the set

[4] See Horty (2012, Chapter 8) for a discussion of the difficulties involved in arriving at a general definition.

$$\begin{aligned} \mathit{Binding}_{\mathcal{W},\mathcal{D},<}(\mathcal{S}) = \{r \in \mathcal{D} :\ & r \in \mathit{Applicable}_{\mathcal{W},\mathcal{D}}(\mathcal{S}),\\ & r \notin \mathit{Conflicted}_{\mathcal{W},\mathcal{D}}(\mathcal{S}),\\ & r \notin \mathit{Defeated}_{\mathcal{W},\mathcal{D},<}(\mathcal{S})\}. \end{aligned}$$

And the concept can again be illustrated with the Tweety example, under the assumption that the agent's scenario is $\mathcal{S}_1 = \emptyset$. Here, the default r_B, supporting the conclusion F, is applicable in the context of this scenario, and it is not conflicted, but as we have just seen, it is defeated by the default r_P, and so not binding. By contrast, the default r_P, supporting the conclusion $\neg F$, is likewise applicable, not conflicted, and not defeated either. This default is, therefore, binding.

5.1.3 Proper Scenarios and Extensions

We can now, at last, provide a working definition of the concept of a proper scenario.[5] Since the binding defaults represent the good reasons, in the context of a particular scenario, it is natural to characterize a proper scenario as one containing all and only the defaults that are themselves binding in the context of that very scenario:

Definition 27 (Proper scenarios) Let $\Delta = \langle \mathcal{W}, \mathcal{D}, < \rangle$ be a fixed priority default theory, and $\mathcal{S}$ some scenario based on this theory. Then $\mathcal{S}$ is a proper scenario allowed by Δ if and only if

$$\mathcal{S} = \mathit{Binding}_{\mathcal{W},\mathcal{D},<}(\mathcal{S}).$$

A reasoning agent that has accepted a set of defaults forming a proper scenario, then, is in an enviable position. Such an agent has already accepted all and only those defaults that the agent recognizes as providing good reasons; the agent, therefore, has no incentive either to abandon any defaults already accepted, or to accept any others – a proper scenario is a fixed point of the agent's reasoning.

Having introduced the concept of a proper scenarios, we can now officially define an extension of a default theory – a conclusion set that a reasoner might arrive at on the basis of that theory – as a set of formulas generated by a proper scenario allowed by that theory:

[5] There are again some complexities involved in the full definition of this idea that we can safely ignore for the purposes of this book; see Horty (2012, Appendix A.1) for discussion and a full definition.

Definition 28 (Extensions) Let $\Delta = \langle \mathcal{W}, \mathcal{D}, < \rangle$ be a fixed priority default theory. Then $\mathcal{E}$ is an extension of Δ if and only if, for some proper scenario $\mathcal{S}$ allowed by this theory,

$$\mathcal{E} = Closure(\mathcal{W} \cup Conclusion(\mathcal{S})).$$

These definitions can be illustrated by returning, one last time, to our two motivating examples. The first, the Tweety Triangle depicted in Figure 5.1, was the theory $\Delta_1 = \langle \mathcal{W}, \mathcal{D}, < \rangle$ where $\mathcal{W} = \{P, P \supset B\}$, where $\mathcal{D} = \{r_B, r_P\}$ with $r_B = B \rightarrow F$ and $r_P = P \rightarrow \neg F$, and where $r_B < r_P$. In our earlier discussion, we noted that, of the four scenarios based on this theory – that is, $\mathcal{S}_1 = \emptyset$, $\mathcal{S}_2 = \{r_B\}$, $\mathcal{S}_3 = \{r_P\}$, and $\mathcal{S}_4 = \{r_B, r_P\}$ – only the third seemed attractive from an intuitive point of view, and we are now in a position to verify that this scenario, and only this scenario, is proper.

The argument proceeds by enumeration. The first scenario, $\mathcal{S}_1 = \emptyset$, cannot be proper since it fails to contain the default r_P, which is binding in the context of this scenario – applicable but neither conflicted nor defeated. The second, $\mathcal{S}_2 = \{r_B\}$, cannot be proper since it contains the default r_B, which is defeated in the context of that scenario, and so not binding. And the fourth, $\mathcal{S}_4 = \{r_B, r_P\}$, cannot be proper either, since each of the two defaults it contains conflicts with the other, so that both are conflicted and neither is binding. Only the third scenario, $\mathcal{S}_3 = \{r_P\}$, is proper, containing all and only the defaults that are binding in the context of that very scenario. As in our previous discussion, we can then see that $\mathcal{E}_3 = Closure(\mathcal{W} \cup \{\neg F\})$ is the unique extension of this default theory, generated by its unique proper scenario. Default reasoning based on the information from the Tweety example thus supports the conclusion $\neg F$, that Tweety cannot fly.

Our second example, the Nixon Diamond depicted in Figure 5.2, was the theory $\Delta_2 = \langle \mathcal{W}, \mathcal{D}, < \rangle$, where $\mathcal{W} = \{Q, R\}$, where $\mathcal{D} = \{r_Q, r_R\}$ with $r_Q = Q \rightarrow P$ and $r_R = R \rightarrow \neg P$, and where $<$ is empty. As the reader can verify, this theory allows two proper scenarios, both $\mathcal{S}_5 = \{r_Q\}$ and $\mathcal{S}_6 = \{r_R\}$. These two proper scenarios generate the two extensions $\mathcal{E}_5 = Closure(\mathcal{W} \cup \{P\})$ and $\mathcal{E}_6 = Closure(\mathcal{W} \cup \{\neg P\})$. Both of these extensions contain Q and R, the initial information from $\mathcal{W}$, according to which Nixon is a Quaker and a Republican, but the first contains P, supported by the default r_Q, according to which Nixon is a pacifist, while the second contains $\neg P$, supported by the default r_R, according to which he is not.

This example illustrates one of the most interesting features of default logic – that a single default theory might allow multiple proper scenarios, which then generate multiple extensions, or conclusion sets. There are a number of ways of interpreting situations like this, in which a default theory supports multiple extensions.[6] The interpretation to be adopted in this book is that each of these different extensions represents an acceptable conclusion set of the agent's default reasoning. This interpretation can be given a deontic cast if we suppose that a reasoning agent is permitted to reach a conclusion on the basis of a particular default theory just in case that conclusion is found in some extension of that theory, and required to reach a conclusion just in case that conclusion is found in every extension of the theory. Returning to the Nixon example, then, the agent is permitted to conclude P, that Nixon is a pacifist, since that statement belongs to the extension $\mathcal{E}_5$, but also permitted to conclude $\neg P$, that Nixon is not a pacifist, since that statement belongs to the extension $\mathcal{E}_6$; the agent is not required to reach either of these conclusions, since neither P nor $\neg P$ belongs to both the extensions $\mathcal{E}_5$ and $\mathcal{E}_6$. In the Tweety example, by contrast, the reasoning agent is both permitted and required to conclude $\neg F$, that Tweety is not able to fly, since this statement belongs to $\mathcal{E}_3$, the unique extension of the underlying default theory.

5.2 Elaborations

5.2.1 Variable Priorities

We have concentrated thus far on fixed priority default theories, in which priority relations among default rules are fixed in advance. In fact, however, some of the most important things we reason about, and reason about by default, are the priorities among the very defaults that guide our reasoning – we offer reasons for taking some of our reasons more seriously than others. Although this process may sound complicated, it turns out that the basic approach can be extended to account for this kind of reasoning in four simple steps.

The first step is to enrich our background language with the resources to enable formal reasoning about priorities among defaults: a new set of individual constants, to be interpreted as names of defaults, together with a relation symbol representing priority. For the sake of simplicity, we will assume that each of these new constants has the form n_X, for some subscript

[6] See Horty (2012, Section 1.3) for a discussion of the options.

X, and that each such constant refers to the default r_X, or in schematic contexts, that the constants $n, n', n''\ldots$ designate the default rules $r, r', r''\ldots$. And we will assume that our language now contains the relation symbol $\prec$, representing the priority relation $<$ among defaults.

To illustrate, consider the ordinary defaults $r = A \rightarrow B$ and $r' = C \rightarrow \neg B$, and then the priority default $r'' = D \rightarrow \quad n \prec n'$. Since n refers to r and n' refers r', what r'' says is that D functions as a reason for the conclusion that $r < r'$, or that r' is to be assigned a higher priority than r. As a result, we would expect that, when all three of these defaults are applicable – that is, when A, C, and D all hold – the default r will generally be defeated by r', since the two defaults have conflicting conclusions. Of course, since r'' is itself a default, the information it provides concerning the priority of r' over r is defeasible and could likewise be conflicted or defeated.

The second step is to shift our attention from theories of the form $\langle \mathcal{W}, \mathcal{D}, < \rangle$ – that is, from fixed priority default theories – to theories containing a set $\mathcal{W}$ of ordinary propositions as well as a set $\mathcal{D}$ of defaults, but no priority relation on the defaults that is fixed in advance. Instead, both $\mathcal{W}$ and $\mathcal{D}$ may contain initial information concerning priority relations among defaults, and then further conclusions about these priorities, like any other conclusions, will be arrived at through default reasoning. Because conclusions about the priorities among defaults might themselves vary depending on other conclusions drawn by the reasoning agent, theories like this are known as variable priority default theories; it is stipulated as part of the definition that the hard information from such a theory must contain each instance of the asymmetry schema

$$(n \prec n') \supset \neg(n' \prec n)$$

in which the variables n and n' are replaced with names of the defaults from the theory:

Definition 29 (Variable priority default theories) A variable priority default theory is a structure of the form $\Delta = \langle \mathcal{W}, \mathcal{D} \rangle$, with $\mathcal{W}$ a set of ordinary propositions and $\mathcal{D}$ a set of defaults, subject to the following conditions: (1) each default r_X from $\mathcal{D}$ is assigned a unique name n_X; (2) the set $\mathcal{W}$ contains each instance of the asymmetry schema in which the variables are replaced with the names of defaults from $\mathcal{D}$.

Now suppose the agent accepts some particular scenario based on a variable priority default theory of this kind; the third step, then, is to lift the priority ordering implicit in that scenario to an explicit ordering that can be used in default reasoning. This is done in the simplest possible way, through the introduction of a derived priority ordering:

Definition 30 (Derived priority ordering) Let $\Delta = \langle \mathcal{W}, \mathcal{D} \rangle$ be a variable priority default theory and $\mathcal{S}$ a scenario based on this theory. Then the priority ordering $<_{\mathcal{S}}$ derived from $\mathcal{S}$ is defined by stipulating that

$$r <_{\mathcal{S}} r' \text{ if and only if } \mathcal{W} \cup Conclusion(\mathcal{S}) \vdash n \prec n'.$$

The statement $r <_{\mathcal{S}} r'$ is taken to mean that r' has a higher priority than r according to the scenario $\mathcal{S}$. The force of the definition, then, is that this relation holds just in case the statement $n \prec n'$ can be derived from the conclusions of the defaults belonging to $\mathcal{S}$, taken together with the hard information from $\mathcal{W}$. Because $\mathcal{W}$ contains all instances of asymmetry, the derived priority relation $<_{\mathcal{S}}$ is guaranteed to be asymmetric.

The fourth and final step is to define the notion of a proper scenario allowed by a variable priority default theory. This is accomplished by leveraging our previous definition of the proper scenarios allowed by fixed priority theories of the form $\langle \mathcal{W}, \mathcal{D}, < \rangle$, where $<$ can be any asymmetric ordering whatsoever. Using this previous definition, we can now stipulate that $\mathcal{S}$ is a proper scenario allowed by the variable priority theory $\Delta = \langle \mathcal{W}, \mathcal{D} \rangle$ just in case $\mathcal{S}$ is a proper scenario, in the previous sense, allowed by the particular fixed priority theory $\langle \mathcal{W}, \mathcal{D}, <_{\mathcal{S}} \rangle$, where $\mathcal{W}$ and $\mathcal{D}$ are carried over from the variable priority theory Δ, and where $<_{\mathcal{S}}$ is the priority relation derived from the scenario $\mathcal{S}$ itself:

Definition 31 (Proper scenarios: variable priority default theories) Let $\Delta = \langle \mathcal{W}, \mathcal{D} \rangle$ be a variable priority default theory and $\mathcal{S}$ a scenario based on this theory. Then $\mathcal{S}$ is a proper scenario allowed by Δ if and only if $\mathcal{S}$ is a proper scenario allowed by the fixed priority default theory $\langle \mathcal{W}, \mathcal{D}, <_{\mathcal{S}} \rangle$, where $<_{\mathcal{S}}$ is the priority relation derived from $\mathcal{S}$ against the background of Δ.

The intuitive picture is this: In searching for a proper scenario, the agent arrives at some scenario $\mathcal{S}$, which then entails conclusions about various aspects of the world, including priority relations among the agent's own defaults. If these derived priority relations can be used to justify the agent in accepting exactly the scenario $\mathcal{S}$ that the agent began with, then that scenario is proper.

These definitions can be illustrated through a variant of our Nixon example in which it is useful to adopt, not the epistemic perspective of a third party trying to figure out whether Nixon is a pacifist, but instead, the practical perspective of a young Nixon trying to decide whether or not to become a pacifist. Suppose, then, that Nixon's practical reasoning takes place against the background of the variable priority default theory $\Delta_3 = \langle \mathcal{W}, \mathcal{D} \rangle$, where $\mathcal{W}$ contains the propositions Q and R, reminding Nixon that he is a Quaker and a Republican – along with, as always in the case of variable priority default theories, appropriate instances of asymmetry – and where $\mathcal{D}$ contains only $r_Q = Q \to P$ and $r_R = R \to \neg P$. Given our current perspective, these two defaults should now be interpreted as providing practical, rather than epistemic, reasons: r_Q tells Nixon that, as a Quaker, he has a reason to become a pacifist, while r_R tells him that, as a Republican, he has a reason not to become a pacifist.

Nothing in this theory allows Nixon to resolve the conflict between these two defaults, and so he is faced with a practical dilemma. Like our earlier representation of the Nixon example as a fixed priority default theory, the current variable priority default theory allows two proper scenarios, the familiar $\mathcal{S}_5 = \{r_Q\}$ and $\mathcal{S}_6 = \{r_R\}$, again generating the extensions $\mathcal{E}_5 = Closure(\mathcal{W} \cup \{P\})$ and $\mathcal{E}_6 = Closure(\mathcal{W} \cup \{\neg P\})$. According to the interpretation of multiple extensions adopted in this book, each of these extensions represents an acceptable outcome of Nixon's practical reasoning, so that he would be justified in choosing to become a pacifist, but also justified in choosing not to become a pacifist.

Imagine, however, that Nixon decides to consult with certain authorities to help him resolve his practical dilemma. Let us suppose that he discusses the problem first with a respected member from his Society of Friends congregation, who tells him that religious concerns are more important than political concerns, so that r_Q should take priority over r_R, but that he also talks with a local official of the Republican Party who tells him just the opposite, that politics is more important than religion, so that r_R should be assigned higher priority than r_Q. Taking QA and RA as the respective statements of Nixon's Quaker and Republican authorities, the advice of these two figures can be represented through the defaults $r_{QA} = QA \to n_R \prec n_Q$ and $r_{RA} = RA \to n_Q \prec n_R$. If we think of the previous defaults r_Q and r_R as *first-order* defaults, providing Nixon with reasons for becoming, or not becoming, a pacifist, the new defaults r_{QA} and r_{RA} can naturally be thought of as *second-order* defaults. They do not provide Nixon with reasons for becoming, or not,

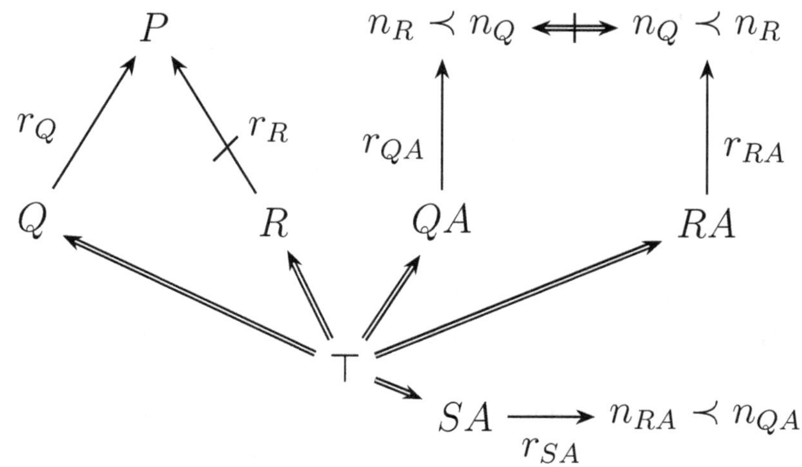

Figure 5.3 Nixon's dilemma

a pacifist. Instead, they provide Nixon with reasons for prioritizing, in certain ways, his first-order reasons for becoming, or not, a pacifist.[7]

At this point, the variable priority default theory that provides the background for Nixon's reasoning is $\Delta_4 = \langle \mathcal{W}, \mathcal{D} \rangle$, where $\mathcal{W}$ contains the propositions Q, R, QA, and RA – according to which Nixon is a Quaker and a Republican, and his religious and political authorities provide the advice they do – and where $\mathcal{D}$ now contains r_Q, r_R, r_{QA}, and r_{RA}. This theory is depicted in the upper region of Figure 5.3. The diamond on the left represents the original conflict between Nixon's religious and political views, which provide reasons favoring and opposing pacifism. The virtual diamond on the right represents the conflict between Nixon's two advisors concerning the proper weight to be assigned to his religious and political reasons, one suggesting that his religious reason should take precedence over his conflicting political reason, the other suggesting the opposite; it follows from the asymmetry schemata contained in $\mathcal{W}$ that these two recommendations stand in direct contradiction.

[7] In Horty (2012, p. 130), I objected to talk of reasons, or defaults, as stratified into levels, on the grounds that, in general, hierarchies among defaults could be tangled, with apparently lower-order defaults bearing on higher-order defaults just as easily as higher-order defaults bear on lower-order defaults. In certain legal and quasi-legal domains, such as those of concern in this book, however, stratification of reasons is at least an ideal, and in these domains, it can be useful to think of reasons, or defaults, as arranged into a strict hierarchy.

This theory now allows the two proper scenarios $\mathcal{S}_7 = \{r_Q, r_{QA}\}$ and $\mathcal{S}_8 = \{r_R, r_{RA}\}$, generating the two extensions $\mathcal{E}_7 = Closure(\mathcal{W} \cup \{P, n_R \prec n_Q\})$, and $\mathcal{E}_8 = Closure(\mathcal{W} \cup \{\neg P, n_Q \prec n_R\})$. Here, the scenario $\mathcal{S}_7$ and its generated extension $\mathcal{E}_7$ represent the outcome in which Nixon accepts the Quaker authority's advice that his religious reason should be assigned higher priority than his political reason, and so, in accord with his religious reason, chooses to become a pacifist; $\mathcal{S}_8$ and $\mathcal{E}_8$ represent the outcome in which Nixon accepts the Republican authority's advice that his political reason should be assigned higher priority than his religious reason, and so, in accord with his political reason, chooses not to become a pacifist. Evidently, Nixon's conflict persists and deepens: he is now faced both with his initial conflicting reasons, as well as further conflicting reasons as to how that initial conflict should be resolved.

Finally, though, let us suppose that Nixon seeks further counsel, this time from his wife, Patricia Nixon, who tells him that the advice of the Quaker authority is to be preferred to that of the Republican authority. If we take SA as the statement made by Nixon's wife, or spousal authority, the force of this advice can be represented through the default $r_{SA} = SA \to n_{RA} \prec n_{QA}$. This new default is not a first-order default like r_Q and r_R, providing Nixon with reasons for becoming, or not, a pacifist. Nor is it a second-order default like r_{QA} or r_{RA}, providing Nixon with reasons for prioritizing his first-order reasons. Instead, r_{SA} is a *third-order* default, recommending a particular prioritization among Nixon's second-order reasons for prioritizing his first-order reasons for becoming, or not, a pacifist.

The variable priority default theory that provides the background for Nixon's reasoning is now $\Delta_5 = \langle \mathcal{W}, \mathcal{D} \rangle$, where $\mathcal{W}$ contains the propositions Q, R, QA, RA, and SA – all of the earlier hard information together with the additional fact of Patricia Nixon's statement – and where $\mathcal{D}$ contains r_Q, r_R, r_{QA}, r_{RA}, and now r_{SA}. This new theory, now represented by the whole of Figure 5.3, allows only the single proper scenario $\mathcal{S}_9 = \{r_Q, r_{QA}, r_{SA}\}$, generating the extension

$$\mathcal{E}_9 = Closure(\mathcal{W} \cup \{P, n_R \prec n_Q, n_{RA} \prec n_{QA}\});$$

the outcome corresponds to the course of action in which Nixon is moved by his wife's advice to take the advice of the Quaker authority more seriously than that of the Republican authority, and so accepts the Quaker authority's recommendation that his religious reason is to be preferred to his political reason, and therefore, on the basis of his religious reasons, chooses to become a pacifist.

5.2.2 Exclusion

We have considered, thus far, only one form of defeat – generally called "rebutting" defeat – according to which a default supporting a conclusion is said to be defeated by a stronger default supporting a conflicting conclusion. There is also a second form of defeat, according to which one default supporting a conclusion is thought to be defeated by another, not because it supports a conflicting conclusion, but because it challenges the connection between the premise and the conclusion of the original default. In the literature on epistemic reasons, this second form of defeat is generally referred to as "undercutting" defeat, and was first pointed out by John Pollock.[8]

The distinction between these two forms of defeat can be illustrated by a standard example. Suppose an object in front of me looks red. Then it is reasonable for me to conclude that it is red, through an application of a general default according to which things that look red tend to be red. But let us imagine two different kinds of confounding circumstances. First of all, a reliable source – so reliable that I trust this source more than my own sense perception – might inform me that the object is not, in fact, red.[9] Or second, I might have taken a drug that makes everything look red.

Now, if the object looks red but the reliable source tells me otherwise, then it is natural to appeal to another default, with the conclusion that the object is not red, since what the reliable source says tends to be true and the reliable source has told me that it is not red. And because, by hypothesis, the reliable source is more reliable than my own perception, this new default would carry higher priority than the original, that whatever looks red tends to be red, and so would defeat this original default in the sense considered so far, by providing a stronger reason for a conflicting conclusion that the object is not red. If the object looks red but I have taken the drug, on the other hand, then it seems again that I am no longer entitled to the conclusion that the object is red. But in this case, the original default is not defeated in the same way. There is no stronger reason for concluding that the object is not red; instead, it is as if the favoring relation represented by the original default is itself severed, so that what was once a reason no longer provides any support for its conclusion.

[8] See Pollock (1970) for an initial discussion; his own treatment of this notion is developed in detail in later work, most notably Pollock (1995).

[9] We can suppose that, as I am well aware, the reliable source may know things that I do not: the object could be illuminated by red lights, a red screen could have been inserted in front of the object, and so on.

This second form of defeat, or something very close to it, is discussed also in the literature on practical reasoning, where it is considered as part of the general topic of "exclusionary" reasons, first introduced by Raz.[10] To motivate the concept, Raz provides a number of examples, but we consider here only the representative case of Colin, who must decide whether to send his son to a private school. We are to imagine that there are various reasons pro and con. On one hand, the school will provide an excellent education for Colin's son, as well as an opportunity to meet a more varied group of friends; on the other hand, the tuition is high, and Colin is concerned that a decision to send his own son to a private school might serve to undermine his support for public education more generally.

However, Raz asks us to imagine that, in addition to these ordinary reasons pro and con, Colin has promised his wife that, in all decisions regarding the education of his son, he will consider only those reasons that bear directly on his son's interests. And this promise, Raz believes, cannot properly be viewed as just another one of the ordinary reasons for sending his son to the private school, like the fact that the school provides a good education. It must be viewed, instead, as a reason of an entirely different sort – a second-order reason, according to Raz, for excluding from consideration all those ordinary, or first-order, reasons that do not bear on the interests of Colin's son. Just as, once I have taken the drug, I should disregard the fact that an object looks red as a reason for concluding that it is red, Colin's promise should lead him, likewise, to disregard those reasons that do not bear on the interests of his son. An exclusionary reason, on this interpretation, is nothing but an undercutting defeater in the practical domain.

Now, how can this phenomenon of undercutting, or exclusion, be understood? The standard practice is to postulate undercutting as a separate, and primitive, form of defeat, to be analyzed alongside the concept of ordinary, or rebutting, defeat; this practice is advocated, most notably, by Pollock.[11] The present account, though, takes a different approach. There remains in our logic only one form of defeat – ordinary defeat, of the sort described earlier. However, the expressive resources of our language are again expanded, ever so slightly, to allow for explicit reasoning about which defaults are, or

[10] See Raz (1975) for his initial discussion; the topic has spawned an extensive secondary literature, notably including Gans (1986), Moore (1989), and Perry (1987, 1989), subsequent elaborations by Raz himself, both in his (1989) and in a postscript to the second edition of his (1975), and a review of the latter by Edmundson (1993).

[11] See Pollock (1995) and the papers cited there.

are not, excluded from consideration, and then the definition of a binding default is modified so that only defaults that are not excluded can be binding. The account can be developed very naturally, this time in three steps.

All of the steps are simple, but the first is the simplest: we introduce a new predicate *Out* into our language, with the intention that, where n is the constant representing the default r, the statement $Out(n)$ expresses the idea that r is undercut, excluded, or otherwise taken out of consideration. To illustrate, consider the ordinary default $r = A \rightarrow B$, and then the exclusionary default $r' = C \rightarrow Out(n')$. Since n refers to r, the force of the default r' is that C functions as a reason for the conclusion that r should be undercut, excluded, or otherwise removed from consideration. As a result, given only these two defaults, and assuming both A and C, we would expect to conclude that the default r should be removed from consideration, and we would expect to conclude nothing at all about B.

An exclusionary default theory, then, is nothing but a default theory with the resources to apply this new *Out* predicate to constants representing its own defaults:

Definition 32 (Exclusionary default theories) An exclusionary default theory is a default theory subject to the following constraints: (1) each default r_X from $\mathcal{D}$ is assigned a unique name n_X; (2) the background language of the theory contains the predicate *Out*.

Although both the fixed priority and variable priority default theories can be exclusionary, we will concentrate here on variable priority exclusionary default theories, which allow both for priorities among defaults to be adjusted and also for defaults to be excluded altogether.

The second step is to specify the defaults that are to be classified as excluded from consideration in the context of some scenario. Again, this task is straightforward: the idea is that a default r is to be excluded from consideration in the context of a scenario just in case that scenario, taken together with the hard information from the underlying theory, entails $Out(n)$, the proposition that r is excluded:

Definition 33 (Exclusion) Let $\Delta = \langle \mathcal{W}, \mathcal{D} \rangle$ be a variable priority exclusionary default theory and $\mathcal{S}$ a scenario based on this theory. Then the defaults from $\mathcal{D}$ that are excluded in the context of the scenario $\mathcal{S}$ are those belonging to the set

$$Excluded_{\mathcal{W},\mathcal{D}}(\mathcal{S}) = \{r \in \mathcal{D} : \mathcal{W} \cup Conclusion(\mathcal{S}) \vdash Out(n)\}.$$

The third and final step is to modify the definition of an applicable default so that only those defaults that are not excluded can be applicable:

Definition 34 (Applicable defaults: revised definition) Let $\Delta = \langle \mathcal{W}, \mathcal{D} \rangle$ be a variable priority exclusionary default theory and $\mathcal{S}$ a scenario based on this theory. Then the defaults from $\mathcal{D}$ that are applicable in the context of $\mathcal{S}$ are those belonging to the set

$$Applicable_{\mathcal{W},\mathcal{D}}(\mathcal{S}) = \{r \in \mathcal{D} : \mathcal{W} \cup Conclusion(\mathcal{S}) \vdash Premise(r) \\ \text{and } r \notin Excluded_{\mathcal{W},\mathcal{D}}(\mathcal{S})\}.$$

This revised notion of applicability has two clauses. A default that is applicable in a certain scenario must, first of all, satisfy our original condition that the premise of the default is entailed in the context of that scenario, but second, the new definition also requires that the default not be excluded. Of course, the revised definition, though formulated with exclusionary default theories in mind, is a conservative generalization of our original definition, since, in any default theory that is not exclusionary, the set of excluded defaults will be empty, so that the revised definition collapses into the original.

Our treatment of exclusion can be illustrated by returning to the epistemic example sketched earlier. Let L, R, and D be the respective propositions that the object before me looks red, that it is red, and that I have taken the drug; and consider the defaults $r_L = L \to R$ and $r_D = D \to Out(n_L)$. According to the first of these defaults, looking red favors the conclusion that the object is red; and according to the second, having taken the drug favors the conclusion that the first default should be removed from consideration. From these materials, we can construct the exclusionary default theory $\Delta_6 = \langle \mathcal{W}, \mathcal{D} \rangle$, where $\mathcal{W}$ includes L, R, and D and where $\mathcal{D} = \{r_L, r_D\}$, to represent the information presented to the reasoning agent.

Exclusionary default theories like these can be depicted as inference graphs in the standard fashion, but also in a new and somewhat more suggestive format in which each link of the form $X \to Out(n)$, where n refers to the default r, is replaced with a link of the form $X \not\to r$, indicating that X favors rejecting the default itself. In the case of our example, then, the default r_D can be depicted through the link $D \not\to (L \to R)$; the entire theory Δ_6 can thus be depicted in standard fashion by the diagram on the left of Figure 5.4, or in our new format by the diagram on the right.

This theory allows four possible scenarios – $\mathcal{S}_{10} = \emptyset$, $\mathcal{S}_{11} = \{r_L\}$, $\mathcal{S}_{12} = \{r_D\}$, and $\mathcal{S}_{13} = \{r_L, r_D\}$ – but we can see that only the third of these, the

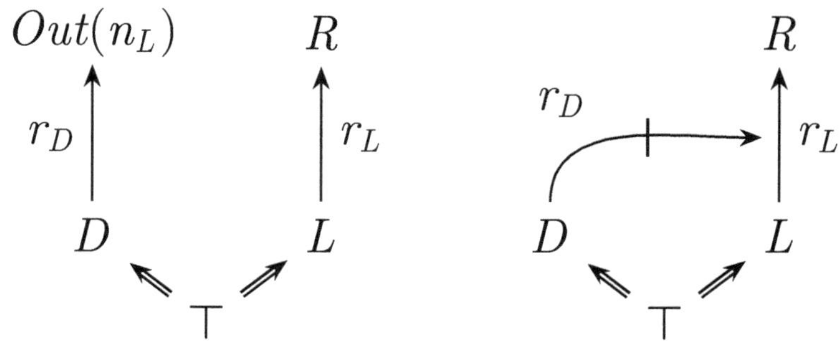

Figure 5.4 An exclusionary default theory

scenario $\mathcal{S}_{12} = \{r_D\}$, is proper. Why? Well, to begin with, the default r_D is binding in the context of this scenario, applicable but neither conflicted nor defeated. But the default r_L is excluded in this same context – r_L belongs to $Excluded_{\mathcal{W},\mathcal{D}}(\mathcal{S}_{12})$ – since $\mathcal{W} \cup Conclusion(\mathcal{S}_{12}) \vdash Out(n_L)$. It thus follows from the revised definition of applicability that r_L, though its premise is entailed, is not applicable in the context of this scenario, and so cannot be binding either. From this, we can conclude that $\mathcal{S}_{12}$ is proper, since it contains all and only the defaults that are binding in that context. As for the other scenarios: it is easy to verify that both r_L and r_D are binding in the context of $\mathcal{S}_{10}$, but neither is contained in that scenario; the default r_D is binding in the context of $\mathcal{S}_{11}$ but not contained in that scenario; and the default r_L is contained in $\mathcal{S}_{13}$, but excluded, and so cannot be applicable or binding.

The unique proper scenario $\mathcal{S}_{12}$ generates the unique extension

$$\mathcal{E}_{12} = Conclusion(\mathcal{W} \cup \{Out(n_L)\}),$$

supporting the conclusion that the default r_L should be excluded from consideration, but no conclusions at all about whether or not the object is red.

5.3 Natural Reasoning about Cases

Having seen how default logic can be interpreted as an account of natural reasoning, and also how the theory can be elaborated to allow for reasoning about priorities and exclusion among reasons, we now turn to the task of using this logic to provide a precise account of constrained natural reasoning. We begin slowly, first developing, in this section, an account of natural reasoning in the absence of any constraints at all, and then exploring, in the next chapter, natural reasoning that involves the constraining force of precedent cases.

5.3.1 Judicial Problems as Default Theories

It is often suggested by those who favor the picture of common law rules as defeasible that courts introduce, with their decisions, rules according to which certain collections of factors favor one side or another by default, though of course, these rules are subject to later exceptions. But this picture does not sit well with the view of factors themselves as having polarities, favoring one side or another. If the factor f_1^π favors the side π, then there is no particular need for a court actually to introduce the factor default rule $\{f_1^\pi\} \rightarrow \pi$, for example. Such a rule would tell us that $\{f_1^\pi\}$ counts as a reason for π, but that is just what it means to say that the factor f_1^π, and so the reason $\{f_1^\pi\}$, favors π – the factor default rule is, in a sense, already built into the favoring relation.

Supposing, then, that we can take factor default rules for granted, we postulate a set $\mathcal{F}$ containing each of these factor defaults – each rule of the form $U \rightarrow s$ where U is a factor reason favoring the side s. For convenience, we refer to the factor default rule $U \rightarrow s$ through a structural descriptor of the form $r_{U_i}^s$, whose superscript s is the side favored by the rule and whose subscript U_i is a set containing the indices of the factors belonging to the premise U of the rule; the factor default $\{f_1^\pi\} \rightarrow \pi$ mentioned above, for example, can be referred to as $r_{\{1\}}^\pi$, and the factor default $\{f_1^\pi, f_2^\pi\} \rightarrow \pi$ can be referred to as $r_{\{1,2\}}^\pi$. For further convenience, and to minimize notation, we omit curly brackets in displaying the set that forms the subscript of the structural descriptor, so that these same factor defaults can be abbreviated as r_1^π and $r_{1,2}^\pi$. Finally, the convention introduced in the previous section for designating default rules can be broadened to factor default rules as well, so that, in general, the rule $r_{U_i}^s$ will be designated in the language by the term $n_{U_i}^s$, and in the case of our examples, the particular rules r_1^π and $r_{1,2}^\pi$ will be designated by the terms n_1^π and $n_{1,2}^\pi$.

We recall from Definition 2, set out in Section 1.1.2, that, if U and V are factor reasons favoring the side s, then V favors s at least a strongly as U – written, $U \leq^s V$ – just in case $U \subseteq V$. This ordering on the basis of strength for a side can be extended from factor reasons to factor default rules by ordering rules along with the premises that form their reasons:

Definition 35 (Strength for a side among factor defaults) Where $r_{U_i}^s$ and $r_{V_i}^s$ are factor defaults favoring the side s, then $r_{V_i}^s$ is at least as strong as $r_{U_i}^s$ – written, $r_{U_i}^s \leq^s r_{V_i}^s$ – if and only if $Premise(r_{U_i}^s) \leq^s Premise(r_{V_i}^s)$.

Combining this ordering with the conventions just established concerning structural descriptors of factor default rules, we can see at once, for example, that the rule $r^{\pi}_{1,2}$ favors the side π at least as strongly as r^{π}_{1} – that is, $r^{\pi}_{1} \leq^{\pi} r^{\pi}_{1,2}$. And just as we have supposed that the language contains the relation symbol $\prec$ representing the priority relation among defaults, we now suppose that the language contains the symbols $\preceq^{s}$ representing strength for a side s among factor defaults favoring s; the fact that $r^{\pi}_{1} \leq^{\pi} r^{\pi}_{1,2}$, for example, can be expressed in the language through the statement $n^{\pi}_{1} \preceq^{\pi} n^{\pi}_{1,2}$.

Returning to our main theme: If courts do not introduce new factor default rules with their decisions – if these factor default rules are already present, implicit in the meaning of factors – then what effect do the decisions of courts have? One natural answer is that these decisions impose a priority ordering on factor default rules, telling us which of these rules are to be viewed as more important than others. This idea, first suggested by Henry Prakken and Giovanni Sartor, has been highly influential in the field of artificial intelligence and law, but it does not give us exactly what we want.[12] Although Prakken and Sartor provide an illuminating account of defeasible reasoning with legal information alone, they do not attempt to develop an account of the way in which this legal information constrains a court's natural reasoning. There is no reference to a court's own values, or to the way in which precedent cases can influence the decisions that a court would otherwise have reached on the basis of its values alone.

To fill this gap, we will introduce a special class of default rules to represent a court's values, as they influence that court's priority ordering among factor reasons and their corresponding default rules. Before beginning, two clarificatory notes will be helpful: First, when I speak of "values," I use this term only in a technical sense, to refer to the court's reasons for ranking one factor reason over another, and so, for ranking one factor default over another; I do not mean to advance any philosophical claims about the relations between reasons and values.[13] And second, the reasoning through which a court's values lead to a priority ordering among factor reasons, and so factor defaults, can, of course, be arbitrarily complex. The present goal, however, is not to understand this complex reasoning itself – that is a matter for future research – but only the way in which the constraints derived from

[12] See Prakken and Sartor (1998).

[13] In particular, values are not reified here as independent objects, as they are in Prakken (2002), Bench-Capon and Sartor (2003), and Grabmair and Ashley (2011), for example.

precedent cases affect the decisions that might have been reached entirely on the basis of the court's own values.

We begin, therefore, by representing the defaults encoding a court's values in the simplest possible way: where $U \rightarrow \bar{s}$ and $V \rightarrow s$ are factor defaults favoring opposite sides, referred to as $r^{\bar{s}}_{U_i}$ and $r^{s}_{V_i}$ and designated within our language as $n^{\bar{s}}_{U_i}$ and $n^{s}_{V_i}$, we define a *value default* as a rule of the form

$$\top \rightarrow n^{\bar{s}}_{U_i} \prec n^{s}_{V_i};$$

the force of this default is that, according to the court's own values, the factor default $r^{s}_{V_i}$ is, by default, assigned a higher priority than the factor default $r^{\bar{s}}_{U_i}$. If we think of factor defaults as first-order default rules, telling us which factor reasons favor which sides, these new value defaults can be thought of a second-order rules, telling us which first-order factor defaults are to be prioritized over which others.

As with factor defaults, value defaults can likewise be referred to through structural descriptors: we will suppose that a value default of the form $\top \rightarrow n^{\bar{s}}_{U_i} \prec n^{s}_{V_i}$ is referred to through the descriptor $r^{s}_{U_i \backslash V_i}$, whose superscript s is the side favored by the factor default to which the value default under consideration assigns higher priority, and whose subscript $U_i \backslash V_i$ contains indices of factors from the premise U of the rule with lower priority, followed by indices of factors from the premise V of the rule with higher priority. Again, our conventions for designating default rules within the language can be broadened to apply to value defaults as well, so that the value default $r^{s}_{U_i \backslash V_i}$ will be designated by the term $n^{s}_{U_i \backslash V_i}$. To illustrate, we return to the factor default $r^{\pi}_{1,2} = \{f^{\pi}_1, f^{\pi}_2\} \rightarrow \pi$ considered earlier, and now consider also the factor default $r^{\delta}_1 = \{f^{\delta}_1\} \rightarrow \delta$. Then the value default $\top \rightarrow n^{\pi}_{1,2} \prec n^{\delta}_1$ – according to which $r^{\pi}_{1,2} < r^{\delta}_1$ holds by default, so that, by default, the factor default r^{δ}_1 is assigned a higher priority than the factor default $r^{\pi}_{1,2}$ – can be referred to through the structural descriptor $r^{\delta}_{1,2\backslash 1}$, and then designated in the language by the term $n^{\delta}_{1,2\backslash 1}$.

Let us now consider the problem facing a court that is free to reason about a particular fact situation entirely on the basis of its own values, without any constraints at all. How can this problem be encoded as a default theory? Well, suppose the fact situation X is presented for adjudication to a court whose values are represented by a set $\mathcal{V}$ of value defaults. In that case, the set $\mathcal{D}_{\mathcal{V}}$ of defaults guiding the court's reasoning will contain the entire set $\mathcal{F}$ of factor defaults, together with the set $\mathcal{V}$ of value defaults representing the court's own reasons for prioritizing some of these factor defaults over others.

The hard information $\mathcal{W}_X$ to which these defaults are applied will include X, the facts at hand, together with a set $\mathcal{O} = \mathcal{O}_1 \cup \mathcal{O}_2 \cup \mathcal{O}_3$ of structural conditions that must be represented explicitly for the default theory to work properly. As indicated, the set $\mathcal{O}$ divides into three components. The first component $\mathcal{O}_1$ contains each instance of the schema $n \preceq^s n'$ where r and r' are factor defaults from $\mathcal{F}$ and $r \leq^s r'$. These statements guarantee that the relation of strength for a side among factor defaults is encoded in the default theory; an example is the statement $n_1^\pi \preceq^\pi n_{1,2}^\pi$, considered earlier. The second component $\mathcal{O}_2$ contains each instance of the two schemata

$$(n \prec n' \wedge n' \preceq^s n'') \supset n \prec n'',$$
$$(n \preceq^s n' \wedge n' \prec n'') \supset n \prec n'',$$

where r, r', and r'' are factor defaults from $\mathcal{F}$. These statements guarantee that the relation of strength for a side among factor defaults favoring the same side interacts properly with the relation of priority among factor defaults favoring opposite sides; an example is the statement $(n_1^\pi \preceq^\pi n_{1,2}^\pi \wedge n_{1,2}^\pi \prec n_1^\delta) \supset n_1^\pi \prec n_1^\delta$, according to which the court will be able to conclude that $r_1^\pi < r_1^\delta$ once it has established that $r_1^\pi <^\pi r_{1,2}^\pi$ and $r_{1,2}^\pi < r_1^\delta$ – in other words, that the rule r_1^δ for the defendant has higher priority than the rule r_1^π for the plaintiff once it has established that $r_{1,2}^\pi$ favors the plaintiff at least as strongly as r_1^π, and that r_1^δ has higher priority than $r_{1,2}^\pi$. The third component $\mathcal{O}_3$ contains the single statement $\neg(s \wedge s')$, where s and s' are the opposing sides of some dispute. This statement simply guarantees that the opposing sides actually stand in formal opposition as well, so that, as a matter of logic, the court cannot decide in favor of both; if the current dispute involves a plaintiff and a defendant, for example, the single statement in the third component would be $\neg(\pi \wedge \delta)$.

Putting these ideas together, we can now define the problem presented by a particular fact situation to a court with a specified set of values, in the absence of any constraints at all, as the variable priority default theory constructed from defaults and hard information in the manner just described:

Definition 36 (Problem presented to court) Let X be a fact situation and $\mathcal{V}$ a set of value defaults. Then the problem presented by the fact situation X to a court with values $\mathcal{V}$ is represented by the variable priority default theory $\Delta_{X,\mathcal{V}} = \langle \mathcal{W}_X, \mathcal{D}_\mathcal{V} \rangle$ where

$$\mathcal{W}_X = X \cup \mathcal{O},$$
$$\mathcal{D}_\mathcal{V} = \mathcal{F} \cup \mathcal{V}.$$

Note that, unlike the fact situation X and the set $\mathcal{V}$ of value defaults, which vary as courts with different values confront different situations, both the set $\mathcal{F}$ of factor defaults and the set $\mathcal{O}$ of structural conditions are fixed in advance, depending only on the particular dispute in question and the underlying set of factors favoring one side of that dispute or another. Therefore, even though these two sets are important components of the theory $\Delta_{X,\mathcal{V}}$ representing the problem presented by the fact situation X to a court with values $\mathcal{V}$, there is no need to decorate this theory further by listing either $\mathcal{F}$ or $\mathcal{O}$ as additional subscripts.

Where the default theory $\Delta_{X,\mathcal{V}}$ represents a problem presented to the court, we can define a *solution to this problem* as a proper scenario allowed by that theory. When presented with a default theory representing a particular problem, then, the court's task is simply to arrive at a solution to the problem, in exactly this sense: a proper scenario allowed by the theory – a coherent set of defaults, or reasons, that then generate an extension containing the conclusions endorsed by the court.

5.3.2 Some Examples

For a concrete illustration, we return to our domestic examples, in which various children would like to stay up and watch TV, and so, as plaintiffs, present different cases to their parents, Jack and Jo, who function as both defendants and adjudicators. The cases presented by the children are characterized through combinations of the factors f_1^π and f_2^π, respectively representing the facts that the child in question is at least nine years old and has completed chores, and f_1^δ and f_2^δ, respectively representing the facts that the child has failed to finish dinner and failed to complete homework.

We start here with the very simple situation $X_6 = \{f_1^\pi, f_1^\delta\}$ presented by Chris, considered earlier in Sections 1.2.4 and 4.2.2. What we know about Chris is that she is at least nine years old but failed to finish dinner, so that, out of the entire set $\mathcal{F}$ of factor defaults, only two are applicable in this situation:

$$r_1^\pi = \{f_1^\pi\} \rightarrow \pi,$$
$$r_1^\delta = \{f_1^\delta\} \rightarrow \delta.$$

In contrast to our earlier discussions, where the situation X_6 was presented to Jack for decision against the background of constraints derived from a previous decision by Jo, we will suppose here either that the background set of cases is empty or that Jack is simply not subject to constraint from these cases, so that he is free to reason about the situation entirely on the basis of his own values.

But what are Jack's values? Well, to keep things simple, let us suppose that Jack's values are represented by the set $\mathcal{V}_{Jack}$ containing exactly the following two value defaults:

$$\begin{aligned} r^{\delta}_{1\backslash 1} &= \top \rightarrow n^{\pi}_{1} \prec n^{\delta}_{1}, \\ r^{\delta}_{1,2\backslash 2} &= \top \rightarrow n^{\pi}_{1,2} \prec n^{\delta}_{2}. \end{aligned}$$

According to the first of these defaults, Jack prioritizes the factor default r^{δ}_{1} over the factor default r^{π}_{1} – that is, he prioritizes failing to finish dinner as a reason for the defendant over being at least nine years of age as a reason for the plaintiff. According to the second, Jack prioritizes the factor default r^{δ}_{2} over the factor default $r^{\pi}_{1,2}$ – that is, he prioritizes failing to complete homework as a reason for the defendant over being at least nine years of age and completing chores, taken together, as a reason for the plaintiff. This set of values – that is, $\mathcal{V}_{Jack} = \{r^{\delta}_{1\backslash 1}, r^{\delta}_{1,2\backslash 2}\}$ – may not be especially rich or interesting, but it is a set of values; perhaps it suggests that Jack is something of a strict disciplinarian, since he tends to prioritize reasons favoring the parents over reasons favoring the children.

Based on this information, the problem presented to Jack by the situation $X_6 = \{f^{\pi}_{1}, f^{\delta}_{1}\}$ can be represented as the default theory $\Delta_{X_6, \mathcal{V}_{Jack}} = \langle \mathcal{W}_{X_6}, \mathcal{D}_{\mathcal{V}_{Jack}} \rangle$ where

$$\begin{aligned} \mathcal{W}_{X_6} &= X_6 \cup \mathcal{O} \\ &= \{f^{\pi}_{1}, f^{\delta}_{1}\} \cup \mathcal{O}, \\ \mathcal{D}_{\mathcal{V}_{Jack}} &= \mathcal{F} \cup \mathcal{V}_{Jack} \\ &= \mathcal{F} \cup \{r^{\delta}_{1\backslash 1}, r^{\delta}_{1,2\backslash 2}\}. \end{aligned}$$

In accord with our definition, the hard information $\mathcal{W}_{X_6}$ from this theory includes the set X_6 of factors characterizing the situation at hand, along with the fixed collection $\mathcal{O}$ of structural conditions; the set $\mathcal{D}_{\mathcal{V}_{Jack}}$ of defaults from the theory includes the entire set $\mathcal{F}$ of factor defaults together with the set $\mathcal{V}_{Jack}$ of value defaults, which prioritize the various

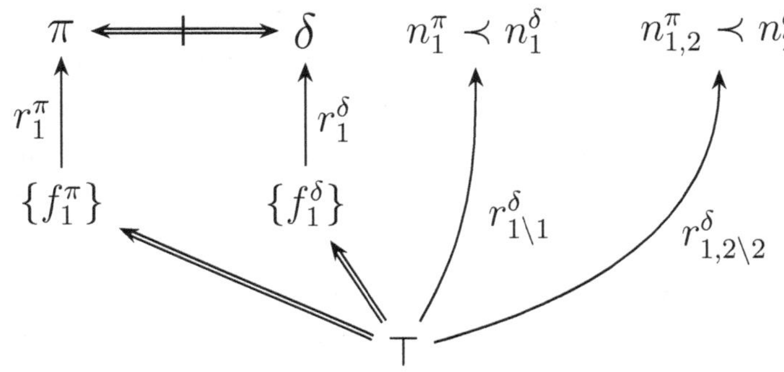

Figure 5.5 Chris and Jack, with values

factor defaults in accord with Jack's own values. This theory is depicted in Figure 5.5.[14]

As it turns out, there is a unique solution to this problem: the theory $\Delta_{X_6, \mathcal{V}_{Jack}}$ allows $\mathcal{S}_{14} = \{r_1^\delta, r_{1\backslash 1}^\delta, r_{1,2\backslash 2}^\delta\}$ as its unique proper scenario, generating the unique extension

$$\mathcal{E}_{14} = Closure(\mathcal{W}_{X_6} \cup \{\delta,\ n_1^\pi \prec n_1^\delta,\ n_{1,2}^\pi \prec n_2^\delta\}),$$

and so supporting the conclusions $n_1^\pi \prec n_1^\delta$ and $n_{1,2}^\pi \prec n_2^\delta$, reflecting Jack's values, as well as the conclusion δ, that the situation is to be decided for the defendant. And this outcome appears to be correct, under the circumstances. Jack is confronted by a plaintiff, Chris, who, although at least nine years of age, has failed to finish his dinner. According to Jack's values, failing to finish dinner carries a higher priority as a reason for the defendant than being at least nine years of age as a reason for the plaintiff. Therefore, reasoning entirely on the basis of his own values, Jack decides for the defendant, the parents, on the grounds that Chris has failed to finish dinner. In addition to determining Jack's conclusion, a decision for the defendant, the scenario $\mathcal{S}_{14}$ provides at least a rudimentary explanation of that conclusion. Why did Jack decide for the defendant? Because, of the two factor reasons that hold in the situation, he assigns higher priority to failing to finish dinner than to having reached nine years of age. Why does Jack assign higher priority to failing to

[14] Note that the inference graphs representing judicial problems are more schematic than those displayed earlier, depicting only selected information that is unique to a particular problem, not all information from the underlying default theory; this graph, for example, does not explicitly depict the structural conditions belonging to $\mathcal{O}$ from the underlying theory $\Delta_{X_6, \mathcal{V}_{Jack}}$.

finish dinner than to having reached nine years of age? Here the explanation stops, because we have not tried to describe how a priority ordering among factor reasons can be derived from an agent's values – we have not tried to provide a full explanation of the court's decision, but we have taken at least a first step along that path, and indicated the direction in which the path can be continued.

The reader is encouraged to verify in detail that the scenario $\mathcal{S}_{14} = \{r_1^{\delta}, r_{1\backslash 1}^{\delta}, r_{1,2\backslash 2}^{\delta}\}$ is in fact the unique proper scenario allowed by the theory $\Delta_{X_6, \mathcal{V}_{Jack}}$, but the central points of this verification are summarized here. In order to show that $\mathcal{S}_{14}$ is the unique proper scenario allowed by the theory, we must show, first, that it is a proper scenario allowed by the theory, and second, that there is no other. First, then: To show that $\mathcal{S}_{14}$ is a proper scenario, we must show that all and only the default rules it contains are binding in that scenario. To show that all the defaults contained in $\mathcal{S}_{14}$ are binding in that scenario, we observe that the two value defaults $r_{1\backslash 1}^{\delta}$ and $r_{1,2\backslash 2}^{\delta}$ are applicable, obviously, since each has the trivial statement $\top$ as antecedent, and are neither conflicted nor defeated, and also that the factor default r_1^{δ} is applicable, since its premise is entailed by the hard information from the default theory, and likewise neither conflicted nor defeated; hence, all defaults from the scenario $\mathcal{S}_{14}$ are binding in that scenario. To show that only defaults from $\mathcal{S}_{14}$ are binding in that scenario, we observe that, apart from r_1^{π}, none of the other factor defaults from $\mathcal{F}$ are even applicable, and that r_1^{π}, although applicable, is both conflicted and defeated; hence, only defaults from $\mathcal{S}_{14}$ are binding in that scenario. And second: To show that $\mathcal{S}_{14}$ is the only proper scenario allowed by the theory $\Delta_{X_6, \mathcal{V}_{Jack}}$, suppose there is another – say, $\mathcal{S}$. Evidently, both of the value defaults $r_{1\backslash 1}^{\delta}$ and $r_{1,2\backslash 2}^{\delta}$ must be contained in $\mathcal{S}$, since both are applicable, and the theory contains no information that conflicts with either. Apart from r_1^{π} and r_1^{δ}, none of the other factor defaults from $\mathcal{F}$ are applicable, and so $\mathcal{S}$ can differ from $\mathcal{S}_{14}$ only by containing r_1^{π} in place of r_1^{δ}. But since, as we have just seen, $\mathcal{S}$ must contain $r_{1\backslash 1}^{\delta}$, according to which the conflicting applicable default r_1^{δ} is assigned higher priority than r_1^{π}, it follows that r_1^{π} is defeated, and so cannot be binding; hence $\mathcal{S}$ cannot be a proper scenario after all, since it would contain a default that is not binding in the context of that scenario.

We conclude this section with five observations concerning the problems presented to courts and the proper scenarios representing their solutions.

First: The scenarios representing solutions to problems presented by certain fact situations might contain value defaults that really have no bearing on those situations – not all of a court's values will bear on every situation confronted by that court. This possibility is already illustrated by the scenario $\mathcal{S}_{14} = \{r^{\delta}_{1}, r^{\delta}_{1\backslash 1}, r^{\delta}_{1,2\backslash 2}\}$ identified above as a solution to the problem presented to Jack by the situation $X_6 = \{f^{\pi}_{1}, f^{\delta}_{1}\}$, which contains the value default $r^{\delta}_{1,2\backslash 2}$, supporting the conclusion $n^{\pi}_{1,2} \prec n^{\delta}_{2}$, that the factor default r^{δ}_{2} is prioritized over the factor default $r^{\pi}_{1,2}$, even though neither of these two factor defaults is applicable in the situation at hand.

Second: Although perhaps obvious, it is worth noting that a court's values need not yield a complete ordering on factor default rules, or factor reasons. The value defaults from $\mathcal{V}_{Jack}$, for example, do not tell us either that the factor default r^{δ}_{1} is to be prioritized over the factor default r^{π}_{2}, or that r^{π}_{2} is to be prioritized over r^{δ}_{1} – Jack's values specify no relation at all between completing chores as a reason for the plaintiff and failing to complete homework as a reason for the defendant.

Third: Unlike the solution $\mathcal{S}_{14} = \{r^{\delta}_{1}, r^{\delta}_{1\backslash 1}, r^{\delta}_{1,2\backslash 2}\}$ to the problem presented by Chris to Jack, which contains only the single factor default r^{δ}_{1} justifying the ultimate decision in favor of the defendant, some problems might allow solutions that contain several such factor defaults, any of which might be taken to justify the ultimate decision. To illustrate, imagine that Jack and Jo have yet another child, Leslie, who is at least nine years of age but has neither finished dinner nor completed homework, and so presents Jack with the situation $X_{36} = \{f^{\pi}_{1}, f^{\delta}_{1}, f^{\delta}_{2}\}$. In this new situation, somewhat richer than that presented by Chris, four factor defaults are now applicable:

$$
\begin{aligned}
r^{\pi}_{1} &= \{f^{\pi}_{1}\} \rightarrow \pi, \\
r^{\delta}_{1} &= \{f^{\delta}_{1}\} \rightarrow \delta, \\
r^{\delta}_{2} &= \{f^{\delta}_{2}\} \rightarrow \delta, \\
r^{\delta}_{1,2} &= \{f^{\delta}_{1}, f^{\delta}_{2}\} \rightarrow \delta.
\end{aligned}
$$

Since Jack's values remain $\mathcal{V}_{Jack} = \{r^{\delta}_{1\backslash 1}, r^{\delta}_{1,2\backslash 2}\}$, we can see that the problem presented by X_{36} to Jack – that is $\Delta_{X_{36}, \mathcal{V}_{Jack}} = \langle \mathcal{W}_{X_{36}}, \mathcal{D}_{\mathcal{V}_{Jack}} \rangle$, where $\mathcal{W}_{X_{36}} = \{f^{\pi}_{1}, f^{\delta}_{1}, f^{\delta}_{2}\} \cup \mathcal{O}$ and $\mathcal{D}_{\mathcal{V}_{Jack}} = \mathcal{F} \cup \{r^{\delta}_{1\backslash 1}, r^{\delta}_{1,2\backslash 2}\}$ – allows the proper scenario $\mathcal{S}_{15} = \{r^{\delta}_{1}, r^{\delta}_{2}, r^{\delta}_{1,2}, r^{\delta}_{1\backslash 1}, r^{\delta}_{1,2\backslash 2}\}$ as its unique solution, again generating

$$
\mathcal{E}_{15} = \mathcal{E}_{14} = \mathit{Closure}(\mathcal{W}_{X_{36}} \cup \{\delta,\ n^{\pi}_{1} \prec n^{\delta}_{1},\ n^{\pi}_{1,2} \prec n^{\delta}_{2}\})
$$

as its unique extension, and again supporting the ultimate decision δ, that the situation is to be decided for the defendant. In contrast to the earlier example, however, where the solution $\mathcal{S}_{14}$ to the problem presented by Chris contained only a single factor default r_1^δ supporting the ultimate decision for the defendant, the proper scenario $\mathcal{S}_{15}$ that functions as a solution to the problem presented by Leslie contains three separate factor defaults – r_1^δ, r_2^δ, and $r_{1,2}^\delta$ – supporting this decision. Suppose Jack needs to select a particular rule to justify his decision. Which one should he choose? We must suppose that Jack is free to choose any of these rules, either one of the broader rules r_1^δ or r_2^δ or the narrower rule $r_{1,2}^\delta$, to justify his decision; this choice is determined – if it is determined at all – by information that is not represented in the current formalism.

Fourth: A court's values might not address the issue presented by some particular situation, and for that reason, fail to determine a unique solution to the problem presented by that situation. To take an extreme case, suppose Chris presents the situation $X_6 = \{f_1^\pi, f_1^\delta\}$, not to Jack, but to another authority – say, Aunt Pat – whose values are represented by the set $\mathcal{V}_{Pat}$ containing the single default

$$r_{2\backslash 2}^\pi = \top \rightarrow n_2^\delta \prec n_2^\pi.$$

As we can see, Aunt Pat prioritizes the factor default r_2^π over the factor default r_2^δ – that is, she prioritizes completing chores as a reason for the plaintiff over failing to complete homework as a reason for the defendant – but has no further opinions regarding the relative priorities of other factor defaults, including those that are actually applicable in the situation presented by Chris. As a result, the problem presented to Aunt Pat by this situation – that is, the theory $\Delta_{X_6,\mathcal{V}_{Pat}} = \langle \mathcal{W}_{X_6}, \mathcal{D}_{\mathcal{V}_{Pat}} \rangle$, where $\mathcal{W}_{X_6} = \{f_1^\pi, f_1^\delta\} \cup \mathcal{O}$ and $\mathcal{D}_{\mathcal{V}_{Pat}} = \mathcal{F} \cup \{r_{2\backslash 2}^\pi\}$ – allows two proper scenarios as solutions, both $\mathcal{S}_{16} = \{r_1^\pi, r_{2\backslash 2}^\pi\}$ and $\mathcal{S}_{17} = \{r_1^\delta, r_{2\backslash 2}^\pi\}$, generating the extensions $\mathcal{E}_{16} = Closure(\mathcal{W}_{X_6} \cup \{\pi, n_2^\delta \prec n_2^\pi\})$ and $\mathcal{E}_{17} = Closure(\mathcal{W}_{X_6} \cup \{\delta, n_2^\delta \prec n_2^\pi\})$. Each of these solutions supports the conclusion $n_2^\delta \prec n_2^\pi$, in accord with Aunt Pat's values, but the first applies the default r_1^π to yield π, a decision for the plaintiff, while the second applies the default r_1^δ to yield δ, a decision for the defendant. According to the interpretation adopted in this book of theories allowing multiple proper scenarios, which then generate multiple extensions, each of these extensions represents an acceptable outcome – Aunt Pat is thus permitted to reach a decision for the plaintiff but also permitted to reach a decision for the defendant.

Fifth, and finally: Rather than failing to address the issues presented by some situation – providing, in effect, too little information – a court's values might seem to provide too much information, suggesting inconsistent rankings among factor defaults applicable in the situation at hand; the result would be that, once again, the default theory representing the problem presented to the court will allow multiple proper scenarios as solutions, which then generate multiple extensions. To illustrate, suppose this time that the situation $X_6 = \{f_1^\pi, f_1^\delta\}$ is presented to yet another authority – say, Uncle Mike – whose values can be represented by the set $\mathcal{V}_{Mike}$ containing the two defaults

$$r^{\pi}_{1\backslash 1} = \top \rightarrow n_1^\delta \prec n_1^\pi,$$
$$r^{\delta}_{1\backslash 1} = \top \rightarrow n_1^\pi \prec n_1^\delta.$$

According to the first of these defaults, Uncle Mike prioritizes the factor default r_1^π over the factor default r_1^δ, but according to the second, he prioritizes r_1^δ over r_1^π – that is, he prioritizes being at least nine years of age as a reason for the plaintiff over failing to finish dinner as a reason for the defendant, while at the same time prioritizing failing to finish dinner as a reason for the defendant over being at least nine years of age as a reason for the plaintiff.

Perhaps it is unfortunate that Uncle Mike's values are inconsistent in this way, but many of us harbor inconsistent values, or conflicting ideals – sometimes the inconsistency in our values is brought into focus only through the consideration of some particular situation; sometimes we are fully aware of the inconsistency in our values, and simply hope to muddle through without encountering a situation that would force us to resolve this inconsistency one way or another. The point here, however, is not to criticize Uncle Mike for his inconsistent values but to show that, even so, there are still solutions available to the problem presented by the current situation. To be explicit, the problem presented to Uncle Mike by the situation X_6 is represented by the theory $\Delta_{X_6,\mathcal{V}_{Mike}} = \langle \mathcal{W}_{X_6}, \mathcal{D}_{\mathcal{V}_{Mike}} \rangle$, where $\mathcal{W}_{X_6} = \{f_1^\pi, f_1^\delta\} \cup \mathcal{O}$ and $\mathcal{D}_{\mathcal{V}_{Mike}} = \mathcal{F} \cup \{r^{\pi}_{1\backslash 1}, r^{\delta}_{1\backslash 1}\}$, depicted in Figure 5.6. This theory allows two proper scenarios as solutions, both $\mathcal{S}_{18} = \{r_1^\pi, r^{\pi}_{1\backslash 1}\}$ and $\mathcal{S}_{19} = \{r_1^\delta, r^{\delta}_{1\backslash 1}\}$, generating the extensions $\mathcal{E}_{18} = Closure(\mathcal{W}_{X_6} \cup \{\pi, n_1^\delta \prec n_1^\pi\})$ and $\mathcal{E}_{19} = Closure(\mathcal{W}_{X_6} \cup \{\delta, n_1^\pi \prec n_1^\delta\})$. The first of these solutions represents the outcome in which Uncle Mike resolves his conflicting values in favor of $r^{\pi}_{1\backslash 1}$, committing himself, at last, to the idea that r_1^π carries higher priority than r_1^δ, and so finding for the plaintiff on the basis of r_1^π; the second solution represents the opposite outcome, in which Uncle Mike resolves the conflict in favor of $r^{\delta}_{1\backslash 1}$, committing himself instead to the idea that r_1^δ carries higher

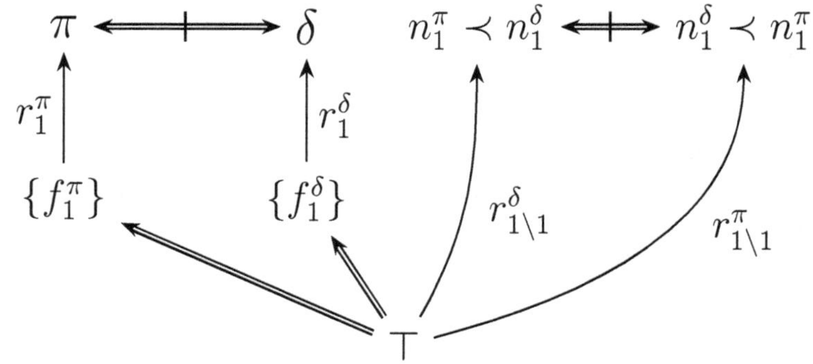

Figure 5.6 Chris and Uncle Mike, with conflicting values

priority than r_1^π, and so finding for the defendant on the basis of r_1^δ. On the current interpretation, once again, each of these outcomes would be acceptable – Uncle Mike is permitted to resolve his conflicting values either way, and so to decide either for the plaintiff or for the defendant.

6 Constraining Natural Reasoning

In Chapter 5, we saw how default logic could be developed as a formal account of natural reasoning in general, and then used to provide an account of natural reasoning about judicial problems. More exactly, we saw how the problem presented by a fact situation to a court with its own particular set of values could be represented as a default theory, and how a solution to that problem could then be arrived at through natural reasoning based entirely on the court's own values. The goal of the current chapter is to show how natural reasoning of this kind can be adapted to respect the constraints derived from a background set of precedent cases – that is, to provide a formal theory of constrained natural reasoning.

The constraints derived from precedent cases can be understood in two ways, as *hard* constraints or as *soft* constraints. We begin by developing an account of precedential constraints as hard, or absolute, in a way that would be appropriate for a court that has no choice but to satisfy these constraints. On the basis of this account, we can establish the central result that a decision arrived at through natural reasoning subject to hard constraints derived from a background case base is guaranteed to satisfy the reason model of constraint. This result confirms our earlier suggestion, from Chapter 4, that constrained natural reasoning is the form of reasoning appropriate to the reason model of constraint; it also shows, as suggested in Chapter 2, that the reason model itself can be reformulated as a defeasible rule model of constraint.

After considering hard constraints, we turn to the more subtle and complex matter of adapting our account of natural reasoning to respect precedential constraints that are softer – suggestive, or persuasive, but not absolute. Finally, we return to the topic of open-textured predicates considered earlier, in Chapter 1, but this time using the tools developed in our treatment of constrained natural reasoning.

6.1 Hard Constraints

6.1.1 Representing Problems with Hard Constraints

The account of hard precedential constraints is relatively simple. The general idea is this: in constructing a default theory to represent the problem presented to a court whose natural reasoning is subject to hard constraints derived from a background case base, the hard information from that default theory is supplemented with a set containing, for each case from the case base, a statement according to which the rule of that case, a particular factor default, is assigned higher priority than the strongest applicable factor default rule favoring the other side.

To see how this set of statements is constructed, we begin with a case $c = \langle X, r, s \rangle$ from a background case base Γ, and consider, first, the rule

$$r = \quad Premise(r) \rightarrow s$$

of that case. According to the conventions for identifying factor default rules introduced earlier, in Section 5.3.1, this rule can be referred to through the structural descriptor $r^{s}_{Premise(r)_i}$, whose subscript $Premise(r)_i$ is the set containing indices of the factors belonging to the premise of the rule and whose superscript s is the side favored by the rule; our conventions then allow us to designate this default rule within the language using the term $n^{s}_{Premise(r)_i}$.

Next, continuing to rely on our notational conventions, and recalling that $X^{\overline{s}}$ is the entire set of factors from X that favor the side $\overline{s}$, the strongest factor default rule

$$X^{\overline{s}} \rightarrow \overline{s}$$

for the losing side of the case $c = \langle X, r, s \rangle$ that is applicable in the fact situation of that case can be referred to through the structural descriptor $r^{\overline{s}}_{X^{\overline{s}}_i}$, whose subscript $X^{\overline{s}}_i$ is the set containing indices of all those factors from X favoring the side $\overline{s}$ and whose superscript $\overline{s}$ is the side favored by the rule; this rule can be designated within the language using the term $n^{\overline{s}}_{X^{\overline{s}}_i}$. How do we know that $r^{\overline{s}}_{X^{\overline{s}}_i}$ is the strongest factor default favoring the side $\overline{s}$ that is applicable in the situation X? Well, suppose that another rule r' favoring $\overline{s}$ even more strongly than $r^{\overline{s}}_{X^{\overline{s}}_i}$ is also applicable in X. Since r' is applicable in X, and favors $\overline{s}$, we know that $Premise(r') \subseteq X^{\overline{s}}$, from which we can conclude by Definition 2 from Section 1.1.2 that $Premise(r') \leq^{\overline{s}} X^{\overline{s}}$ holds as a relation among reasons, and so by Definition 35 from Section 5.3.1 that $r' \leq^{\overline{s}} r^{\overline{s}}_{X^{\overline{s}}_i}$

holds as a relation among rules – in other words, that the rule $r^{\overline{s}}_{X^{\overline{s}}_i}$ favors the side $\overline{s}$ at least as strongly as the rule r', contrary to assumption.

Since $r^{s}_{Premise(r)_i}$ is the rule of the case $c = \langle X, r, s\rangle$, then, and $r^{\overline{s}}_{X^{\overline{s}}_i}$ is the strongest applicable rule for the other side, the fact that the rule of the case has a higher priority than the strongest applicable rule for the other side can be expressed through the statement

$$r^{\overline{s}}_{X^{\overline{s}}_i} \; < \; r^{s}_{Premise(r)_i},$$

which can itself be encoded into the language of our theory with the formula

$$n^{\overline{s}}_{X^{\overline{s}}_i} \; \prec \; n^{s}_{Premise(r)_i},$$

where the constants $n^{\overline{s}}_{X^{\overline{s}}_i}$ and $n^{s}_{Premise(r)_i}$ designate the corresponding rules, and where $\prec$ is our linguistic representation of priority among rules. Using this representational schema, we can then collect together into the set

$$\mathcal{H}_{\Gamma} \; = \; \{n^{\overline{s}}_{X^{\overline{s}}_i} \prec n^{s}_{Premise(r)_i} \; : \; \langle X, r, s\rangle \in \Gamma\}$$

the various statements according to which, for each case from the background case base Γ, the rule of that case carries higher priority than the strongest rule for the other side that is applicable in the fact situation of that case. The statements from $\mathcal{H}_{\Gamma}$ represent the hard constraints derived from the case base Γ.

To illustrate, we construct the set of statements representing hard constraints derived from the case base $\Gamma_4 = \{c_4\}$, with $c_4 = \langle X_4, r_4, s_4\rangle$, where $X_4 = \{f^{\pi}_1, f^{\pi}_2, f^{\delta}_1\}$, where $r_4 = \{f^{\pi}_1\} \rightarrow \pi$, and where $s_4 = \pi$. Here, the rule r_4 of the case can be represented through the structural descriptor r^{π}_1, and since $X^{\delta}_4 = \{f^{\delta}_1\}$, the strongest applicable rule for the other side – that is, $\{f^{\delta}_1\} \rightarrow \delta$ – can be represented through the structural descriptor r^{δ}_1. The fact that the rule of the particular case c_4 is assigned a higher priority than the strongest applicable rule for the opposite side – that is, the fact that $r^{\delta}_1 < r^{\pi}_1$ – can then be encoded into the language through the statement $n^{\delta}_1 \prec n^{\pi}_1$. And since c_4 is the only case belonging to Γ_4, the set of hard constraints derived from the case base contains this statement alone:

$$\mathcal{H}_{\Gamma_4} = \{n^{\delta}_1 \prec n^{\pi}_1\}.$$

We can now carry through with our plan of constructing a default theory to represent the problem facing a court that is reasoning about a fact situation on the basis of its own values, but under hard constraints derived from a background case base. As suggested, this default theory is like that set out earlier, in Definition 36 from Section 5.3.1, except that the hard information from the theory is now supplemented with constraints derived from the background case base:

Definition 37 (Problem presented to court under hard constraints) Let X be a fact situation, $\mathcal{V}$ a set of value defaults, and Γ a case base. Then the problem presented by the fact situation X to a court with values $\mathcal{V}$ under hard constraints $\mathcal{H}_\Gamma$ derived from Γ is represented by the variable priority default theory $\Delta_{X,\mathcal{V},\mathcal{H}_\Gamma} = \langle \mathcal{W}_{X,\mathcal{H}_\Gamma}, \mathcal{D}_\mathcal{V} \rangle$ where

$$\begin{aligned} \mathcal{W}_{X,\mathcal{H}_\Gamma} &= X \cup \mathcal{H}_\Gamma \cup \mathcal{O}, \\ \mathcal{D}_\mathcal{V} &= \mathcal{F} \cup \mathcal{V}. \end{aligned}$$

Just as before, where the theory $\Delta_{X,\mathcal{V},\mathcal{H}_\Gamma}$, represents a problem presented to the court under hard constraints derived from a background case base, we will again define a *solution to this problem* as a proper scenario allowed by that theory. Our claim, then, is that a court working with a theory of this kind, searching for a solution, can legitimately be described as engaged in a process of constrained natural reasoning: the court is reasoning in the natural way, on the basis of its own values, except that, when those values conflict with decisions reached in previous cases, the court must defer to those previous decisions.

It was suggested earlier, in Section 4.1, that constrained natural reasoning is the form of reasoning appropriate to the reason model of constraint, and we are now in a position to confirm that suggestion. As we recall, the function of the reason model – formulated precisely in Definition 7 from Section 1.2.2 – is to characterize, given a fact situation presented to a court against a background case base, the rules on the basis of which a court is permitted to justify a decision. Now imagine that the court, reasoning about some fact situation on the basis of its own values but against the background of hard constraints derived from a consistent case base, first defines the default theory representing the problem it faces, and then finds its way to some solution, a particular proper scenario allowed by that theory. We can then conclude that, in the sense of permission at work in the reason model, the court is permitted to base its decision on any factor default rule belonging to that proper scenario:

Observation 12 Where X is a fact situation, $\mathcal{V}$ is a set of value defaults, and Γ is a consistent case base, let the default theory $\Delta_{X,\mathcal{V},\mathcal{H}_\Gamma}$ represent the problem presented by the fact situation X to a court with values $\mathcal{V}$ under hard constraints $\mathcal{H}_\Gamma$ derived from Γ. Then, if r is a factor default rule, it follows that: if r belongs to some proper scenario allowed by the theory $\Delta_{X,\mathcal{V},\mathcal{H}_\Gamma}$, the reason model of constraint on rule selection permits the court, against the background of the case base Γ, to base its decision in the situation X on the rule r.

This result shows that, given a problem posed by some fact situation to a court, with its own particular values but reasoning with hard constraints, if a factor default rule belongs to some solution to the default theory representing that problem – that is, some proper scenario allowed by the theory – then a decision on the basis of that factor default will be permitted by the reason model. Does the converse hold: can we conclude that, if a decision based on a factor default rule is permitted by the reason model, then that factor default will belong to some proper scenario allowed by the theory representing the problem presented to the court? No, we cannot. Certain factor defaults, even if they lead to decisions that would be permitted by the reason model, might not appear in any solutions to the problem presented to the court, because the court's own values eliminate the proper scenarios that would have contained those factor defaults. What we can conclude, though, is that, if a court sets aside its own values in constructing the default theory that represents the problem it faces – so that the court is, in effect, reasoning with the empty set of values – then the appropriate biconditional holds: a factor default rule will belong to some proper scenario allowed by that default theory just in case a decision based on that rule is permitted by the reason model:

Observation 13 Where X is a fact situation, $\emptyset$ is the empty set of value defaults, and Γ is a consistent case base, let the default theory $\Delta_{X,\emptyset,\mathcal{H}_\Gamma}$ represent the problem presented by the fact situation X to a court with values $\emptyset$ under hard constraints $\mathcal{H}_\Gamma$ derived from Γ. Then, if r is a factor default rule, it follows that: r belongs to some proper scenario allowed by the theory $\Delta_{X,\emptyset,\mathcal{H}_\Gamma}$ if and only if the reason model of constraint on rule selection permits the court, against the background of the case base Γ, to base its decision in the situation X on the rule r.

Before moving on to concrete examples, let us step back and consider the meaning of these two observations. We have already seen, in a sense, two ways of formulating the reason model of constraint – the canonical formulation in Definition 7, but also our formulation of the standard model in Definition 17 from Section 3.1.3, which turned out to be equivalent to the canonical formulation. This section provides a third. Once again, the function of the reason model is to characterize, given a fact situation X presented to a court against a background case base Γ, the rules on the basis of which the court is permitted to justify a decision. And as it turns out, the account presented in this section does exactly that. Given a situation X and a consistent case base Γ, and supposing the court's own set of values is empty, Definition 37 provides a recipe for constructing the default theory $\Delta_{X,\emptyset,\mathcal{H}_\Gamma}$ to represent the problem facing the court, and then Observation 13 tells us that the court is permitted to base its decision on a particular factor default rule just in case that rule belongs to some proper scenario allowed by the theory $\Delta_{X,\emptyset,\mathcal{H}_\Gamma}$. The account presented in this section therefore identifies the very same set of rules characterized earlier, in the canonical Definition 7 and also in Definition 17, but this time using the machinery of default logic – it can thus be seen as providing yet another formulation of the reason model, this time as a defeasible rule model of constraint.

Of course, taken simply as a formulation of the reason model, the current account is considerably more complicated than that provided by the canonical Definition 7. But it is also richer, in two ways. First, by placing the matter in the overall framework of default logic, this account helps us understand, not just the constraints derived from a background case base, but how a court might reason its way to a solution satisfying those constraints. And second, as Observation 12 shows, the current account helps us understand how the court might have to adapt, or constrain, its own natural reasoning, on the basis of its own values, to arrive at such a solution.

6.1.2 Some Examples

For illustration, we return to the situation presented by Chris to Jack, considered most recently in Section 5.3.2. This time, however, as in our earlier discussions of this example from Sections 1.2.4 and 4.2.2, we suppose that Jack confronts the situation against the background of a case base containing the decision previously reached by Jo in the case of Emma: we suppose, that is, that Jack now confronts the situation $X_6 = \{f_1^\pi, f_1^\delta\}$ presented by Chris against the background of the case base $\Gamma_4 = \{c_4\}$ containing Jo's earlier decision $c_4 = \langle X_4, r_4, s_4 \rangle$, where $X_4 = \{f_1^\pi, f_2^\pi, f_1^\delta\}$, where $r_4 = \{f_1^\pi\} \rightarrow \pi$, and where $s_4 = \pi$. As a reminder, f_1^π and f_2^π represent, respectively, the facts that the child in question is at least nine years old and has completed chores, while f_1^δ and f_2^δ represent the fact that the child has failed to finish dinner and failed to complete homework. Chris, then, is at least nine but failed to finish dinner, while Emma was also at least nine, completed chores, but likewise failed to finish dinner.

Jack's values, discussed in Chapter 5, are represented by the set $\mathcal{V}_{Jack}$ containing the two value defaults

$$r^{\delta}_{1\backslash 1} = \top \rightarrow n^{\pi}_{1} \prec n^{\delta}_{1},$$

$$r^{\delta}_{1,2\backslash 2} = \top \rightarrow n^{\pi}_{1,2} \prec n^{\delta}_{2};$$

again, these defaults reflect Jack's view that failing to finish dinner carries higher priority as a reason for the defendant than having reached the age of nine as a reason for the plaintiff, and also, though it has no bearing on this example, that failing to complete homework carries higher priority as a reason for the defendant than having reached the age of nine and completed chores, taken together, as a reason for the plaintiff. And as we have now seen, the hard constraints derived from the case base Γ_4 are those contained in the set $\mathcal{H}_{\Gamma_4} = \{n^{\delta}_{1} \prec n^{\pi}_{1}\}$. Following the recipe set out in Definition 37, then, the problem presented to Jack by the situation $X_6 = \{f^{\pi}_{1}, f^{\pi}_{2}\}$ under hard constraints derived from Γ_4 can be represented as the theory $\Delta_{X_6, \mathcal{V}_{Jack}, \mathcal{H}_{\Gamma_4}} = \langle \mathcal{W}_{X_6, \mathcal{H}_{\Gamma_4}}, \mathcal{D}_{\mathcal{V}_{Jack}} \rangle$ where

$$\begin{aligned} \mathcal{W}_{X_6, \mathcal{H}_{\Gamma_4}} &= X_6 \cup \mathcal{H}_{\Gamma_4} \cup \mathcal{O} \\ &= \{f^{\pi}_{1}, f^{\delta}_{1}\} \cup \{n^{\delta}_{1} \prec n^{\pi}_{1}\} \cup \mathcal{O}, \\ \mathcal{D}_{\mathcal{V}_{Jack}} &= \mathcal{F} \cup \mathcal{V}_{Jack} \\ &= \mathcal{F} \cup \{r^{\delta}_{1\backslash 1}, r^{\delta}_{1,2\backslash 2}\}. \end{aligned}$$

The hard information $\mathcal{W}_{X_6, \mathcal{H}_{\Gamma_4}}$ from this theory includes both the set X_6 characterizing the situation at hand and the fixed collection $\mathcal{O}$ of ordering statements, but now also the set $\mathcal{H}_{\Gamma_4}$ of hard constraints derived from the background case base; the set $\mathcal{D}_{\mathcal{V}_{Jack}}$ of defaults includes the set $\mathcal{F}$ of factor defaults together with the set $\mathcal{V}_{Jack}$ of defaults representing Jack's values. This theory is depicted in Figure 6.1.

The theory $\Delta_{X_6, \mathcal{V}_{Jack}, \mathcal{H}_{\Gamma_4}}$ allows, as its unique solution, the proper scenario $\mathcal{S}_{20} = \{r^{\pi}_{1}, r^{\delta}_{1,2\backslash 2}\}$, generating the unique extension

$$\mathcal{E}_{20} = Closure(\mathcal{W}_{X_6, \mathcal{H}_{\Gamma_4}} \cup \{\pi, n^{\pi}_{1,2} \prec n^{\delta}_{2}\}),$$

and so supporting the conclusion π, that the situation is to be decided for the plaintiff. Since this proper scenario contains the factor default r^{π}_{1}, it follows from Observation 12 that a decision based on r^{π}_{1} is permitted by the

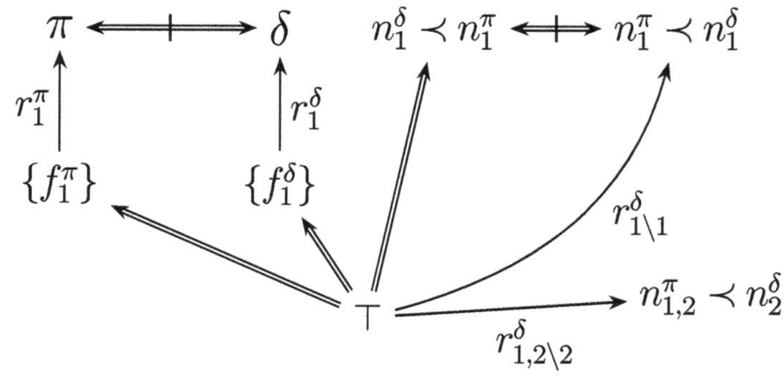

Figure 6.1 Chris and Jack, with hard constraints

reason model of constraint on rule selection – in other words, according to Definition 7, that the augmented case base $\Gamma_4 \cup \{\langle X_6, r_1^\pi, \pi\rangle\}$ is consistent.

In order to understand how hard constraints from a background case base can shape a court's natural reasoning, it is useful to compare the proper scenario $\mathcal{S}_{20} = \{r_1^\pi, r_{1,2\backslash 2}^\delta\}$ allowed by the current theory $\Delta_{X_6, \mathcal{V}_{Jack}, \mathcal{H}_{\Gamma_4}}$ with the proper scenario $\mathcal{S}_{14} = \{r_1^\delta, r_{1\backslash 1}^\delta, r_{1,2\backslash 2}^\delta\}$ allowed by the theory $\Delta_{X_6, \mathcal{V}_{Jack}}$, considered in Section 5.3.2, in which the same situation $X_6 = \{f_1^\pi, f_1^\delta\}$ was presented to Jack in a setting that did not involve constraints from a background case base, so that Jack was free to reason entirely on the basis of his own values. That earlier proper scenario, generating the extension

$$\mathcal{E}_{14} = Closure(\mathcal{W}_{X_6} \cup \{\delta,\ n_1^\pi \prec n_1^\delta,\ n_{1,2}^\pi \prec n_2^\delta\}),$$

contained the value default $r_{1\backslash 1}^\delta$, supporting the conclusion $n_1^\pi \prec n_1^\delta$, reflecting Jack's own view that failing to finish dinner as a reason for the defendant carries higher priority than having reached the age of nine as a reason for the plaintiff, and so driving his decision for the defendant in that situation. Unfortunately for Jack, the hard information $\mathcal{W}_{X_6, \mathcal{H}_{\Gamma_4}}$ from the current theory $\Delta_{X_6, \mathcal{V}_{Jack}, \mathcal{H}_{\Gamma_4}}$ now contains the statement $n_1^\delta \prec n_1^\pi$ as a constraint derived from Jo's previous decision, telling us exactly the opposite, that having reached the age of nine carries higher priority as a reason for the plaintiff than failing to finish dinner as a reason for the defendant. As a result, Jack's value default $r_{1\backslash 1}^\delta$ cannot appear in any proper scenario allowed by the current theory – technically, this default is conflicted. And because the hard information from this theory tells us that r_1^π has a higher priority than r_1^δ, it follows that r_1^δ, supporting the conclusion δ, cannot appear in any proper scenario either – technically, it is defeated. Instead, and contrary to his own values, Jack is now forced to conclude π, a decision for the plaintiff, on the basis of the default r_1^π.

For a second illustration, we return to our initial domestic example, the situation presented by Max to Jack against the background of the decision already reached by Jo in the case of Emma, discussed in the Introduction and first presented formally in Section 1.2.3. As we recall, Max, like Emma, has reached the age of nine and completed chores but failed to finish dinner, and in addition, failed to complete homework. We therefore suppose that Jack now faces the situation $X_5 = \{f_1^\pi, f_2^\pi, f_1^\delta, f_2^\delta\}$ presented by Max against the background of the case base $\Gamma_4 = \{c_4\}$ containing, once again, Jo's earlier decision $c_4 = \langle X_4, r_4, s_4\rangle$, where $X_4 = \{f_1^\pi, f_2^\pi, f_1^\delta\}$, where $r_4 = \{f_1^\pi\} \rightarrow \pi$, and where $s_4 = \pi$. Since this situation is richer than that presented by Chris, more factor defaults are applicable: favoring the plaintiff, we have the three defaults

$$\begin{aligned} r_1^\pi &= \{f_1^\pi\} \rightarrow \pi, \\ r_2^\pi &= \{f_2^\pi\} \rightarrow \pi, \\ r_{1,2}^\pi &= \{f_1^\pi, f_2^\pi\} \rightarrow \pi, \end{aligned}$$

and favoring the defendant, the three defaults

$$\begin{aligned} r_1^\delta &= \{f_1^\delta\} \rightarrow \delta, \\ r_2^\delta &= \{f_2^\delta\} \rightarrow \delta, \\ r_{1,2}^\delta &= \{f_1^\delta, f_2^\delta\} \rightarrow \delta. \end{aligned}$$

Following our recipe, again, the problem presented to Jack by the situation X_5 under hard constraints derived from the case base Γ_4 can be represented by the theory $\Delta_{X_5, \mathcal{V}_{Jack}, \mathcal{H}_{\Gamma_4}} = \langle \mathcal{W}_{X_5, \mathcal{H}_{\Gamma_4}}, \mathcal{D}_{\mathcal{V}_{Jack}}\rangle$, where

$$\begin{aligned} \mathcal{W}_{X_5, \mathcal{H}_{\Gamma_4}} &= X_5 \cup \mathcal{H}_{\Gamma_4} \cup \mathcal{O} \\ &= \{f_1^\pi, f_2^\pi, f_1^\delta, f_2^\delta\} \cup \{n_1^\delta \prec n_1^\pi\} \cup \mathcal{O}, \\ \mathcal{D}_{\mathcal{V}_{Jack}} &= \mathcal{F} \cup \mathcal{V}_{Jack} \\ &= \mathcal{F} \cup \{r_{1\backslash 1}^\delta, r_{1,2\backslash 2}^\delta\}. \end{aligned}$$

This theory allows, as its unique solution, the proper scenario $\mathcal{S}_{21} = \{r_2^\delta, r_{1,2}^\delta, r_{1,2\backslash 2}^\delta\}$, generating the unique extension

$$\mathcal{E}_{21} = Closure(\mathcal{W}_{X_5, \mathcal{H}_{\Gamma_4}} \cup \{\delta, n_{1,2}^\pi \prec n_2^\delta\}),$$

and so supporting the conclusion δ, that the situation is to be decided for the defendant. Since this proper scenario contains two factor defaults, r_2^δ and

$r^{\delta}_{1,2}$, it again follows from Observation 12 that the reason model would permit a decision based on either of these defaults – that both $\Gamma_4 \cup \{\langle X_5, r^{\delta}_{2}, \delta\rangle\}$ and $\Gamma_4 \cup \{\langle X_5, r^{\delta}_{1,2}, \delta\rangle\}$ are consistent.

Why is it that, in the case of Max, Jack is able to decide for the defendant in accord with his values, but unable to do so in the case of Chris? Well, in the situation presented by Chris, only two factor defaults are applicable: r^{π}_{1}, favoring the plaintiff on grounds of age, and r^{δ}_{1}, favoring the defendant on grounds of failing to finish dinner. And although Jack's values support the idea that failing to finish dinner is a more important reason than age, leading Jack to prioritize r^{δ}_{1} over r^{π}_{1}, it is already settled as a hard constraint derived from the background case base that age is a more important reason than failing to finish dinner, or that r^{π}_{1} is to be prioritized over r^{δ}_{1}. Jack therefore has no choice but to decide for the plaintiff on the basis of r^{π}_{1}. By contrast, a number of other factor defaults are applicable in the situation presented by Max, including r^{δ}_{2}, favoring the defendant on grounds of failing to complete homework, which Jack prioritizes over the factor default $r^{\pi}_{1,2}$, favoring the plaintiff on grounds of age and completion of chores taken together, and so over r^{π}_{1} and r^{π}_{2} taken individually, favoring the plaintiff on grounds of age and favoring the plaintiff on ground of completion of chores. In this situation, Jack's values are consistent with the hard constraints derived from the background case base – there is no conflict between prioritizing failure to complete homework over age, while at the same time prioritizing age over failure to finish dinner. Since there is no conflict between his values and prior hard constraints, Jack is free to decide this situation for the defendant on the basis of r^{δ}_{2}, or even on the basis of the stronger $r^{\delta}_{1,2}$, in accord with his values.

So far, we have illustrated Observation 12, according to which, once a default theory is formulated to represent the problem posed by a fact situation to a court with its particular values, but under hard constraints from a background case base, a decision based on any factor default belonging to any proper scenario allowed by that theory will be permitted by the reason model. But we have not illustrated Observation 13, according to which, if the court sets its own values aside in formulating the default theory representing the problem, then the converse holds as well: if a decision based on some factor default is permitted by the reason model, then that factor default will belong to some proper scenario allowed by the default theory.

To illustrate this latter observation, we consider again the situation $X_5 = \{f^{\pi}_{1}, f^{\pi}_{2}, f^{\delta}_{1}, f^{\delta}_{2}\}$ presented by Max to Jack against the background of the case base Γ_4 containing Jo's earlier decision, but this time imagine that, in constructing the default theory to represent the problem he faces, Jack sets his own values aside. Following the recipe set out in Definition 37, but substituting the empty set $\emptyset$ for the set $\mathcal{V}_{Jack}$ of Jack's values, the resulting problem can be represented as the default theory $\Delta_{X_5,\emptyset,\mathcal{H}_{\Gamma_4}} = \langle \mathcal{W}_{X_5,\mathcal{H}_{\Gamma_4}}, \mathcal{D}_{\emptyset}\rangle$ in which

$$\begin{aligned}\mathcal{W}_{X_5,\mathcal{H}_{\Gamma_4}} &= X_5 \cup \mathcal{H}_{\Gamma_4} \cup \mathcal{O}\\ &= \{f_1^{\pi}, f_2^{\pi}, f_1^{\delta}, f_2^{\delta}\} \cup \{n_1^{\delta} \prec n_1^{\pi}\} \cup \mathcal{O},\\ \mathcal{D}_{\emptyset} &= \mathcal{F} \cup \emptyset\\ &= \mathcal{F}.\end{aligned}$$

Unlike the previous theory $\Delta_{X_5,\mathcal{V}_{Jack},\mathcal{H}_{\Gamma_4}}$, which takes Jack's values into account, the current $\Delta_{X_5,\emptyset,\mathcal{H}_{\Gamma_4}}$ allows two solutions: the two proper scenarios $\mathcal{S}_{22} = \{r_1^{\pi}, r_2^{\pi}, r_{1,2}^{\pi}\}$ and $\mathcal{S}_{23} = \{r_2^{\delta}, r_{1,2}^{\delta}\}$, representing two solutions to the problem at hand, and generating the two extensions

$$\begin{aligned}\mathcal{E}_{22} &= Closure(\mathcal{W}_{X_5,\mathcal{H}_{\Gamma_4}} \cup \{\pi\}),\\ \mathcal{E}_{23} &= Closure(\mathcal{W}_{X_5,\mathcal{H}_{\Gamma_4}} \cup \{\delta\}).\end{aligned}$$

The second of these solutions, $\mathcal{S}_{23}$, is an analogue of the unique solution $\mathcal{S}_{21} = \{r_2^{\delta}, r_{1,2}^{\delta}, r_{1,2\backslash 2}^{\delta}\}$ allowed by the previous $\Delta_{X_5,\mathcal{V}_{Jack},\mathcal{H}_{\Gamma_4}}$, except that $\mathcal{S}_{23}$ is missing the value default $r_{1,2\backslash 2}^{\delta}$, since none of Jack's value defaults figure in the definition of the current problem. However, the first solution, $\mathcal{S}_{22}$, is entirely new; it has no analogue among the proper scenarios allowed by the previous theory, since the presence of the default $r_{1,2\backslash 2}^{\delta}$ among Jack's values entails that each of the factor defaults belonging to this proper scenario would have to be defeated.

As promised, this example can be used to illustrate Observation 13, according to which, against the background of the case base Γ_4, the reason model permits a decision on the basis of a factor default rule in the situation X_5 just in case that factor default belongs to some proper scenario – either $\mathcal{S}_{22}$ or $\mathcal{S}_{23}$ – allowed by the theory $\Delta_{X_5,\emptyset,\mathcal{H}_{\Gamma_4}}$. To verify this result, we first note that a decision based on any factor default that is actually applicable in the situation X_5 is permitted by the reason model, with the sole exception of the rule r_1^{δ}; next, we note that all the applicable factor defaults, again with the exception of r_1^{δ}, belong either to $\mathcal{S}_{22}$ or to $\mathcal{S}_{23}$.

We close this section with a general point. As we have seen in our discussion of the theories $\Delta_{X_6\mathcal{V}_{Jack},\mathcal{H}_{\Gamma_4}}$ from the current section and $\Delta_{X_6,\mathcal{V}_{Jack}}$ from Section 5.3.2, representing the problems presented by Chris to Jack with or without constraints but in both cases taking Jack's values into account, the presence of constraints derived from a background case base rules out certain solutions that would have been allowed based on Jack's values alone. And as we have seen in our discussion of the theories $\Delta_{X_5, \mathcal{V}_{Jack}, \mathcal{H}_{\Gamma_4}}$ and $\Delta_{X_5, \emptyset, \mathcal{H}_{\Gamma_4}}$ from the current section, including or setting aside Jack's values but in both cases respecting constraints from the background case base, the presence of values likewise rules out certain solutions that would have been allowed based on case base constraints alone. From this standpoint, the pressures exerted by constraints and values may seem to be equivalent, since both values and constraints rule out solutions that would otherwise have been allowed. But of course, they are not equivalent: hard constraints derived from a background case base are prioritized over a court's values. The goal of a court engaged in constrained natural reasoning is, first, to satisfy these hard constraints, and then, to the extent possible, to satisfy its own values.

6.2 Soft Constraints

6.2.1 Motivation

We now turn from hard precedential constraints to softer, or weaker, constraints – persuasive, but not absolute.

Since there is, as we have now established, a precise correspondence between the reason model of constraint and the account developed here of natural reasoning with hard constraints, it is sensible to wonder why we should bother with soft constraints at all. One answer is that an account of reasoning with soft constraints helps us understand the problem faced by a court with the authority to overrule earlier decisions. A court with this authority, contemplating the possibility of overruling an earlier decision in some new situation, is not simply unconstrained: it cannot just reason about the new situation entirely on the basis of its own values, as if the earlier decision had never been reached. But since the court has the authority to overrule, it is not subject to hard constraints derived from the previous decision either. How, then, can we make logical sense of the problem confronting this court – how can we understand its reasoning?

Consider an analogy. In the game of American football, governed by the rules of the National Football League, field officials reach judgments concerning play on the field in real time, as the game progresses. But League rules also allow for replay officials, who are able to stop the game clock in order to review videos of events about which the field officials have already reached decisions, and who have the authority to overrule these decisions – but only if "clear and obvious video evidence" shows that the decisions reached by these field officials were incorrect.[1]

Suppose the question at hand is whether the football carried by a player crossed the plane of the goal line before that player's knee hit the ground, so that, if so, the player scored a touchdown. And suppose that field officials operate with a preponderance of standard, according to which a play is to be classified as a touchdown just in case their credence that the ball crossed the goal line before the player's knee hit the ground is at least .5, but that, in this particular situation, since the field official's credence was only .48, the play was not classified as a touchdown. Now imagine that, as the result of a challenge, this decision comes before a replay official, who operates with a standard according to which there is "clear and obvious video evidence" that the play should be classified as a touchdown just in case, upon review of the video, the official's credence that the ball crossed the goal line before the player's knee hit the ground is .9 or greater. Finally, suppose that, after video review, the replay official has a very high credence that the ball crossed the goal line before the player's knee hit the ground – perhaps a credence of .85 – but not quite high enough that the evidence supplied by the video counts as clear and obvious. In that case, although the replay official would happily conclude under ordinary circumstances, or in the role of a field official, that the play should be classified as a touchdown, and in fact has the authority to overrule the field official's decision that it was not, the heightened standards of evidence governing replay review would not allow the replay official to classify the play as a touchdown.

This example illustrates one way in which earlier decisions might still constrain later authorities, even if those later authorities have the power to overrule earlier decisions: by shifting the applicable standards so that, rather than working with evidence in an ordinary way, the later authorities require much stronger evidence than usual in order to justify a judgment that overrules an earlier decision. Can this model be applied to the kind of legal or quasi-legal issues considered here – can a court with the authority to overrule earlier decisions be thought of along the lines of a replay official in football?

Not really. Talk of credence, evidence, and standards of evidence makes most sense in situations in which we are reasoning about facts in the

[1] See Rule 15, Section 2, Article 1 of Goodell (2020).

world that exist independently of our deliberations, but are uncertain about those facts, and are working with evidence in order to reduce our level of uncertainty. The football example is like this. Here, we can suppose that, as a matter of fact, the football either crossed the goal line before the player's knee touched the ground or it did not. The various officials are reasoning on the basis of their evidence to determine the fact of the matter, but the fact is what it is independent of any deliberations by these officials.

The kind of situations we are concerned with in this book, and of concern in common law reasoning more generally, are not like that. In our domestic examples, for instance, it is not as if there are prior facts of the matter about whether the children are allowed to stay up and watch TV, and the parents are working with the available evidence to discover what those facts are. Instead, the parents, through their deliberations and decisions, are constructing the household normative system in such a way that the various children either are or are not allowed to stay up and watch TV – what will later become the facts of the matter are constructed, in a progressive fashion, through these decisions. Or consider the question discussed earlier, in Section 1.3.2, and which we will return to shortly, about whether or not the Super Scoop is a vessel. If we can agree that "vessel" is an open-textured predicate, then again, there may be no prior fact of the matter: on Hart's view, the Super Scoop may lie in the predicate's penumbra, or on the view advocated here, prior decisions may neither require nor forbid the classification of the Super Scoop as a vessel. The different courts investigating the question, would then best be thought of, not as working with evidence to discover whether the Super Scoop is or is not a vessel but as considering whether it is better to extend the predicate "vessel" so that it includes or excludes the Super Scoop – again, the task is constructive, or constitutive, rather than epistemic.[2]

[2] The position set out in this paragraph – that judgments of the kind under consideration are constructive, rather than epistemic – is what I think of as the most natural position, but the opposing position has been occupied as well, in both philosophy of language and legal theory. In philosophy of language, Williamson (1994) defends an epistemic view of vagueness, according to which there is a prior fact of the matter concerning whether vague predicates, such as "tall" or "bald," do or do not apply to some particular individual, whether or not speakers of the language are aware of this fact. As far as I know, Williamson has not explicitly extended his epistemic view of vague predicates to open-textured predicates of the kind under consideration, but it would be a natural extension. In legal theory, Dworkin (1967, 1975) has advanced, in opposition to Hart's views on open texture, a "one right answer" thesis, according to which there are supposed to be determinate answers to legal questions – including questions concerning applicability of

In cases like this, where the issue does not seem to center around evidence at all, we cannot understand how a court could be constrained by a decision it has the power to overrule by imagining, as in the football example, that the court is forced by that earlier decision to apply heightened evidential standards. Still, it is possible to fashion an account very much like that found in the football example even in situations in which the enterprise is constructive, rather than epistemic. A familiar conception of our reasoning in these situations, which I have characterized elsewhere as the "weighing conception," asks us to assume that the reasons favoring each side carry a kind of weight, where weight is a measure of normative force in roughly the same way that credence is a measure of epistemic certainty.[3] It is then imagined that the weight of the reasons favoring one side can meaningfully be compared to the weight of the reasons favoring the other, and that a decision should be made for the side whose reasons carry greater weight.

Against the background of a weighing conception of reasoning like this, we can now suppose – just as a replay official is constrained to apply heightened epistemic standards in order to overrule a field official – that a court with the authority to overrule is constrained to do so only on the basis of heightened normative standards, requiring that the reasons supporting its decisions carry, not just greater weight but significantly greater weight, than the reasons supporting the other side. Indeed, this is exactly the idea behind an influential proposal by Stephen Perry, who suggests that a court

> nevertheless will not depart from a prior holding unless it is first satisfied that the collective weight of the reasons supporting the opposite result is of greater strength, to some specified degree, than the weight which would otherwise be required to reach that result on the ordinary balance of reasons. The intuitive idea is that a court is bound by a previous decision unless it is convinced that there is a *strong* reason for holding otherwise.[4]

open-textured predicates, such as "vessel" – and the function of courts is to discover, rather than construct, those answers.

[3] See the Introduction to Horty (2012) for my characterization of the weighing conception of reasoning, and the various essays in Lord and Maguire (2016) for a wide-ranging discussion of reasons and their weight.

[4] Perry (1987, p. 222). Note that Perry offers this proposal, not as an interpretation of the reasoning required for a court to overrule a previous decision, but as an interpretation, within Dworkin's overall framework, of the binding force of ordinary precedent. Although I adapt Perry's proposal to account for the reasoning of a court with the authority to overrule a precedent, rather than ordinary reasoning on the basis of precedent, Perry's own interpretation provides us with another reason for the study of soft constraints –

To provide a concrete illustration of this proposal, we return to the situation presented by Chris, the third child, who has reached the age of nine, failed to finish dinner, and asks to stay up and watch TV. Again, the question arises against the background of a previous judgment by Jo in the case of Emma, decided for the plaintiff on the grounds that – as we can now suppose, in accord with the weighing conception – having reached the age of nine carries greater weight as a reason for the plaintiff than failing to finish dinner carries as a reason for the defendant. This time, however, let us imagine that Chris's request is put, not to Jack, who is bound by Jo's decision, but to yet another member of the family – say, Grandmother – who has the authority (or thinks she does) to overrule earlier decisions by the parents. And let us imagine further that Grandmother places great value on order in the household, feels strongly that children should eat the meals prepared for them, and so assigns the following weights to the reasons at work in the case of Chris: having reached the age of nine carries a weight of 5 for the plaintiff, while failing to finish dinner carries a weight of 7 for the defendant.

According to the weighing conception of reasoning, because Grandmother assigns greater weight to the reasons favoring the defendant than to those favoring the plaintiff, it would follow under ordinary circumstances that she should decide this case for the defendant, and so deny Chris's request. Perry's proposal, however, is that, precisely because Grandmother would then be overruling a previous decision by Jo, a decision for the defendant would require reasons that carry, not just greater weight, but greater weight "to some specified degree, than the weight which would otherwise be required to reach that result on the ordinary balance of reasons." Suppose this specified degree is 3 – that, in order to overrule a previous decision, the reasons supporting the desired outcome must outweigh the opposing reasons by a degree of 3. It would then follow in this case that, although the reasons for the defendant in fact outweigh those for the plaintiff, they do so only by a degree of 2, and so fail to outweigh the opposing reasons to the degree necessary to justify Grandmother in overruling Jo's earlier decision.

This account of Perry's offers an attractive way of understanding how, in the normative domain, just as in the epistemic domain, even courts with the authority to overrule previous decisions can be constrained by those decisions – by being forced to apply heightened normative standards in order

it may offer a way of understanding the force of ordinary precedents within Dworkin's framework.

to overrule.[5] Taking Perry's account as a starting point, we now generalize it in two ways.

To motivate the first generalization, we begin by noting that the strength of the reasons supporting a particular decision can be seen, from the other side, as a measure of how wrong it would be to make the opposite decision. Perry's account, then, according to which overruling an earlier decision is allowed only when the judgment it recommends is opposed by reasons that are strong to a specified degree, or sufficiently strong, can be seen as identifying some particular property that justifies overruling an earlier case – the property of being, not just wrong, but wrong to a specified degree, or sufficiently wrong. Returning to our example, Grandmother can be understood as concluding that, although Jo's earlier decision in the case of Emma was indeed wrong, it does not satisfy the further property of being sufficiently wrong, so that overruling is not justified.

Once we accept the idea that a decision can be overruled when it satisfies the particular property of being sufficiently wrong, it is then natural to generalize by imagining that there might be other properties that could likewise justify a court in overruling a previous decision. On this more general view, then, a court could overrule an earlier decision as long as it is able to identify some special property or reason – some "special justification" – for overruling that decision, above and beyond the property of being, merely, wrong.[6] This special justification might involve, as in Perry's account, only the claim that

[5] In fact, Perry's own presentation of his proposal is, superficially at least, somewhat different. Rather than supposing that reasoning against the background of a precedent decision forces us to apply heightened normative standards in order to reach a result that violates precedent, Perry suggests instead that the background precedent forces us to assign different, and lower, weights to the reasons that would favor violating the precedent – we are to reason "*as if* the first-order reason in question had a different weight than in fact one thinks it has" (1987, p. 222). This way of presenting the proposal is, however, equivalent to that described in the text, as we can illustrate with our example of Chris and Grandmother, where Chris's age carries a weight of 5 for the plaintiff and his failure to finish dinner carries a weight of 7 for the defendant. As described in the text, Grandmother is forced to decide for the plaintiff because, although the reason favoring the defendant outweighs the reason favoring the plaintiff, it does not do so by the specified degree of 3. Perry could arrive at the same outcome by decrementing the weight assigned to reasons contrary to precedent by this same specified degree, requiring in this case that, although Chris's failure to finish dinner carries a weight of 7, Grandmother should reason "as if" its weight were actually 4 – so that, on this re-weighted analysis, the reasons for the defendant would no longer outweigh those for the plaintiff.

[6] See Schauer (2009, pp. 57–60) for discussion; for further discussion of the idea that overruling requires some special justification, see, for example, Kozel (2018).

the decision is not just wrong, but sufficiently wrong. But other justifications for overruling could be available as well. Raz illustrates the kind of reasons that might count as special justifications when, after noting that courts cannot simply overrule earlier decisions "whenever they consider that on the balance of reasons it would be better to do so," he writes:

> They may change them only for certain kinds of reasons. They may change them, for example, for being unjust, for iniquitous discrimination, for being out of step with the court's conception of the body of laws to which they belong.[7]

Other writers have argued that a court might be justified in overruling an earlier decision based, for example, on social or technological changes since the time of that decision, or on the grounds that the earlier decision failed to command acceptance either in the courts or in society at large; some originalists have suggested that a court is justified in overruling any decision that conflicts with the constitution's original meaning.[8]

Since the exact range of considerations that count as special justifications is a matter of substantive legal debate, we take no stand on the issue, but simply postulate – as our first generalization of Perry's account – that some set of properties serves this purpose, so that, if it can be established that one of these properties applies to a previous decision, the court is then justified in overruling that decision.

Turning to our second generalization, we recall that Perry's account is built on top of the weighing conception of reasoning, according to which reasons are assigned definite weights, which can be manipulated and compared using arithmetical operations. Indeed, the account depends on the weighing conception, since it relies on the idea of meaningful cardinal comparisons among the weights of reasons – that some reasons are not just stronger than others, but stronger to a specified degree. Although there may be occasions on which the assignment of definite, numerical weights to reasons makes sense (imagine, for example, that we can rescue just one to two lifeboats, the first containing twenty-five souls and the second only three), I have argued in my earlier treatment of the weighing conception that this is not always possible, and that, instead, we may often be able to speak only of a

[7] Raz (1975, p. 140); see also Raz (1979, p. 114), where the passage is repeated in a slightly different context, and pp. 189–192 of the same book, where the ideas set out in this passage are modified and expanded.

[8] See, for example, Lawson (1994) and Barnett (2005).

priority relation among reasons, not numerical weights.[9] To illustrate with our current example: Grandmother might simply prioritize failing to finish dinner as a reason for the defendant over having reached the age of nine as a reason for the plaintiff, simply judging that failing to finish dinner is the more important of the two reasons, without assigning to either of these reasons a definite numerical weight. As our second generalization, then, we separate our account from the weighing conception of reasoning.

Putting these two generalizations together, we arrive at an account of the way in which courts can be constrained by decisions they have the authority to overrule that is rooted in Perry's, but different. The account can be summed up as follows: Previous decisions provide constraints, but these constraints are soft, or defeasible, not hard. In order to overrule one of these previous decisions, a court must supply a special justification. This special justification may be, as in Perry's account, that the judgment suggested by the previous decision is sufficiently wrong, but it may be a different kind of justification entirely. Finally, once a special justification is supplied, so that the previous decision can be overruled, and the defeasible constraint derived from that decision removed from consideration, the court is then free to reason about the current situation in any natural way, and is not restricted to the weighing conception of reasoning.

Implementing this account of soft constraints within our formal theory of constrained natural reasoning is, evidently, going to be complex – but also, quite possibly, illuminating. Readers who are impatient with complexity, or skeptical of any resulting illumination, are invited to skip ahead to Section 6.3. But for readers who are more tolerant of complexity and more optimistic of illumination, a formal implementation of the account of soft constraint sketched here is now provided.

6.2.2 Implementation

In Section 6.1.1, on hard constraints, we supposed that the hard information from the default theory representing a judicial problem was to be supplemented with a set containing, for each precedent case, a statement according to which the rule of that case is assigned higher priority than the strongest applicable rule for the other side. In the present setting, these

[9] For further skepticism that assignment of numerical weights to normative reasons makes sense, even in what might seem to be clear cases, such as the lifeboat example, see Taurek (1977).

hard constraints will be replaced by soft constraints, carrying the same information, but now in the form of defaults.

To be precise, given a case $c = \langle X, r, s\rangle$, we recall from the previous section that the priority of the rule $r^{s}_{Premise(r)_i}$ of the case over the strongest applicable rule $r^{\overline{s}}_{X^{\overline{s}}_i}$ for the other side was expressed through the statement $r^{\overline{s}}_{X^{\overline{s}}_i} < r^{s}_{Premise(r)_i}$, and then encoded in the language of our theory through the formula $n^{\overline{s}}_{X^{\overline{s}}_i} \prec n^{s}_{Premise(r)_i}$, with the constants $n^{\overline{s}}_{X^{\overline{s}}_i}$ and $n^{s}_{Premise(r)_i}$ designating the corresponding rules, and with $\prec$ representing the priority relation among rules. In order to convey the same information in a softer way, rather than including this formula along with the hard information of the underlying theory, and so taking it as a hard constraint, we place it in the conclusion of a *case default* derived from the case $c = \langle X, r, s\rangle$, and having the form

$$n(c) \rightarrow n^{\overline{s}}_{X^{\overline{s}}_i} \prec n^{s}_{Premise(r)_i}.$$

The premise $n(c)$ of this default should be thought of as a statement of our language expressing the proposition that the case c was decided as it was – that the situation X was decided for the side s on the basis of the rule r. What the case default tells us, then, is that the decision reached in the case c provides a reason for the conclusion $n^{\overline{s}}_{X^{\overline{s}}_i} \prec n^{s}_{Premise(r)_i}$, or for prioritizing the rule $r^{s}_{Premise(r)_i}$ over the rule $r^{\overline{s}}_{X^{\overline{s}}_i}$. As with factor defaults and value defaults, case defaults can be referred to through structural descriptors: the case default displayed above will be referred to through the descriptor r^{s}_{c}, whose superscript s is the winning side of the case from which the default is derived, and whose subscript c indicates that case itself; extending our notational conventions once more, this case default can be designated in our language with the term n^{s}_{c}.

Just as we had previously collected the hard constraints derived from the case base Γ into the set $\mathcal{H}_\Gamma$, we can now collect the case defaults expressing soft constraints derived from that case base into the set

$$\mathcal{S}_\Gamma = \{r^{s}_{c} : c = \langle X, r, s\rangle \text{ and } c \in \Gamma\}.$$

Since case defaults will have, as their premises, statements describing the precedent cases from Γ, when it comes time to construct the default theory representing a problem with soft constraints, these statements will have to be contained in that theory; more exactly, the hard information from such a theory will now include the set

$$n(\Gamma) = \{n(c) \ : \ c \in \Gamma\}$$

of statements asserting simply that the cases from Γ were decided as they were, and so guaranteeing that the case defaults from $\mathcal{S}_\Gamma$ will be applicable.

To illustrate these various concepts, we begin by returning to $c_4 = \langle X_4, r_4, s_4 \rangle$, representing Jo's decision in the situation presented by Emma, where $X_4 = \{f_1^\pi, f_2^\pi, f_1^\delta\}$, where $r_4 = \{f_1^\pi\} \rightarrow \pi$, and where $s_4 = \pi$. As usual, f_1^π and f_2^π represent the respective propositions that the child in question has reached the age of nine and has completed chores, and f_1^δ represents the proposition that the child failed to finish dinner, so that, this case is one in which Jo decided for the plaintiff, Emma, on the grounds that she has reached the age of nine. Here, the rule r_4 of the case can be represented through the structural descriptor r_1^π, and the strongest applicable rule for the other side – that is, $\{f_1^\delta\} \rightarrow \delta$ – through the structural descriptor r_1^δ; these two rules are then designated in our language with the terms n_1^π and n_1^δ. The case default derived from this case is therefore

$$r_{c_4}^\pi = n(c_4) \rightarrow n_1^\delta \prec n_1^\pi.$$

According to this default, the decision reached in the case c_4 provides a reason for the conclusion $n_1^\delta \prec n_1^\pi$ – that is, for the conclusion that the factor default r_1^π is to be prioritized over the factor default r_1^δ, or that having reached the age to nine as a reason for the plaintiff is to be prioritized over failing to finish dinner as a reason for the defendant.

Continuing our illustration by turning to the familiar case base $\Gamma_4 = \{c_4\}$, we now have

$$\mathcal{S}_{\Gamma_4} = \{r_{c_4}^\pi\}$$

as the set of soft constraints derived from this case base. And as we have seen, any default theory representing a problem with soft constraints derived from Γ_4 would have to include the single statement belonging to

$$n(\Gamma_4) = \{n(c_4)\}$$

in its hard information, so that the default $r_{c_4}^\pi$ from $\mathcal{S}_{\Gamma_4}$ will be applicable.

Like value defaults, case defaults can be thought of as second-order default rules. Just as value defaults provide reasons, based on a court's values, for prioritizing certain first-order factor defaults over others, case defaults also provide reasons for prioritizing certain first-order factor defaults over others, but this time the reasons are based on precedent decisions. Of course, the priorities recommended by case defaults can conflict with those recommended by value defaults. Consider, once again, Jack, whose values are represented by the set $\mathcal{V}_{Jack}$ containing the two value defaults

$$r^{\delta}_{1\backslash 1} = \top \rightarrow n^{\pi}_{1} \prec n^{\delta}_{1},$$

$$r^{\delta}_{1,2\backslash 2} = \top \rightarrow n^{\pi}_{1,2} \prec n^{\delta}_{2};$$

and suppose that Jack is now working against the background of soft constraints derived from the case base Γ_4, containing the decision c_4, so that the case default r^{π}_{c4} is applicable as well. Then according to $r^{\delta}_{1\backslash 1}$, the first of Jack's value defaults, the factor default r^{δ}_{1} is to be prioritized over the factor default r^{π}_{1} – failing to finish dinner as a reason for the defendant is to be prioritized over having reached the age to nine as a reason for the plaintiff. But according to the case default r^{π}_{c4}, as we have just seen, r^{π}_{1} is to be prioritized over r^{δ}_{1} – having reached the age to nine as a reason for the plaintiff is to be prioritized over failing to finish dinner as a reason for the defendant. Suppose, then, that Jack is faced with a situation in which both of the conflicting factor defaults r^{π}_{1} and r^{δ}_{1} are applicable. Which should he apply?

The answer is that a court reasoning under the constraints of precedent, even soft constraints, is generally required – at least by default – to prioritize rulings of precedent decisions over its own values, and so to prioritize case defaults over value defaults. How do we capture this idea? As we have seen, where $c = \langle X, r, s \rangle$ is a precedent decision, the case default r^{s}_{c} is a second-order rule according to which, by default, the rule of that case, favoring the side s, should be prioritized over the strongest rule favoring $\bar{s}$, the other side, that holds in the fact situation of that case. And suppose that $r^{\bar{s}}_{U_i \backslash V_i}$ is a value default according to which the factor default $r^{\bar{s}}_{V_i}$ favoring the side $\bar{s}$ is prioritized over the factor default $r^{s}_{U_i}$ favoring the other side. With these case and value defaults designated in the language through the terms n^{s}_{c} and $n^{\bar{s}}_{U_i \backslash V_i}$, a *precedent default* can now be defined as a rule of the form

$$\top \rightarrow n^{\bar{s}}_{U_i \backslash V_i} \prec n^{s}_{c},$$

according to which the statement $n^{\bar{s}}_{U_i \backslash V_i} \prec n^{s}_{c}$ holds by default, so that, as a default, the case default r^{s}_{c} is prioritized over the value default $r^{\bar{s}}_{U_i \backslash V_i}$.

Like factor, value, and case defaults, precedent defaults can be referred to with structural descriptors: the precedent default displayed above will be referred to through the descriptor $r^{s}_{(U_i \backslash V_i) \backslash c}$, whose superscript s matches the winning side of the case default r^{s}_{c} to which the precedent default assigns higher priority, and whose subscript $(U_i \backslash V_i)\backslash c$ is composed of the subscript $U_i \backslash V_i$ of the value default $r^{\bar{s}}_{U_i \backslash V_i}$ to which the precedent default assigns lower priority, followed by the case c from which the higher priority case default is derived; continuing to extend our convention, this precedent default can be designated within our language as $n^{s}_{(U_i \backslash V_i)\backslash c}$.

If factor defaults are first-order rules and both value defaults and case defaults are second-order rules, telling us that certain first-order rules are to be prioritized over others, then precedent defaults can be thought of as *third-order* rules, telling us that certain second-order rules are to be prioritized over others.[10] What the rule $r^{s}_{(U_i \backslash V_i)\backslash c}$ tells us is that the prioritization on first-order factor defaults supported by the second-order case default r^{s}_{c} is itself to be prioritized over the prioritization on first-order factor defaults supported by the second-order value default $r^{\bar{s}}_{U_i \backslash V_i}$.

Returning to our example, since Jack is subject to soft constraints derived from the case base Γ_4, we now suppose that his reasoning is guided by the precedent default

$$r^{\pi}_{(1\backslash 1)\backslash c4} = \top \rightarrow n^{\delta}_{1\backslash 1} \prec n^{\pi}_{c4},$$

supporting the conclusion $n^{\delta}_{1\backslash 1} \prec n^{\pi}_{c4}$, according to which the prioritization of the first-order factor default r^{π}_{1} over the first-order factor default r^{δ}_{1} that is supported by the second-order case default r^{π}_{c4} is itself to be prioritized over the prioritization of r^{δ}_{1} over r^{π}_{1} that is supported by the second-order value default $r^{\delta}_{1\backslash 1}$, or by Jack's own values. If Jack is presented, then, with a situation in which both of the conflicting factor defaults r^{π}_{1} and r^{δ}_{1} are applicable, it follows that what he should do – at least by default – is this: in accord with the precedent default $r^{\pi}_{(1\backslash 1)\backslash c4}$, he should accept the prioritization of the case default r^{π}_{c4} over his own value default $r^{\delta}_{1\backslash 1}$, and then, in accord with the case default r^{π}_{c4}, accept the prioritization of the factor default r^{π}_{1} over the factor default r^{δ}_{1}, and then, in accord with the factor default r^{π}_{1}, decide for the plaintiff.

Of course, the particular rule $r^{\pi}_{(1\backslash 1)\backslash c4}$ is just one of the precedent defaults guiding Jack's reasoning, telling us that the particular case default r^{π}_{c4} is to be prioritized over the particular value default $r^{\delta}_{1\backslash 1}$. More generally, we require that any case default favoring one side is to be prioritized over any value

[10] Perry (1987, p. 224), by contrast, describes precedent as a second-order rule, telling the court how to reason with first-order rules – in particular, as we have seen, that it should reason as if the weight carried by reasons supporting the side contrary to precedent were lower than it actually is.

default favoring the other side; this is accomplished by defining, given a set $\mathcal{V}$ of values and a case base Γ, the entire set

$$\mathcal{P}_{\mathcal{V},\Gamma} = \{r^{s}_{(U_i\backslash V_i)\backslash c} : r^{\bar{s}}_{U_i\backslash V_i} \in \mathcal{V} \text{ and } r^{s}_{c} \in \mathcal{S}_{\Gamma}\}$$

of precedent defaults derived from $\mathcal{V}$ and Γ, containing separate precedent defaults according to which each case default r^{s}_{c} derived from a case c from Γ favoring the side s is, by default, prioritized over each value default $r^{\bar{s}}_{U_i\backslash V_i}$ belonging to $\mathcal{V}$ favoring the side $\bar{s}$. For illustration, we turn again to Jack, working against the background of the case base $\Gamma_4 = \{c_4\}$ containing only a single case, but whose set of values $\mathcal{V}_{Jack} = \{r^{\delta}_{1\backslash 1}, r^{\delta}_{1,2\backslash 2}\}$ contains the two value defaults displayed above. The set of precedent defaults derived from $\mathcal{V}_{Jack}$ and Γ_4 is therefore

$$\mathcal{P}_{\mathcal{V}_{Jack},\Gamma_4} = \{r^{\pi}_{(1\backslash 1)\backslash c_4}, r^{\pi}_{(1,2\backslash 2)\backslash c_4}\}$$

containing, in addition to the rule $r^{\pi}_{(1\backslash 1)\backslash c_4}$ considered above and prioritizing the case default $r^{\pi}_{c_4}$ over the value default $r^{\delta}_{1\backslash 1}$, also the precedent default

$$r^{\pi}_{(1,2\backslash 2)\backslash c_4} = \top \to n^{\delta}_{1,2\backslash 2} \prec n^{\pi}_{c_4}$$

prioritizing the case default $r^{\pi}_{c_4}$ over the value default $r^{\delta}_{1,2\backslash 2}$.

Having introduced both case defaults and precedent defaults, we are nearly ready to define the problem presented to a court with the authority to overrule previous decisions, but not quite. Our informal account of soft constraints, recall, is based on the idea that overruling a precedent case requires some special justification – or as we have interpreted the idea, that overruling requires that the case must satisfy a particular predicate representing one of these special justifications. Let us therefore suppose our language contains a set

$$\mathcal{Q} = \{Q_1, Q_2, \ldots, Q_n\}$$

of such predicates. Where Q is one of these predicates and c is a case, the fact that the case c satisfies the predicate Q might be taken to mean, for example, that c is not just wrong but sufficiently wrong, or, as in Raz's view, that c violates fundamental principles of justice, that c involves iniquitous discrimination, or that c is out of step with the body of laws to which it belongs – or perhaps, continuing with the list of candidate special justifications mentioned earlier, that c has been rendered obsolete by social or technological change, that c has failed to command wide acceptance, or even that c conflicts with the original meaning of the constitution. Again, since identification of the considerations that might justify overruling a precedent decision is a matter of substantive legal debate, we take no stand on the issue but simply postulate some set of predicates representing these special justifications.

Suppose that a case c satisfies one of these special justification predicates Q – that is, suppose $Q(c)$. Then how, within our formal account, can this fact allow a court to evade the precedential constraints deriving from this case? There are a number of ways to achieve this result, but we choose one that is particularly simple, and that echoes the view explored earlier, in Section 4.2.1, that an overruled case is "wiped off the slate," or removed "root and branch." Considering the case $c = \langle X, r, s\rangle$, then, let us ask: what would it mean to overrule the case c in this sense – to wipe it from the slate, or remove it root and branch? Well, two things. First, we would have to take the case default r^s_c derived from the case itself out of consideration; recalling our treatment of exclusion from Section 5.2.2, this can be accomplished by introducing the statement

$$Out(n^s_c),$$

according to which this case default is excluded. Second, we would also have to remove from consideration each precedent default that happens to prioritize the case default r^s_c over some value default supporting the opposite side; this can be accomplished by introducing the statement

$$\bigwedge\{Out(n^s_{(U_i\backslash V_i)\backslash c}) : r^{\bar{s}}_{U_i\backslash V_i} \in \mathcal{V}\}$$

conjoining together the entire collection of statements of the form $Out(n^s_{(U_i\backslash V_i)\backslash c})$ and so excluding each precedent default $r^s_{(U_i\backslash V_i)\backslash c}$ that prioritizes the case default r^s_c over some value default $r^{\bar{s}}_{U_i\backslash V_i}$ favoring the other side.

We can now define default rules that introduce both of these statements, thus removing a case root and branch, once it is established that there is a special justification for overruling that case. Formally, where $c = \langle X, r, s\rangle$ is a case and Q is a special justification predicate whose satisfaction justifies overruling, we define a *special justification default* as a rule of the form

$$Q(c) \rightarrow Out(n^s_c) \wedge \bigwedge\{Out(n^s_{(U_i\backslash V_i)\backslash c}) : r^{\bar{s}}_{U_i\backslash V_i} \in \mathcal{V}\}$$

according to which the fact that $Q(c)$ provides a reason for excluding the case default r^s_c that carries the soft constraint derived from c, as well as all precedent defaults of the form $r^s_{(U_i\backslash V_i)\backslash c}$ that prioritize the case default r^s_c over opposing value defaults from the set $\mathcal{V}$ of values. These special justification defaults can be thought of as *fourth-order* rules, telling us that certain third-order precedent defaults, as well as second-order case defaults, must be taken out of consideration.

If we fix the set $\mathcal{V}$ of values in question as those of the court to which a judicial problem is presented, the special justification displayed above can be referred to through the structural descriptor $r_{c\backslash Q}$ whose subscript $c\backslash Q$ contains the case being overruled followed by the special justification for overruling it. The entire set of special justification defaults can then be collected together as

$$\mathcal{J}_{\Gamma,\mathcal{Q}} = \{r_{c\backslash Q} : c \in \Gamma \text{ and } Q \in \mathcal{Q}\},$$

containing rules that tell us, for each case c from a background case base Γ and for each predicate Q from the set $\mathcal{Q}$ of special justifications, if it can be established that that case satisfies such a special justification predicate, that the court then has a reason for excluding all defaults bearing on that case from consideration – in other words, for overruling the case.

For a concrete illustration, we now consider, not Jack, but Grandmother – since we have assumed that Grandmother, unlike Jack, has the authority to overrule previous decisions. To keep things simple, we will suppose that the set $\mathcal{V}_{Gmother}$ of defaults representing Grandmother's values contains only the single value default

$$r^{\delta}_{1\backslash 1} = \top \rightarrow n^{\pi}_{1} \prec n^{\delta}_{1};$$

Grandmother's sole concern, then, is that r^{δ}_{1} should be prioritized over r^{π}_{1}, or that failing to finish dinner as a reason for the defendant should be prioritized over having reached the age to nine as a reason for the plaintiff. And we will suppose that Grandmother, with her values, is also working against soft constraints derived from the background case base $\Gamma_4 = \{c_4\}$. Like Jack, then, she is subject to the single case default from the set

$$\mathcal{S}_{\Gamma_4} = \{r^{\pi}_{c_4}\}$$

and then to the set

$$\mathcal{P}_{\mathcal{V}_{Gmother},\Gamma_4} = \{r^{\pi}_{(1\backslash 1)\backslash c_4}\}$$

of precedent defaults, prioritizing this case default, by default, over her own value default.

Since Grandmother has the authority to overrule previous decisions, however, the special justification predicates that might support a decision to overrule are also relevant to her situation. Let us imagine that these predicates are those contained in the set $\mathcal{Q} = \{Q_1, Q_2\}$, where we might as well suppose that $Q_1(c)$ means that the case c is out of step with the body of decisions to which it belongs, and that $Q_2(c)$ means that c has failed to command wide acceptance. Then, following our recipe, the special justification defaults bearing on Grandmother's situation are those belonging to the set

$$\mathcal{J}_{\Gamma_4,\mathcal{Q}} = \{r_{c_4\backslash Q_1}, r_{c_4\backslash Q_2}\},$$

where

$$\begin{aligned} r_{c_4\backslash Q_1} &= Q_1(c_4) \rightarrow Out(n^{\pi}_{c_4}) \wedge Out(n^{\pi}_{(1\backslash 1)\backslash c_4}), \\ r_{c_4\backslash Q_2} &= Q_2(c_4) \rightarrow Out(n^{\pi}_{c_4}) \wedge Out(n^{\pi}_{(1\backslash 1)\backslash c_4}). \end{aligned}$$

What these defaults tell us is that, if it can be established that the decision c_4 satisfies one of the special justification predicates – if it is out of step with other decisions, or has failed to command wide acceptance – then this provides a reason for Grandmother to overrule that decision, in the sense that, in her deliberations, she can exclude from consideration both the derived case default $r^{\pi}_{c_4}$ and the precedent default $r^{\pi}_{(1\backslash 1)\backslash c_4}$ that might have prioritized this case default over her own values.

We are now, at last, in a position to define a problem presented by a fact situation to a court with a specified set of values, under soft constraints derived from a background case base, with precedential constraints according to which constraints derived from the case base are prioritized over the court's own values but also with a set of special justifications on the basis of which earlier decisions can be overruled:

Definition 38 (Problem presented to court under soft constraints) Let X be a fact situation, $\mathcal{V}$ a set of value defaults, Γ a case base, and $\mathcal{Q}$ a set of special justifications recognized as sufficient to allow overruling of previous decisions. Then a problem presented by the fact situation X to a court with values $\mathcal{V}$, under soft constraints $\mathcal{S}_\Gamma$ derived from Γ, with precedent defaults $\mathcal{P}_{\mathcal{V},\Gamma}$ prioritizing previous decisions over the court's own values but also with special justification defaults $\mathcal{J}_{\Gamma,\mathcal{Q}}$ allowing the court to overrule earlier decisions, is a variable priority exclusionary default theory $\Delta_{X,\mathcal{V},\Gamma,\mathcal{S}_\Gamma,\mathcal{P}_{\mathcal{V},\Gamma},\mathcal{J}_{\Gamma,\mathcal{Q}}} = \langle \mathcal{W}_{X,\Gamma}, \mathcal{D}_{\mathcal{V},\mathcal{S}_\Gamma,\mathcal{P}_{\mathcal{V},\Gamma},\mathcal{J}_{\Gamma,\mathcal{Q}}}\rangle$ where

$$\begin{aligned} \mathcal{W}_{X,\Gamma} &\text{ includes } X \cup n(\Gamma) \cup \mathcal{O}, \\ \mathcal{D}_{\mathcal{V},\mathcal{S}_\Gamma,\mathcal{P}_{\mathcal{V},\Gamma},\mathcal{J}_{\Gamma,\mathcal{Q}}} &\text{ includes } \mathcal{F} \cup \mathcal{V} \cup \mathcal{S}_\Gamma \cup \mathcal{P}_{\mathcal{V},\Gamma} \cup \mathcal{J}_{\Gamma,\mathcal{Q}}. \end{aligned}$$

Note that, in contrast to the problems previously defined in Definitions 36 and 37, in the absence of any constraints at all or under hard constraints, the default theories representing a problem under soft constraints are not specified exactly but only in terms of what information they include. The reason for this is that the court must be able to conclude, or fail to conclude, that a special justification predicate applies to a background decision; we need to allow that the reasoning involved – which could be complex, and which we do not consider here – may draw on sources of information other than those explicitly listed.

As usual, where the theory $\Delta_{X,\mathcal{V},\Gamma,\mathcal{S}_\Gamma,\mathcal{P}_{\mathcal{V},\Gamma},\mathcal{J}_{\Gamma,\mathcal{Q}}}$ represents a problem of this kind, we will define a *solution to the problem* as a proper scenario allowed by the theory.

This concept of a problem presented to a court under soft constraints can be illustrated with two examples. Imagine, first, that the situation $X_6 = \{f_1^\pi, f_1^\delta\}$ is presented by Chris to Grandmother, with her set $\mathcal{V}_{Gmother} = \{r_{1\backslash 1}^\delta\}$ of values, against the background of the case base $\Gamma_4 = \{c_4\}$, and with $\mathcal{Q} = \{Q_1, Q_2\}$ as special justifications. This problem can be represented through the default theory

$$\Delta_{X_6,\mathcal{V}_{Gmother},\Gamma_4,\mathcal{S}_{\Gamma_4},\mathcal{P}_{\mathcal{V}_{Gmother},\Gamma_4},\mathcal{J}_{\Gamma_4,\mathcal{Q}}} = \langle \mathcal{W}_{X_6,\Gamma_4}, \mathcal{D}_{\mathcal{V}_{Gmother},\mathcal{S}_{\Gamma_4},\mathcal{P}_{\mathcal{V}_{Gmother},\Gamma_4},\mathcal{J}_{\Gamma_4,\mathcal{Q}}}\rangle$$

where

$$\begin{aligned}
\mathcal{W}_{X_6,\Gamma_4} &= X_6 \cup n(\Gamma_4) \cup \mathcal{O} \\
&= \{f_1^\pi, f_1^\delta\} \cup \{n(c_4)\} \cup \mathcal{O}, \\
\mathcal{D}_{\mathcal{V}_{Gmother},\mathcal{S}_{\Gamma_4},\mathcal{P}_{\mathcal{V}_{Gmother},\Gamma_4},\mathcal{J}_{\Gamma_4,\mathcal{Q}}} &= \mathcal{F} \cup \mathcal{V}_{Gmother} \cup \mathcal{S}_{\Gamma_4} \cup \mathcal{P}_{\mathcal{V}_{Gmother},\Gamma_4} \cup \mathcal{J}_{\Gamma_4,\mathcal{Q}} \\
&= \mathcal{F} \cup \{r_{1\backslash 1}^\delta\} \cup \{r_{c_4}^\pi\} \cup \{r_{(1\backslash 1)\backslash c_4}^\pi\} \cup \{r_{c_4\backslash Q_1}, r_{c_4\backslash Q_2}\}.
\end{aligned}$$

The hard information $\mathcal{W}_{X_6,\Gamma_4}$ from this theory includes the set X_6 describing the situation presented by Chris, the set $n(\Gamma_4)$ characterizing the background case base, and the set $\mathcal{O}$ of structural conditions. The set $\mathcal{D}_{\mathcal{V}_{Gmother},\mathcal{S}_{\Gamma_4},\mathcal{P}_{\mathcal{V}_{Gmother},\Gamma_4},\mathcal{J}_{\Gamma_4,\mathcal{Q}}}$ of defaults includes the set of factor defaults from $\mathcal{F}$ that are applicable in the situation, the set $\mathcal{V}_{Gmother}$ of Grandmother's value defaults, the set $\mathcal{S}_{\Gamma_4}$ of case defaults representing soft constraints derived from the background case base Γ_4, the set $\mathcal{P}_{\mathcal{V}_{Gmother},\Gamma_4}$ of precedent defaults prioritizing the soft constraints derived from this case base over Grandmother's value defaults, and finally, the set $\mathcal{J}_{\Gamma_4,\mathcal{Q}}$ of special justification defaults, enabling Grandmother to exclude the constraints deriving from a background case from Γ_4 whenever that case satisfies one of the special justification predicates belonging to $\mathcal{Q}$. This theory is depicted in the inference graph from Figure 6.2.

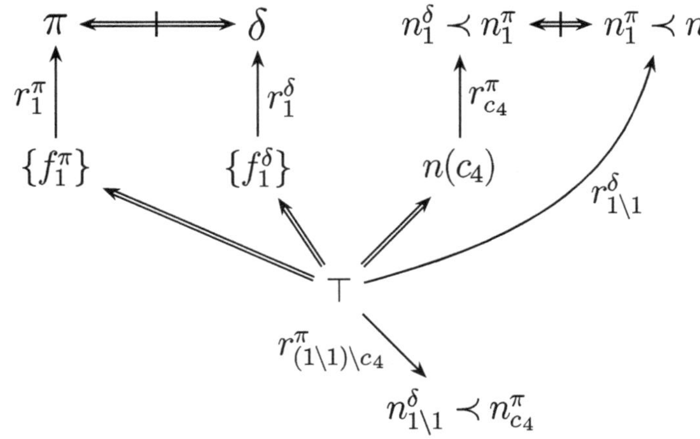

Figure 6.2 Chris and Grandmother, with soft constraints

The theory $\Delta_{X_6, \mathcal{V}_{Gmother}, \Gamma_4, \mathcal{S}_{\Gamma_4}, \mathcal{P}_{\mathcal{V}_{Gmother}, \Gamma_4}, \mathcal{J}_{\Gamma_4}, \mathcal{Q}}$ allows as its unique solution the proper scenario

$$\mathcal{S}_{24} = \{r_1^\pi, r_{c_4}^\pi, r_{(1\backslash 1)\backslash c_4}^\pi\},$$

generating the extension

$$\mathcal{E}_{24} = Closure(\mathcal{W}_{X_6, \Gamma_4} \cup \{\pi, n_1^\delta \prec n_1^\pi, n_{1\backslash 1}^\delta \prec n_{c_4}^\pi\}).$$

According to this solution, what Grandmother ought to do is this: in accord with the precedent default $r_{(1\backslash 1)\backslash c_4}^\pi$, she should accept the prioritization recommended by the case default $r_{c_4}^\pi$ over that recommended by her own value default $r_{1\backslash 1}^\delta$, and then, in accord with the case default $r_{c_4}^\pi$, accept the prioritization of the factor default r_1^π over the factor default r_1^δ, and then, in accord with the factor default r_1^π, decide for the plaintiff. Note that, in this example, Grandmother is led by constraints deriving from the previous case c_4, Jo's decision concerning Emma, to decide for the plaintiff, even though this decision runs contrary to her own values, and even though she has the authority to overrule the case; the reason for this is that she is unable to establish any special justification for overruling the previous case – the theory does not support either $\mathcal{Q}_1(c_4)$ or $\mathcal{Q}_2(c_4)$.

Suppose, however, that Grandmother is able to conclude that there is some special justification for overruling Jo's previous decision – suppose, for example, she concludes that this decision is out of step with the body of decisions to which it belongs, or that $\mathcal{Q}_1(c_4)$. Since we are not considering the complex reasoning that might lead Grandmother to this conclusion, we will simply include this statement along with the hard information representing

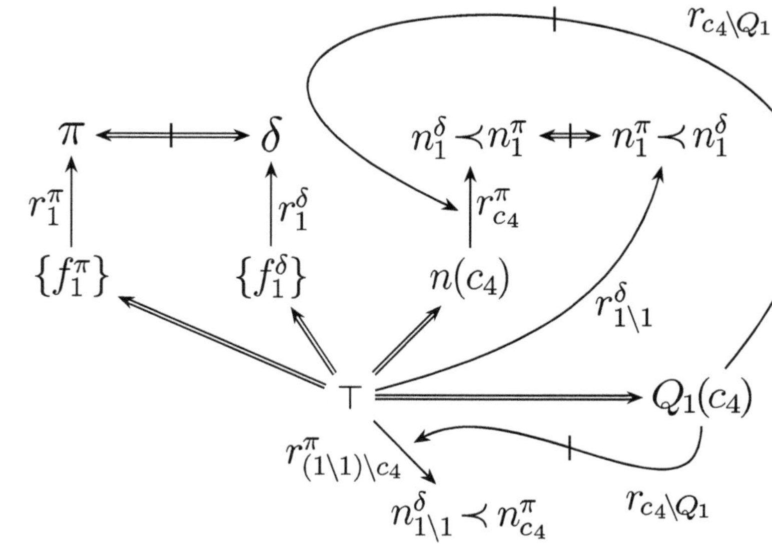

Figure 6.3 Chris and Grandmother, with soft constraints and a special justification

the problem presented by the situation. This leads us, as our second example, to the theory

$$\Delta'_{X_6,\mathcal{V}_{Gmother},\mathcal{S}_{\Gamma_4},\mathcal{P}_{\mathcal{V}_{Gmother},\Gamma_4},\mathcal{J}_{\Gamma_4,\mathcal{Q}}} = \langle \mathcal{W}'_{X_6,\Gamma_4}, \mathcal{D}_{\mathcal{V}_{Gmother}}, \mathcal{S}_{\Gamma_4}, \mathcal{P}_{\mathcal{V}_{Gmother},\Gamma_4}, \mathcal{J}_{\Gamma_4,\mathcal{Q}} \rangle,$$

exactly like the theory just considered, with the very same set of defaults, but in which the hard information

$$\mathcal{W}'_{X_6,\Gamma_4} = X_6 \cup n(\Gamma_4) \cup \mathcal{O} \cup \{Q_1(c_4)\}$$

now contains, in addition to the facts of the situation, a description of the background case base, and the standard structural conditions, also the statement $Q_1(c_4)$. This new theory is depicted in the inference graph from Figure 6.3, exactly like the graph from Figure 6.2, except that the diagram now depicts the special justification default $r_{c_4\backslash Q_1}$ along a strict link indicating that the statement $Q_1(c_4)$, which forms the premise of this default, follows from the hard information contained in the theory.[11]

[11] Since neither $Q_1(c_4)$ nor $Q_2(c_4)$ could be established in the previous theory, and in order to reduce diagrammatic clutter, the links representing the corresponding special justification default $r_{c_4\backslash Q_1}$ and $r_{c_4\backslash Q_2}$ are not depicted in Figure 6.2; likewise, the link representing $r_{c_4\backslash Q_2}$ is not depicted in Figure 6.3, since the special justification $Q_2(c_4)$ cannot be established in the current theory.

The new theory $\Delta'_{X_6, \mathcal{V}_{Gmother}, \Gamma_4, \mathcal{S}_{\Gamma_4}, \mathcal{P}_{\mathcal{V}_{Gmother}, \Gamma_4}, \mathcal{J}_{\Gamma_4}, \mathcal{Q}}$ now allows as its unique solution the proper scenario

$$\mathcal{S}_{25} = \{r^{\delta}_{1}, r^{\delta}_{1\backslash 1}, r_{c4\backslash Q_1}\},$$

generating the extension

$$\mathcal{E}_{25} = Closure(\mathcal{W}_{X_6, \Gamma_4} \cup \{\delta, n^{\pi}_{1} \prec n^{\delta}_{1}, Out(n^{\pi}_{c4}), Out(n^{\pi}_{(1\backslash 1)\backslash c4})\}).$$

According to this new solution, and based on her conclusion $Q_1(c_4)$, or that the decision reached in the previous case c_4 was out of step with the body of decisions to which it belongs, Grandmother now accepts the special justification default $r_{c4\backslash Q_1}$, which excludes both the case default r^{π}_{c4} and the precedent default $r^{\pi}_{(1\backslash 1)\backslash c4}$ that might have prioritized this case default over her own value default; she is therefore free to reason about the case on the basis of her own value default $r^{\delta}_{1\backslash 1}$, according to which the factor default r^{δ}_{1} is to be prioritized over the factor default r^{π}_{1}, and then, in accord with the factor default r^{δ}_{1}, to decide the case for the defendant.

Although the formalization sketched here is complex, we must remember that the process of natural reasoning with soft constraints is itself complex, so that it would be surprising if a formal treatment were simple. A high-level summary may be helpful: First, then, a situation typically supports various, and conflicting, factor defaults – first-order rules according to which the factors reasons that hold in that situation favor one side or the other. A particular court's values are then represented by value defaults, second-order rules which provide reasons for prioritizing some factor defaults over others. A court deciding a case entirely on the basis of its own values, represented by its own set of value defaults, is engaging in purely natural reasoning. Next, looking beyond a particular court's own values, there are also other reasons for prioritizing factor defaults. Precedent cases likewise provide reasons for favoring certain factor reasons over others. These reasons are represented here by case defaults, which, like value defaults, are also second-order rules recommending prioritizations among first-order factor defaults. Of course, the prioritization recommended by a case default might conflict with that derived from a court's own values – the court might disagree with the decisions reached in some previous case. In the modern common law, however, the doctrine of precedent then functions as a reason for favoring those reasons derived from the precedent case over those reasons derived from the court's own values. This doctrine is represented here as a collection of third-order default rules, which provide the court with reasons for prioritizing the prioritization recommended by case defaults over the prioritization recommended by its own value defaults. Finally, our account of soft constraints allows that cases satisfying certain properties – special justification predicates – can be overruled. This possibility is captured by fourth-order special justification defaults, according to which, if a case satisfies such a property, that fact provides a reason for removing from consideration both the case default derived from that case and also any precedent default prioritizing that case default over a conflicting value default.

6.3 Open Texture: Waismann

6.3.1 Evidences

We now return to the topic of open-textured predicates considered earlier, in Section 1.3, but using the tools developed in our treatment of constrained natural reasoning. The concept of open texture is generally associated, particularly among legal philosophers, with the work of Hart, which formed the focus of our previous discussion. In fact, though, the concept had already been introduced in an earlier article by Friedrich Waismann, setting out an objection to the verification theory of meaning for empirical statements.[12] Although the verification theory never had a single canonical formulation, and its competing formulations were subject to numerous refinements, the central idea is clear enough: For a statement to be meaningful, it has to be analyzable in terms of statements that are closely connected to experience, and so verifiable, or privileged in some other way. Waismann illustrates this idea with a hypothetical analysis according to which the statement that some object a is a cat can be analyzed in terms of the statements that it looks like a cat, feels furry, and purrs – leading to a definition along the following lines, in which the defining statement on the right is supposed to be, if not actually experiential, then at least closer to experience than the defined statement on the left:

$$Cat(a) =_{df} LooksLikeCat(a) \wedge FeelsFurry(a) \wedge Purrs(a).$$

During the middle of the previous century, the verification theory of meaning was subject to intense discussion, as well as intense criticism.[13]

[12] Waismann (1945).

[13] Nelson (1954) begins with the statement, "During the last two decades probably no other one topic in philosophy has received more consideration than has the verification theory of meaning" (p. 182).

Much of this criticism centered around expressive limitations of the more experiential language in terms of which empirical statements were supposed to be analyzed, focusing in particular on the question whether the meaning of empirical statements could actually be reconstructed in a restricted language of this kind. The problem raised by Waismann, however, is different, and more fundamental. He does not argue that empirical statements cannot be analyzed within some more experiential language because of its expressive limitations. Instead, he argues that empirical statements cannot be analyzed at all – the idea of definitional analysis of empirical statements is itself mistaken, Waismann maintains, due to the open-textured nature of empirical predicates.

What is open texture? The characterization offered here relies on two assumptions. The first, which is implicit in Waismann's article, is that the application of an empirical predicate to an object is justified, or not, on the basis of some description of that object. This assumption, although worth drawing out explicitly, is supposed to be routine: if asked to justify the statement that some object is a cat, for example, a speaker might point out that it looks like a cat, that it is furry like a cat, and that it purrs.

The second assumption – an idea Waismann describes as the "*essential incompleteness* of an empirical description" – is more crucial. He illustrates the idea by imagining how he might try to characterize a familiar object:

> If I had to describe [my] right hand . . . I may say different things of it: I may state its size, its shape, its color, its tissue, the chemical compound of its bones, its cells, and perhaps add some more particulars; but however far I go, I shall never reach a point where my description will be completed: logically speaking, it is always possible to extend the description by adding some detail or other. Every description stretches, as it were, into a horizon of open possibilities: however far I go, I shall always carry this horizon with me.[14]

By contrast, as Waismann explains, a triangle can be described completely, by specifying the length of its three sides; once such a description is provided, "nothing can be added to it that is not included in, or at variance with, the data." Likewise, a melody can be described completely, using musical notation (setting aside, he says, matters of interpretation), and a game of chess can be described completely as a sequence of moves.

[14] Waismann (1945, p. 4).

Waismann's second assumption, then, is simply that empirical objects are not like this. They cannot be described completely – no matter how complete a description may seem, something further can always be added, and something, moreover, that might affect the application of an empirical predicate to that object:

> Such cases serve merely to set off the nature of an empirical description by the contrast: there is no such thing as completeness in the case in which I describe my right hand, or the character of a person; I can never exhaust all the details nor foresee all possible circumstances which would make me modify or retract my statement.[15]

On the basis of these assumptions, we can now explicate Waismann's concept of an open-textured predicate in this way: the predicate P is *open-textured* just in case, given any description of an object a on the basis of which we can reasonably apply P to a, it is always possible consistently to extend this description in such a way that it is no longer reasonable to apply P to a.[16] And this explication allows us to see exactly why Waismann would think of empirical predicates as uniformly open textured – because, given his assumption of essential incompleteness of empirical description, it follows that any characterization of some object on the basis of which an empirical predicate would be reasonably applied to that object can be extended in such a way that that predicate would be reasonably withdrawn.

This point can be illustrated by returning to Waismann's original example, which he sets out to show why the phenomenon of open texture should lead us to reject the analysis, or definition, of a cat as an object that looks like a cat, is furry, and purrs – or indeed, any such definition. As Waismann argues, any description of some object that satisfies this definition, leading us to conclude that the object is a cat, could then, in accord with the essential incompleteness of empirical description, be supplemented with

[15] Ibid.

[16] Shapiro and Roberts (2019a) offer a different explication: "P exhibits *open texture* if it is possible for there to be an object a such that nothing concerning the established use of P, and nothing concerning the non-linguistics facts, determines that P holds of a, nor does anything determine that P fails to hold of a" (p. 190). I believe this explication and that presented in the text are largely equivalent. Both emphasize the idea that no collection of facts can guarantee the applicability of P to a, though Shapiro and Roberts focus on the entire collection of relevant facts taken as a whole, while I focus on the partial descriptions formed as these facts accumulate. The point of my formulation is to emphasize the explicitly nonmonotonic nature of judgments involving open-textured predicates – later information can force revisions to these judgments.

further information that would lead us to conclude that it is not, in fact, a cat. He supports this possibility by imagining that we first verify that the object looks like a cat, is furry, and purrs, but that we then learn that it "grew to a gigantic size," or perhaps, "under certain conditions, it could be revived from death."[17] In either case, even though the object continues to satisfy the original definition, Waismann concludes that we might reasonably withdraw our judgment that it is a cat.[18]

There are many other similar examples, both in Waismann and in the work of his contemporaries. Waismann goes on to imagine the case of "a being that looks like a man, speaks like a man, behaves like a man, and is only one span tall – shall I say it is a man?"[19] And then, a substance that looks like gold and satisfies all chemical tests for gold, but which emits a new sort of radiation. J. L. Austin considers how we would react if, after verifying, using the appropriate definitional standards, that some object is a goldfinch, it then "does something outrageous" – explodes, or quotes Virginia Woolf.[20] And Wittgenstein imagines a situation in which what seems to be a chair suddenly disappears, then reappears, then disappears again, and asks:

> Have you rules ready for such cases – rules saying whether one may use the word "chair" to include this kind of thing? But do we miss them when we use the word "chair"; and are we to say that we do not really attach any meaning to this word, because we are not equipped with rules for every possible application of it?[21]

[17] Waismann (1945, p. 2).

[18] Although Waismann himself does not offer a formal definition of open texture, at one point, he distinguishes open texture from vagueness by writing that open texture is "something like the *possibility of vagueness*" (1945, p. 3). This characterization is echoed by a number of writers, such as Williamson (1994, p. 90) and Schauer (2013, p. 199), and is sometimes taken as definitional. The point of Waismann's gnomic phrase seems to be that, while vague terms, such as "tall" or "bald," allow actual contested cases, predicates such as "cat" do not: there are no real contested cases for the applicability of "cat" – the situations Waismann imagines to establish the open texture of this predicate are mere logical possibilities. While this is a fair point concerning "cat" and similar predicates, I do not think the distinction Waismann calls attention to – between actual versus merely possible contested cases – can usefully figure in a definition of open texture, since so many of the open-textured predicates found in the law and elsewhere do allow for actual contested cases. These include the examples discussed earlier, in Section 1.3, such as "clean" as applied to Max's room, or "potato chips" as applied to Pringles, or "vessel" as applied to the Super Scoop.

[19] Waismann (1945, p. 3).

[20] Austin (1946, p. 160).

[21] Wittgenstein (1953, Section 80).

This phenomenon of open texture raises a number of questions, of which we focus on two.[22] The first is this: lacking a definitional analysis, or as Wittgenstein says, "rules for every possible application," how do we work with these open-textured concepts at all – how do we actually determine whether an object is, for example, a cat, a man, a piece of gold, a goldfinch, or a chair? Waismann's answer is that concepts like these can be approached only through partial definitions, which explicitly fail to cover every case:

> We introduce a concept and limit it in some directions; for instance, we define gold in contrast to some other metals such as alloys. This suffices for our present needs, and we do not probe any farther. We tend to overlook the fact that there are always other directions in which the concept has not been defined. And if we did, we could imagine conditions which would necessitate new limitations. In short, it is not possible to define a concept like gold with absolute precision, i.e. in such a way that every nook and cranny is blocked against entry or doubt. That is what is meant by open texture of a concept.[23]

One could be forgiven for thinking that the scenarios used by philosophers such as Waismann, Austin, and Wittgenstein to motivate the phenomenon of open texture – gigantic cats, exploding goldfinches, disappearing chairs – are too contrived to be taken seriously. But, even setting aside the legal predicates mentioned in our earlier discussion, similar examples appear in a number of other domains, including the sciences. Many of us can recall, for instance, that the dwarf planet Pluto was once classified as a planet. In 2006, this classification was withdrawn by the International Astronomical Union (IAU) on the grounds that, although Pluto satisfied the existing definition of a planet, it did not satisfy a new criterion that the IAU had identified as important: Pluto failed to "clear the neighborhood" around its orbit – in other words, it shared its orbital space with bodies of similar size. This shift in status suggested that a new definitional analysis was required for the concept of a planet, so that Pluto could be properly excluded, and indeed, such a proposal was formulated.[24] However, one group within the IAU, the

[22] Others are explored in a series of papers by Shapiro and Roberts, including their (2019a), mentioned above, as well as Shapiro and Roberts (2018, 2019b).

[23] Waismann (1945, p. 3).

[24] See Resolution B5 (Definition of a Planet in the Solar System), passed at the August 2006 meeting of the IAU; available at www.iau.org/static/resolutions/ResolutionGA26-5-6.pdf

Working Group on Extrasolar Planets (WGESP), resisted the call for a new analysis, at least in the case of planets outside our own solar system:

> Rather than try to construct a detailed definition of a planet which is designed to cover all future possibilities, the WGESP has agreed to restrict itself to developing a working definition applicable to the cases where there already are claimed detections .... As new claims are made in the future, the WGESP will weigh their individual merits and circumstances, and will try to fit the new objects into the WGESP definition of a "planet," revising this definition as necessary. This is a gradualist approach with an evolving definition.[25]

In effect, what the WGESP proposed was that the concept of a planet should be regarded as open-textured and treated exactly as Waismann recommends: the concept should be "limited in some directions" in a way that "suffices for present needs," while still allowing for the possibility that future cases will force the concept to be modified in unexpected ways.

The second of the two questions considered here, prompted by the phenomenon of open texture, is this: supposing that we accept Waismann's view of open-textured concepts as limited in some directions but still allowing for unexpected avenues of development, what becomes of the traditional philosophical project of definitional analysis – or in verificationist language, the project of formulating verification conditions for empirical statements? What work is left for the philosopher to do? Waismann has an interesting response to this question as well:

> How, then, should we formulate the 'method of verification' – that is, the connection between a proposition p and the statements $s_1, s_2, \ldots, s_n$ which are evidences for it? I propose to say that the evidences $s_1, s_2, \ldots, s_n$ *speak for* or *against* the proposition p, that they *strengthen* or *weaken* it, which does not mean that they prove or disprove it strictly.[26]

On Waismann's view, then, what remains of the definitional, or verificationist, project from traditional philosophy is simply the identification and classification of the "evidences," as he calls them, that speak for or against the application of an open-textured predicate to some individual. Put schematically, rather than attempting to analyze the statement $P(a)$ through a traditional definition of the form

[25] Boss et al. (2007).
[26] Waismann (1945, p. 7).

$$P(a) =_{df} S_1(a) \wedge S_2(a) \wedge \ldots \wedge S_n(a),$$

which provides necessary and sufficient conditions for the truth of that statement, Waismann's idea is that the analytic project should focus on identifying those statements $S_1^P(a), \ldots, S_i^P(a)$ that count as evidences strengthening the claim that $P(a)$, along with those statements $S_1^{P'}(a), \ldots, S_j^{P'}(a)$ that count as evidences weakening that claim. Or returning to our initial example for illustration, Waismann's view is that we should abandon any attempt to analyze the proposition that a is a cat through a traditional definition of the form

$$Cat(a) =_{df} LooksLikeCat(a) \wedge FeelsFurry(a) \wedge Purrs(a),$$

displayed earlier, according to which the statement on the right is supposed to supply necessary and sufficient conditions for the statement on the left. Instead, what he suggests is that the project of analysis should be limited to the identification of statements such as

$LooksLikeCat(a)$,
$FeelsFurry(a)$,
$Purrs(a)$

that count as evidences strengthening the conclusion that a is a cat, as well as statements such as, following Waismann's own discussion,

$BecomesGigantic(a)$,
$RevivedFromDead(a)$,

that would naturally be taken as evidences weakening the conclusion.

This suggestion of Waismann's now raises two further issues – both of which, however, our analysis of constrained natural reasoning now provides us with the tools to resolve. The first issue concerns reasoning. Standard logic, together with the standard theory of definitions, shows us how to reason with definitional analyses of the usual kind in order to determine, for instance, whether or not the object a is a cat.[27] But on Waismann's view, the best we can hope for from an analysis is a catalog of evidences strengthening or weakening the conclusion that a is a cat. How, then, are we supposed to reason with these various evidences – how do the evidences bearing on the question interact to support the conclusion that a is, or is not, a cat?

[27] The usual reference for the standard theory of definitions is Leśniewski (1930), although the matter was already set out in Frege (1893, Section 33). A textbook presentation can be found in Suppes (1957), and a philosophical exposition and discussion in Belnap (1993).

Our framework provides a natural response. First, Waismann's evidences can be understood as factors, favoring the application either of a predicate or of its contrary to some individual; the statements that the object a looks like a cat, feels furry, or purrs would be factors favoring the conclusion that a is a cat, while the statements that a becomes gigantic or is revived from the dead would be factors favoring the contrary conclusion. Next, collections of factors uniformly favoring one conclusion or the other can be taken as reasons supporting that conclusion, and so as premises of factor defaults; for example,

$$\{LooksLikeCat(a), Purrs(a)\} \rightarrow Cat(a)$$

would be a factor default according to which the statements that a looks like a cat and purrs, taken together, is a reason for concluding that a is a cat, while

$$\{BecomesGigantic(a)\} \rightarrow NotCat(a)$$

would be a factor default according to which the statement that a becomes gigantic is a reason for the contrary conclusion. Finally, we can suppose that reasoning then proceeds in accord with default logic, on the basis of a default theory of the kind explored here – with hard information containing the factors characterizing some object, with factor defaults bearing on the application of open-textured predicates to that object, as well as, possibly, value defaults reflecting the reasoner's prioritization of those factor defaults.

This suggestion – that Waismann's evidences support conclusions in accord with default logic – not only shows how reasoning with these evidences might proceed, but also helps us understand a complex passage from Waismann's article in which he can now be seen, in retrospect, as searching for a kind of default, or nonmonotonic, logic.[28] But the suggestion

[28] The passage occurs in a complex paragraph from Waismann (1945, p. 8), where he considers a scientific example in which conclusions depend, not only on laws, facts, and boundary conditions but on an additional consideration of "*no other disturbing factors being present*." Waismann is puzzled by this additional consideration, since "we never make use of this premise: it never forms part of the body of premisses: it does not enter the process of deduction" and goes on to wonder whether it should be "termed a premise at all; what a queer sort of premiss this is, which is never made use of!" In fact, the issues that Waismann is wrestling with here are exactly the issues that puzzled early researchers in nonmonotonic reasoning, and whose solution led to the first successful nonmonotonic logics. For example, in the simple default logic set out in Section 5.1 the inference from the premise that Tweety is a bird to the conclusion that Tweety flies can be said to depend,

also leads to a second issue. As we recall from our initial discussion of default logic, in Section 5.1.3, default theories can allow multiple proper scenarios, generating multiple conclusion sets, or extensions. Suppose, for example, it is part of our hard information that the object *a* looks like a cat and purrs, but also that it becomes gigantic, so that both of the defaults displayed above are applicable. In the absence of any additional information about priorities, the resulting theory would allow two proper scenarios, generating two extensions, one supporting the conclusion that *a* is a cat, the other supporting the conclusion that *a* is not a cat. According to our interpretation of situations like this, where a default theory allows different extensions supporting conflicting conclusion, the reasoner is permitted to accept as a conclusion any statement contained in any of these extensions – so that, in this situation, the reasoner would be permitted to conclude that *a* is a cat on the grounds that it looks like a cat and purrs, but also permitted to conclude that *a* is not a cat on the grounds of its gigantic size.

Of course, for an individual reasoning with Waismann's evidences, it is natural to suppose that some proper scenarios, and so some extensions, would be ruled out by a prioritization among factor defaults derived from that reasoner's values – in our current example, it is natural to suppose that the factor default based on gigantic size would be prioritized over the factor default based on looking like a cat and purring, thus eliminating the extension containing the conclusion that *a* is a cat. But we cannot expect that any particular reasoner's values should be strong enough to rule out multiple extensions in every situation. In addition, different reasoners will have different values, leading them to prioritize factor defaults in different ways, allowing different proper scenarios that generate different extensions – so that, even if each individual reasoner does arrive at a unique extension, there is no guarantee that different reasoners will arrive at the same unique extension.

in a sense, on the absence of the disturbing information that Tweety is a penguin. But the fact that Tweety is not a penguin does not function as an additional premise in this inference – any more than the fact that Tweety is not a baby bird, a sick bird, or a bird with weights attached to its legs. At the end of the paragraph under consideration, Waismann writes, of a conclusion *s* arrived at in this way, on the basis of the absence of disturbing information, that: "Saying that the class of premisses is not 'closed' and that *therefore* the conclusion is lacking in stringency comes, in my view, to the same thing as saying that *s* is not a logical consequence of the premisses as far as they are stated." And from a modern perspective, we can now see that this is exactly right: *s* is not a logical consequence of the premises – it follows from the premises by default reasoning.

The question thus arises: if reasoning about open-textured predicates on the basis of Waismann's evidences is to be understood as a form of default reasoning, and default reasoning permits different reasoners to arrive at different extensions, supporting different conclusions, then why is there so much agreement, in the vast run of situations, concerning the proper applicability of open-textured predicates – why is our use of these open-textured predicates, generally, so stable and predictable? How is this coordination achieved? There are surely many forces at work. But a hypothesis emerging from the current framework is that one of these forces is this: our judgments are stable because, even when our values are not aligned, any particular decision concerning the applicability of an open-textured predicate takes place against an extensive background of previous applications of that predicate, which constrain new applications in exactly the same way that a court's decision in a new situation is constrained, often contrary to its own values, by decisions reached in precedent cases.

6.3.2 An Example

In order to illustrate this kind of lexical constraint, possibly contrary to a speaker's own values, we now step away from gigantic cats, exploding goldfinches, and disappearing chairs to focus on the more mundane legal question, considered earlier, in Section 1.3.2, of whether or not the Super Scoop is to be classified as a vessel. As we recall from that discussion, the statements v and v' represent the contrary judgments that some object under consideration either is or is not a vessel. Among factors favoring the conclusion v, that the object is a vessel, we let f_1^v indicate that it has a captain and crew and f_2^v that it is subject to Coast Guard regulations. Among factors favoring the conclusion v', that the object is not a vessel, we let $f_1^{v'}$ indicate that it is not capable of self-propulsion, $f_2^{v'}$ that its primary business is not navigation, and $f_3^{v'}$ that it has been largely stationary for at least a month.

Using this notation, the Super Scoop, we recall, gives rise to the situation $X_8 = \{f_1^v, f_2^v, f_1^{v'}, f_2^{v'}\}$, with four factors as evidences, indicating that this object has a captain and crew and is subject to Coast Guard regulations, but is neither capable of self-propulsion nor used primarily for navigation. Of the set $\mathcal{F}$ of factor defaults constructible on the basis of the factors considered, then, the applicable factor defaults favoring the conclusion v, that the Super Scoop is a vessel, are

$$r_1^v = \{f_1^v\} \rightarrow v,$$
$$r_2^v = \{f_2^v\} \rightarrow v,$$
$$r_{1,2}^v = \{f_1^v, f_2^v\} \rightarrow v,$$

while the applicable factor defaults favoring v', the contrary conclusion, are

$$r_1^{v'} = \{f_1^{v'}\} \rightarrow v',$$
$$r_2^{v'} = \{f_2^{v'}\} \rightarrow v',$$
$$r_{1,2}^{v'} = \{f_1^{v'}, f_2^{v'}\} \rightarrow v'.$$

Now, how can this situation be cast as a problem presented to a court? Well, suppose, for instance, that the set $\mathcal{V}_{Court}$ representing the court's values contains the single value default

$$r_{1,2\backslash 2}^v = \top \rightarrow n_{1,2}^{v'} \prec n_2^v,$$

indicating that the court prioritizes the factor default r_2^v over the factor default $r_{1,2}^{v'}$ – the court, in other words, prioritizes the fact that the object is subject to Coast Guard regulations as a reason for concluding that it is a vessel over the fact that it is neither capable of self-propulsion nor primarily involved in navigation as a reason to the contrary. And let us begin by imagining that the court is free to address the problem presented by the Super Scoop entirely on the basis of its own values, without constraint. In that case, following the recipe set out in Definition 36 from Section 5.3.1, the problem presented to the court can be represented as the theory $\Delta_{X_8, \mathcal{V}_{Court}} = \langle \mathcal{W}_{X_8}, \mathcal{D}_{\mathcal{V}_{Court}} \rangle$ where

$$\begin{aligned}
\mathcal{W}_{X_8} &= X_8 \cup \mathcal{O} \\
&= \{f_1^v, f_2^v, f_1^{v'}, f_2^{v'}\} \cup \mathcal{O}, \\
\mathcal{D}_{\mathcal{V}_{Court}} &= \mathcal{F} \cup \mathcal{V}_{Court} \\
&= \mathcal{F} \cup \{r_{1,2\backslash 2}^v\}.
\end{aligned}$$

Here, the set $\mathcal{W}_{X_8}$ of hard information contains the various factors, or evidences, characterizing the Super Scoop, along with the usual structural conditions; the set $\mathcal{D}_{\mathcal{V}_{Court}}$ contains the factor defaults constructible from these evidences, as well as the single value default representing the court's prioritization of these factor defaults.

This theory allows as its unique solution the proper scenario $\mathcal{S}_{26} = \{r_1^v, r_2^v, r_{1,2}^v, r_{1,2\backslash 2}^v\}$, generating the unique extension

$$\mathcal{E}_{26} = Closure(\mathcal{W}_{X_8} \cup \{v, n_{1,2}^{v'} \prec n_2^v\}),$$

and so supporting the conclusion v, that the Super Scoop is a vessel, as well as the fact that r_2^v is to be prioritized over $r_{1,2}^{v'}$. In accord with its values, the court defers to the Coast Guard and concludes that the Super Scoop is a vessel on the grounds that it is subject to Coast Guard regulations.

Suppose, however, that – as in our earlier discussion, and also in fact – the court confronts the problem presented by the Super Scoop under hard constraints derived from the previous decision in the case of the Betty F. This decision was represented earlier as $c_7 = \langle X_7, r_7, s_7 \rangle$, where $X_7 = \{f_1^v, f_2^v, f_1^{v'}, f_2^{v'}, f_3^{v'}\}$, where $r_7 = \{f_2^{v'}\} \rightarrow v'$, and where $s_7 = v'$. The Betty F, then, was characterized as an object exactly like the Super Scoop except that, in addition, it had remained stationary for at least a month; and it was decided by the previous court that the Betty F should be classified as not a vessel, on the grounds that its primary business was not navigation. As before, we will suppose that the background case base is $\Gamma_7 = \{c_7\}$, containing the case of the Betty F alone.

In accord with the account set out in Section 6.1.1, the hard constraints derived from this case base are contained in the set $\mathcal{H}_{\Gamma_7} = \{n_{1,2}^v \prec n_2^{v'}\}$, so that, following the recipe from Definition 37, the problem presented to the court by the Super Scoop under these hard constraints can be represented as the theory $\Delta_{X_8, \mathcal{V}_{Court}, \mathcal{H}_{\Gamma_7}} = \langle \mathcal{W}_{X_8, \mathcal{H}_{\Gamma_7}}, \mathcal{D}_{\mathcal{V}_{Court}} \rangle$ where

$$
\begin{aligned}
\mathcal{W}_{X_8, \mathcal{H}_{\Gamma_7}} &= X_8 \cup \mathcal{H}_{\Gamma_7} \cup \mathcal{O} \\
&= \{f_1^v, f_2^v, f_1^{v'}, f_2^{v'}\} \cup \{n_{1,2}^v \prec n_2^{v'}\} \cup \mathcal{O}, \\
\mathcal{D}_{\mathcal{V}_{Court}} &= \mathcal{F} \cup \mathcal{V}_{Court} \\
&= \mathcal{F} \cup \{r_{1,2\backslash 2}^v\}.
\end{aligned}
$$

This problem is exactly like the problem $\Delta_{X_8, \mathcal{V}_{Court}}$, just considered, except that the hard information $\mathcal{W}_{X_8, \mathcal{H}_{\Gamma_7}}$ now includes the hard constraints derived from Γ_7.

This new theory now allows as its unique solution the proper scenario $\mathcal{S}_{27} = \{r_1^{v'}, r_2^{v'}, r_{1,2}^{v'}\}$, generating the extension

$$
\mathcal{E}_{27} = Closure(\mathcal{W}_{X_8, \mathcal{H}_{\Gamma_7}} \cup \{v'\}),
$$

and so supporting v', the decision that the Super Scoop is not a vessel. The court's own prioritization of r_2^v over $r_{1,2}^{v'}$ conflicts with the hard constraint that $r_2^{v'}$, and so $r_{1,2}^{v'}$, is to be prioritized over $r_{1,2}^v$, and so over r_2^v. The court must, therefore, abandon the prioritization recommended by its own values, reason instead on the basis of the hard constraint, and so conclude that the Super Scoop is not appropriately classified as a vessel.

This example illustrates how, in the legal setting, constraints derived from previous decisions force coordination in the application of open-textured predicates. The hypothesis under consideration here is that the use of open-textured predicates in natural languages is constrained in a similar way: Over the course of a conversation, which can last for seconds or for centuries, a stock of prior applications of open-textured predicates – a case base – is established. Individuals who wish to participate in this conversation, rather than starting a new one, are then required to use these predicates in a way that respects the constraints established in their previous applications.

Of course, even as a hypothesis, this proposal would need to be explored in much more detail – there are many ways in which the use of open-textured predicates in natural language differs from their use in the law, of which we mention four.

First: In a legal setting, the set of precedent cases bearing on applicability of an open-textured predicate is carefully documented and curated; if questions arise, there are recognized methods of argument for determining whether or not some previous decision functions as an authoritative precedent in a new situation. In the more fluid setting of a natural language, by contrast, we could expect the set of precedent cases constraining the use of open-textured predicates to be indefinite, local, and changing; speakers might exercise creativity by flouting norms – ignoring previous cases that should count as precedents, or granting authority to previous cases that should not.

Second: While the authority of past decisions over present cases in the law is carefully documented, the nature of the authority on the basis of which previous uses of open-textured predicates might constrain current uses in natural language is much less clear. My suspicion is that these constraints result from an unnoticed, or at least underexplored, principle of conversational coordination in natural language, which leads to coordination in the use of open-textured predicates.[29] If this suspicion, or something like it, is correct, then the legal doctrine of precedent, like so much else in the law,

[29] For a central account of meaning coordination in natural language, see, of course, Lewis (1969), who himself appeals to precedent but only as a mechanism for aligning mutual expectations. Empirical research along these lines can be found in Clark and Marshall (1981) and Clark and Wilkes-Gibbs (1986), and then in Garrod and Anderson (1987), who introduce the term "entrainment" for the kind of meaning coordination under consideration; this term was later adopted in Clark (1991) and Ludlow (2014). The current suggestion is that a precedent is more than just a kind of signpost for use by speakers to coordinate expectations, but that, instead, precedential constraint has a normative force,

can be seen as a more stylized, self-conscious, and rigorous development of a mechanism that is already at work in our everyday interactions.

Third: While the uses of open-textured predicates in the law are often subject to hard constraints derived from precedent cases, we could expect that the constraints governing open-textured predicates in natural language are, for the most part, soft. If the model of soft constraint described in the previous section can be adapted to natural language more generally, we would then be faced with the question: what, in this case, are the special justifications that would allow competent speakers to overrule existing constraints concerning the applicability of open-textured predicates? What special justifications, for example, did the astronomers from the IAU appeal to in deciding to overrule existing constraints concerning applicability of the predicate "planet" in the case of Pluto?

Fourth and finally: According to the account of constrained natural reasoning developed here, courts involved in legal reasoning are thought of as attempting to advance certain values, subject to constraints derived from previous decisions. Values thus play a central role in the account, and in the more paradigmatically legal examples, it is easy to identify the conflicting values underlying a particular dispute: the alligator/ocelot example from Section 4.3, for instance, involves a balance between the values of safety and property rights. But what values could be at stake in disputes concerning applicability of ordinary open-textured predicates?

Well, in many situations, these disputes also have a quasi-legal character. Consider the situation described in our earlier discussion of open texture, from Section 1.3, where Jack and Jo allow Max to go out and play with his friends on Saturday morning only if his room is clean. Here, it is easy to imagine that what Jack and Jo value is a neat and orderly house, while Max, who cares nothing of neatness or order, values only playing with his friends – and that the balance between these two values is arrived at, at least on Saturday mornings, through a series of decisions concerning appropriate applicability of the predicate "clean." Not all disputes concerning the applicability of open-textured predicates have this quasi-legal character, however. A wide range of other values might be involved. Often, the particular value at stake is simply the value of maintaining a useful concept, and in these situations, disputes concerning applicability of an open-textured predicate can be seen as disputes concerning ways in which the concept expressed by

explicated here by the reason model, in bringing about what Garrod, Anderson, Clark, and Ludlow refer to as meaning entrainment.

that predicate can most usefully be developed. This concern is highlighted in our astronomical example, where the astronomers from the IAU explicitly argued that the application conditions of the predicate "planet" should be adjusted to exclude Pluto on the grounds that the resulting concept of a planet would be more useful than a concept that continued to include Pluto.[30]

[30] See Egré and O'Madagain (2019) for a formal measure of concept utility according to which the new concept of a planet excluding Pluto has greater utility than the original.

7 Dimensions and Magnitudes

In this final chapter, we explore one way in which the models of precedential constraint studied here can be generalized to a richer representational setting, in which situations are described, not in terms of statements that either do or do not hold, but in terms of features that may be present, or not, to a particular degree. More exactly: The situations considered thus far have been characterized in terms of factors – where a factor, as we have seen, is a legally significant property, or proposition, that may or may not hold in a particular situation but that, when it does hold, always favors the same side in a dispute. In many cases, however, it seems more natural to characterize the situations under consideration, not in terms of factors but in terms of *dimensions* – where a dimension can be thought of as an ordered set of legally significant values, with the ordering among values reflecting the extent to which that value favors one side or another. While a factor is binary, then, either holding or not in any situation, and uniform in polarity, always favoring a single side when it does hold, a dimension can take on different values in different situations, and the polarity associated with a given value can be indeterminate.

In order to illustrate the difference between factors and dimensions, we return to the domain of trade-secrets law – studied extensively within artificial intelligence and law, and described earlier in Section 1.1.1. In this domain, a dispute generally concerns the issue whether the defendant has gained an unfair competitive advantage over the plaintiff through the misappropriation of a trade secret. To secure a judgment, the plaintiff is required to establish, not only that certain information was misappropriated by the defendant, but also that the misappropriated information was in fact a trade secret; and here, a number of considerations can be brought to bear. One relevant consideration is whether the defendant has, or has not, signed a nondisclosure agreement. This consideration can naturally be represented as a factor – say, the proposition that a nondisclosure agreement was signed – since this proposition either holds or does not hold, and, if it does, always supports the plaintiff's contention that the information is a genuine trade secret. Another consideration concerns the extent to which the information alleged to be a trade secret has already been disclosed to outsiders. This consideration is best represented as a dimension, with the possible values along that dimension – the number of outsiders to whom the information was disclosed – arranged in such a way that disclosure to more and more outsiders progressively strengthens the case for the defendant, since it provides stronger support for the idea that the information in question was not in fact a secret.

A third consideration concerns measures taken to protect the information purported to be a trade secret – again best represented as a dimension, with protective measures as values, and these values ordered in such a way that stronger measures provide stronger support for the plaintiff's claim that the information was indeed a trade secret. Imagine that the information in question is data stored on a disk, and consider four possible values along the protective measures dimension: (1) the plaintiff has taken no protective measures, (2) the plaintiff has encrypted the disk, (3) the plaintiff has locked the disk in a safe, (4) the plaintiff has both encrypted the disk and locked it in a safe. These four values could naturally be ordered so that the second and third provide stronger support for the plaintiff than the first, but are incomparable to each other, and the fourth provides stronger support for the plaintiff than all the others.

The last example highlights three useful points about dimensions. It shows, first of all, that the values along a dimension need not correspond to a numerical range, but can be entirely qualitative, and second, that the ordering among these values need not be linear. Third, the example provides a clear illustration of the fact that the polarity, or side favored, by some particular value along a dimension can be indeterminate. Consider a case in which the protective measures dimension takes the second value listed above: the disk was encrypted but not locked away. It is easy to imagine the plaintiff arguing that this value supports the conclusion that the information was indeed a trade secret, since, after all, it was encrypted. It is also easy to imagine the defendant arguing that the same value supports the conclusion that the information was not a trade secret, since it was merely encrypted, and not locked away as well.

The distinction between factors and dimensions raises important issues within the field of artificial intelligence and law itself. On one hand, many major case-based legal reasoning systems support reasoning based on dimensions, not just factors, and most researchers in the field believe that full dimensional resources are necessary for an adequate representation of legal information.[1] But on the other hand, the most promising formal analyses of case-based reasoning – such as that of Prakken and Sartor – rely on factors alone, without any account of the connection between these factors and the underlying dimensional information.[2]

The point can be illustrated with one of Prakken and Sartor's own hypothetical examples concerning the issue whether an individual who has spent time in a foreign country has changed fiscal domicile for income tax purposes. Among the considerations bearing on this issue is the duration of the individual's stay abroad, where greater duration provides stronger support for change of domicile. Here, it is natural to represent duration as a dimension that can take on a variety of values – the individual might have stayed in the foreign country for a week, a month, six months, a year, five years, and so on. But in fact, Prakken and Sartor bypass the full range of available values and deal with this dimensional information, instead, only through the introduction of a pair of factors – "long-duration" and "short-duration" – where the first favors change of fiscal domicile and the second favors no change. Now of course, it is sensible to assume that a long duration abroad should favor change of domicile, and that a short duration should favor no change, but that leaves open the question whether any particular duration should count as long or as short. Suppose an individual has lived in a foreign country for thirteen months. Does a period abroad of that length count as a long duration, and so favor change of fiscal domicile, or does it count as a short duration, and so favor lack of change? This is exactly the kind of question that should itself be subject to legal argument, rather than settled through representational convention.

Even if the problem of relating factors to underlying dimensional information is real, however, it may appear to be only a minor problem, and easily solvable. This seems to be what Prakken and Sartor themselves thought.[3] But in a brief but important paper, Trevor Bench-Capon sets out a number of arguments that raise real concerns about the possibility of handling dimensional

1 See both Bench-Capon and Rissland (2001) and Rissland and Ashley (2002) for arguments supporting the importance of dimensions in legal knowledge representation.

2 Prakken and Sartor (1998).

3 Speaking of dimensions, as well as hypotheticals, Prakken and Sartor write that "there are no theoretical objections to extending our analysis with these features" (1998, p. 279).

information in the kind of rule-based systems used by Prakken and Sartor.[4] The purpose of this chapter, then, is simply to demonstrate one way in which the formal analyses of precedential constraint described in this book can be generalized to accommodate dimensional information as well. Developing this generalization will require us to address two crucial problems, both noted by Bench-Capon. The first is that, as already emphasized, no particular value along a dimensional scale necessarily favors one side or the other, in the way that factors do. The second is that, if several dimensions are present, weakness for a side along one dimension can be offset by strength for that side along another.

The chapter begins with an exposition of the dimensional framework itself. We then show how both the reason model and the a fortiori model of constraint can be defined within this new framework. Our previous definition of the reason model seems, at first, to generalize very naturally to the new framework, but then a problem develops: the reason model and the a fortiori model, which were distinct before, now collapse into one another. Analysis of this problem will show that developing the reason model within a framework – such as the dimensional framework – in which there are nontrivial structural relations among reasons themselves may require the definition of a more complex priority ordering on reasons.

7.1 The Dimensional Framework

For the sake of clarity, to heighten contrast, we refer in this chapter to the central framework we have been working in thus far, set out formally in Section 1.1, as the *ordinary framework*. In this ordinary framework, as we have seen, situations are characterized as collections of factors. By contrast, we now define an alternative *dimensional framework*, in which situations are described in terms of values along a number of dimensions.[5]

7.1.1 Dimensions

We start by postulating a set $D = \{d_1, d_2, \ldots, d_n\}$ of dimensions relevant to some area of dispute. For each dimension, we assume an ordered set of values,

[4] Bench-Capon (1999).

[5] The same framework that is described here as "ordinary," in contrast to the dimensional framework, is also referred to as "defeasible" in Chapter 3, where it stands in contrast to the strict framework.

ranging from those favoring the side s to those favoring the side $\overline{s}$. Where p and q are particular values along some dimension, we take the statement

$$p \trianglelefteq^s q$$

to mean that the value q on this dimension favors the side s at least as strongly as the value p.[6] The strength ordering on dimension values is assumed to satisfy the partial-order conditions of reflexivity, transitivity, and antisymmetry

$$p \trianglelefteq^s p,$$
$$p \trianglelefteq^s q \text{ and } q \trianglelefteq^s r \text{ implies } p \trianglelefteq^s r,$$
$$p \trianglelefteq^s q \text{ and } q \trianglelefteq^s p \text{ implies } p = q,$$

as well as a duality condition

$$p \trianglelefteq^s q \text{ if and only if } q \trianglelefteq^{\overline{s}} p,$$

according to which q favors the side s at least as strongly as p just in case p favors the opposing side $\overline{s}$ at least as strongly as q.

This notation can be illustrated by returning to Prakken and Sartor's fiscal domicile example: imagine that the plaintiff is an individual's native country, which is arguing against change of domicile in order to tax the individual's income, and that the defendant is that individual, who is arguing for change of domicile in order to pay, let us suppose, the lower tax rate available in a foreign country. Here, two possible values along the dimension representing the period of residence abroad are, say, half a year and two and a half years, or six months and thirty months. If these values are denoted simply as 6 and 30, we then have $30 \trianglelefteq^{\pi} 6$, since the shorter period abroad favors the plaintiff's argument against change of domicile; duality then tells us that $6 \trianglelefteq^{\delta} 30$, or that the longer period abroad favors the individual's argument in favor of change. Of course, period of residence abroad would not be the only dimension bearing on the issue of change of fiscal domicile. Another might be proportion of income earned from organizations based in the country of residence, during that period. Two possible values along this dimension might be, say, 50 percent and 60 percent. If we denote these values simply as 50 and 60, then we would have $60 \trianglelefteq^{\pi} 50$, and by duality $50 \trianglelefteq^{\delta} 60$,

6 For strict representational accuracy, this notation should carry some indication of the dimension under consideration, so that the statement $p \trianglelefteq^s_{d_i} q$, for example, would mean that the value q on the particular dimension d_i favors the side s at least as strongly as p. We omit explicit mention of the dimension under consideration, however, both because it is generally clear from context and to avoid further notational complexity.

since a smaller proportion of income earned abroad favors the plaintiff's argument against change while a larger proportion favors the defendant's argument in favor of change.

Where p is a value along the dimension d, the pair $\langle d, p \rangle$ is a *value assignment*, according to which the dimension d takes on the value p. In contrast to an ordinary fact situation, defined earlier as a set of ordinary factors, a *dimensional fact situation*

$$X = \{\langle d, p \rangle : d \in D\}$$

can be defined as a set of values assignments, one for each dimension, subject to the condition that if $\langle d, p \rangle$ and $\langle d, p' \rangle$ both belong to X, then $p = p'$. A dimensional fact situation, in other words, is a function mapping each dimension to a value along that dimension. We take $X(d)$ as the value assigned to the dimension d in the fact situation X, where this idea is defined in the usual way:

$$X(d) = p \text{ if and only if } \langle d, p \rangle \in X.$$

To illustrate: if d_1 and d_2 are the dimensions representing length of time in a foreign country and proportion of income earned from organizations based in that country, then $X_{37} = \{\langle d_1, 30 \rangle, \langle d_2, 60 \rangle\}$ is the dimensional fact situation presented by an individual who has spent thirty months in a foreign country while earning 60 percent of his or her income from organizations based in that country. We would therefore have $X_{37}(d_1) = 30$ and $X_{37}(d_2) = 60$.

7.1.2 Magnitude Factors

The central conceptual problem presented by the dimensional framework is that, while ordinary fact situations are constructed out of ordinary factors, always favoring one side or the other, dimensional fact situations are constructed out of value assignments, which need not, intrinsically, favor any particular side. There is nothing about the period of thirty months, for example, to indicate that this length of time abroad should count either in favor of or against change of fiscal domicile – one court might feel that thirty months favors change because it is longer than a year, while another feels that it tells against change because it is shorter than five years. This problem will be addressed through the introduction of a different class of factors, like ordinary factors in possessing a definite polarity, but keyed to the value assignments found in dimensional fact situations.

To motivate the proposal, consider a situation, such as that represented above as $X_{37} = \{\langle d_1, 30\rangle, \langle d_2, 60\rangle\}$, in which an individual has been living in a foreign country for thirty months while earning 60 percent of his or her income from foreign organizations. Now suppose a court focuses on length of time abroad as the most important of these two dimensions. How would such a court decide, in this situation, whether a period of thirty months abroad is sufficient to justify a change of fiscal domicile? The suggestion explored here is that the court might focus on some particular salient, or meaningful, value along this particular dimension – a *reference value* – and then justify its decision by comparing the value of the dimension in the current fact situation to that reference value. Suppose, for instance, that the value of one year stands out, for the court, as a sufficient length of time to justify a change of fiscal domicile. Taking this value as a reference value, the court could then justify its decision in the current situation by ruling for change of fiscal domicile, and so in favor of the defendant, on the grounds that the actual period of residence in the foreign country favors the defendant at least as much as a period of one year.

This proposition – to spell it out, the proposition that the actual period of residence abroad favors the defendant at least as much as a period of one year – is a kind of factor: it either holds or does not hold in any fact situation, and always favors the same side, the defendant, when it does hold. Generalizing from our example, then, where p is some value along the dimension d, we now introduce the concept of a *magnitude factor favoring the side* s, as a statement of the form

$$M^s_{d,p}$$

carrying the meaning that: the actual value assigned to the dimension d favors the side s as least as strongly as the value p. Continuing to take d_1 as the dimension representing length of time abroad, then, the magnitude factor at work in our example can be expressed as $M^{\delta}_{d_1,12}$, the proposition that the actual value assigned to d_1 in the situation at hand favors the defendant at least as much as a value of one year, or twelve months – or more simply, that the defendant spent at least a year, or twelve months, abroad.

Now consider again a magnitude factor of the form $M^s_{d,p}$, according to which the actual value assigned to the dimension d favors the side s as least as strongly as the value p. Since the value assigned to the dimension d in some situation X is simply $X(d)$, and since this value favors the side s at least as strongly as p whenever $p \trianglelefteq^s X(d)$, the conditions under the factor

$M^s_{d,p}$ holds in the situation X – or more technically, X satisfies $M^s_{d,p}$ – can be defined as follows:

Definition 39 (Magnitude factor satisfaction) Where X is a dimensional fact situation and $M^s_{d,p}$ is a magnitude factor, X satisfies $M^s_{d,p}$ – written, $X \models M^s_{d,p}$ – if and only if $p \trianglelefteq^s X(d)$.

Returning to our example, we can see that $X_{37} \models M^{\delta}_{d_1,12}$, since $X_{37}(d_1) = 30$ and since $12 \trianglelefteq^{\delta} 30$ – that is, a period abroad of thirty months favors change of domicile, and so the defendant, at least as much as a period of twelve months.

There is one oddity that deserves mention. In our example, the factor $M^{\delta}_{d_1,12}$ – that the defendant spent at least a year abroad – does seem to represent a real consideration in favor of the defendant, since a year, as a reference value, is a significant length of time. But what if a magnitude factor were keyed to a less significant reference value, such as a single month, or even a single day? A month, or a day, is surely a much less significant value on the dimensional scale – could it even serve as a reference value at all? In fact, yes. We propose no formal restrictions bearing on the intuitive significance of the reference point: any value on the dimensional scale will do. But is this sensible? Can we really suppose that the proposition that an individual has spent at least a single day abroad should count as a factor favoring a judgment for change of fiscal domicile? To this question there is a simple response. To say that a factor favors a particular side does not necessarily mean that it favors that side very strongly. We can allow that the proposition that an individual has spent at least a day abroad counts as a reason supporting change of fiscal domicile – after all, the proposition rules out periods of less than a day, and holds in all longer periods – while still insisting that it is an exceptionally weak reason, likely to be outweighed by just about any serious reason favoring the other side.[7]

7.1.3 Reasons, Rules, and Cases

Once these magnitude factors have been introduced, we can now, following the pattern from the ordinary framework, define a *magnitude reason favoring the side s* as a set of magnitude factors favoring that side, and a *magnitude reason* as a magnitude reason favoring one side or the other. To illustrate: $\{M^{\delta}_{d_1,12}, M^{\delta}_{d_2,50}\}$ is a magnitude reason favoring the defendant, since all of

[7] I owe this form of argument, or perhaps this argument itself, to Schroeder (2007).

the magnitude factors it contains favor the defendant, but $\{M^{\delta}_{d_1,12}, M^{\pi}_{d_2,50}\}$ is not a reason, since it contains factors favoring different sides. As with ordinary reasons, magnitude reasons are to be interpreted conjunctively, so that the reason $\{M^{\delta}_{d_1,12}, M^{\delta}_{d_2,50}\}$, for example, tells us that some individual under consideration spent at least twelve months abroad while earning at least 50 percent of his or her income from foreign organizations; and again, reasons containing only a single factor coincide in meaning with the factor they contain, so that the reason $\{M^{\delta}_{d_1,12}\}$, for example, carries the same meaning as the factor $M^{\delta}_{d_1,12}$.

Now what of satisfaction and strength relations among magnitude reasons? Here there are complications. Earlier – in Definitions 1 and 2 from Section 1.1.2 – we introduced the ideas of satisfaction and strength for ordinary reasons in terms of simple set-theoretic inclusions, stipulating that an ordinary reason U holds in an ordinary fact situation X just in case $U \subseteq X$ and that, of two ordinary reasons U and V favoring the same side, V is at least as strong as U just in case $U \subseteq V$. But these definitions will no longer work in the dimensional framework. We cannot say that a magnitude reason U holds in a dimensional fact situation X just in case $U \subseteq X$ because magnitude reasons and dimensional fact situations are not objects of the same type – magnitude reasons are sets of magnitude factors, while dimensional fact situations are sets of value assignments. And we cannot say that the magnitude reason V is at least as strong as U just in case $U \subseteq V$ either, because, as we will see, there are meaningful relations of strength among magnitude reasons even when neither is a subset of the other. In response to these complications, we now reformulate our previous treatment of reason satisfaction and strength in the ordinary framework in a more general fashion that will apply in the dimensional framework as well.

To begin with, then, let us stipulate that an ordinary factor holds in an ordinary fact situation – or that the situation satisfies the factor – just in case that factor is contained in the fact situation:

Definition 40 (Ordinary factor satisfaction) Where X is an ordinary fact situation and f^s_i is an ordinary factor, X satisfies f^s_i – written, $X \models f^s_i$ – if and only if f^s_i belongs to X.

A more general notion of reason satisfaction can then be arrived at simply by lifting the idea of satisfaction from factors to reasons, or sets of factors, by stipulating that a situation satisfies a set of factors whenever it satisfies each factor from that set:

Definition 41 (Reason satisfaction: generalized) Where X is a fact situation and U is a reason, X satisfies U – written, $X \models U$ – if and only if X satisfies each factor contained in U.

Turning to strength among reasons, it is natural, first of all, to introduce a notion of reason entailment by stipulating that one reason entails another whenever any situation that satisfies the first of these reasons also satisfies the second:

Definition 42 (Reason entailment) Where U and V are reasons, V entails U – written, $V \Vdash U$ – if and only if, for any fact situation X, whenever $X \models V$, we also have $X \models U$.

And we can then generalize our earlier notion of strength for a side among reasons by stipulating that one reason is at least as strong as another whenever, in the sense just defined, the first of these reasons entails the second:

Definition 43 (Strength for a side among reasons: generalized) Where U and V are reasons for the side s, then V is at least as strong a reason as U for s – written, $U \leq^s V$ – if and only if $V \Vdash U$.

It is easy to see that the new notions of reason satisfaction and strength set out in Definitions 41 and 43 coincide, in the ordinary framework, with the previous notions from Definitions 1 and 2. This can be established by verifying, first, where X is an ordinary fact situation and U is an ordinary reason, that $X \models U$ in the sense of Definition 41 just in case the Definition 1 condition that $U \subseteq X$ is met, and second, where U and V are ordinary reasons, that $U \leq^s V$ in the sense of Definition 43 just in case the Definition 2 condition that $U \subseteq V$ is likewise satisfied. Although they coincide with the previous notions in the ordinary setting, however, the new notions of reason satisfaction and strength from Definitions 41 and 43 are sufficiently general that – if we start with the Definition 39 account of magnitude factor satisfaction rather than the Definition 40 account of ordinary factor satisfaction – these definitions yield accounts of satisfaction and strength that apply sensibly in the dimensional framework as well.

Beginning with satisfaction and recalling the previous dimensional fact situation $X_{37} = \{\langle d_1, 30\rangle, \langle d_2, 60\rangle\}$: Definition 41 allows us to see, for example, that $X_{37} \models \{M^{\delta}_{d_1,12}, M^{\delta}_{d_2,50}\}$, since each of the factors belonging to the magnitude reason $\{M^{\delta}_{d_1,12}, M^{\delta}_{d_2,50}\}$ holds in this fact situation. What this definition allows us to see, in other words, is that a fact situation in which some individual spent thirty months abroad while earning 60 percent of his or her income from foreign sources satisfies the magnitude reason according to which that individual spent at least twelve months abroad while earning at least 50 percent of income from foreign sources. And we can note that, in contrast to the account provided in the earlier Definition 1, this notion of satisfaction does not depend on a subset relation between the reason and the fact situation – we do not have, of course, anything like $\{M^{\delta}_{d_1,12}, M^{\delta}_{d_2,50}\} \subseteq X_{37}$.

Turning next to strength: Definition 43 allows us to see, for example, that $\{M^{\delta}_{d_1,12}\} \leq^{\delta} \{M^{\delta}_{d_1,30}\}$, since any situation that satisfies $\{M^{\delta}_{d_1,30}\}$ will satisfy $\{M^{\delta}_{d_1,12}\}$ as well – in other words, that residing in a foreign country for at least thirty months provides a reason for change of residence, and so for the defendant, that is at least as strong as that provided by residing in a foreign country for at least twelve months. And we can note again that, in contrast to the account provided by the earlier Definition 2, this strength relation holds even though there is no subset relation between the reasons involved – we do not have $\{M^{\delta}_{d_1,12}\} \subseteq \{M^{\delta}_{d_1,30}\}$.

At this point, having introduced dimensional fact situations, magnitude factors, and magnitude reasons, we can now complete our treatment of the dimensional framework in a way that confirms to the pattern set out earlier, in our Section 1.1 exposition of the ordinary framework. Specifically: If U is a magnitude reason favoring the side s, we can define $U \rightarrow s$ as a *magnitude rule*, where this rule is interpreted defeasibly, just like an ordinary rule, and where the functions $Premise$ and $Conclusion$ picking out the premise and conclusion of this rule are defined as before. Following our earlier pattern, we will say that a magnitude rule is *applicable* in a dimensional fact situation just in case the magnitude reason that forms its premise holds in that fact situation. And we can then define a *dimensional case* as a triple $c = \langle X, r, s \rangle$, where X is a dimensional fact situation, r is a magnitude rule justifying a particular outcome, and s is the case outcome itself. As before, we have three functions – *Facts*, *Rule*, and *Outcome* – mapping cases into their component parts. And we again require, as a coherence condition on the concept of a case, both that the rule of the case should apply to its fact situation and that the conclusion of the case rule should match the case outcome, so that, with c as above, $X \models Premise(r)$ and $Conclusion(r) = s$.

These ideas can be illustrated by the dimensional case $c_{37} = \langle X_{37}, r_{37}, s_{37} \rangle$, with the familiar $X_{37} = \{\langle d_1, 30 \rangle, \langle d_2, 60 \rangle\}$ as its underlying dimensional fact situation, with $r_{37} = \{M^{\delta}_{d_1,12}\} \rightarrow \delta$ as its magnitude rule, and with

$s_{37} = \delta$ as its outcome, a decision for the defendant. The case, then, is one in which, confronted with an individual who has spent two and a half years, or thirty months, abroad, and during that period earned 60 percent of his or her income from foreign organizations, the court ruled for change of fiscal domicile, and so in favor of the defendant, on the grounds that the individual spent at least a year, or twelve months, abroad. Note that this case satisfies both of our coherence conditions, since the premise of the case rule holds in the fact situation of the case and the conclusion of this rule coincides with the case outcome.

Finally, and again following the pattern of ordinary framework, we define a *dimensional case base* Γ as a set of dimensional cases.

7.2 Constraint

We now explore ways in which our previous notions of constraint can be adapted to the dimensional framework, concentrating on two previous models: the a fortiori model and the reason model.

7.2.1 The A Fortiori Model

According to the a fortiori model, defined for the ordinary framework in Section 3.3, a court is required to decide a new fact situation for a particular side whenever the new situation is at least as strong for that side as the fact situation from an existing case that has already been decided for that side. This model, as noted earlier, depends on an ordering through which different fact situations can be compared in strength for one side or another. And in the ordinary framework, with ordinary fact situations defined as collections of ordinary factors, an appropriate ordering was introduced in Definition 20 from Section 3.3.1. Because it is cast in terms of set-theoretic inclusions, however, that earlier ordering, is no longer applicable in the dimensional framework. Fortunately, it is plain how the new definition should go: the dimensional fact situation Y should now be defined to be at least as strong as the dimensional fact situation X whenever the value of Y is at least as strong as the value of X along every dimension from D, the entire set of dimensions. Continuing to use $\leq^s$ to represent strength for a side s, this new definition can be stated formally as follows:

Definition 44 (Strength for a side among fact situations: dimensional) Let X and Y be dimensional fact situations. Then Y is at least as strong as X for the side s – written, $X \leq^s Y$ – if and only if $X(d) \trianglelefteq^s Y(d)$ for every dimension d from D.

And once this new concept of strength for a side is in place, our previous statement of the a fortiori model in terms of strength for a side, set out in Definition 21 from Section 3.3.2, can be carried over to the dimensional framework without change.

This model can be illustrated in the dimensional framework by taking as background the dimensional case base $\Gamma_{26} = \{c_{37}\}$, containing only the familiar $c_{37} = \langle X_{37}, r_{37}, s_{37}\rangle$, where $X_{37} = \{\langle d_1, 30\rangle, \langle d_2, 60\rangle\}$, where $r_{37} = \{M^{\delta}_{d_1,12}\} \rightarrow \delta$, and where $s_{37} = \delta$. Let us imagine that, against this background, the court confronts the new situation $X_{38} = \{\langle d_1, 36\rangle, \langle d_2, 65\rangle\}$, representing a state of affairs in which an individual spent three years in a foreign country while earning 65 percent of his or her income from foreign organizations. Comparing this fresh situation to the earlier X_{37}, our new Definition 44 tells us that $X_{37} \leq^{\delta} X_{38}$, or that X_{38} is at least as strong for the defendant as X_{37}, since $30 \trianglelefteq^{\delta} 36$ along the dimension d_1 and $60 \trianglelefteq^{\delta} 65$ along the dimension d_2 – a longer period in the foreign country favors the defendant, and so does a greater proportion of income earned from foreign organizations. The previous Definition 21 then tells us that the a fortiori model of constraint requires a decision for the defendant in the situation X_{38}, since this new situation is at least as strong for the defendant as X_{37}, the fact situation from a previous case that was already decided for the defendant.

7.2.2 The Reason Model

The a fortiori model of constraint, then, can be adapted in a straightforward way to the dimensional framework, but what about the reason model? The key idea underlying the reason model, we recall, is that later courts are required only to reach decisions that are consistent with the priority ordering among reasons already established by cases within a background case base. But how, in the dimensional framework, is a priority ordering among reasons to be determined by the decision in a precedent case?

Here, it seems that – once the notions of reason satisfaction and strength for a side among reasons have been reformulated to apply in the dimensional framework, as well as the ordinary framework – the series of definitions set out in Sections 1.2.1 and 1.2.2 to characterize the reason model can be transposed to the dimensional setting very simply. To spell it out: According to Definition 7, the reason model permits a court, faced with a fresh fact situation and working against the background of an existing case base, to reach a particular decision in that situation only if that decision maintains consistency of the background case base. A case base is consistent, according to Definition 6, as long as the priority ordering derived from that case base does not rank each of a pair of reasons as higher in priority than the other, where the priority ordering derived from a case base is set out in Definition 5, which itself relies on the central concept, from Definition 4, of the priority ordering on reasons derived from a single case. This latter definition draws on the ideas of reason satisfaction and strength for a side among reasons from our new Definitions 41 and 43, which themselves bottom out, in the ordinary setting, in the treatment of ordinary factor satisfaction from Definition 40 and, in the dimensional setting, in the new treatment of magnitude factor satisfaction from Definition 39.

According to this transposition, then, the entire structure of the reason model is identical in the ordinary and dimensional frameworks, differing only at the very bottom level, with different accounts of satisfaction for ordinary and magnitude factors. And on the basis of this structural similarity, it can be verified that the helpful Observation 5, established in Section 2.2.1 for the reason model in the ordinary framework, holds in the dimensional framework as well.

To illustrate the reason model in the more complex dimensional framework, let us begin with the familiar $c_{37} = \langle X_{37}, r_{37}, s_{37} \rangle$ – where $X_{37} = \{\langle d_1, 30\rangle, \langle d_2, 60\rangle\}$, where $r_{37} = \{M^{\delta}_{d_1,12}\} \rightarrow \delta$, and where $s_{37} = \delta$ – and again ask what information is carried by this case; what is the court telling us with its decision? According to the reason model, the answer is that, with its decision for the defendant on the basis of the rule r_{37}, the court is telling us, first of all, that $Premise(r_{37}) = \{M^{\delta}_{d_1,12}\}$, the reason for its decision, carries higher priority than any reason for the plaintiff that holds in X_{37}, the fact situation of the case, and second, that any reason for the defendant that is itself at least as strong as $Premise(r_{37})$ must likewise carry higher priority than any reason for the plaintiff that holds in this situation.

We now consider two examples, each of which is based on the background case base $\Gamma_{26} = \{c_{37}\}$, containing c_{37} as its sole member. The fact situation from this case can be depicted as a point in the dimensional space from Figure 7.1, with the horizontal and vertical axes representing the dimensions d_1 and d_2, length of time abroad and proportion of income earned abroad, and with values along each dimension more distant from the origin favoring

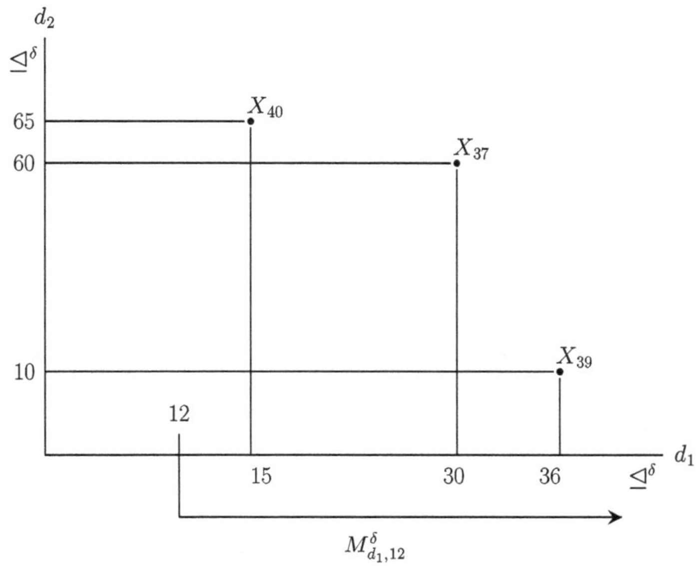

Figure 7.1 $r_{37} = \{M^\delta_{d_1,12}\} \rightarrow \delta$

the defendant more strongly; the diagram also indicates the range of situations in which $Premise(r_{37}) = \{M^\delta_{d_1,12}\}$ holds, so that the rule r_{37} of the case applies.

For our first example, imagine that a court confronts the new fact situation $X_{39} = \{\langle d_1, 36\rangle, \langle d_2, 10\rangle\}$, also depicted in Figure 7.1, representing a defendant who easily satisfies the rule of the c_{37} court by spending a full three years abroad, but during that period earned only 10 percent of his or her income abroad. In considering this situation, the court might be struck by the remarkably low proportion of income earned abroad and suppose that this possibility had not been foreseen by the c_{37} court when it formulated its rule based solely on length of stay. The new court might, therefore, hope to distinguish on this basis, ruling against change of domicile, and so in favor of the plaintiff, on the grounds that no more than, say, 25 percent of income was earned abroad. This decision would be represented by the case $c_{39} = \langle X_{39}, r_{39}, s_{39}\rangle$, where X_{39} is as above, where $r_{39} = \{M^\pi_{d_2,25}\} \rightarrow \pi$, and where $s_{39} = \pi$.

Is the new court permitted to rule as it prefers? It is, according to the reason model, since the resulting case base $\Gamma_{26} \cup \{c_{39}\}$ is consistent. This fact can be verified as follows: Suppose $\Gamma_{26} \cup \{c_{39}\}$ were inconsistent. Since the case base contains only two cases, c_{37} and c_{39}, it would then follow by Observation 5 that both $Premise(r_{39}) <_{c_{37}} Premise(r_{37})$

and $Premise(r_{37}) <_{c_{39}} Premise(r_{39})$. By Definition 4, the first of these priority relations requires that $X_{37} \models Premise(r_{39})$, which holds just in case $25 \trianglelefteq^{\pi} X_{37}(d_2)$ by Definitions 41 and 39, the evaluation rules for reasons and magnitude factors. From this we have $25 \trianglelefteq^{\pi} 60$, since $X_{37}(d_2) = 60$. Our domain assumptions, however, tell us that $60 \trianglelefteq^{\pi} 25$, since a smaller proportion of income earned from foreign organizations favors the plaintiff as least as much as a larger proportion. And then antisymmetry of the $\trianglelefteq^{\pi}$ relation tells us that $25 = 60$, which is false.

Even in light of this formal verification, however, it is still worth asking exactly why, from an intuitive standpoint, this decision for the plaintiff in the situation X_{39} should be consistent with the background case base – since, after all, the contrary rule r_{37} from the previous case applies in the new situation. The answer is that, according to the reason model, the previous c_{37} decision is interpreted to mean only that the reason $Premise(r_{37}) = \{M^{\delta}_{d_1,12}\}$ – or of course, any other reason for the defendant that is at least as strong – must be assigned a higher priority than any reason for the plaintiff that holds in X_{37}, the fact situation of that case. But the new situation X_{39} presents new reasons for the plaintiff that do not hold in the previous situation – such as the reason $Premise(r_{39}) = \{M^{\pi}_{d_2,25}\}$ itself. And it is not inconsistent for a new court to decide that one of these new reasons carries a higher priority than the premise of the previous rule. In particular, the new court might consistently decide that earning no more than 25 percent of income abroad is a stronger reason against change of domicile than spending at least a year abroad is in favor of change of domicile, leading to the decision c_{39} and so to the proposition $Premise(r_{37}) <_{c_{39}} Premise(r_{39})$.

For our second example, still working against the background of the case base $\Gamma_{26} = \{c_{37}\}$, consider the new fact situation $X_{40} = \{\langle d_1, 15\rangle, \langle d_2, 65\rangle\}$, again depicted in Figure 7.1, representing a defendant who spent fifteen months abroad while earning 65 percent of income abroad. Imagine that this situation comes before a court that evaluates change of domicile cases against very high standards for proportion of income earned abroad – suppose, in fact, that the court feels that change of domicile requires earning more than 75 percent of income abroad. A court like this would prefer to rule in favor of the plaintiff in the situation X_{40} on the grounds that the defendant fails the 75 percent test. This decision would be represented by the case $c_{40} = \langle X_{40}, r_{40}, s_{40}\rangle$, where X_{40} is as above, where $r_{40} = \{M^{\pi}_{d_2,75}\} \rightarrow \pi$, and where $s_{40} = \pi$.

Again we ask whether the court is permitted to rule as it prefers, and the answer this time is that it cannot, since the resulting case base $\Gamma_{26} \cup \{c_{40}\}$ is inconsistent. To see this, we note that the pair of cases c_{37} and c_{40} belonging to this case base would generate an inconsistent ordering on the premises of its case rules, since each of these rules would then hold in the fact situation of the other case, where the other rule was preferred. More exactly, we have $X_{37} \models Premise(r_{40})$ and also $Premise(r_{37}) \leq^{\delta} Premise(r_{37})$, of course, from which it follows that $Premise(r_{40}) <_{c_{37}} Premise(r_{37})$; likewise we have $X_{40} \models Premise(r_{37})$ and also $Premise(r_{40}) \leq^{\pi} Premise(r_{40})$, from which it follows that $Premise(r_{37}) <_{c_{40}} Premise(r_{40})$. What this example illustrates is that the court is not permitted to find for the plaintiff in the situation X_{40} on the basis of proportion of income earned abroad, since any reason favoring the plaintiff on the basis of proportion of income that holds in X_{40} would already have to hold in X_{37}.

7.3 Collapse and Recovery

7.3.1 Collapse

So far, so good – but now consider a third example. Still assuming $\Gamma_{26} = \{c_{37}\}$ as a background case base – with $c_{37} = \langle X_{37}, r_{37}, s_{37}\rangle$ where $X_{37} = \{\langle d_1, 30\rangle, \langle d_2, 60\rangle\}$, where $r_{37} = \{M^{\delta}_{d_1,12}\} \rightarrow \delta$, and where $s_{37} = \delta$ – imagine that the previous situation $X_{40} = \{\langle d_1, 15\rangle, \langle d_2, 65\rangle\}$ now comes before a court that cares little about proportion of income earned abroad, but applies much stricter standards than the c_{37} court for length of time abroad. Imagine, in fact, that the new court would prefer to rule against change of domicile in this situation, and so for the plaintiff, on the grounds that the defendant failed to spend more than two years abroad – that is, that the actual period abroad favors the plaintiff at least as much as a period of two years, or twenty-four months. The resulting decision would be represented by the new case $c_{41} = \langle X_{41}, r_{41}, s_{41}\rangle$, where $X_{41} = X_{40}$, where $r_{41} = \{M^{\pi}_{d_1,24}\} \rightarrow \pi$, and where $s_{41} = \pi$.

Is this new court permitted to rule as it prefers? Yes, according to the reason model, since the resulting case base $\Gamma_{26} \cup \{c_{41}\}$ is consistent – this can be established by an argument parallel to that set out just above to establish the consistency of $\Gamma_{26} \cup \{c_{39}\}$. Of course, there is, quite plainly, a disagreement of sorts between the previous c_{37} court and the current c_{41} court, since the c_{37} court bases its decision on the rule that any period of a year or longer abroad is sufficient to justify change of fiscal domicile, while the c_{41} court relies on the rule that there is no change of domicile as long as the period abroad is two years or less. But at least according to our current formulation of the reason model, a disagreement like this does not rise to the level of inconsistency.

This fact reflects a more general result about the relation, in the dimensional framework, between the a fortiori model and the reason model. An analogue to the earlier Observation 10, established in Section 3.3.3 for the ordinary framework, continues to hold in the dimensional framework:

Observation 14 Let Γ be a consistent dimensional case base and X a dimensional fact situation confronting the court. Then against the background of Γ, if the a fortiori model of constraint requires the court to decide X for the side s, the reason model of constraint also requires the court to decide X for the side s.

What this observation tells us is that, in the dimensional setting as well as the ordinary setting, a fortiori constraint entails reason constraint: in any situation in which the a fortiori model requires the court to reach a decision for some side, the reason model requires a decision for that same side. As we saw in the discussion following the earlier Observation 10, the converse does not hold in the ordinary setting: a court can be required by the reason model to reach a decision for a particular side even though that decision is not required by the a fortiori model. Once we move to the full dimensional setting, however, it turns out that the converse of the analogous Observation 14 holds as well: not only does a fortiori constraint entail reason constraint, but reason constraint entails a fortiori constraint. The two models of constraint, which are distinct in the ordinary setting, now collapse into one.

Observation 15 Let Γ be a consistent dimensional case base and X a dimensional fact situation confronting the court. Then against the background of Γ, if the reason model of constraint requires the court to decide X for the side s, the a fortiori model of constraint also requires the court to decide X for the side s.

Although this observation will be verified formally in the appendix, it is worth illustrating here with an example that contains the germ of the full proof. Again working against the background of the case base $\Gamma_{26} = \{c_{37}\}$ – containing $c_{37} = \langle X_{37}, r_{37}, s_{37}\rangle$, where $X_{37} = \{\langle d_1, 30\rangle, \langle d_2, 60\rangle\}$, where r_{37} is

$\{M^{\delta}_{d_1,12}\} \rightarrow \delta$, and where s_{37} is δ – let us now suppose the court confronts the new situation $X_{42} = \{\langle d_1, 29\rangle, \langle d_2, 65\rangle\}$. This new situation is similar to the situation $X_{41} = \{\langle d_1, 15\rangle, \langle d_2, 65\rangle\}$, just considered. Compared to the fact situation X_{37} from c_{37}, the single case from the background case base, both X_{41} and X_{42} are stronger for the defendant along the dimension d_2, proportion of income earned abroad. In contrast to X_{41}, however, which is considerably weaker for the defendant along the dimension d_1, length of time abroad, the new X_{42} is only very slightly weaker for the defendant along this dimension – here, the individual spent twenty-nine months abroad rather than thirty, a difference of only a single month.

Still, since there is some dimension along which X_{42} is not at least as strong for the defendant as the fact situation X_{37} from c_{37}, this case cannot form the basis of an a fortiori argument for the defendant in the new situation. A decision for the defendant is not, therefore, required by the a fortiori model, and what Observation 15 tells us is that a decision for the defendant cannot then be required by the rule model either – there must be some rule on the basis of which the court can consistently decide for the plaintiff. How do we construct such a rule? As it turns out, if X_{42} is weaker along any dimension than the fact situation from c_{37}, then this weakness – however slight, however limited in extent – can be used to form a rule consistently supporting the plaintiff. In this particular situation, there is nothing to prevent the court from ruling for the plaintiff on the basis of the reason $\{M^{\pi}_{d_1,29}\}$ – that the individual spent no more than twenty-nine months abroad. The resulting decision would be represented by the case $c_{42} = \langle X_{42}, r_{42}, s_{42}\rangle$, where X_{42} is as above, where $r_{42} = \{M^{\pi}_{d_1,29}\} \rightarrow \pi$, and where $s_{42} = \pi$. The reader can verify that the augmented case base $\Gamma_{26} \cup \{c_{42}\}$ is consistent, so that this decision is permitted by the reason model.

7.3.2 Modifying the Reason Model

How should we respond to this collapse, within the dimensional framework, of the reason model of constraint into the a fortiori model? When I first noticed this problem, I was willing to accept it, and explored what might be thought as "pragmatic" means of differentiating the two models, rather than altering the definition of the reason model itself.[8] A number of other writers, however, criticized this approach, arguing that the collapse of the reason and result models shows that the reason model itself must be modified, and

[8] See Horty (2019, Section 4) for some of these pragmatic suggestions.

mapping out alternative approaches of their own.[9] Although I still think there is something to be said for the original definition of the reason model, I now agree that the collapse is sufficiently unintuitive that this model, initially formulated within the ordinary framework, must be modified to function properly within the more complex dimensional setting, which allows nontrivial structural relations among reasons.

In order to motivate the proposed modification, let us return to the rationale for the original reason model, and especially to its conclusion that the case base $\Gamma_{26} \cup \{c_{41}\}$, considered just above in Section 7.3.1, is consistent – where, as a reminder, $\Gamma_{26} = \{c_{37}\}$ with $c_{37} = \langle X_{37}, r_{37}, s_{37}\rangle$, where $X_{37} = \{\langle d_1, 30\rangle, \langle d_2, 60\rangle\}$, where $r_{37} = \{M^{\delta}_{d_1,12}\} \rightarrow \delta$, and where $s_{37} = \delta$; and with $c_{41} = \langle X_{41}, r_{41}, s_{41}\rangle$, where $X_{41} = \{\langle d_1, 15\rangle, \langle d_2, 65\rangle\}$, where $r_{41} = \{M^{\pi}_{d_1,24}\} \rightarrow \pi$, and where $s_{41} = \pi$. How could anyone think that the case base $\Gamma_{26} \cup \{c_{41}\}$ is consistent, or that c_{41} could be consistent with c_{37}? How could anyone think, in light of the earlier c_{37} decision for change of domicile on the grounds that the defendant spent at least a year abroad, that a later court could consistently decide in c_{41} against change of domicile on the grounds that the defendant in that case, who did in fact spend at least a year abroad, failed to stay abroad for two years?

Well, to understand how this c_{41} decision could be regarded as consistent with the earlier c_{37}, on the reason model, let us recall our initial example from Section 7.2.2, where, against the background of the same c_{37} decision for change of domicile on the grounds that the defendant spent at least a year abroad, a later court decided against change of domicile in $c_{39} = \langle X_{39}, r_{39}, s_{39}\rangle$ – where $X_{39} = \{\langle d_1, 36\rangle, \langle d_2, 10\rangle\}$, where $r_{39} = \{M^{\pi}_{d_2,25}\} \rightarrow \pi$, and where $s_{39} = \pi$ – on the grounds that the defendant in that case, who had spent at least a year abroad, failed to earn at least 25 percent of his or her income abroad. In that example, we concluded that the c_{39} decision was consistent with the earlier c_{37} decision because the new situation X_{39} presented new reasons for the plaintiff – in particular, the reason $Premise(r_{39}) = \{M^{\pi}_{d_2,25}\}$, or that the defendant had failed to earn at least 25 percent of income abroad – that did not hold in the earlier situation X_{37}. Because these new reasons failed to hold in the earlier situation, they were, therefore, not ordered relative to the reason $Premise(r_{37}) = \{M^{\delta}_{d_1,12}\}$, justifying the earlier decision, and so could consistently be assigned a higher priority than this earlier reason.

9 See, especially, Bench-Capon and Atkinson (2017, 2018) and Rigoni (2018).

With this argument for consistency in mind, we can return to the current example, where, as it turns out, exactly the same argument can be deployed to support the conclusion that the c_{41} decision is consistent with the earlier c_{37}. To be precise: the new situation X_{41} likewise presents new reasons for the plaintiff – in particular, $Premise(r_{41}) = \{M^{\pi}_{d_1,24}\}$, or that the defendant failed to stay abroad for at least two years – that do not hold in the earlier situation X_{37}, that were therefore not ordered relative to the reason $Premise(r_{37}) = \{M^{\delta}_{d_1,12}\}$, justifying the earlier decision, and so can likewise consistently be assigned a higher priority than this earlier reason.

The reason model argument to establish the consistency of c_{39} with the earlier c_{37} seems, therefore, to work equally well at establishing the consistency of c_{41} with c_{37}. It follows that if we want to allow consistency between c_{39} and c_{37}, but not between c_{41} and c_{37}, we will have to modify the reason model to reflect some difference between c_{39} and c_{41}. But what could the relevant difference be? Given that c_{37} had been justified with the reason $Premise(r_{37}) = \{M^{\delta}_{d_1,12}\}$, and neither $Premise(r_{39}) = \{M^{\pi}_{d_2,25}\}$ nor $Premise(r_{41}) = \{M^{\pi}_{d_1,24}\}$ held in the earlier situations, respectively X_{39} and X_{41}, what basis could we have for later allowing $Premise(r_{39}) = \{M^{\pi}_{d_2,25}\}$ but not $Premise(r_{41}) = \{M^{\pi}_{d_1,24}\}$, to be consistently assigned a higher priority than the original $Premise(r_{37}) = \{M^{\delta}_{d_1,12}\}$? The proposal set out here is based on the idea that the additional structural information present in the dimensional framework suggests a more complex ordering among reasons, according to which, as a result of the c_{37} decision, the reason $Premise(r_{37}) = \{M^{\delta}_{d_1,12}\}$ must be assigned a priority higher than that of $Premise(r_{41}) = \{M^{\pi}_{d_1,24}\}$ but not higher than that of $Premise(r_{39}) = \{M^{\pi}_{d_2,25}\}$, so that, in the later cases, $Premise(r_{39}) = \{M^{\pi}_{d_2,25}\}$ can consistently be ranked above $Premise(r_{37}) = \{M^{\delta}_{d_1,12}\}$ but $Premise(r_{41}) = \{M^{\pi}_{d_1,24}\}$ cannot.

How can this more complex priority ordering be defined? Our characterization moves through two steps. The first is entirely notational: where V is a reason favoring the side s, we let

$$\overline{V} = \{M^{\overline{s}}_{d,p} \; : \; M^{s}_{d,p} \in V\}$$

be a reason favoring the side $\overline{s}$, built from magnitude factors addressing the same dimensions as those in V and using the same reference values, but favoring the opposite side. To illustrate: where $Premise(r_{37}) = \{M^{\delta}_{d_1,12}\}$ is a reason favoring the defendant on the grounds that they spent a year or more abroad, $\overline{Premise(r_{37})} = \{M^{\pi}_{d_1,12}\}$ is a reason favoring the plaintiff on the grounds that the defendant spent a year or less abroad.

Next, and more substantially, where $c = \langle X,r,s\rangle$ is a dimensional case decided for the side s with the reason $Premise(r)$ as justification, and W is a reason favoring the opposite side $\bar{s}$, we stipulate that $Premise(r)$ is to be assigned a higher priority than W on the basis of the decision c – that is, $W <_c Premise(r)$ – whenever $W \leq^{\bar{s}} \overline{Premise(r)}$. The intuition behind this stipulation is this: By appealing to $Premise(r)$ to justify its decision for s, the court is implicitly asserting that $Premise(r)$ carries higher priority as a reason for s than $\overline{Premise(r)}$ does as a reason for $\bar{s}$. And then, of course, since $W \leq^{\bar{s}} \overline{Premise(r)}$, we know that $\overline{Premise(r)}$ is at least as strong a reason as W for $\bar{s}$, from which it follows – given that $Premise(r)$ carries higher priority for s than $\overline{Premise(r)}$ does for $\bar{s}$ – that $Premise(r)$ must likewise carry higher priority for s than W does for $\bar{s}$.

For a concrete illustration, we return to the problem presented by our third example: ruling out consistency of c_{41} with the earlier c_{37} by showing why $Premise(r_{41}) = \{M^{\pi}_{d_1,24}\}$ cannot consistently be ranked above $Premise(r_{37}) = \{M^{\delta}_{d_1,12}\}$. By appealing to $Premise(r_{37}) = \{M^{\delta}_{d_1,12}\}$ to justify a judgment for the defendant, the c_{37} court is implicitly asserting that $Premise(r_{37}) = \{M^{\delta}_{d_1,12}\}$ carries higher priority as a reason for the defendant than $\overline{Premise(r_{37})} = \{M^{\pi}_{d_1,12}\}$ does for the plaintiff, or that $\overline{Premise(r_{37})} <_{c_{37}} Premise(r_{37})$ – spending a year or more abroad carries higher priority for the defendant than spending a year or less abroad for the plaintiff. Turning now to $Premise(r_{41}) = \{M^{\pi}_{d_1,24}\}$, it is easy to verify first that $\{M^{\pi}_{d_1,12}\} \Vdash \{M^{\pi}_{d_1,24}\}$, so that $\{M^{\pi}_{d_1,24}\} \leq^{\pi} \{M^{\pi}_{d_1,12}\}$, or that $Premise(r_{41}) \leq^{\pi} \overline{Premise(r_{37})}$ – spending a year or less abroad is at least as strong a reason for the plaintiff as spending two years or less abroad. Then this, along with the previous $\overline{Premise(r_{37})} <_{c_{37}} Premise(r_{37})$ yields the further conclusion $Premise(r_{41}) <_{c_{37}} Premise(r_{37})$ – spending a year or more abroad carries higher priority for the defendant than spending two years or less abroad for the plaintiff. In other words, our new stipulation allows us to conclude that the court's decision in c_{37} entails that $Premise(r_{37}) = \{M^{\delta}_{d_1,12}\}$ carries higher priority than $Premise(r_{41}) = \{M^{\pi}_{d_1,24}\}$, so that, as desired, $Premise(r_{41}) = \{M^{\pi}_{d_1,24}\}$ can no longer consistently be prioritized over $Premise(r_{37}) = \{M^{\delta}_{d_1,12}\}$.

Our suggested modification, taking dimensional information into account, can now be incorporated very simply into our original definition of the priority ordering among reasons derived from a case:

Definition 45 (Priority ordering derived from a case: modified) Let $c = \langle X,r,s\rangle$ be a case, and let W and Z be reasons favoring the sides $\bar{s}$ and

s respectively. Then the relation $<_c$ representing the priority ordering on reasons derived from the case c is defined by stipulating that $W <_c Z$ if and only if either (1a) $X \models W$ or (1b) $W \leq^{\bar{s}} \overline{Premise(r)}$, and (2) $Premise(r) \leq^{s} Z$.

The modified reason model, appropriate for the dimensional setting, then results simply by replacing the original Definition 4 from Section 1.2.1 with this new Definition 45, leaving everything else unchanged.

It is easy to see that this modified reason model agrees with the original in our first and second examples, from Section 7.2.2. In our third example, from Section 7.3.1, where the original model yields the troubling result that the case base $\Gamma_{26} \cup \{c_{41}\}$ is consistent, or that the later decision c_{41} is consistent with the earlier c_{37}, the modified reason model yields the more natural result that this decision is inconsistent. More exactly, we have $Premise(r_{37}) <_{c_{41}} Premise(r_{41})$, since (1a) $X_{41} \models Premise(r_{37})$ and of course (2) $Premise(r_{41}) \leq^{\pi} Premise(r_{41})$. But we also have $Premise(r_{41}) <_{c_{37}} Premise(r_{37})$, since, although (1a) $X_{37} \models Premise(r_{41})$ fails, we now have (1b) $Premise(r_{41}) \leq^{\pi} \overline{Premise(r_{37})}$ and (2) $Premise(r_{37}) \leq^{\delta} Premise(r_{37})$.

In order to see how this modified reason model works with reasons addressing multiple dimensions, we consider two additional examples. Suppose a court faced once more with the familiar fact situation $X_{37} = \{\langle d_1, 30\rangle, \langle d_2, 60\rangle\}$ again decides for the defendant, but this time on the basis of the more restrictive consideration that the defendant both spent at least a year abroad and earned at least 50 percent of income abroad. This decision can be represented through the new case $c_{43} = \langle X_{43}, r_{43}, s_{43}\rangle$, where $X_{43} = X_{37}$, where $r_{43} = \{M^{\delta}_{d_1,12}, M^{\delta}_{d_2,50}\} \rightarrow \delta$, and where $s_{43} = \delta$. The fact situation and rule from this case are depicted in Figure 7.2.

Against the background of the case base $\Gamma_{27} = \{c_{43}\}$ containing this case, consider the new fact situations $X_{44} = \{\langle d_1, 15\rangle, \langle d_2, 55\rangle\}$ and $X_{45} = \{\langle d_1, 15\rangle, \langle d_2, 35\rangle\}$, also depicted in Figure 7.2. Suppose the court wishes to decide X_{44} for the plaintiff on the grounds that the defendant failed to spend at least two years abroad, a decision that would be represented through the case $c_{44} = \langle X_{44}, r_{44}, s_{44}\rangle$, where X_{44} is as above, where $r_{44} = \{M^{\pi}_{d_1,24}\} \rightarrow \pi$, and where $s_{44} = \pi$. According to the modified version of the reason model, though not the original, this decision would be inconsistent with Γ_{27}. We have $Premise(r_{44}) <_{c_{43}} Premise(r_{43})$, since (1b) $Premise(r_{44}) \leq^{\delta} \overline{Premise(r_{43})}$ and (2) $Premise(r_{43}) \leq^{\delta} Premise(r_{43})$. But we also have $Premise(r_{43}) <_{c_{44}} Premise(r_{44})$, since (1a) $X_{44} \models Premise(r_{43})$ and (2) $Premise(r_{44}) \leq^{\pi} Premise(r_{44})$.

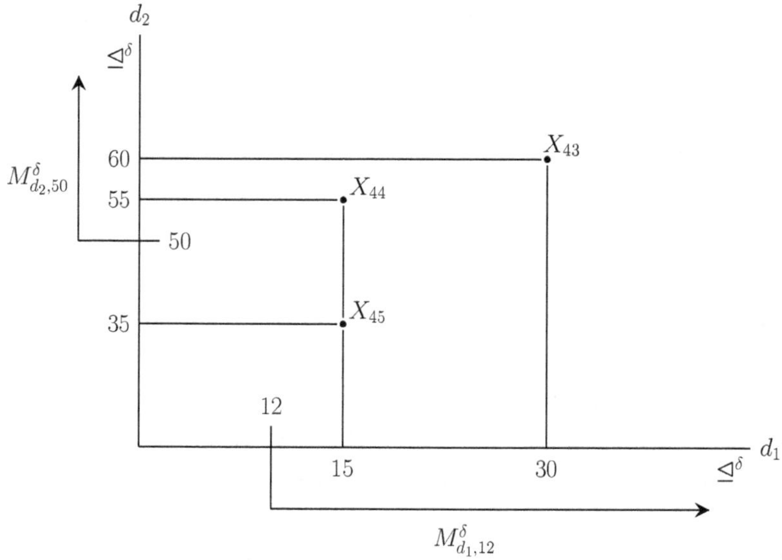

Figure 7.2 $r_{43} = \{M^{\delta}_{d_1,12}, M^{\delta}_{d_2,50}\} \rightarrow \delta$

On the other hand, suppose the court wishes to decide X_{45} for the plaintiff for exactly the same reason, because the defendant failed to spend at least two years abroad, leading to $c_{45} = \langle X_{45}, r_{45}, s_{45}\rangle$, where X_{45} is as above, where $r_{45} = \{M^{\pi}_{d_1,24}\} \rightarrow \pi$, and where $s_{45} = \pi$. This time the decision would be consistent with Γ_{27}. We again have $Premise(r_{45}) <_{c_{43}} Premise(r_{43})$, since (1b) $Premise(r_{45}) \leq^{\pi} \overline{Premise(r_{43})}$ and (2) $Premise(r_{43}) \leq^{\delta} Premise(r_{43})$. But we do not have $Premise(r_{43}) <_{c_{45}} Premise(r_{45})$, since although (2) $Premise(r_{45}) \leq^{\pi} Premise(r_{45})$ holds, of course, both (1a) $X_{45} \models Premise(r_{43})$ and (1b) $Premise(r_{43}) \leq^{\delta} \overline{Premise(r_{45})}$ fail.

The proposed modification, then, separates the reason model from the a fortiori model and yields more attractive outcomes in certain situations, such as those explored in our third example, but it raises interesting conceptual questions of its own. Consider, one last time, the case $c_{37} = \langle X_{37}, r_{37}, s_{37}\rangle$ – where $X_{37} = \{\langle d_1, 30\rangle, \langle d_2, 60\rangle\}$, where $r_{37} = \{M^{\delta}_{d_1,12}\} \rightarrow \delta$, and where $s_{37} = \delta$ – in which the court confronting a defendant who had spent two and a half years abroad found for change of domicile on the grounds that the defendant had stayed abroad for at least a year. Now imagine that a new court confronting the new situation $X_{46} = \{\langle d_1, 6\rangle, \langle d_2, 60\rangle\}$, in which a defendant has spent a mere six months abroad, rules against change of domicile, and so for the plaintiff, on the grounds that the defendant had stayed abroad for less than two years. This decision would be represented by the case

$c_{46} = \langle X_{46}, r_{46}, s_{46} \rangle$, where X_{46} is as above, where $r_{46} = \{M^{\pi}_{d_1,24}\} \rightarrow \pi$, and where $s_{46} = \pi$. According to the modified reason model proposed here, but not according to the original, these two cases would be inconsistent – so that a court could not, for example, consistently reach the c_{46} decision against the background of a case base containing c_{37}. It is striking, however, that neither of the rules from these two cases is applicable in the fact situation from the other – that is, r_{37} is not applicable in X_{46} and r_{46} is not applicable in X_{37}. Any inconsistency must therefore result entirely from structural relations between the case rules themselves, contrary to what many feel is the common law idea that inconsistency is not an abstract feature of rule systems but arises only from the application of rules to particular, concrete situations.

Appendix

A.1 Cases and Fact Situations

1. $c_1 = \langle X_1, r_1, s_1 \rangle$, where $X_1 = \{f_1^{\pi}, f_2^{\pi}, f_1^{\delta}, f_2^{\delta}\}$, where $r_1 = \{f_1^{\pi}\} \rightarrow \pi$, and where s_1 is π. Introduced in Section 1.1.1.
2. $c_2 = \langle X_2, r_2, s_2 \rangle$, where $X_2 = \{f_1^{\pi}, f_2^{\pi}, f_1^{\delta}, f_2^{\delta}, f_3^{\delta}\}$, where $r_2 = \{f_1^{\delta}, f_2^{\delta}\} \rightarrow \delta$, and where $s_2 = \delta$. Introduced in Section 1.2.2.
3. $c_3 = \langle X_3, r_3, s_3 \rangle$, where $X_3 = \{f_1^{\pi}, f_2^{\pi}, f_1^{\delta}, f_2^{\delta}, f_3^{\delta}\}$, where $r_3 = \{f_1^{\delta}, f_3^{\delta}\} \rightarrow \delta$, and where $s_3 = \delta$. Introduced in Section 1.2.2.
4. $c_4 = \langle X_4, r_4, s_4 \rangle$, where $X_4 = \{f_1^{\pi}, f_2^{\pi}, f_1^{\delta}\}$, where $r_4 = \{f_1^{\pi}\} \rightarrow \pi$, and where $s_4 = \pi$. Introduced in Section 1.2.3.
5. $c_5 = \langle X_5, r_5, s_5 \rangle$, where $X_5 = \{f_1^{\pi}, f_2^{\pi}, f_1^{\delta}, f_1^{\delta}\}$, where $r_5 = \{f_2^{\delta}\} \rightarrow \delta$, and where $s_5 = \delta$. Introduced in Section 1.2.3.
6. $X_6 = \{f_1^{\delta}, f_1^{\delta}\}$. Introduced in Section 1.2.4.
7. $c_7 = \langle X_7, r_7, s_7 \rangle$, where $X_7 = \{f_1^{\upsilon}, f_2^{\upsilon}, f_1^{\upsilon'}, f_2^{\upsilon'}, f_3^{\upsilon'}\}$, where $r_7 = \{f_2^{\upsilon'}\} \rightarrow \upsilon'$, and where $s_7 = \upsilon'$. Introduced in Section 1.3.2.
8. $c_8 = \langle X_8, r_8, s_8 \rangle$, where $X_8 = \{f_1^{\upsilon}, f_2^{\upsilon}, f_1^{\upsilon'}, f_2^{\upsilon'}\}$, where $r_8 = \{f_2^{\upsilon'}\} \rightarrow \upsilon'$, and where $s_8 = \upsilon'$. Introduced in Section 1.3.2.
9. $c_9 = \langle X_9, r_9, s_9 \rangle$, where $X_9 = \{f_1^{\pi}, f_2^{\pi}, f_3^{\pi}, f_1^{\delta}, f_3^{\delta}, f_4^{\delta}\}$, where $r_9 = \{f_1^{\delta}, f_3^{\delta}\} \rightarrow \delta$, and where $s_9 = \delta$. Introduced in Section 2.1.2.
10. $c_{10} = \langle X_{10}, r_{10}, s_{10} \rangle$, where $X_{10} = \{f_1^{\pi}, f_2^{\pi}, f_3^{\pi}, f_1^{\delta}, f_3^{\delta}, f_4^{\delta}\}$, where $r_{10} = \{f_3^{\pi}\} \rightarrow \pi$, and where $s_{10} = \pi$. Introduced in Section 2.1.2.
11. $c_{11} = \langle X_{11}, r_{11}, s_{11} \rangle$, where $X_{11} = \{f_1^{\pi}, f_2^{\pi}, f_3^{\pi}, f_1^{\delta}, f_3^{\delta}, f_4^{\delta}\}$, where $r_{11} = \{f_4^{\delta}\} \rightarrow \delta$, and where $s_{11} = \delta$. Introduced in Section 2.1.2.
12. $c_{12} = \langle X_{12}, r_{12}, s_{12} \rangle$, where $X_{12} = \{f_1^{\pi}, f_1^{\delta}, f_3^{\delta}\}$, where $r_{12} = \{f_1^{\pi}\} \rightarrow \pi$, and where $s_{12} = \pi$. Introduced in Section 2.1.3.
13. $c_{13} = \langle X_{13}, r_{13}, s_{13} \rangle$, where $X_{13} = \{f_1^{\pi}, f_1^{\delta}, f_2^{\delta}\}$, where $r_{13} = \{f_1^{\pi}\} \rightarrow \pi$, and where $s_{13} = \pi$. Introduced in Section 2.2.2.
14. $c_{14} = \langle X_{14}, r_{14}, s_{14} \rangle$, where $X_{14} = \{f_1^{\pi}, f_1^{\delta}\}$, where $r_{14} = \{f_1^{\delta}\} \rightarrow \delta$, and where $s_{14} = \delta$. Introduced in Section 2.2.2.

15. $c_{15} = \langle X_{15}, r_{15}, s_{15} \rangle$, where $X_{15} = \{f_1^{\pi}, f_2^{\delta}\}$, where $r_{15} = \{f_1^{\pi}\} \rightarrow \pi$, and where $s_{15} = \pi$. Introduced in Section 2.2.2.
16. $c_{16} = \langle X_{16}, r_{16}, s_{16} \rangle$, where $X_{16} = \{f_1^{\pi}, f_2^{\delta}\}$, where $r_{16} = \{f_2^{\delta}\} \rightarrow \delta$, and where $s_{16} = \delta$. Introduced in Section 2.2.2.
17. $c_{17} = \langle X_{17}, r_{17}, s_{17} \rangle$, where $X_{17} = \{f_1^{\pi}, f_1^{\delta}\}$, where $r_{17} = \{f_1^{\pi}\} \rightarrow \pi$, and where $s_{17} = \pi$. Introduced in Section 2.2.3.
18. $c_{18} = \langle X_{18}, r_{18}, s_{18} \rangle$, where $X_{18} = \{f_1^{\pi}, f_2^{\delta}\}$, where $r_{18} = \{f_2^{\delta}\} \rightarrow \delta$, and where $s_{18} = \delta$. Introduced in Section 2.2.3.
19. $c_{19} = \langle X_{19}, r_{19}, s_{19} \rangle$, where $X_{19} = \{f_2^{\pi}, f_2^{\delta}\}$, where $r_{19} = \{f_2^{\pi}\} \rightarrow \pi$, and where $s_{19} = \pi$. Introduced in Section 2.2.3.
20. $c_{20} = \langle X_{20}, r_{20}, s_{20} \rangle$, where $X_{20} = \{f_2^{\pi}, f_1^{\delta}\}$, where $r_{20} = \{f_1^{\delta}\} \rightarrow \delta$, and where $s_{20} = \delta$. Introduced in Section 2.2.3.
21. $c_{21} = \langle X_{21}, r_{21}, s_{21} \rangle$, where $X_{21} = \{f_1^{\pi}, f_2^{\pi}, f_1^{\delta}, f_2^{\delta}\}$, where $r_{21} = \{f_1^{\pi}\} \Rightarrow \pi$, and where $s_{21} = \pi$. Introduced in Section 3.1.2.
22. $c_{22} = \langle X_{22}, r_{22}, s_{22} \rangle$, where $X_{22} = \{f_1^{\pi}, f_2^{\pi}, f_1^{\delta}, f_2^{\delta}, f_3^{\delta}\}$, where $r_{22} = \{f_1^{\delta}, f_3^{\delta}\} \Rightarrow \delta$, and where $s_{22} = \delta$. Introduced in Section 3.1.2.
23. $c_{23} = \langle X_{23}, r_{23}, s_{23} \rangle$, where $X_{23} = \{f_1^{\pi}, f_2^{\pi}, f_4^{\delta}\}$, where $r_{23} = \{f_4^{\delta}\} \Rightarrow \delta$, and where $s_{23} = \delta$. Introduced in Section 3.1.2.
24. $c_{24} = \langle X_{24}, r_{24}, s_{24} \rangle$, where $X_{24} = \{f_1^{\pi}, f_2^{\pi}, f_1^{\delta}\}$, where $r_{24} = \{f_1^{\pi}\} \Rightarrow \pi$, and where $s_{24} = \pi$. Introduced in Section 3.1.2.
25. $c_{25} = \langle X_{25}, r_{25}, s_{25} \rangle$, where $X_{25} = \{f_1^{\pi}, f_2^{\pi}, f_1^{\delta}, f_1^{\delta}\}$, where $r_{25} = \{f_2^{\delta}\} \Rightarrow \delta$, and where $s_{25} = \delta$. Introduced in Section 3.1.2.
26. $c_{26} = \langle X_{26}, r_{26}, s_{26} \rangle$, where $X_{26} = \{f_1^{\pi}, f_2^{\pi}, f_1^{\delta}, f_2^{\delta}, f_3^{\delta}\}$, where $r_{26} = \{f_1^{\delta}, f_2^{\delta}\} \Rightarrow \delta$, and where $s_{26} = \delta$. Introduced in Section 3.1.3.
27. $X_{27} = \{f_1^{\pi}, f_2^{\pi}, f_2^{\delta}\}$. Introduced in Section 3.3.1.
28. $c_{28} = \langle X_{28}, r_{28}, s_{28} \rangle$, where $X_{28} = \{f_1^{\pi}, f_2^{\pi}, f_1^{\delta}, f_2^{\delta}\}$, where $r_{28} = \{f_1^{\delta}\} \Rightarrow \delta$, and where $s_{28} = \delta$. Introduced in Section 4.2.1.
29. $c_{29} = \langle X_{29}, r_{29}, s_{29} \rangle$, where $X_{29} = \{f_1^{\pi}, f_2^{\pi}, f_1^{\delta}, f_2^{\delta}\}$, where $r_{29} = \{f_1^{\delta}\} \rightarrow \delta$, and where $s_{29} = \delta$. Introduced in Section 4.2.1.
30. $c_{30} = \langle X_{30}, r_{30}, s_{30} \rangle$, where $X_{30} = \{f_1^{\pi}, f_1^{\delta}\}$, where $r_{30} = \{f_1^{\delta}\} \Rightarrow \delta$, and where $s_{30} = \delta$. Introduced in Section 4.2.2.
31. $c_{31} = \langle X_{31}, r_{31}, s_{31} \rangle$, where $X_{31} = \{f_1^{\pi}, f_1^{\delta}\}$, where $r_{31} = \{f_1^{\delta}\} \rightarrow \delta$, and where $s_{31} = \delta$. Introduced in Section 4.2.2.
32. $c_{32} = \langle X_{32}, r_{32}, s_{32} \rangle$, where $X_{32} = \{f_1^{\pi}, f_1^{\delta}\}$, where $r_{32} = \{f_1^{\pi}\} \rightarrow \pi$, and where $s_{32} = \pi$. Introduced in Section 4.3.2.
33. $c_{33} = \langle X_{33}, r_{33}, s_{33} \rangle$, where $X_{33} = \{f_1^{\pi}, f_1^{\delta}, f_2^{\delta}\}$, where $r_{33} = \{f_1^{\delta}\} \rightarrow \delta$, and where $s_{33} = \delta$. Introduced in Section 4.3.2.

34. $c_{34} = \langle X_{34}, r_{34}, s_{34}\rangle$, where $X_{34} = \{f_1^\pi, f_1^\delta, f_2^\delta\}$, where $r_{34} = \{f_2^\delta\} \rightarrow \delta$, and where $s_{34} = \delta$. Introduced in Section 4.3.2.
35. $c_{35} = \langle X_{35}, r_{35}, s_{35}\rangle$, where $X_{35} = \{f_1^\pi, f_1^\delta, f_2^\delta\}$, where $r_{35} = \{f_1^\delta, f_2^\delta\} \rightarrow \delta$, and where $s_{35} = \delta$. Introduced in Section 4.3.2.
36. $X_{36} = \{f_1^\pi, f_1^\delta, f_2^\delta\}$. Introduced in Section 5.3.2.
37. $c_{37} = \langle X_{37}, r_{37}, s_{37}\rangle$, where $X_{37} = \{\langle d_1, 30\rangle, \langle d_2, 60\rangle\}$, where $r_{37} = \{M^\delta_{d_1,12}\} \rightarrow \delta$, and where $s_{37} = \delta$. Introduced in Section 7.1.3.
38. $X_{38} = \{\langle d_1, 36\rangle, \langle d_2, 65\rangle\}$. Introduced in Section 7.2.1.
39. $c_{39} = \langle X_{39}, r_{39}, s_{39}\rangle$, where $X_{39} = \{\langle d_1, 36\rangle, \langle d_2, 10\rangle\}$, where $r_{39} = \{M^\pi_{d_2,25}\} \rightarrow \pi$, and where $s_{39} = \pi$. Introduced in Section 7.2.2.
40. $c_{40} = \langle X_{40}, r_{40}, s_{40}\rangle$, where $X_{40} = \{\langle d_1, 15\rangle, \langle d_2, 65\rangle\}$, where $r_{40} = \{M^\pi_{d_2,75}\} \rightarrow \pi$, and where $s_{40} = \pi$. Introduced in Section 7.2.2.
41. $c_{41} = \langle X_{41}, r_{41}, s_{41}\rangle$, where $X_{41} = \{\langle d_1, 15\rangle, \langle d_2, 65\rangle\}$, where $r_{41} = \{M^\pi_{d_1,24}\} \rightarrow \pi$, and where $s_{41} = \pi$. Introduced in Section 7.3.1.
42. $c_{42} = \langle X_{42}, r_{42}, s_{42}\rangle$, where $X_{42} = \{\langle d_1, 29\rangle, \langle d_2, 65\rangle\}$, where $r_{42} = \{M^\pi_{d_1,29}\} \rightarrow \pi$, and where $s_{42} = \pi$. Introduced in Section 7.3.1.
43. $c_{43} = \langle X_{43}, r_{43}, s_{43}\rangle$, where $X_{43} = \{\langle d_1, 30\rangle, \langle d_2, 60\rangle\}$, where $r_{43} = \{M^\delta_{d_1,12}, M^\delta_{d_2,50}\} \rightarrow \delta$, and where $s_{43} = \delta$. Introduced in Section 7.3.2.
44. $c_{44} = \langle X_{44}, r_{44}, s_{44}\rangle$, where $X_{44} = \{\langle d_1, 15\rangle, \langle d_2, 55\rangle\}$, where $r_{44} = \{M^\pi_{d_1,24}\} \rightarrow \pi$, and where $s_{44} = \pi$. Introduced in Section 7.3.2.
45. $c_{45} = \langle X_{45}, r_{45}, s_{45}\rangle$, where $X_{45} = \{\langle d_1, 15\rangle, \langle d_2, 35\rangle\}$, where $r_{45} = \{M^\pi_{d_1,24}\} \rightarrow \pi$, and where $s_{45} = \pi$. Introduced in Section 7.3.2.
46. $c_{46} = \langle X_{46}, r_{46}, s_{46}\rangle$, where $X_{46} = \{\langle d_1, 6\rangle, \langle d_2, 60\rangle\}$, where $r_{46} = \{M^\pi_{d_1,24}\} \rightarrow \pi$, and where $s_{46} = \pi$. Introduced in Section 7.3.2.

A.2 Observations and Proofs

Observation 1 Let Γ be a consistent case base and X a fact situation confronting the court. Then there exists some rule r applicable in X and supporting the side s such that the augmented case base $\Gamma \cup \{\langle X, r, s\rangle\}$ is consistent.

Proof Where Γ is a consistent case base and X a fact situation confronting the court, assume for contradiction that there is no rule r applicable in X and supporting s such that $\Gamma \cup \{\langle X, r, s\rangle\}$ is consistent. Then in particular, where $r_1 = X^s \rightarrow s$ and $r_2 = X^{\overline{s}} \rightarrow \overline{s}$ are applicable rules leading to the decisions $c_1 = \langle X, r_1, s\rangle$ and $c_2 = \langle X, r_2, \overline{s}\rangle$, both $\Gamma \cup \{\langle X, r_1, s\rangle\}$ and $\Gamma \cup \{\langle X, r_2, \overline{s}\rangle\}$ must be inconsistent. Because $\Gamma \cup \{\langle X, r_1, s\rangle\}$ is inconsistent while Γ is consistent, it follows from Observation 5 that there is some case $c_3 = \langle X_3, r_3, \overline{s} \rangle$ in Γ such that (1) $Premise(r_3) <_{c_1} Premise(r_1)$ and (2) $Premise(r_1) <_{c_3} Premise(r_3)$; likewise, because $\Gamma \cup \{\langle X, r_2, \overline{s} \rangle\}$ is inconsistent while Γ consistent, there is some case $c_4 = \langle X_4, r_4, s \rangle$ in Γ such that (3) $Premise(r_4) <_{c_2} Premise(r_2)$ and (4) $Premise(r_2) <_{c_4} Premise(r_4)$.

From (1), it follows as part of Definition 4 that (5) $X \models Premise(r_3)$; likewise, it follows from (2) that (6) $X_3 \models Premise(r_1)$, from (3) that (7) $X \models Premise(r_4)$, and from (4) that (8) $X_4 \models Premise(r_2)$. From (5) we can conclude by Definition 1 that $Premise(r_3) \subseteq X$, and then because $Premise(r_3) \subseteq F^{\overline{s}}$, that $Premise(r_3) \subseteq X^s = Premise(r_2)$, or that (9) $Premise(r_3) \subseteq Premise(r_2)$; likewise, we can conclude from (6) that (10) $Premise(r_1) \subseteq X_3$, from (7) that $Premise(r_4) \subseteq X^s = Premise(r_1)$, or that (11) $Premise(r_4) \subseteq Premise(r_1)$, and from (8) that (12) $Premise(r_2) \subseteq X_4$.

From (9) and (12), we have $Premise(r_3) \subseteq X_4$. This tells us by Definition 1 again that $X_4 \models Premise(r_3)$, which, together with the obvious $Premise(r_4) \leq^s Premise(r_4)$, yields (13) $Premise(r_3) <_{c_4} Premise(r_4)$ by Definition 4. Likewise, from (10) and (11), we have $Premise(r_4) \subseteq X_3$, telling us that $X_3 \models Premise(r_4)$, which, together with the obvious $Premise(r_3) \leq^{\overline{s}} Premise(r_3)$, yields (14) $Premise(r_4) <_{c_3} Premise(r_3)$.

But because both c_3 and c_4 belong to Γ, it follows from (13) and (14) that Γ is inconsistent, contrary to assumption. ■

Observation 2 Let Γ be a consistent case base with *Rule*(Γ) the set of rules contained in this case base, and let X be a fact situation in which none of the rules from *Rule*(Γ) is applicable. Then where r is some newly formulated rule applicable in X and supporting the side s, the augmented case base $\Gamma \cup \{\langle X, r, s \rangle\}$ is also consistent.

Proof Let Γ be a consistent case base such that no rule from *Rule*(Γ) is applicable in the fact situation X, and assume for contradiction that $\Gamma \cup \{\langle X, r, s \rangle\}$ is inconsistent, where r is some newly formulated rule applicable in X and supporting s. Then where $c = \langle X, r, s \rangle$, because $\Gamma \cup \{\langle X, r, s \rangle\}$ is inconsistent while Γ is consistent, it follows from Observation 5 that there must be some case $c' = \langle Y, r', \overline{s} \rangle$ in Γ such that $Premise(r') <_c Premise(r)$ and $Premise(r) <_{c'} Premise(r')$. From $Premise(r') <_c Premise(r)$, however, it follows as part of Definition 4 that $X \models Premise(r')$, but then, since r' belongs to *Rule*(Γ), some rule from *Rule*(Γ) is applicable in X, contrary to assumption. ■

Observation 3 Let Γ be a consistent case base with *Rule*(Γ) the set of rules contained in this case base, X a fact situation confronting the court, and r a rule from *Rule*(Γ), supporting the side s, that is binding in the context of Γ. Then the augmented case base $\Gamma \cup \{\langle X,r,s\rangle\}$ is consistent.

Proof Let Γ be a consistent case base, X a fact situation, and r a rule from *Rule*(Γ) that is binding in the context of Γ, and assume for contradiction that $\Gamma \cup \{\langle X,r,s\rangle\}$ is inconsistent. Then where $c = \langle X,r,s\rangle$, because $\Gamma \cup \{\langle X,r,s\rangle\}$ is inconsistent while Γ is consistent, it follows from Observation 5 that there must be some case $c' = \langle Y,r',\bar{s}\rangle$ in Γ such that $Premise(r') <_c Premise(r)$ and $Premise(r) <_{c'} Premise(r')$.

Now, three facts: First, from $Premise(r') <_c Premise(r)$, it follows as part of Definition 4 that $X \models Premise(r')$, so that the rule r' is applicable in X. Second, from $Premise(r) <_{c'} Premise(r')$, it follows by Definition 9 that $r <_\Gamma r'$, or that the case base Γ assigns a higher priority to the rule r' than to the rule r'. And third, the rules r and r' support opposite sides. Putting these facts together, we conclude by Definition 10 that the rule r, although applicable in X, is defeated in the context of Γ, since *Rule*(Γ) contains the rule r' that is also applicable in X, carries higher priority than r, and supports a conflicting conclusion. Since r is defeated, it follows by Definition 11 that it is not binding in X after all, contrary to assumption. ■

Observation 4 Let Γ be a consistent case base, X a fact situation confronting the court, and $\langle Y,r,s\rangle$ a case from Γ such that the rule r of that case is binding in X in the context of Γ. Then, if we suppose, where r' is a rule applicable in X and supporting the side $\bar{s}$, that the case base $\Gamma \cup \{\langle X,r',\bar{s}\rangle\}$ is consistent, it follows that we do not have $Y \models Premise(r')$.

Proof Where Γ be a consistent case base, X a new fact situation, and $\langle Y,r,s\rangle$ a case from Γ such that the rule r of that case is binding in X in the context of Γ, and where r' is a rule applicable in X and supporting the side $\bar{s}$ with the case base $\Gamma \cup \{\langle X,r',\bar{s}\rangle\}$ consistent, assume for contradiction that $Y \models Premise(r')$. Let $c = \langle Y,r,s\rangle$ and $c' = \langle X,r',\bar{s}\rangle$. Since r is applicable in X, we have $X \models Premise(r)$, which, together with the obvious $Premise(r') \leq^{\bar{s}} Premise(r')$ yields $Premise(r) <_{c'} Premise(r')$ by Definition 4. But if $Y \models Premise(r')$, then, together with the obvious $Premise(r) \leq^s Premise(r)$, Definition 4 likewise yields $Premise(r') <_c Premise(r)$, so that $\Gamma \cup \{\langle X,r',\bar{s}\rangle\}$ cannot be consistent, contrary to assumption. ■

Lemma 1 Where X is a fact situation and U and V are reasons favoring the side s, suppose that $X \models U$ and $V \leq^s U$. Then $X \models V$.

Proof This simple fact is supplied with two verifications, first for our initial definitions of reason satisfaction and strength for a side among reasons from Section 1.1.2 and then for our generalized definitions of these same concepts from Section 7.1.3.

Where X is a fact situation and U and V are reasons favoring the side s, then: First, according to our initial Definitions 1 and 2, what $X \models U$ means is that $U \subseteq X$ and what $V \leq^s U$ means is that $V \subseteq U$. From this, it follows at once by transitivity of set inclusion that $V \subseteq X$, or that $X \models V$. And second, according to our more general treatment from Definitions 42 and 43, what $V \leq^s U$ means is that $X \models U$ entails $X \models V$ for any fact situation X, where a reason satisfaction statement of the form $X \models U$ is now set out more generally in Definition 41. Regardless of the details of this more general treatment of satisfaction, however, it again follows at once from the quantificational treatment of the statement $V \leq^s U$ that this statement together with $X \models U$ entails $X \models V$. ■

Observation 5 Let Γ be a case base. Then Γ is inconsistent if and only if there are cases $c = \langle X, r, s\rangle$ and $c' = \langle Y, r', \overline{s}\rangle$ belonging to Γ such that $Premise(r') <_c Premise(r)$ and $Premise(r) <_{c'} Premise(r')$.

Proof Right to left is obvious. For left to right, suppose that Γ is an inconsistent case base. Then by Definitions 5 and 6, there are cases $c = \langle X, r, s\rangle$ and $c' = \langle Y, r', \overline{s}\rangle$ belonging to Γ such that $U <_c V$ and $V <_{c'} U$ for some reasons U and V. Since $U <_c V$, we have (1) $X \models U$ and (2) $Premise(r) \leq^s V$ by Definition 4. Likewise, since $V <_{c'} U$, we have (3) $Y \models V$ and (4) $Premise(r') \leq^{\overline{s}} U$. From (1) and (4), Lemma 1 tells us that $X \models Premise(r')$, which, together with the obvious $Premise(r) \leq^s Premise(r)$, yields $Premise(r') <_c Premise(r)$ by Definition 4. But likewise, from (2) and (3), Lemma 1 tells us that $Y \models Premise(r)$, which, together with $Premise(r') \leq^{\overline{s}} Premise(r')$, yields $Premise(r) <_{c'} Premise(r')$. ■

Lemma 2 If r is a defeasible rule and r^+ its corresponding strict rule, then where X is a fact situation, $X \models Premise(r)$ if and only if $X \models Premise^s(r^+)$. Likewise, if r is a strict rule and r^- its corresponding defeasible rule, then where X is a fact situation, $X \models Premise^s(r)$ if and only if $X \models Premise(r^-)$.

Proof Although worth highlighting because of its role in the proof of the following Observation, this fact is obvious from the definitions in Section

3.2.2, since, if r is defeasible, then $Premise(r)$ is $Premise^s(r^+)$, and if r is strict, then $Premise^s(r)$ is $Premise(r^-)$. ■

Observation 6 Let Γ be a defeasible case base. Then Γ is consistent if and only if the corresponding strict case base Γ^k is accommodation consistent. Likewise, let Γ be a strict case base. Then Γ is accommodation consistent if and only if the corresponding defeasible case base Γ^k is consistent.

Proof The proof has two parts.

Part 1: Assuming that Γ is a defeasible case base, the corresponding strict case base Γ^k is Γ^+. We show that Γ is consistent if and only if Γ^+ is accommodation consistent.

Part 1A: Left to right. Assume that the defeasible case base Γ is consistent. To show that the strict case base Γ^+ is accommodation consistent, in accord with Definition 16, we must establish that the refinement $(\Gamma^+)^*$ of Γ^+ is itself a case base. By Step 4 of the construction from Definition 15, the refinement $(\Gamma^+)^*$ is arrived at from Γ^+ by replacing each case of the form $c = \langle X, r, s\rangle$ from Γ^+ with a new structure of the form $c^* = \langle X, r^*, s\rangle$, where r^* is the modified rule $Premise^s(r) \wedge D_c \Rightarrow s$. Since all of the rule modifications involved in moving from Γ^+ to $(\Gamma^+)^*$ lead to rules supporting the same outcomes as the original, unmodified rules, we can verify that $(\Gamma^+)^*$ is a case base simply by establishing that, for each $c^* = \langle X, r^*, s\rangle$ from $(\Gamma^+)^*$, constructed as above by modifying $c = \langle X, r, s\rangle$ from Γ^+, the modified rule r^* continues to be applicable in the fact situation X – that is, that $X \models Premise(r^*)$, or that $X \models Premise^s(r) \wedge D_c$. We know, of course, that $X \models Premise^s(r)$, since the original $c = \langle X, r, s\rangle$ is a case, so that $X \models Premise(s)$. In order to show that $X \models Premise^s(r) \wedge D_c$, therefore, we need only show that $X \models D_c$.

It follows from Steps 2 and 3 of the construction from Definition 15 that establishing that $X \models D_c$ amounts to showing, for each $c' = \langle Y, r', \bar{s}\rangle$ from Γ_c^+, where $c = \langle X, r, s\rangle$, that $Premise^{\bar{s}}(r')$ is not applicable in X, or that $X \models Premise^{\bar{s}}(r')$ fails. So assume for contradiction that (1) $X \models Premise^{\bar{s}}(r')$ for some particular $c' = \langle Y, r', \bar{s}\rangle$ from Γ_c^+. Since $c' = \langle Y, r', \bar{s}\rangle$ belongs to Γ_c^+, we know from Step 1 of the construction that (2) $Y \models Premise^s(r)$.

Because Γ^+ is the strict case base corresponding to the defeasible Γ, and since Γ^+ contains the strict cases $c = \langle X, r, s\rangle$ and $c' = \langle Y, r', \bar{s}\rangle$, we know from the definition of Γ^+ that Γ must contain defeasible cases of the form $c'' = \langle X, r'', s\rangle$ and $c''' = \langle Y, r''', \bar{s}\rangle$, where $(r'')^+ = r$ and $(r''')^+ = r'$. From (1) and $(r''')^+ = r'$, then, Lemma 2 tells us that $X \models Premise(r''')$, which, together with the obvious $Premise(r'') \leq^s Premise(r'')$, entails (3)

$Premise(r''') <_{c''} Premise(r'')$. Likewise, from (2) and $(r'')^+ = r$, Lemma 2 tells us that $Y \models Premise(r'')$, which, together with the obvious $Premise(r''') \leq^{\overline{s}} Premise(r''')$, entails (4) $Premise(r'') <_{c'''} Premise(r''')$. But since c'' and c''' belong to the defeasible case base Γ, it follows from (3) and (4) that this case base must be inconsistent, contrary to our assumption that Γ is consistent.

Since the assumption that (1) leads to a contradiction, we can conclude, therefore, that $X \models D_c$, from which it follows – retracing our previous reasoning in the opposite direction – that $X \models Premise^s(r) \wedge D_c$, or that $X \models Premise(r^*)$, so that $c^* = \langle X, r^*, s\rangle$ is a case, that $(\Gamma^+)^*$ is a case base, and that Γ^+ is accommodation consistent.

Part 1B: Right to left. Assume for contraposition that the defeasible case base Γ is inconsistent. It then follows by Observation 5 that Γ contains cases $c = \langle X, r, s\rangle$ and $c' = \langle Y, r', \overline{s}\rangle$ such that (1) $Premise(r') <_c Premise(r)$ and (2) $Premise(r) <_{c'} Premise(r')$. By Definition 4, it follows from (1) that (3) $X \models Premise(r')$ and from (2) that (4) $Y \models Premise(r)$. Because Γ^+ is the strict case base corresponding to the defeasible case base Γ, we know that Γ^+ contains strict cases $c'' = \langle X, r'', s\rangle$ and $c''' = \langle Y, r''', \overline{s}\rangle$ corresponding to the defeasible cases $c = \langle X, r, s\rangle$ and $c' = \langle Y, r', \overline{s}\rangle$, with $r^+ = r''$ and $(r')^+ = r'''$. By Lemma 2, then, it follows from (3) and $(r')^+ = r'''$ that (5) $X \models Premise^{\overline{s}}(r''')$, and from (4) and $r^+ = r''$ that (6) $Y \models Premise^s(r'')$.

Where Γ^+ is the strict case base corresponding to Γ, it follows from Definition 16 that Γ^+ is accommodation consistent if and only if its refinement $(\Gamma^+)^*$ is itself a case base. So consider the particular item $(c'')^* = \langle X, (r'')^*, s\rangle$ from $(\Gamma^+)^*$, constructed from the case $c'' = \langle X, r'', s\rangle$ in accord with Definition 15, so that $(r'')^* = Premise^s(r'') \wedge D_{c''} \rightarrow s$. And let us ask: is $(c'')^*$ itself a case? Well, Step 1 of the construction from Definition 15, together with (6), tells us that c''' belongs to $\Gamma^+_{c''}$, and then Steps 2, 3, and 4 allow us to conclude that $\neg Premise^{\overline{s}}(r''')$ is one of the conjuncts of $D_{c''}$, and so of the new rule $(r'')^*$. From (5), however, we know that $X \models \neg Premise^{\overline{s}}(r''')$ fails, from which it follows that $X \models D_{c''}$ fails as well, as does $X \models Premise((r'')^*)$. As a result, the rule of $(c'')^*$ does not apply to its facts, from which it follows that $(c'')^*$ is not a case, so that $(\Gamma^+)^*$ is not a case base, and therefore, that Γ^+ is not accommodation consistent.

From the assumption that Γ is inconsistent, then, it follows that Γ^+ is not accommodation consistent, so that, by contraposition, we know that, if Γ^+ is accommodation consistent, then Γ must be consistent.

Part 2: Assuming that Γ is a strict case base, the corresponding defeasible case base Γ^k is Γ^-. We must also show, then, that Γ is accommodation consistent if and only if Γ^- is consistent. The proof of this part, however, involves reasoning similar to that found in the proof of Part 1, and is omitted. ■

Observation 7 Let Γ be a consistent defeasible case base and X a fact situation confronting the court. Then against the background of Γ, the reason model permits the court to base its decision in X on the defeasible rule r, applicable in X and supporting the side s, if and only if, against the background of the corresponding strict case base Γ^k, the standard model permits the court to base its decision in X on the corresponding strict rule r^k, also applicable in X and supporting s. Likewise, let Γ be an accommodation consistent strict case base and X a fact situation confronting the court. Then against the background of Γ, the standard model permits the court to base its decision in X on the strict rule r, applicable in X and supporting the side s, if and only if, against the background of the corresponding defeasible case base Γ^k, the standard model permits the court to base its decision in X on the corresponding defeasible rule r^k, also applicable in X and supporting s.

Proof Suppose that the case base Γ and the rule r are defeasible, so that the corresponding strict case base Γ^k is Γ^+ and the corresponding strict rule r^k is r^+. By Definition 7, what it means to say that the reason model permits the court to base its decision in the situation X on the rule r, applicable in X and supporting the side s, is that $\Gamma \cup \{\langle X, r, s\rangle\}$ is consistent. By Definition 17, what it means to say that the standard model permits the court to base its decision in the situation X on the rule r^+, also applicable in X and supporting the side s, is that $\Gamma^+ \cup \{\langle X, r^+, s\rangle\}$ is accommodation consistent. From Observation 6, we know that $\Gamma \cup \{\langle X, r, s\rangle\}$ is consistent if and only if $(\Gamma \cup \{\langle X, r, s\rangle\})^+$ is accommodation consistent. But $(\Gamma \cup \{\langle X, r, s\rangle\})^+$ is simply $\Gamma^+ \cup \{\langle X, r^+, s\rangle\}$. It therefore follows that $\Gamma \cup \{\langle X, r, s\rangle\}$ is consistent if and only if $\Gamma^+ \cup \{\langle X, r^+, s\rangle\}$ is accommodation consistent, or that the reason model permits a decision in X on the basis of r if and only if the standard model permits a decision in X on the basis of r^+. We must also show, where Γ and r are strict, so Γ^k is Γ^- and r^k is r^-, that, against the background of Γ, the standard model permits a decision in X on the basis of r if and only if, against the background of Γ^-, the reason model permits a decision in X on the basis r^-. The reasoning in this direction, however, is similar and omitted. ■

Observation 8 Let Γ be a consistent defeasible case base and X a fact situation confronting the court. Then against the background of Γ, the reason model permits the court to decide X for the side s if and only if, against the background of the corresponding strict case base Γ^k, the standard model permits the court to decide X for the same side. Likewise, let Γ be an accommodation consistent strict case base and X a fact situation confronting the court. Then against the background of Γ, the standard model permits the court to decide X for some the side s if and only if, against the background of the corresponding defeasible case base Γ^k, the reason model permits the court to decide X for the same side.

Proof Let Γ be a consistent defeasible case base so that the corresponding strict case base is Γ^+, and let X be a fact situation confronting the court. By Definition 8, the reason model of constraint on decision permits the court, against the background of Γ, to decide X for the side s if and only if the reason model of constraint on rule selection permits the court to decide X on the basis of some rule supporting that side. By Definition 18, the standard model of constraint on decision permits the court, against the background of Γ^+, to decide X for the side s if and only if the standard model of constraint on rule selection permits the court to decide X on the basis of some rule supporting that side. But by Observation 7, the reason model permits the court, against the background of Γ, to decide X on the basis of some rule r supporting s if and only if the standard model permits the court, against the background of Γ^+, to decide X on the basis of the corresponding rule r^+, likewise supporting s. We must also show, where Γ is strict, so Γ^k is Γ^-, that, against the background of Γ, the standard model permits a decision in X for s if and only if, against the background of Γ^-, the reason model likewise permits a decision in X for s. The reasoning in this direction, however, is similar and omitted. ■

Observation 9 Let Γ be a case base containing two precedent cases of the form $c = \langle X, r, s\rangle$ and $c' = \langle Y, r', \overline{s}\rangle$, where $X \leq^s Y$. Then Γ is inconsistent.

Proof Suppose Γ contains cases of the form $c = \langle X, r, s\rangle$ and $c' = \langle Y, r', \overline{s}\rangle$, where $X \leq^s Y$. Because c is a case, by our coherence conditions on cases, particularly the requirement that the rule of a case must be applicable to its facts, we have $X \models Premise(r)$, or $Premise(r) \subseteq X$ by Definition 3, and then by the definition of a rule we have $Premise(r) \subseteq F^s$, so that $Premise(r) \subseteq X^s$. From this we have (1) $Premise(r) \leq^s X^s$ by Definition 2. Because $X \leq^s Y$, we have $Y^{\overline{s}} \subseteq X^{\overline{s}}$ from Definition 20, and then since $X^{\overline{s}} \subseteq X$, we have $Y^{\overline{s}} \subseteq X$, which entails (2) $X \models Y^{\overline{s}}$ by Definition 1. Together, (1) and (2) yield (3) $Y^{\overline{s}} <_c X^s$ by Definition 4. In the same way, because c' is a case, we have $Y \models Premise(r')$, or $Premise(r') \subseteq Y$ by Definition 3, and then by the definition of a rule we have $Premise(r') \subseteq F^{\overline{s}}$, so that $Premise(r') \subseteq Y^{\overline{s}}$. From this we have (4) $Premise(r') \leq^{\overline{s}} Y^{\overline{s}}$ by Definition 2. Because $X \leq^{s} Y$, we also have $X^{s} \subseteq Y^{s}$ from Definition 20, and then since $Y^{s} \subseteq Y$, we have $X^{s} \subseteq Y$, which entails (5) $Y \models X^{s}$ by Definition 1. Together, (4) and (5) yield (6) $X^{s} <_{c'} Y^{\overline{s}}$ by Definition 4. And then, since Γ contains both c and c', it follows from (3) and (6) that Γ is inconsistent, by Definitions 5 and 6. ■

Observation 10 Let Γ be a consistent case base and X a fact situation confronting the court. Then against the background of Γ, if the a fortiori model of constraint requires the court to decide X for the side s, the reason model of constraint also requires the court to decide X for the side s.

Proof Where Γ is a consistent case base and X a fact situation confronting the court, suppose the a fortiori model of constraint requires the court to decide X for the side s. What this means, by Definition 21, is that Γ contains some case of the form $\langle Y, r, s \rangle$ for which $Y \leq^{s} X$. Now assume for contradiction that the reason model does not require the court to decide s for the side s. Then by Definition 8, the court is permitted to base its decision on some rule r' supporting the opposite side $\overline{s}$ – that is, by Definition 7, that the case base $\Gamma \cup \{\langle X, r', \overline{s} \rangle\}$ is consistent. But since Γ already contains the decision $\langle Y, r, s \rangle$ with $Y \leq^{s} X$, it follows from Observation 9 that $\Gamma \cup \{\langle X, r', \overline{s} \rangle\}$ must be inconsistent, so that our assumption leads to a contradiction. ■

Observation 11 Let Γ be a consistent set of cases of the form $\langle X, r, s \rangle$ in each of which the case rule r has the form $X^{s} \rightarrow s$, and let Y be a fact situation confronting the court. Then against the background of Γ, the reason model of constraint requires the court to decide Y for some particular side if only if the a fortiori model of constraint requires the court to decide Y for that same side.

Proof We have already seen, in Observation 10, that, in general, if the a fortiori model requires a decision for a particular side, then the reason model requires a decision for that same side. It remains only to show that, under the assumption that each rule r in a case $\langle X, r, s \rangle$ has the form $X^{s} \rightarrow s$, then, if the reason model requires a decision for a particular side, the a fortiori model requires a decision for that same side.

Under this assumption, then, suppose that Γ is a consistent case base against the background of which the reason model requires a court confronting a situation Y to decide for the side s. What this means, according to Definition 8, is that there is no rule r supporting the side $\overline{s}$ on the basis of which the court is permitted to decide the situation Y – or, by Definition 7, that augmenting Γ with a decision of the form $c = \langle Y, r, \overline{s}\rangle$ renders the case base inconsistent. From this, Observation 5 tells us that Γ must already contain a case $c' = \langle X, r', s\rangle$ such that (1) $Premise(r') <_c Premise(r)$ and (2) $Premise(r) <_{c'} Premise(r')$.

From (1), we know by Definition 4 that $Y \models Premise(r')$, or $Premise(r') \subseteq Y$ by Definitions 1, and then since $Premise(r') \subseteq F^s$ by the definition of a rule, that (3) $Premise(r') \subseteq Y^s$. By our assumption concerning the nature of rules, however, $Premise(r') = X^s$, so that (3) tells us (4) $X^s \subseteq Y^s$. In the same way, from (2), we know that $X \models Premise(r)$, so $Premise(r) \subseteq X$, and then since $Premise(r) \subseteq F^{\overline{s}}$, that (5) $Premise(r) \subseteq X^{\overline{s}}$. Again, though, by our special assumption, we have $Premise(r) = Y^{\overline{s}}$, so that (5) tells us (6) $Y^{\overline{s}} \subseteq X^{\overline{s}}$. Together (4) and (6) yield $X \leq^s Y$ by Definition 20, and so, since the case $c' = \langle X, r', s\rangle$ already belongs to Γ, it follows from Definition 21 that the a fortiori model requires the court to reach a decision for the side s in the situation Y. ■

Lemma 3 Where X is a fact situation, $\mathcal{V}$ is a set of value defaults, Γ is a consistent case base, let the default theory $\Delta_{X,\mathcal{V},\mathcal{H}_\Gamma}$ represent the problem presented by the fact situation X to a court with values $\mathcal{V}$ under hard constraints $\mathcal{H}_\Gamma$ derived from Γ, and let $\mathcal{S}$ be any scenario based on this theory. Then:

1. If $X \models Premise(r)$, then $r \in \mathit{Applicable}_{\mathcal{W}_{X,\mathcal{H}_\Gamma},\mathcal{D}_\mathcal{V}}(\mathcal{S})$;
2. If there is some rule r' in $\mathcal{S}$ such that $Conclusion(r) \neq Conclusion(r')$, then $r \in \mathit{Conflicted}_{\mathcal{W}_{X,\mathcal{H}_\Gamma},\mathcal{D}_\mathcal{V}}(\mathcal{S})$;
3. If $Premise(r') <_\Gamma Premise(r)$, then $r' <_\mathcal{S} r$;
4. If there is some rule r' in $\mathcal{F}$ such that (a) $X \models Premise(r')$, (b) $Premise(r) <_\Gamma Premise(r')$, and (c) $Conclusion(r) \neq Conclusion(r')$, then $r \in \mathit{Defeated}_{\mathcal{W}_{X,\mathcal{H}_\Gamma},\mathcal{D}_\mathcal{V},<_\mathcal{S}}(\mathcal{S})$.

Proof Where X, $\mathcal{V}$, and Γ are as in the statement of the Lemma, $\Delta_{X,\mathcal{V},\mathcal{H}_\Gamma} = \langle \mathcal{W}_{X,\mathcal{H}_\Gamma}, \mathcal{D}_\mathcal{V}\rangle$, and $\mathcal{S}$ is some scenario based on this theory, we prove the parts of the Lemma separately.

Part 1: Suppose $X \models Premise(r)$, so that $Premise(r) \subseteq X$ by Definition 1. Then $X \vdash Premise(r)$, since $Premise(r)$ is interpreted as a conjunction. But then, since $X \subseteq \mathcal{W}_{X,\mathcal{H}_\Gamma} \cup Conclusion(\mathcal{S})$, it follows that $\mathcal{W}_{X,\mathcal{H}_\Gamma} \cup Conclusion(\mathcal{S}) \vdash Premise(r)$, or that $r \in \mathit{Applicable}_{\mathcal{W}_{X,\mathcal{H}_\Gamma},\mathcal{D}_\mathcal{V}}(\mathcal{S})$.

Part 2: Where $Conclusion(r) = s$, suppose $\mathcal{S}$ contains a rule r' with $Conclusion(r') = \overline{s}$. Since r' belongs to $\mathcal{S}$, then, we have $Conclusion(\mathcal{S}) \vdash \overline{s}$, and then since $\neg(s \wedge \overline{s})$ belongs to $\mathcal{O}_3$ and so to $\mathcal{W}_{X,\mathcal{H}_\Gamma}$, we have $\mathcal{W}_{X,\mathcal{H}_\Gamma} \cup Conclusion(\mathcal{S}) \vdash \overline{s} \wedge \neg(s \wedge \overline{s})$, from which it follows that $\mathcal{W}_{X,\mathcal{H}_\Gamma} \cup Conclusion(\mathcal{S}) \vdash \neg s$, so that $\mathcal{W}_{X,\mathcal{H}_\Gamma} \cup Conclusion(\mathcal{S}) \vdash \neg Conclusion(r)$, or that $r \in \mathit{Conflicted}_{\mathcal{W}_{X,\mathcal{H}_\Gamma},\mathcal{D}_\mathcal{V}}(\mathcal{S})$.

Part 3: Suppose $Premise(r') <_\Gamma Premise(r)$. Then there is some $c = \langle X, r, s\rangle$ in Γ with $Premise(r') \subseteq X^{\overline{s}}$, from which it follows that $r^{\overline{s}}_{Premise(r')_i} \preceq^{\overline{s}} r^{\overline{s}}_{X^{\overline{s}}{}_i}$, so that the formula $n^{\overline{s}}_{Premise(r')_i} \preceq^{\overline{s}} n^{\overline{s}}_{X^{\overline{s}}{}_i}$ belongs to $\mathcal{O}_1$ and so to $\mathcal{W}_{X,\mathcal{H}_\Gamma}$. From $c = \langle X, r, s\rangle$, again, we also have $X^{\overline{s}} <_c Premise(r)$, so that the formula $n^{\overline{s}}_{X^{\overline{s}}{}_i} \prec n^{s}_{Premise(r)_i}$ belongs to $\mathcal{H}_\Gamma$ and so to $\mathcal{W}_{X,\mathcal{H}_\Gamma}$. Finally, we know that the formula

$$(n^{\overline{s}}_{Premise(r')_i} \preceq^{\overline{s}} n^{\overline{s}}_{X^{\overline{s}}{}_i} \wedge n^{\overline{s}}_{X^{\overline{s}}{}_i} \prec n^{s}_{Premise(r)_i}) \supset n^{\overline{s}}_{Premise(r')_i} \prec n^{s}_{Premise(r)_i}$$

belongs to $\mathcal{O}_2$ and so to $\mathcal{W}_{X,\mathcal{H}_\Gamma}$, so that

$$\mathcal{W}_{X,\mathcal{H}_\Gamma} \cup Conclusion(\mathcal{S}) \vdash n^{\overline{s}}_{Premise(r')_i} \prec n^{s}_{Premise(r)_i}.$$

From this, by Definition 30, we have $r^{\overline{s}}_{Premise(r')_i} <_\mathcal{S} r^{s}_{Premise(r)_i}$, but since $r^{\overline{s}}_{Premise(r')_i}$ is just the rule r' and $r^{s}_{Premise(r)_i}$ is just the rule r, this entails that $r' <_\mathcal{S} r$.

Part 4: Suppose there is some rule r' in $\mathcal{F}$ satisfying conditions (a), (b), and (c). From (a), we know that $r' \in \mathit{Applicable}_{\mathcal{W}_{X,\mathcal{H}_\Gamma},\mathcal{D}_\mathcal{V}}(\mathcal{S})$. From (b) we know that $r <_\mathcal{S} r'$. And from (c), we know through an argument similar to that in the proof of Part 2, that $\mathcal{W}_{X,\mathcal{H}_\Gamma} \cup \{Conclusion(r')\} \vdash \neg Conclusion(r)$. Combining these results, we can conclude that $r \in \mathit{Defeated}_{\mathcal{W}_{X,\mathcal{H}_\Gamma},\mathcal{D}_\mathcal{V},<_\mathcal{S}}(\mathcal{S})$. ■

Observation 12 Where X is a fact situation, $\mathcal{V}$ is a set of value defaults, and Γ is a consistent case base, let the default theory $\Delta_{X,\mathcal{V},\mathcal{H}_\Gamma}$ represent the problem presented by the fact situation X to a court with values $\mathcal{V}$ under hard constraints $\mathcal{H}_\Gamma$ derived from Γ. Then, if r is a factor default rule, it follows that: if r belongs to some proper scenario allowed by the theory $\Delta_{X,\mathcal{V},\mathcal{H}_\Gamma}$, the reason model of constraint on rule selection permits the court, against the background of the case base Γ, to base its decision in the situation X on the rule r.

Proof Where X is a fact situation, $\mathcal{V}$ a set of value defaults, Γ a consistent case base, and $\Delta_{X,\mathcal{V},\mathcal{H}_\Gamma} = \langle \mathcal{W}_{X,\mathcal{H}_\Gamma}, \mathcal{D}_\mathcal{V}\rangle$ the variable priority default theory representing the problem presented by X to a court with values $\mathcal{V}$ under hard constraints $\mathcal{H}_\Gamma$, suppose that $\mathcal{S}$ is a proper scenario allowed by this theory and that r is some factor default belonging to $\mathcal{S}$. By Definition 7, establishing that the reason model permits a decision in X on the basis of r requires showing that the augmented case base $\Gamma \cup \{\langle X, r, s\rangle\}$ is consistent, where s is the side supported by r. So let us suppose for contradiction that this augmented case base is inconsistent.

If $\Gamma \cup \{\langle X, r, s\rangle\}$ is inconsistent, it follows from Observation 5 that, where $c = \langle X, r, s\rangle$, there is also some case $c' = \langle Y, r', \bar{s}\rangle$ already belonging to Γ such that (1) $Premise(r) <_{c'} Premise(r')$ and (2) $Premise(r') <_{c} Premise(r)$. From (2), we have (3) $X \models Premise(r')$ by Definition 7. From (1), because c' belongs to Γ, we have (4) $Premise(r) <_{\Gamma} Premise(r')$ by Definition 5. And of course (5) $Conclusion(r) \neq Conclusion(r')$. By Part 4 of Lemma 3, then, (3), (4), and (5) tell us that $r \in Defeated_{\mathcal{W}_{X,\mathcal{H}_\Gamma}, \mathcal{D}_{\mathcal{V}}, <_{\mathcal{S}}}(\mathcal{S})$ – that is, by Definition 25, that r is defeated in the context of the scenario $\mathcal{S}$, so that, by Definition 26, r cannot be binding in the context of this scenario either. Since $\mathcal{S}$, then, contains a rule that is not binding in the context of that scenario, it follows by Definition 27 that $\mathcal{S}$ cannot be a proper scenario allowed by the fixed priority default theory $\langle \mathcal{W}_{X,\mathcal{H}_\Gamma}, \mathcal{D}_{\mathcal{V}}, <_{\mathcal{S}}\rangle$, and so by Definition 31 that $\mathcal{S}$ cannot be a proper scenario allowed by the variable priority theory $\Delta_{X,\mathcal{V},\mathcal{H}_\Gamma} = \langle \mathcal{W}_{X,\mathcal{H}_\Gamma}, \mathcal{D}_{\mathcal{V}}\rangle$, contrary to our initial assumption. ■

Lemma 4 Where X is a fact situation, $\emptyset$ is the empty set of value defaults, and Γ is a consistent case base, let the default theory $\Delta_{X,\emptyset,\mathcal{H}_\Gamma}$ represent the problem presented by the fact situation X to a court with values $\emptyset$ under hard constraints $\mathcal{H}_\Gamma$ derived from Γ, and let $\mathcal{S}$ be any scenario based on this theory that does not contain defaults r and r' such that $Conclusion(r) \neq Conclusion(r')$. Then:

1. If $r \in Applicable_{\mathcal{W}_{X,\mathcal{H}_\Gamma}, \mathcal{D}_\emptyset}(\mathcal{S})$, then $X \models Premise(r)$;
2. If $r \in Conflicted_{\mathcal{W}_{X,\mathcal{H}_\Gamma}, \mathcal{D}_\emptyset}(\mathcal{S})$, then there is some rule r' in $\mathcal{S}$ such that $Conclusion(r) \neq Conclusion(r')$;
3. If $r <_{\mathcal{S}} r'$, then $Premise(r) <_{\Gamma} Premise(r')$;
4. If $r \in Defeated_{\mathcal{W}_{X,\mathcal{H}_\Gamma}, \mathcal{D}_\emptyset, <_{\mathcal{S}}}(\mathcal{S})$, then there is some rule r' in $\mathcal{F}$ such that (a) $X \models Premise(r')$, (b) $Premise(r) <_{\Gamma} Premise(r')$, and (c) $Conclusion(r') \neq Conclusion(r)$.

Proof Let X, $\emptyset$, and Γ be as in the statement of the Lemma, $\Delta_{X,\emptyset,\mathcal{H}_\Gamma} = \langle \mathcal{W}_{X,\mathcal{H}_\Gamma}, \mathcal{D}_\emptyset\rangle$, and $\mathcal{S}$ some scenario based on this theory satisfying the conditions of the Lemma. We note first that, by Definition 37, the set $\mathcal{D}_\emptyset$ of defaults from the theory $\Delta_{X,\emptyset,\mathcal{H}_\Gamma}$ coincides with the set $\mathcal{F}$ of factor defaults, so that any scenario based on this theory is simply some subset of $\mathcal{F}$. And second, we note that, as long as Γ is consistent and the scenario $\mathcal{S}$ does not contain defaults r and r' such that $Conclusion(r) \neq Conclusion(r')$, the set

$\mathcal{W}_{X,\mathcal{H}_\Gamma} \cup Conclusion(\mathcal{S})$ is logically consistent. We can now sketch the proof of the Lemma in parts.

Part 1: Suppose $r \in Applicable_{\mathcal{W}_{X,\mathcal{H}_\Gamma},\mathcal{D}_\emptyset}(\mathcal{S})$. Then $\mathcal{W}_{X,\mathcal{H}_\Gamma} \cup Conclusion(\mathcal{S}) \vdash Premise(r)$, where $\mathcal{W}_{X,\mathcal{H}_\Gamma} = X \cup \mathcal{H}_\Gamma \cup \mathcal{O}$. But $Premise(r)$ is a set of factors. And since none of the statements in $\mathcal{H}_\Gamma$, $\mathcal{O}$, or $Conclusion(\mathcal{S})$ mention factors, and since $\mathcal{W}_{X,\mathcal{H}_\Gamma} \cup Conclusion(\mathcal{S})$ is consistent, we can conclude that $\mathcal{W}_{X,\mathcal{H}_\Gamma} \cup Conclusion(\mathcal{S}) \vdash Premise(r)$ only if $X \vdash Premise(r)$. And since factors are atomic, with no logical structure, it follows from $X \vdash Premise(r)$ that $Premise(r) \subseteq X$, or that $X \models Premise(r)$.

Part 2: Suppose $r \in Conflicted_{\mathcal{W}_{X,\mathcal{H}_\Gamma},\mathcal{D}_\emptyset}(\mathcal{S})$, so that $\mathcal{W}_{X,\mathcal{H}_\Gamma} \cup Conclusion(\mathcal{S}) \vdash \neg s$ where $Conclusion(r) = s$. But the set $\mathcal{W}_{X,\mathcal{H}_\Gamma} \cup Conclusion(\mathcal{S})$ is consistent, and the statements from $\mathcal{W}_{X,\mathcal{H}_\Gamma} = X \cup \mathcal{H}_\Gamma \cup \mathcal{O}$ do no allow us to conclude either s or s'. Therefore $\mathcal{W}_{X,\mathcal{H}_\Gamma} \cup Conclusion(\mathcal{S}) \vdash \neg s$ holds only if $Conclusion(\mathcal{S})$ contains s', from which $\neg s$ follows by the statement $\neg(s \wedge s')$, contained in $\mathcal{O}$. But s' belongs to $Conclusion(\mathcal{S})$ only if $\mathcal{S}$ contains some rule r' supporting s', so that $Conclusion(r) \neq Conclusion(r')$.

Part 3: By Definition 30, what $r <_{\mathcal{S}} r'$ means, in the current setting, is that $\mathcal{W}_{X,\mathcal{H}_\Gamma} \cup Conclusion(\mathcal{S}) \vdash n \prec n'$. We can establish the result, therefore, by showing by induction on length of shortest proof of $n \prec n'$ from $\mathcal{W}_{X,\mathcal{H}_\Gamma} \cup Conclusion(\mathcal{S})$ that (*) if $\mathcal{W}_{X,\mathcal{H}_\Gamma} \cup Conclusion(\mathcal{S}) \vdash n \prec n'$, then $Premise(r) <_\Gamma Premise(r')$.

For the base case, suppose the length of shortest proof of $n \prec n'$ from $\mathcal{W}_{X,\mathcal{H}_\Gamma} \cup Conclusion(\mathcal{S})$ is 1, so that the statement $n \prec n'$ itself belongs to $\mathcal{H}_\Gamma$. In that case, $n \prec n'$ has the form $n^{\bar{s}}_{X^{\bar{s}}_i} \prec n^{s}_{Premise(r)_i}$ for some case $c = \langle X, r, s\rangle$ from Γ. From the fact that Γ contains this case, however, we have $X^{\bar{s}} <_\Gamma Premise(r)$. But since $Premise(r^{\bar{s}}_{X^{\bar{s}}_i}) = X^{\bar{s}}$ and $Premise(r^{s}_{Premise(r)_i}) = Premise(r)$, this allows us to conclude that $Premise(r^{\bar{s}}_{X^{\bar{s}}_i}) <_\Gamma Premise(r^{s}_{Premise(r)_i})$.

For the inductive step, suppose (*) holds for all statements of form $n \prec n'$ whose shortest proof from $\mathcal{W}_{X,\mathcal{H}_\Gamma} \cup Conclusion(\mathcal{S})$ has length i or less, and suppose that the statement $n \prec n'$ in particular has a shortest proof of length $i + 1$. There are two cases. First, $n \prec n'$ might have the form $n^{\bar{s}}_{U_i} \prec n^{s}_{V_i}$ and follow from the statement

$$(n^{\bar{s}}_{U_i} \preceq n^{\bar{s}}_{W_i} \wedge n^{\bar{s}}_{W_i} \prec n^{s}_{V_i}) \supset n^{\bar{s}}_{U_i} \prec n^{s}_{V_i},$$

found in $\mathcal{O}_2$, together with the statements $n^{\bar{s}}_{U_i} \preceq n^{\bar{s}}_{W_i}$, found in $\mathcal{O}_1$, and $n^{\bar{s}}_{W_i} \prec n^{s}_{V_i}$. In this case, the statement $n^{\bar{s}}_{W_i} \prec n^{s}_{V_i}$ must have a proof of length i or less so that we know by hypothesis that $Premise(r^{\bar{s}}_{W_i}) <_\Gamma Premise(r^{s}_{V_i})$, or that (1) $W <_\Gamma V$. From the fact that the statement $n^{\bar{s}}_{U_i} \preceq n^{\bar{s}}_{W_i}$ belongs to $\mathcal{O}_1$, it follows from the definition of this set that (2) $U \leq^{\bar{s}} W$. But then (1) and (2) entail $U <_\Gamma V$ – or that $Premise(r^{\bar{s}}_{U_i}) <_\Gamma Premise(r^{s}_{V_i})$. In the second case $n \prec n'$ again has the form $n^{\bar{s}}_{U_i} \prec n^{s}_{V_i}$ but this time follows from the statement

$$(n^{\bar{s}}_{U_i} \prec n^{s}_{W_i} \wedge n^{s}_{W_i} \preceq n^{s}_{V_i}) \supset n^{\bar{s}}_{U_i} \prec n^{s}_{V_i},$$

found in $\mathcal{O}_2$, together with the statements $n^{s}_{W_i} \preceq n^{s}_{V_i}$, found in $\mathcal{O}_1$, and $n^{\bar{s}}_{U_i} \prec n^{s}_{W_i}$. The reasoning in this case is similar.

Part 4: Suppose $r \in Defeated_{\mathcal{W}_{X,\mathcal{H}_\Gamma},\mathcal{D}_\mathcal{V},<_\mathcal{S}}(\mathcal{S})$, so that there is some $r' \in \mathcal{D}_\emptyset$ such that $r' \in Applicable_{\mathcal{W}_{X,\mathcal{H}_\Gamma}}(\mathcal{S})$, $r <_\mathcal{S} r'$, and $\mathcal{W}_{X,\mathcal{H}_\Gamma} \cup \{Conclusion(r')\} \vdash \neg Conclusion(r)$. We know that $\mathcal{D}_\emptyset$ is $\mathcal{F}$, so that $r' \in \mathcal{F}$. Because $r' \in Applicable_{\mathcal{W}_{X,\mathcal{H}_\Gamma}}(\mathcal{S})$, we have (a) $X \models Premise(r')$ from Part 1 of the current Lemma. Because $r <_\mathcal{S} r'$, we have (b) $Premise(r) <_\Gamma Premise(r')$ from Part 3. And because $\mathcal{W}_{X,\mathcal{H}_\Gamma} \cup \{Conclusion(r')\} \vdash \neg Conclusion(r)$, we know that (c) $Conclusion(r) \neq Conclusion(r')$ by reasoning similar to that found in Part 2. ■

Observation 13 Where X is a fact situation, $\emptyset$ is the empty set of value defaults, and Γ is a consistent case base, let the default theory $\Delta_{X,\emptyset,\mathcal{H}_\Gamma}$ represent the problem presented by the fact situation X to a court with values $\emptyset$ under hard constraints $\mathcal{H}_\Gamma$ derived from Γ. Then, if r is a factor default rule, it follows that: r belongs to some proper scenario allowed by the theory $\Delta_{X,\emptyset,\mathcal{H}_\Gamma}$ if and only if the reason model of constraint on rule selection permits the court, against the background of the case base Γ, to base its decision in the situation X on the rule r.

Proof Let X be a fact situation, $\emptyset$ the empty set of value defaults, Γ a consistent case base, and $\Delta_{X,\emptyset,\mathcal{H}_\Gamma} = \langle \mathcal{W}_{X,\mathcal{H}_\Gamma}, \mathcal{D}_\emptyset \rangle$ the variable priority default theory representing the problem presented by X to a court with values $\emptyset$ under hard constraints $\mathcal{H}_\Gamma$. It follows from Observation 12 that, if a factor default rule belongs to some proper scenario allowed by $\Delta_{X,\emptyset,\mathcal{H}_\Gamma}$, then the reason model permits a decision in X based on that rule. To verify the other direction, we suppose that the reason model permits a decision in X based on the particular factor default rule r^* – that is, by Definition 7, that $\Gamma \cup \{\langle X, r^*, s\}$ is consistent, where r^* supports the side s – and reason our way to the conclusion that r^* belongs to some proper scenario allowed by $\Delta_{X,\emptyset,\mathcal{H}_\Gamma}$.

To begin with, given the rule r^* and recalling that $\mathcal{F}$ is the entire set of factor defaults, we define the set

$$\begin{aligned}\mathcal{S}^* = \{r \in \mathcal{F} : &(1)\ X \models \mathit{Premise}(r),\\ &(2)\ \mathit{Conclusion}(r) = \mathit{Conclusion}(r^*),\\ &(3)\ \text{there is no } r' \in \mathcal{F} \text{ such that}\\ &\qquad (a)\ X \models \mathit{Premise}(r'),\\ &\qquad (b)\ \mathit{Premise}(r) <_\Gamma \mathit{Premise}(r'),\\ &\qquad (c)\ \mathit{Conclusion}(r') \neq \mathit{Conclusion}(r)\}.\end{aligned}$$

Our argument then has two parts, first establishing that $\mathcal{S}^*$ is a proper scenario allowed by $\Delta_{X,\emptyset,\mathcal{H}_\Gamma}$, and second, showing r^* belongs to $\mathcal{S}^*$.

Part 1: In order to establish that $\mathcal{S}^*$ is a proper scenario allowed by the variable priority theory $\Delta_{X,\emptyset,\mathcal{H}_\Gamma} = \langle \mathcal{W}_{X,\mathcal{H}_\Gamma}, \mathcal{D}_\emptyset \rangle$, we must show, by Definition 31, that $\mathcal{S}^*$ is a proper scenario allowed by the fixed priority theory $\langle \mathcal{W}_{X,\mathcal{H}_\Gamma}, \mathcal{D}_\emptyset, <_{\mathcal{S}^*} \rangle$. What this means, by Definition 27, is that

$$\mathcal{S}^* = \mathit{Binding}_{\mathcal{W}_{X,\mathcal{H}_\Gamma}, \mathcal{D}_\emptyset, <_{\mathcal{S}^*}}(\mathcal{S}^*),$$

or together with Definition 26, that the following identity holds:

$$\begin{aligned}\mathcal{S}^* = \{r \in \mathcal{D}_\emptyset : &(4)\ r \in \mathit{Applicable}_{\mathcal{W}_{X,\mathcal{H}_\Gamma}, \mathcal{D}_\emptyset}(\mathcal{S}^*),\\ &(5)\ r \notin \mathit{Conflicted}_{\mathcal{W}_{X,\mathcal{H}_\Gamma}, \mathcal{D}_\emptyset}(\mathcal{S}^*),\\ &(6)\ r \notin \mathit{Defeated}_{\mathcal{W}_{X,\mathcal{H}_\Gamma}, \mathcal{D}_\emptyset, <_{\mathcal{S}^*}}(\mathcal{S}^*)\}.\end{aligned}$$

Since, by Definition 37, the set $\mathcal{D}_\emptyset$ of defaults from the theories under consideration coincides with the set $\mathcal{F}$ of factor defaults, we can establish this identity by showing that the conjunction of (1), (2), and (3) is equivalent to the conjunction of (4), (5), and (6). It is also worth noting that we can make use of Lemma 4 in our reasoning, since we know by (2) that the set $\mathcal{S}^*$ does not contain rules r and r' such that $\mathit{Conclusion}(r) \neq \mathit{Conclusion}(r')$.

First, then, suppose that (1), (2), and (3). From (1), it follows that (4) by Part 1 of Lemma 3. Next, if (5) fails, so that $r \in \mathit{Conflicted}_{\mathcal{W}_{X,\mathcal{H}_\Gamma}, \mathcal{D}_\emptyset}(\mathcal{S}^*)$, it follows from Part 2 of Lemma 4 that $\mathcal{S}^*$ must contain rules r and r' supporting different sides, contrary to (2), which tells us all rules from $\mathcal{S}^*$ support the side supported by r^*. Hence, (2) entails (5). Finally, if (6) fails, so that $r \in \mathit{Defeated}_{\mathcal{W}_{X,\mathcal{H}_\Gamma}, \mathcal{D}_\emptyset, <_{\mathcal{S}^*}}(\mathcal{S}^*)$, then Part 4 of Lemma 4 tells us that there is some rule r' in $\mathcal{F}$ satisfying the conditions (a), (b), and (c) specified there, contrary to (3). Hence (3) entails (6). From (1), (2), and (3), therefore, we have (4), (5), and (6).

Next, suppose that (4), (5), and (6). From (4), it follows that (1) by Part 1 of Lemma 4. If (2) fails, so that $\mathcal{S}^*$ contains rules supporting different sides, it follows from Part 2 of Lemma 3 that $r \in \mathit{Conflicted}_{\mathcal{W}_{X,\mathcal{H}_\Gamma}, \mathcal{D}_\emptyset}(\mathcal{S}^*)$, contrary to (5). Hence (5) entails (2). Finally, if (3) fails, so that there is some rule r'

in $\mathcal{F}$ satisfying the conditions (a), (b), and (c) specified there, it follows from Part 4 of Lemma 3 that $r \in \mathit{Defeated}_{\mathcal{W}_{X},\mathcal{H}_{\Gamma},\mathcal{D}_{\emptyset},<_{\mathcal{S}^*}}(\mathcal{S}^*)$, contrary to (6). Hence (6) entails (3). From (4), (5), and (6), therefore, we have (1), (2), and (3).

Part 2: In order to establish that r^* belongs to $\mathcal{S}^*$, let us assume for contradiction that r^* does not belong to $\mathcal{S}^*$, and then – reflecting on the definition of $\mathcal{S}^*$ – we can ask: why not? Well, because r^* is defined as the rule of the case $c = \langle X, r^*, s \rangle$, we have $X \models Premise(r)$, so that (1) holds. We also have $Conclusion(r^*) = Conclusion(r^*)$, so that (2) holds. So if r^* does not belong to $\mathcal{S}^*$, it must be because (3) fails – there must be some factor default r' such that (3a) $X \models Premise(r')$, (3b) $Premise(r^*) <_{\Gamma} Premise(r')$, and (3c) $Conclusion(r') \neq Conclusion(r^*)$. From (3a), however, together with the trivial $Premise(r^*) \leq^{s} Premise(r^*)$, we can conclude that $Premise(r') <_{c} Premise(r^*)$ by Definition 4. But from this conclusion, together with (3b), it follows that the augmented case base $\Gamma \cup \{\langle X, r^*, s \rangle\}$ is inconsistent, or by Definition 7, that, against the background of Γ, the reason model does not permit a decision in the situation X on the basis of the rule r^*, contrary to our initial assumption. ■

Observation 14 Let Γ be a consistent dimensional case base and X a dimensional fact situation confronting the court. Then against the background of Γ, if the a fortiori model of constraint requires the court to decide X for the side s, the reason model of constraint also requires the court to decide X for the side s.

Proof Consider a dimensional case base Γ and fact situation X, where the a fortiori model of constraint requires a decision for s. Then by Definition 21, there must be some case $c = \langle Y, r, s \rangle$ from Γ such that $Y \leq^{s} X$, which means, in the dimensional setting, by Definition 44, that $Y(d) \trianglelefteq^{s} X(d)$ for each dimension d. Now assume for contradiction that the reason model does not require a decision for s in the situation X. Then it must be possible to consistently decide X for $\bar{s}$ – that is, by Definitions 7 and 8, there must be some rule r' favoring $\bar{s}$ such that $\Gamma \cup \{c'\}$ is consistent where $c' = \langle X, r', \bar{s} \rangle$.

We can verify that $Y \models Premise(r')$ by showing that Y satisfies each magnitude factor from $Premise(r')$, as follows. Suppose $M^{\bar{s}}_{d,p}$ is a magnitude factor from $Premise(r')$. Then since c' is a case, we have $X \models M^{\bar{s}}_{d,p}$, that is, $p \trianglelefteq^{\bar{s}} X(d)$. By assumption, we have $Y(d) \trianglelefteq^{s} X(d)$, which yields $X(d) \trianglelefteq^{\bar{s}} Y(d)$ by duality of the ordering relation on dimension values. By transitivity, this and the previous inequality then tell us that $p \trianglelefteq^{\bar{s}} Y(d)$, or that $Y \models M^{\bar{s}}_{d,p}$. In the same way, we can verify that $X \models Premise(r)$ by showing that X satisfies each magnitude factor from $Premise(r)$. Suppose $M^s_{d,p}$ is a magnitude factor from $Premise(r)$. Then since c is a case, we have $Y \models M^s_{d,p}$, or $p \trianglelefteq^s Y(d)$. We again have $Y(d) \trianglelefteq^s X(d)$ by assumption, and then $p \trianglelefteq^s X(d)$ by transitivity, so that $X \models M^s_{d,p}$.

Since $Y \models Premise(r')$, and of course $Premise(r) \leq^s Premise(r)$, we have $Premise(r') <_c Premise(r)$ by Definition 4. Likewise, since $X \models Premise(r)$, and of course $Premise(r') \leq^{\bar{s}} Premise(r')$, we have $Premise(r) <_{c'} Premise(r')$. But together, these two conclusions tell us that $\Gamma \cup \{c'\}$ is inconsistent, contrary to assumption. ■

Observation 15 Let Γ be a consistent dimensional case base and X a dimensional fact situation confronting the court. Then against the background of Γ, if the reason model of constraint requires the court to decide X for the side s, the a fortiori model of constraint also requires the court to decide X for the side s.

Proof We reason by contraposition. Consider a dimensional case base Γ and fact situation X, where the a fortiori model of constraint does not require a decision for s. Then there is no case c in Γ such that $Outcome(c) = s$ and $Facts(c) \leq^s X$. In other words, for every c from Γ with $Outcome(c) = s$, it is not the case that $Facts(c)(d) \trianglelefteq^s X(d)$ for each dimension d – that is, for each such case c, there is some dimension d for which $Facts(c)(d) \trianglelefteq^s X(d)$ fails. We show that the reason model cannot require a decision for s in the situation X either, by constructing a rule r favoring $\bar{s}$ such that $\Gamma \cup \{c\}$ is consistent where $c = \langle X, r, \bar{s} \rangle$.

If there are no cases in Γ that have been decided for s, then r can be any rule at all favoring $\bar{s}$ whose premise is satisfied by X, so we focus on the more interesting situation in which there are, in fact, cases c from Γ such that $Outcome(c) = s$. For each such case c, let us define d_c as a representative dimension for which $Facts(c)(d_c) \trianglelefteq^s X(d_c)$ fails. (It follows from the argument in the previous paragraph that there is at least one such dimension; if there are more than one, d_c can be chosen arbitrarily.) We know, therefore, that (*) $Facts(c)(d_c) \trianglelefteq^s X(d_c)$ fails for each c from Γ such that $Outcome(c) = s$.

Now consider the magnitude factor

$$M^{\bar{s}}_{d_c,\, X(d_c)},$$

which holds in any situation in which the value of that situation along the dimension d_c favors the side $\bar{s}$ at least as strongly as $X(d_c)$ – that is, at least as strongly as the value of the situation X along the dimension d_c. We form the rule r by collecting together all the factors of this form for each case c from Γ such that $Outcome(c) = s$. More precisely, we take

$$r = \{M^{\bar{s}}_{d_c,\ X(d_c)} : c \in \Gamma \text{ and } Outcome(c) = s\} \rightarrow \bar{s}.$$

In order to establish that $c = \langle X, r, \bar{s} \rangle$ is a case, we verify that $X \models Premise(r)$ by showing that X satisfies each magnitude factor from $Premise(r)$. But this is trivial, since $X \models M^{\bar{s}}_{d_c,\ X(d_c)}$ just in case $X(d_c) \trianglelefteq^{\bar{s}} X(d_c)$, which is an instance of the reflexivity property of the value ordering.

Next, we establish that $\Gamma \cup \{c\}$ is consistent. Suppose otherwise. In that case, Observation 5 tells us that there is some $c' = \langle Y, r', s \rangle$ belonging to Γ such that $Premise(r') <_c Premise(r)$ and $Premise(r) <_{c'} Premise(r')$. But $Premise(r) <_{c'} Premise(r')$ requires that $Y \models Premise(r)$, which is impossible. Why? Because, since c' is a case from Γ with $Outcome(c') = s$, we know that $Premise(r)$ contains a magnitude factor of the form $M^{\bar{s}}_{d_{c'},\ X(d_{c'})}$, which Y would have to satisfy. But $Y \models M^{\bar{s}}_{d_{c'},\ X(d_{c'})}$ just in case $X(d_{c'}) \trianglelefteq^{\bar{s}} Y(d_{c'})$, which is equivalent by duality of the value ordering to $Y(d_{c'}) \trianglelefteq^{s} X(d_{c'})$, which is equivalent, since $Facts(c') = Y$, to $Facts(c')(d_{c'}) \trianglelefteq^{s} X(d_{c'})$, which we know to be false by (*) above. ■

Bibliography

Aleven, Vincent (1997). *Teaching Case-Based Argumentation through a Model and Examples*. PhD thesis, Intelligent Systems Program, University of Pittsburgh.

Aleven, Vincent and Ashley, Kevin (1997). Evaluating a learning environment for case-based argumentation skills. In *Proceedings of the Sixth International Conference on Artificial Intelligence and Law (ICAIL-97)*, pp. 170–179. The Association for Computing Machinery Press.

Alexander, Larry (1989). Constrained by precedent. *Southern California Law Review*, 63:1–64.

Alexander, Larry and Sherwin, Emily (2001). *The Rule of Rules: Morality, Rules, and the Dilemmas of Law*. Duke University Press.

(2008). *Demystifying Legal Reasoning*. Cambridge University Press.

Ashley, Kevin (1990). *Modeling Legal Argument: Reasoning with Cases and Hypotheticals*. The MIT Press.

Austin, J. L. (1946). Other minds. *Proceedings of the Aristotelian Society*, 20: 148–187.

Baker, Gordon (1977). Defeasibility and meaning. In Hacker, Peter and Raz, Joseph, editors, *Law, Morality, and Society: Essays in Honour of H. L. A Hart*, pp. 26–57. Oxford University Press.

Barnett, Randy (2005). Trumping precedent with original meaning: not as radical as it sounds. *Constitutional Commentary*, 22:257–270.

Belnap, Nuel (1993). On rigorous definitions. *Philosophical Studies*, 72: 115–146.

Bench-Capon, Trevor (1991). Practical legal expert systems: the relation between a formalisation of law and expert knowledge. In Bennun, M. and Narayanan, A., editors, *Computers, Law, and AI*, pp. 191–201. Ablex Publishers.

(1999). Some observations on modelling case based reasoning with formal argument models. In *Proceedings of the Sixth International Conference on Artificial Intelligence and Law (ICAIL-99)*, pp. 36–42. The Association for Computing Machinery Press.

(2002). The missing link revisited: the role of teleology in representing legal argument. *Artificial Intelligence and Law*, 10:79–94.

(2017). Hypo's legacy: introduction to the virtual special issue. *Artificial Intelligence and Law*, 25:205–250.

Bench-Capon, Trevor and Atkinson, Katie (2017). Dimensions and values for legal CBR. In *Proceedings of the Thirtieth International Conference on Legal Knowledge and Information Systems (JURIX 2017)*, pp. 27–32. IOS Press.

(2018). Lessons from implementing factors with magnitude. In *Proceedings of the Thirty First International Conference on Legal Knowledge and Information Systems (JURIX 2018)*, pp. 11–20. IOS Press.

Bench-Capon, Trevor and Rissland, Edwina (2001). Back to the future: dimensions revisited. In *The Fourteenth Annual Conference on Legal Knowledge and Information Systems (JURIX-2001)*, pp. 41–52. IOS Press.

Bench-Capon, Trevor and Sartor, Giovanni (2003). A model of legal reasoning with cases incorporating theories and values. *Artificial Intelligence*, 150(1–2):97–143.

Berman, Donald and Hafner, Carole (1993). Representing teleological structure in case-based legal reasoning: the missing link. In *Proceedings of the Fourth International Conference on Artificial Intelligence and Law (ICAIL-93)*, pp. 50–59. The Association for Computing Machinery Press.

Bix, Brian (1991). H. L. A Hart and the open texture of language. *Law and Philosophy*, 10:51–72.

Boss, Alan, Butler, Paul, Hubbard, William, et al. (2007). Working group on extrasolar planets. In *Reports on Astronomy 2002-2005: Proceedings of the IAU Symposium*, pp. 183–186. International Astronomical Union.

Broughton, Gabriel (2019). Vertical precedents in formal models of precedential constraint. *Artificial Intelligence and Law*, 27:253–307.

Burton, Steven (1985). *An Introduction to Law and Legal Reasoning*. Little, Brown, and Company.

(1988). Professor MacCormick's claim regarding universalization in law. In Faralli, Carla and Pattaro, Enrico, editors, *Reason in Law: Proceedings of the Conference Held in Bologna, 12–15 December 1984*. A. Giuffrè.

Canavotto, Ilaria (2022). Precedential constraint derived from inconsistent case bases. In *Proceedings of the Thirty-fifth Annual Conference on Legal Knowledge and Information Systems (JURIX 2022)*, pp. 23–32.

Clark, Herbert (1991). Words, the world, and their possibilities. In Pomerantz, James and Lockhead, Gregory, editors, *The Perception of Structure*, pp. 263–277. American Psychological Association.

Clark, Herbert and Marshall, Catherine (1981). Definite reference and mutual knowledge. In Joshi, Aravind, Sag, Ivan, and Webber, Bonnie, editors, *Elements of Discourse Understanding*, pp. 10–63. Cambridge University Press.

Clark, Herbert and Wilkes-Gibbs, Deanna (1986). Referring as a collaborative process. *Cognition*, 22:1–39.

Cohen, Adam (2009). The Lord Justice hath ruled: Pringles are potato chips. *The New York Times*, May 31, 2009.

Cross, Rupert and Harris, J. W. (1991). *Precedent in English Law*. Oxford University Press. Fourth edition.

Cumming, Samuel (2023). Semantic reasons. *Nous*, 57:641–666.

Dancy, Jonathan (1993). *Moral Reasons*. Basil Blackwell Publisher.

(2004). *Ethics Without Principles*. Oxford University Press.

Dickson, Julie (2016). Interpretation and coherence in legal reasoning. In Zalta, Edward, editor, *The Stanford Encyclopedia of Philosophy (Winter 2016 Edition)*. Stanford University. Available at http://plato.stanford.edu/archives/spr2016/-entries/legal-reas-interpret/.

Dung, Phan Minh (1995). On the acceptability of arguments and its fundamental role in nonmonotonic reasoning, logic programming, and *n*-person games. *Artificial Intelligence*, 77:321–357.

Duxbury, Neil (2005). *The Nature and Authority of Precedent*. Cambridge University Press.

Dworkin, Ronald (1967). The model of rules. *The University of Chicago Law Review*, 35:14–46. Reprinted in Dworkin (1977), pp. 14–45.

(1975). Hard cases. *Harvard Law Review*, 99:1057–1109. Reprinted in Dworkin (1977), pp. 81–130.

(1977). *Taking Rights Seriously*. Harvard University Press.

Edmundson, William (1993). Rethinking exclusionary reasons: a second edition of Joseph Raz's 'Practical Reason and Norms'. *Law and Philosophy*, 12:329–343.

Egré, Paul and O'Madagain, Cathal (2019). Concept utility. *The Journal of Philosophy*, 116:525–554.

Eisenberg, Melvin (1988). *The Nature of the Common Law*. Harvard University Press.

Elbourne, Paul (2011). *Meaning: A Slim Guide to Semantics*. Oxford University Press.

Endicott, Timothy (2000). *Vagueness in Law*. Oxford University Press.

(2022). Law and language. In Zalta, Edward, editor, *The Stanford Encyclopedia of Philosophy (Spring 2022 Edition)*. Stanford University. Available at http://plato.stanford.edu/archives/spr2022/entries/law-language/.

Fodor, Jerry, Garrett, Merrill, Walker, Edward, and Parkes, Cornelia (1980). Against definitions. *Cognition*, 8:263–367.

Frege, Gottlob (1893). *Grundgesetze der Arithmetik*, volume 1. Verlag Hermann Pohle. Partially translated in Furth (1964).

Furth, Montgomery, editor (1964). *Frege: The Basic Laws of Arithmetic*. University of California Press.

Gans, Chaim (1986). Mandatory rules and exclusionary reasons. *Philosophia*, 615:373–394.

Garrod, Simon and Anderson, Anthony (1987). Saying what you mean in dialogue: a study in conceptual and semantic co-ordination. *Cognition*, 27:181–218.

Goodell, Roger (2020). *Official Playing Rules of the National Football League*. National Football League.

Goodhart, Arthur (1930). Determining the *ratio decidendi* of a case. *Yale Law Journal*, 40:161–183.

(1959). The ratio decidendi of a case. *The Modern Law Review*, 22:117–124.

Grabmair, Matthias and Ashley, Kevin (2011). Faciliting case comparison using value judgments and intermediate legal concepts. In *Proceedings of the Thirteenth International Conference on Artificial Intelligence and Law (ICAIL-11)*, pp. 161–170. The Association for Computing Machinery Press.

Hare, R. M. (1952). *The Language of Morals*. Oxford University Press.

(1963). *Freedom and Reason*. Oxford University Press.

Hart, H. L. A. (1958). Positivism and the separation of law and morals. *Harvard Law Review*, 71:593–629.

(1961). *The Concept of Law*. Oxford University Press. Second edition published in 1994; pagination refers to the second edition.

Horty, John (1999). Precedent, deontic logic, and inheritance. In *Proceedings of the Seventh International Conference on Artificial Intelligence and Law (ICAIL-99)*, pp. 63–72. The Association for Computing Machinery Press.

(2004). The result model of precedent. *Legal Theory*, 10:19–31.

(2011). Rules and reasons in the theory of precedent. *Legal Theory*, 17:1–33.

(2012). *Reasons as Defaults*. Oxford University Press.

(2015). Constraint and freedom in the common law. *Philosopher's Imprint*, 15(25):1–27.

(2016). Reasoning with precedent as constrained natural reasoning. In Lord, Errol and Maguire, Barry, editors, *Weighing Reasons*, pp. 193–212. Oxford University Press.

(2017). Reasoning with dimensions and magnitudes (preliminary version). In *Proceedings of the Sixteenth International Conference on Artificial Intelligence and Law (ICAIL-2017)*, pp. 109–118. The Association for Computing Machinery Press.

(2019). Reasoning with dimensions and magnitudes. *Artificial Intelligence and Law*, 27:307–345.

(2021). Modifying the reason model. *Artificial Intelligence and Law*, 29:271–285.

(2022). Grant Lamond's account of precedent: a personal encounter. In McBride, Mark and Penner, James, editors, *New Essays on the Nature of Legal Reasoning*, pp. 139–160. Hart Publishing.

(2023). How does precedent constrain? In Endicott, Timothy, Kristjánsson, Hafsteinn Dan, and Lewis, Sebastian, editors, *Philosophical Foundations of Precedent*, pp. 185–197. Oxford University Press.

(2024). Precedent and open texture. In Green, Leslie and Leiter, Brian, editors, *Oxford Studies in Philosophy of Law*, volume 5. Oxford University Press.

Horty, John and Bench-Capon, Trevor (2012). A factor-based definition of precedential constraint. *Artificial Intelligence and Law*, 20:181–214.

Keil, Geert and Poscher, Ralf (2016). *Vagueness and Law: Philosophical and Legal Perspectives*. Oxford University Press.

Kornhauser, Lewis and Sager, Lawrence (1986). Unpacking the court. *Yale Law Journal*, 96:82–117.

Kozel, Randy (2018). Special justifications book review symposium: settled versus right: A theory of Precedent. *Constitutional Commentary*, 33:471–491.

Lamond, Grant (2005). Do precedents create rules? *Legal Theory*, 11:1–26.

(2006). Precedent and analogy in legal reasoning. In Zalta, Edward, editor, *The Stanford Encyclopedia of Philosophy (Spring 2016 Edition)*. Stanford University. Available at http://plato.stanford.edu/archives/spr2016/entries/legal-reas-prec/.

(2022). Revisiting the reasons account of precedent. In McBride, Mark and Penner, James, editors, *New Essays on the Nature of Legal Reasoning*, pp. 113–138. Hart Publishing.

Lawson, Gary (1994). The constitutional case against precedent. *Harvard Journal of Law and Public Policy*, 17:23–34.

Leśniewski, Stanislaw (1930). Über definitionen in der sogenannten Theory der Deduktion. *Sprawozdania z posiedzen Towarzystwa Naukowego Warzawskiego*, 23:289–309.

Levi, Edward (1949). *An Introduction to Legal Reasoning*. The University of Chicago Press.

Lewis, David (1969). *Convention: A Philosophical Study*. Harvard University Press.

List, Christian (2012). The theory of judgment aggregation: an introductory review. *Synthese*, 187:179–207.

Lord, Errol and Maguire, Barry (2016). An opinionated guide to the weight of reasons. In Lord, Error and Maguire, Barry, editors, *Weighing Reasons*, pp. 3–24. Oxford University Press.

Ludlow, Peter (2014). *Living Words: Meaning Underdetermination and the Dynamic Lexicon*. Oxford University Press.

Lyons, David (1999). Open texture and the possibility of legal interpretation. *Law and Philosophy*, 18:297–309.

MacCormick, Neil (1978). *Legal Reasoning and Legal Theory*. Oxford University Press.

(1987). Why cases have *rationes* and what these are. In Goldstein, Laurence, editor, *Precedent in Law*, pp. 155–182. Oxford University Press.

(1991). On open texture in law. In Amslek, Paul and MacCormick, Neil, editors, *Controversies about Law's Ontology*, pp. 72–83. Edinburgh University Press.

Maguire, Barry (2016). The value-based theory of reasons. *Ergo*, 3:233–262.

McCarty, L. Thorne (1997). Some arguments about legal arguments. In *Proceedings of the Sixth International Conference on Artificial Intelligence and Law (ICAIL-97)*, pp. 215–224. The Association for Computing Machinery Press.

Minker, Jack (1988). On indefinite databases and the closed world assumption. In *Proceedings of the Sixth Conference on Automated Deduction*, pp. 292–308. Springer Verlag, Lecture Notes in Computer Science.

Montrose, J. L. (1956). Distinguishing cases and the limits of ratio decidendi. *The Modern Law Review*, 19:525–530.

(1957a). Ratio decidendi and the House of Lords. *The Modern Law Review*, 20: 124–130.

(1957b). The ratio decidendi of a case. *The Modern Law Review*, 20:587–595.

Moore, Michael (1989). Authority, law, and Razian reasons. *Southern California Law Review*, 62:827–896.

Mullins, Robert (2020). Protected reasons and precedential constraint. *Legal Theory*, 26:40–61.

Nelson, Everett (1954). The verification theory of meaning. *Philosophical Review*, 63:182–192.

Perry, Stephen (1987). Judicial obligation, precedent, and the common law. *Oxford Journal of Legal Studies*, 7:215–257.

(1989). Second-order reasons, uncertainty, and legal theory. *Southern California Law Review*, 62:913–994.

Pollock, John (1970). The structure of epistemic justification. In *Studies in the Theory of Knowledge*, American Philosophical Quarterly Monograph Series, number 4, pp. 62–78. Basil Blackwell Publisher, Inc.

(1995). *Cognitive Carpentry: A Blueprint for How to Build a Person*. The MIT Press.

Prakken, Henry (2002). An exercise in formalising teleological case-based reasoning. *Artificial Intelligence and Law*, 10:113–133.

(2021). A formal analysis of some factor- and precedent-based accounts of precedential constraint. *Artificial Intelligence and Law*, 29:559–581.

Prakken, Henry and Sartor, Giovanni (1998). Modelling reasoning with precedents in a formal dialogue game. *Artificial Intelligence and Law*, 6:231–287.

(2015). Law and logic: a review from an argumentation perspective. *Artificial Intelligence*, 227:214–245.

Raz, Joseph (1972). Legal principles and the limits of law. *The Yale Law Journal*, 81:823–854.

(1975). *Practical Reason and Norms*. Hutchinson and Company. Second edition with new Postscript printed in 1990 by Princeton University Press, and reprinted by Oxford University Press in 2002; pagination refers to the Oxford edition.

(1979). *The Authority of Law*. Oxford University Press.

(1989). Facing up: a reply. *Southern California Law Review*, 62:1153–1235.

Reiter, Raymond (1978). On closed world data bases. In Gallaire, Hervre and Minker, Jack, editors, *Logic and Data Bases*, pp. 119–140. Plenum Publishing Corporation.

(1980). A logic for default reasoning. *Artificial Intelligence*, 13:81–132.

Richardson, Henry (1990). Specifying norms as a way to resolve concrete ethical problems. *Philosophy and Public Affairs*, 19:279–310.

Rigoni, Adam (2014). Common-law judicial reasoning and analogy. *Legal theory*, 20:133–156.

(2015). An improved factor based approach to precedential constraint. *Artificial Intelligence and Law*, 23:133–160.

(2018). Representing dimensions within the reason model of precedent. *Artificial Intelligence and Law*, 26:1–22.

Rissland, Edwina (1990). Artificial intelligence and law: stepping stones to a model of legal reasoning. *The Yale Law Journal*, 99:1957–1981.

Rissland, Edwina and Ashley, Kevin (1987). A case-based system for trade secrets law. In *Proceedings of the First International Conference on Artificial Intelligence and Law (ICAIL-87)*, pp. 60–66. The Association for Computing Machinery Press.

(2002). A note on dimensions and factors. *Artificial Intelligence and Law*, 10:65–77.

Sartor, Giovanni (2010). Doing justice to rights and values: teleological reasoning and proportionality. *Artificial Intelligence and Law*, 18:175–215.

Schauer, Frederick (1987). Precedent. *Stanford Law Review*, 39:571–605.

(1989). Is the common law law? *California Law Review*, 77:455–471.

(1991). *Playing by the Rules: A Philosophical Examination of Rule-Based Decision-Making in Law and Life*. Oxford University Press.

(2008). A critical guide to vehicles in the park. *New York University Law Review*, 83:1109–1134.

(2009). *Thinking Like a Lawyer*. Harvard University Press.

(2013). On the open texture of law. *Grazer Philosophische Studien*, 87:197–215.

Schiappa, Edward (2003). *Defining Reality: Definitions and the Politics of Meaning*. Southern Illinois University Press.

Schroeder, Mark (2007). Weighting for a plausible Humean theory of reasons. *Nous*, 41:110–132.

Shapiro, Stewart and Roberts, Craige (2018). Open texture, and its ramifications for logic and semantics. Unpublished manuscript.

(2019a). Open texture and analyticity. In Makovec, Dejan and Shapiro, Stewart, editors, *Friedrich Waismann: The Open Texture of Analytic Philosophy*, pp. 189–210. Palgrave Macmillan.

Shapiro, Stewart and Roberts, Craige (2019b). Open texture and mathematics. Unpublished manuscript.

Simpson, A. W. B. (1957). The ratio decidendi of a case. *The Modern Law Review*, 20:413–415.

(1958). The ratio decidendi of a case. *The Modern Law Review*, 21:155–160.
(1959). The ratio decidendi of a case. *The Modern Law Review*, 22:453–457.
(1961). The *ratio decidendi* of a case and the doctrine of binding precedent. In Guest, A. G., editor, *Oxford Essays in Jurisprudence*, pp. 148–175. Oxford University Press.
Suppes, Patrick (1957). *Introduction to Logic*. D. van Nostrand Publishing Company.
Taurek, John (1977). Should the numbers count? *Philosophy and Public Affairs*, 6:293–316.
Tur, Richard (2001). Defeasibilism. *Oxford Journal of Legal Studies*, 21:355–368.
Twining, William and Miers, David (2010). *How to Do Things with Rules*. Cambridge University Press. Fifth edition.
Waismann, Frederich (1945). Verifiability. In *Proceedings of the Aristotelian Society, Supplementary Volume 19*, pp. 119–150. Harrison and Son. Reprinted in Anthony Flew, editor, *Logic and Language*, pp. 117–144, Blackwell Publishing Company, 1951; pagination refers to this version.
Williamson, Timothy (1994). *Vagueness*. Routledge.
Wittgenstein, Ludwig (1953). *Philosophical Investigations*. Basil Blackwell.

Index

For EU product safety concerns, contact us at Calle de José Abascal, 56–1°,
28003 Madrid, Spain or eugpsr@cambridge.org.

www.ingramcontent.com/pod-product-compliance
Lightning Source LLC
LaVergne TN
LVHW081934200926
848484LV00009B/2426

* 9 7 8 1 0 0 9 3 5 6 5 0 3 *